SPIRITUAL
LEADERSHIP

Moving
People
on to God's
Agenda

SPIRITUAL
LEADERSHIP

REVISED &
EXPANDED

HENRY & RICHARD
BLACKABY

B&H
PUBLISHING GROUP
Nashville, Tennessee

ISBN: 978–1–4336–6918–7

Published by B&H Publishing Group
Nashville, Tennessee

Dewey Decimal Classification: 303.3
Subject Heading: LEADERSHIP \ SPIRITUAL LIFE \ SUCCESS

Unless otherwise stated, Scripture quotations have been
taken from the Holman Christian Standard Bible®, Copyright
© 1999, 2000, 2002, 2003, by Holman Bible Publishers.
Used by permission. Holman Christian Standard Bible®,
Holman CSB® and HCSB® are federally registered trademarks
of Holman Bible Publishers.

Quotations marked KJV are from the Kings James Version.

1 2 3 4 5 6 7 8 ◆ 15 14 13 12 11

Contents

Acknowledgments

To have released a book on leadership in 2001 seems, on reflection, to have been fortuitous. What followed the events of 9/11 was a decade-long societal debate about the desperate need for robust leadership in government, business, military, home, and church. Everyone had an opinion, and reams of additional books and theories hit bookstore shelves with tsunami-like vigor. We could not have known when we wrote the original version of Spiritual Leadership: Moving People On to God's Agenda in 2001 that it would be so widely and enthusiastically received. We have been truly overwhelmed by how God has used it to encourage leaders around the world. We have personally handed the book to world leaders. A group of state senators read the book a chapter a week and discussed it in the state capitol building. Bible colleges as widespread as in the USA, South Africa, and the Philippines have used it as a textbook. Pastors have approached us at conferences and shown us their dog-eared copies. Christian CEOs have used it as a guide to know how to lead their Fortune 500 companies to honor God. Parenting organizations as well as Christian school faculties have studied the book. We have been privileged to teach its truths on six continents. Since many new theories and books on leadership have emerged since this volume was first released, we were asked to update and expand it to address many of the issues and theories that have dominated leadership thinking in recent years.

We are keenly aware that we did not write this book alone. God has placed along our path many amazing people who have enriched us, added texture to our lives, and infused joy to our journey.

At the top of our list, as always, are our wives. Henry and Marilynn reached a milestone this year—their fiftieth anniversary. Richard and Lisa have been married twenty-seven years. Being married to us has not been easy! We tend to work too hard and too long. Our travels keep us away from home for frequent and extended periods of time. Nevertheless, God knew what kind of lifelong companions we needed to add flavor and laughter to our lives and ministry. They have stood faithfully beside us when life proved difficult. Lisa has always done an outstanding job editing whatever we have written. No words are adequate to express our love for our soul mates.

We are also grateful for the many leaders God has placed around us over the years. We were both blessed to grow up in homes where we could sincerely affirm that our father was the greatest man of God we knew. Thankfully time has not altered those opinions. As teenagers we were blessed with leaders who loved us and taught us how to walk closely with God. In university and seminary God introduced amazing friends into our journey. As we launched out in ministry, denominational leaders, fellow pastors, and godly laypeople encouraged us to keep growing. At every stage of our lives, we could name friends, colleagues, and leaders who challenged us to strive for higher levels in our personal growth and leadership.

Throughout the course of our ministries, we have been privileged to meet some of the finest government, business, home, and church leaders in the world. They have added rich new dimensions to our perspectives and understanding of leadership. Over the last decade we have been blessed to work with Mac McQuiston at the CEO Forum who invited us to invest in the lives of some of the finest Christian CEOs in corporate America.

We are also grateful to those who carefully read through this revised manuscript and offered invaluable suggestions. These include Tom Blackaby, Rick Fisher, Hermann Brandt, Brett Pyle, and Bill Bliss. These men have also contributed much to the Spiritual Leadership Network operated by

Blackaby Ministries International www.blackaby.org which helps church, business, and home leaders move those they lead on to God's agenda.

This book was not written in a few months but over a lifetime. The space needed to list the people to whom we are indebted would double the length of this volume. We have been most fortunate to have journeyed with such outstanding people thus far in our lives. We will be forever indebted to the countless "ordinary" people who shared their extraordinary experiences and insights with us through conversations in conference centers, churches, hotel lobbies, airplanes, and living rooms around the world. We hope these truths impact your life and inspire you to rise to new levels of leadership, just as they have done with us.

Henry and Richard Blackaby
Blackaby Ministries International

Preface

Richard's daughter Carrie (nineteen) has never seen herself as a leader. As the baby of her family and the only girl, she has bravely endured two older, tormenting brothers her entire life. She claims her only aspirations are to purchase designer clothes and to look beautiful (which she does!). Ask her if she sees herself as a "leader" and she rolls her pretty eyes. Then when she turned sixteen, she had a wild, crazy, spontaneous inspiration. She invited three friends over to her house one Friday and announced that she was going to dye a strip of her hair . . . pink.

The other three girls were soon on the phone asking permission from their mothers to follow suit. Richard's home was transformed into a beauty salon. Word spread throughout the church youth group. Additional friends came by the house on Saturday, hair dye in hand. On Sunday morning Carrie sat in church beside *seven* other girls, all of whom were now sporting the latest fashion trend. Carrie is a leader. She just doesn't realize it yet.

Do you view yourself as a leader? Odds are if you picked up this book, you suspect you have the potential to lead others. However, this book is intended not only for those who fit the traditional leader profile but also for "ordinary" people who believe their world needs to change but who are not exactly sure what, if any, role they should play in that transformation. Perhaps your children's behavior concerns you or you feel your family is somehow "off course." Maybe you are burdened over the present condition of your neighborhood, city, or nation.

You may strongly sense that your church or denomination is adrift from its original mission and needs to make major adjustments. It could be that the company for which you work is grossly underperforming. Leadership is about people who choose to make a difference. It often is not flamboyant, and it usually doesn't involve spellbinding speeches or dramatic actions. If you make the place where you live, work, study, and worship better, then you are a leader. And, if ever this world needed leaders, it is now.

A weak, declining organization teeters on the brink of disbandment; then a new leader arrives and everything changes. The leader doesn't do all the work, but peoples' performance and morale improves. A collective sense of relief and hope now pervades the atmosphere. Developments that eluded previous administrators for years are accomplished in weeks with a new leader at the helm.

How can the same collection of people languish under one leader and flourish under another? The very people who were previously the most disillusioned now generate the most results. The difference has little to do with the problems, limitations, or personnel. It has everything to do with good leadership. The fact is, whether they are chairing a church committee, leading a corporation, or rearing their children, some men and women are successful no matter what challenge they undertake while others suffer chronic failure and wallow in mediocrity.

Over the years we have repeatedly observed this phenomenon. The contrast between weak and strong leaders has always intrigued us. We are convinced that most organizations have potential for growth and success. The key is leadership. That's why we have invested years in developing and encouraging leaders. We spend a great deal of time with emerging leaders at the front end of their careers—men and women who wonder if they "have what it takes" to be leaders. We also counsel people from various walks of life who struggle with feelings of failure and regret because they have not realized their hopes and dreams. We also talk with troubled executives who have achieved notable worldly success but worry their lives are making little difference in their families or God's kingdom. It is sadly ironic how many clerics have gained ecclesiastical renown while their own children soundly rejected their faith.

Despite voluminous rhetoric on the subject, the world is disoriented to what constitutes successful leadership. The Bible, however, has much to say about the subject. We have examined the Scriptures and studied the lives of effective leaders, both current and historical, to identify clear biblical principles that lead to effective leadership. As we have shared these truths around the world, we've seen men and women return to their leadership roles with renewed vigor and vision. Why? Because as in every other aspect of life, when people seek and follow God's ways, they experience profound results.

Bookstore shelves overflow with leadership tomes, and we have read scores of them. We will review helpful leadership insights found in both secular and Christian writings. We'll also consider successful leaders from various walks of life including business, military, government, and church leaders who demonstrate healthy leadership. Nevertheless, we believe crucial leadership truths are being overlooked. Moreover we are concerned that many Christian leaders are reading secular books and accepting their teachings uncritically.

Much secular leadership theory is based on presuppositions that may appear sound yet promote ideas contrary to the Scriptures. Secular and spiritual leaders may use similar methods, but spiritual leadership includes dimensions absent from secular leadership. Spiritual leaders who merely use secular methods may experience some degree of worldly success, but they will not fulfill their calling as spiritual leaders.

We wrote this book for spiritual leaders whether they lead Christian or secular organizations. Since this book was first published in 2001, hundreds of men and women have approached us with their stories. They were discouraged and prepared to resign their leadership positions, yet they retained a heartfelt desire for God to use their lives to make a positive difference in their organizations. As we helped them examine the Scriptures, leaders from all over the world have found encouragement and direction for their lives and organizations. The reason? They discovered God's agenda.

The guidelines we present are for *all* Christians whom God has called to be spiritual leaders. Holding a leadership position in a Christian organization does not make you a spiritual leader. Nor does working a secular occupation preclude you from being a spiritual leader at your workplace. *Spiritual leadership is not an occupation: it is a calling.* Christian businesspeople—physicians, educators, politicians, and parents—should be spiritual leaders. No matter what their occupations, more and more men and women are taking their calling as spiritual leaders seriously, and they are dramatically impacting the world and extending God's kingdom. We will share some of their stories with you.

According to the Bible, God is not necessarily looking for leaders, at least not in the sense we might think. He is looking for servants (Isa. 59:16; Ezek. 22:30).

When God finds people willing to serve as he leads them, the possibilities are limitless. People everywhere are looking for someone to lead them into God's purposes, God's way. People will follow spiritual leaders who know how to lead them according to God's agenda.

Since the original publication of this book in 2001, we have been asked to revise and update it. Over the last decade we've observed God moving dramatically among leaders, especially pastors, CEOs, military chaplains, school administrators, prayer leaders, and men's and family ministries. We have traveled to numerous countries and met with a wide array of world leaders. In these pages we'll share much of what we have learned. Every chapter has been significantly reworked; numerous new illustrations have been included, and a significant number of modern leadership issues are addressed. Two important new chapters have been added. If you benefited from the original volume, we pray you will receive additional encouragement and insight from this revised and expanded volume.

As you read this book, we pray you will accept the challenge to be that man or woman God is seeking. We hope you will experience the incredible joy and satisfaction of knowing God is using your life as his instrument to build his kingdom and to change your world.

Chapter One

The Leader's Challenge

Mike sat in stunned silence alone in the boardroom. He had appointments to keep, but now they seemed irrelevant. He remained frozen in his chair, trying to process the painful events of the previous hour. Mike was CEO of a sporting goods company. He was a young man—in his early thirties—bright, creative, and, he thought, good at his job. Moreover, he was a committed Christian with a strong work ethic. He'd always considered his faith to be an asset to his career. But the morning's executive team meeting shattered that assumption. What began as a routine weekly meeting escalated into an acrimonious dispute, revealing a pervasive undercurrent of resentment toward him—more specifically toward his Christian beliefs. A clear line was drawn, with his executive team demanding he keep his faith out of his business decisions.

First, the vice president for human resources announced a revision to the company benefits to include medical coverage for therapeutic abortions. He urged Mike to herald the new policy as a public relations tool. Then Barbara from marketing announced a new advertising campaign, one using women in provocative sexual poses to advertise a men's product. Mike felt he had no choice but to veto both recommendations.

That's when the floodgates opened and his colleagues' hostility spewed forth. "What right did he have to impose his conservative religious beliefs on the company and its staff who did not share his personal values? His stance on the abortion policy was archaic, chauvinistic, and discriminating. This was the company's opportunity to show it was progressive and sensitive to its employees' needs. The sex angle on the television ad was certain to be more effective than the "family friendly" campaign Mike advocated. His staff seemed united on one thing—Mike's agenda for the company did not match theirs.

Mike was bewildered. His leadership team was talented and experienced. Yet most of them were not Christians, and he knew some of them were even disdainful of the Christian faith. Mike knew how important a unified team was to company success. If an insurrection of his executive leaders ensued, his board of directors would most likely assume Mike was unfit for the CEO role. His job was in jeopardy. He had to act quickly. Was there anything he could do? He worried about legal issues if he stood by his convictions. It had never been easy taking a stand for his faith at work, but he'd always tried to honor God at his job. Now it no longer seemed possible. Maybe he should face the reality that his job and his faith could not coexist in a secular environment and resign.

Pastor Edwards could barely withhold his tears. He could still hear the deacons' footsteps echo down the hallway as they marched from his office. The group had arrived unexpectedly and demanded an audience. Their spokesperson, the chairman of the deacons, began the charge. "Many" people were upset over his leadership style, and it appeared "things" had deteriorated to the point that it was best for everyone involved if he immediately resigned from the church.

A second member of the self-appointed tribunal read off a lengthy litany of concerns. Two years ago when Edwards enthusiastically accepted the call to serve as pastor of the medium-sized congregation, he was aware that the church had some problems. After all, every church has issues. He was young and his faith was strong. He sincerely believed that prayer, biblical preaching, and loving ministry to his congregants would revive the ailing church. But the problems worsened. Land mines were exploding everywhere he stepped. Several families requested more modern music in the services and he had obliged. In doing so he inadvertently alienated other families who were now withholding their tithes as well as their service until the music was changed back to their preferred style. One of the deacons was rumored to be in an adulterous relationship. When Edwards had approached him privately about the subject, the offended deacon had appealed to his friends and polarized the entire deacon body. The alarmed deacons accused Edwards of witch hunting. No one denied there was substance to the rumor, but they argued that this man had great influence in the community. They pointed out the sad truth that the church could ill afford another public scandal. When Edwards proposed hiring a part-time youth pastor, a battle erupted. Various interest groups in the church clamored for expanded ministry—for seniors, for choir members, for college students, for the divorced, and for children. Even his preaching had come under fire—too long, not enough humor, too much humor, too academic, too shallow . . . Edwards had grown weary under the stress, but he remained strong in his belief that, if he persevered, the problems would eventually sort themselves out. That was before this visit. Their words deeply wounded him: "As representatives of this church, we feel obliged to tell you that the best thing you can do for our church is to resign immediately. If you do so, we can give you a decent severance and let you keep your health insurance while you circulate your résumé to other churches. There may be a church out there who appreciates your style of leadership . . ." The pastor slumped into his chair with his face in his hands. What more could he have done? He had worked to the point of exhaustion for this congregation. He had sacrificed time with his wife and children, spending most evenings at church meetings, counseling people in distress, or visiting potential members. He knew where the church should be heading, but he simply could not get the people to support his efforts. He felt like a total failure and wondered if he had been misguided to enter the ministry in the first place.

Leadership: The Challenge

Leadership. Everyone experiences it, or the lack of it, daily. The media bombards us with news of new terrorist threats, economic crises, political compromise, and moral failures. Church attendance is declining and Christian values are being publicly ridiculed. Would-be leaders vehemently criticize current office-holders while assuring the public that if given the chance, *they* could resolve the ominous issues that threaten it. Being a leader in such an environment is a daunting task. Bookstores boast rows of books on leadership, but there is still no consensus on exactly what it is. Those expected to follow grow impatient with leaders who fail to resolve their problems and increasingly frustrated as their organizations continue to flounder. Struggling leaders agonize, knowing that others resent them and blame them for their organizations' impotence and decline. Countless discouraged leaders would quit their jobs today, but they need the income and they fear the same problems would engulf them in their new jobs. In an online survey conducted by *USA Today*, people were asked: "If you won the lottery, would you quit your job?" 45.4 percent responded "Definitely." 18.9 percent answered "Probably." Only 10.9 percent said "Definitely not."[1] Clearly most people are working solely for the income and not out of a sense of calling. Many people today would concede that leading is no fun. Christian leaders carry the additional burden that they are not only failing their people but God. They feel guilty because they lack the faith to move their organization forward, yet they are afraid to move on lest they are no more successful in their new venture. Is there any hope for leaders who are not experiencing fulfillment or reaching the potential God intends for them? If anything can revolutionize today's Christian leaders, it is when they understand God's design for those he calls to lead.

During the American Revolutionary era, John Adams complained, "We have not men fit for the times."[2] On December 23, 1776, the iconoclastic writer, Thomas Paine wrote: "These are the times that try men's souls: The summer soldier and the sunshine patriot will, in this crisis, shrink from the service of his country; but he that stands it NOW, deserves the love and thanks of man and woman . . . yet we have this consolation with us, that the harder the conflict, the more glorious the triumph."[3] Certainly the twenty-first century holds unprecedented opportunities for leaders to make a dramatic difference in their world. However, the challenges leaders are facing have never been more complex or hazardous. James Canton in his book, *The Extreme Future*, suggests the top five factors that will define the "extreme" future: speed, complexity, risk, change and surprise.[4] While the future holds untold numbers of opportunities and obstacles, we believe society is experiencing three current issues that will have profound implications for those attempting to lead organizations into the future.

Technology

The Western world has been on a never-ending quest to enhance its quality of life. Scientific breakthroughs used to be infrequent, but now they occur regularly. The rapidity of technological advance is likewise accelerating the speed of change in every arena of life. It is becoming much more difficult for people to incorporate the latest technological advances into their lifestyle and business. We have not even accommodated the latest technological innovation before a newer, more sophisticated hybrid is announced. If you have been using a cell phone for the last decade, try to remember your first one. A decade-old cell phone is downright prehistoric!

What does the dizzying rate of technological advance mean for today's leaders? First, they must be comfortable with change. When Richard was a seminary president, he was informed that seminaries were changing so rapidly that every five years these institutions were morphing into something new. If leaders were not constantly reinventing themselves, they would soon be obsolete. To make matters worse, seminaries were notorious for their traditionally *slow* rate of change!

Business leaders know that fierce competition and shareholders hungry for immediate profits in a global market make rapid adaption necessary. Phil Rosenzweig in his book *The Halo Effect* suggests that companies that are largely technology driven find it almost impossible to stay at the top of their market due to clones, intense competition, and changing technology.[5] Business leaders can't afford to fall asleep at the wheel or they will wake up in a junkyard.

Digitalization is rapidly speeding up most aspects of our lives and creating impatient consumers with demanding expectations. Sophisticated technology has made communication both a blessing and a curse. Electronic messages provide instant access to leaders anywhere in the world. In times past people sent messages to leaders and then waited for days or even weeks for a reply. People accepted delayed responses as a matter of course.

Past leaders could take time to ponder their decisions and consult with advisors before responding. The dynamics of communication have drastically changed. The moment someone sends an electronic message, they know that within seconds they could (and therefore should) receive a reply.

A church youth minister we know messaged six of his youth fifteen minutes into their first class period when all cell phones are verboten. He received a reply from all six in less than two minutes. Busy leaders can return from a lunch appointment to discover dozens of messages awaiting them, all expecting an immediate reply. In any airport you see harried executives deplaning and consulting their cell phones to discover that while they traveled the first leg of their business trip, their in-box was filling up with urgent messages, most of them demanding a reply before they board their next flight. Cell phones can be tremendously helpful to leaders as they maintain close contact with their people, but beleaguered executives and pastors are discovering that those devices designed to make their work less burdensome follow them everywhere, even on their vacations.

Past leaders had certain times in their day when they were inaccessible. During such times they could reflect on their situation and make decisions about their next course of action. Technology makes today's leaders constantly and instantly accessible. It becomes almost impossible to reflect or to think deeply on a matter due to constant notifications of incoming messages. The pressure to make rapid decisions and maintain steady communication can intimidate even the most capable leader.

The rise of the Information Age has inundated leaders with new knowledge that must be processed immediately. They are bombarded with information and advice on leadership and management theory as well as data pertaining to their particular field. An exhausting parade of consultants claims that if busy executives will simply follow their proposed steps, they will be guaranteed success. Of course, their competitors are also being invited to embrace the same new technology and methodology. Company leaders are facing intense pressure to adopt the best technology and systems quickly so they are not left behind the early adopters. As Brad Szollose observes: "Being able to learn faster is the key to success in the twenty-first century."[6]

Leaders wanting to improve their skills and expand their knowledge base have virtually limitless opportunities. But where does one begin? Which book do they read next? Which seminar is a must? Which management trend vociferously advocated now will be passé next year? Such a bombardment of information, much of which is contradictory, can cause leaders to grow cynical.

While the Information Age has given leaders valuable new tools with which to lead, it has also placed heavy, unprecedented demands on them. No wonder many leaders express frustration that they are always hopelessly behind. Gordon Sullivan and Michael Harper have suggested the defining characteristic of the Information Age is not speed but the "compression of time."[7] It is not that events are necessarily moving faster but that there is less time for leaders to respond to those events, putting enormous pressure on them.

Technology has created another growing challenge. Today's management is mostly drawn from Baby Boomers. However, the Millennial Generation (born between 1980–2000), is the largest generation in American history, boasting 77.9 million people.[8] Brad Szollose coined the term *liquid leadership* to describe how current managers will have to adjust their leadership styles to manage this emerging, technologically savvy, and relationally oriented generation.[9]

The church is certainly not immune to pressures created by technology. Traditionally, the local minister was one of the best educated people in the community with one of the largest personal libraries. While those listening to the sermon might not always agree with the message, it was difficult to dispute the minister's facts. Today's congregants can google illustrations and facts stated from the pulpit to verify their veracity before the minister has stepped down from the platform. Parishioners can now have more information on their laptops than the most studious ministers used to house in their libraries.

Modern churches are embracing technology with gusto. PowerPoint presentations and video clips are commonplace. People can text questions to the minister during the service and give their offering using their debit card in the church foyer. There is increased ecclesiastical competition with the rise of the megachurch. Now church members can watch celebrated preachers on television or the Internet, making their own local preacher seem ordinary at best. With so many great sermons at one's fingertips, the thought of going to all the trouble of driving to church and searching for a parking place seems increasingly unnecessary.

Globalization

Craig Johnson claims globalization may well be the most important trend of the twenty-first century.[10] He is not alone. In 2005, Thomas L. Friedman declared the world was "flat."[11] He suggested that the lowering of the former communist walls to the west—along with the advent of the World Wide Web, the proliferation of the personal computer, the development of fiber optic cable, and work flow software—ushered the world into its third major era around the year 2000.[12] While the debate about what globalization involves is still intense, many of the geographic, political, social, and technological walls that used to separate people have clearly come crashing down.

Now a small, family-run store in South Korea can do business internationally. More significantly, it can compete with much larger companies in the United States. Adversely, a terrorist hiding in a cave in Afghanistan can direct an attack that brings skyscrapers on the other side of the world tumbling down. A computer virus generated in Iran can cripple computers around the world in a matter of hours. A downturn in the Southeastern Asia economy can cause layoffs in Midwestern American towns shortly thereafter. A customer service call placed in Detroit may well be answered by someone in India. With the advent of the Internet and personal computers, your child's math tutor may as well be sitting at a laptop in Bangalore as at your kitchen table. The world has indeed flattened.

As with any change, one person's disaster is another person's opportunity. Because the world is more interconnected than before, those seeking to exert a global impact have unprecedented opportunities. Small businesses that used to merely strive to be one of the top three companies in their region are now eyeing the world for new markets. Churches that used to think their mission field was their local parish are now using technology to impact some of the remotest places on earth.

Diversity

While the United States has been a favored destination for immigrants for centuries, the infamous "melting pot" has not been producing a homogenous nation. There was a time when American presidents could quote a verse from the Bible and most citizens understood the reference. But that time is gone. There was also an age when moral standards and views toward traditional institutions such as the family and church were widely accepted. However, American society has grown extremely diverse and fragmented.

Likewise, as immigrants from the poorest nations of the world pour into Europe and its traditionally homogenous nations, a radical transformation is occurring. Recently we were in the Netherlands; and during a free afternoon in Amsterdam, we set out to visit a local European bakery. We walked for several blocks and came upon three bakeries, all of them Arabic. Switzerland recently passed a law restricting the height of minarets above mosques because they were beginning to dominate the skylines. Europe is changing.

What does this mean for leaders? Taylor Cox concludes that managing diversity will be the core of modern organizational leadership.[13] CEOs will direct a workforce far more diverse than that overseen by their predecessors. Executives cannot assume their employees share their values, worldview, work ethic, sexual orientation, or goals. Craig Johnson points out the challenge of making ethical decisions in the corporate world when "every ethnic group, nation, and religion approaches moral dilemmas from a different perspective . . . what is perfectly acceptable to members of one group may raise serious ethical concerns for another."[14]

The great challenge will be to build a unified team or corporate culture when the worldviews of your team members emanate from every conceivable vantage point. This dilemma also exists within the church. One might assume that a congregation holding the same theology would naturally be unified. But Christians today are widely divided on social, political, and moral issues stemming from a broad spectrum of experience and backgrounds.

This growing diversity will complicate every field of leadership in the future. The term *politically correct* has entered our vocabulary to mean a decision or action that doesn't upset anyone's specialized interests or agenda. How can difficult decisions or progress be made with so many obstacles or such broad criteria? While the external issues assaulting organizations are increasingly varied and complex, the internal complexity of modern organizations makes it increasingly difficult for them to develop a unified response to any issue.[15]

Effective leadership has become the panacea for every challenge society faces. Whether politics, religion, business, education, or law, the universally expressed need is for leaders who will meet the challenges confronting today's organizations. The issue is not a shortage of people willing to lead. The problem is an increasing skepticism among followers over whether today's executives can truly lead. Warren Bennis observed, "At the heart of America is a vacuum into which self-anointed saviors have rushed."[16] People know intuitively that claiming to be a leader or holding a leadership position does not make someone a leader. People are warily looking for leaders they can trust.

Leadership: In Politics

For several decades the public has been expressing a growing distrust of political leaders. These are not easy times for governments. The world's complexity increases at exponential speed. Political alliances are in constant flux. Threats of nuclear, biological, and chemical terrorism are a frightening possibility. A severe downturn in the global economy can devastate nations overnight. Violence is epidemic. Natural disasters have decimated entire cities. Social norms previously assumed are now publicly ridiculed. Societal plagues such as drugs and domestic violence seem immune to government solutions. Government debts continue to escalate while leaders are unwilling to make unpopular decisions.

Morally, society has deteriorated to the point that like those in the prophet Jeremiah's time, the people have forgotten how to blush (Jer. 6:15; 8:12). Such daunting realities have generated a dire need for leaders who can be trusted and who are capable of addressing a multitude of social, political, economic, and spiritual ills. People are weary of politicians who make promises they are either unwilling or unable to keep. Concern for reelection or holding on to their office can motivate some leaders more than making the best decisions for their constituents.

Society longs for statesmen, but it generally receives politicians. Statesmen are leaders who uphold what is right regardless of the effect on their popularity. Statesmen speak out to achieve the greatest good for their people, not to identify with the shifting winds of popular opinion. Statesmen promote the general good rather than regional or personal self-interest. Statesmen can make unpopular decisions when they are called for, but in the long run they are widely respected for their integrity and for following their convictions.

Harry Truman was a statesman. He left the presidency with a low rating in public opinion polls, yet history evaluates him as an effective leader during a dangerous and turbulent time. Politicians may win elections; nevertheless, future generations often deride them for their lack of character and ineffective leadership.

Warren Bennis suggests that the American Revolutionary era produced at least six world-class leaders—Franklin, Washington, Adams, Jefferson, Hamilton, and Madison.[17] For a national population of only three million, that was an impressive number. If the United States enjoyed the same ratio of world-class leaders to its current population today, it would boast over five hundred such statesmen. In recent years the term *great* has not been the adjective of choice in describing many political leaders. If there was ever a time that called for statesmen rather than politicians, this is it.

Leadership: In Business

The business world is searching for effective leaders as fervently as is the political world. Technology continues to revolutionize the way people do business. The global economy has mushroomed. National economies have become integrated to the point that a financial meltdown in Asia can have instant, stunning repercussions on businesses in North America.

Diversity is the pervasive characteristic of the North American workforce. Employees represent numerous ethnic groups. More and more people are trading in their desks for laptops so they can work at home or while they travel. Charles Handy observes, "The challenge for tomorrow's leaders is to manage an organization that is not there in any sense in which we are used to."[18] It requires enormous effort to create a corporate culture in which every employee feels a vital part of the team.

More and more work is outsourced to other companies; freelance and project people are becoming more popular. Yesterday's workplace was a specific location where employees came together for eight hours a day. The majority of jobs were performed for one reason—a paycheck. Personal fulfillment, though a factor, was secondary. All that has changed. Today's workplace is a forum for people to express themselves and to invest their efforts into something that contributes positively to society. People no longer choose jobs based merely on salary and benefits. They seek companies with corporate values that match their personal values.

Daniel Goleman suggests: "Except for the financially desperate, people do not work for money alone. What also fuels their passion for work is a larger sense of purpose or passion. Given the opportunity, people gravitate to what gives them meaning, to what engages to the fullest their commitment, talent, energy, and skill."[19] Accordingly, many people have embarked on multiple careers. Robert Greenleaf reflects on the shift in employee focus: "All work exists as much for the enrichment of the life of the worker as it does for the service of the one who pays for it."[20] Consequently, employees expect much more from their leaders than they did in years past.

The complex and critical issues facing today's marketplace only exacerbate the need for effective leaders. Modern business leaders are expected to peer into the turbulent economic future and make the necessary adjustments to avoid disaster for their companies. They must mold productive, cohesive teams out of the most variegated workforce in history. Leaders are expected to continually upgrade their skills and adjust to dizzying daily changes in the business world.

Businesses call on their leaders to understand and guide their industries though the workplace is filled with specialists who themselves require constant retraining to stay current in their fields. Is it any wonder companies cannot find men and women qualified to lead them into an uncertain future? Is it surprising that the salaries of CEOs have risen astronomically in comparison to the wages of laborers?

In December 2000, Home Depot hired Bob Nardelli to bring order to the rapidly growing company. Nardelli was a high-level executive for General Electric and on the short list to replace Jack Welch as its CEO. Home Depot valued Nardelli's ability and paid handsomely for it, providing him a total salary package of $30 million a year. This placed him fifty-sixth among America's highest paid CEOs for 2005. Nardelli had nine private parking places at the corporate office as well as a private elevator to his office. Five years later, despite overall company growth, Nardelli was fired and given a $210 million severance package.[21]

In July 1999, Hewlett-Packard Company named Carli Fiorina chief executive officer. The first woman to lead a Fortune 20 company, Fiorina immediately became a highly visible chief executive and she remained so throughout her tenure at the company. When she was hired, HP's stock price was $52 per share, and when she left five and a half years later in February 2005, it was $21 per share—a loss of over 60 percent of the stock's value. During that same time period, the stock price of HP's competitor, Dell, increased from $37 to $40 per share. Hewlett-Packard showed Fiori the door and paid her more than $20 million in severance.[22]

Rapacious for profit, companies not only pay enormous salaries; they sometimes ignore the warning signs of unethical or illegal practices. The business community has its share of scandals: Enron, Worldcom, and Bernie Maddoff had their misbehavior largely ignored as long as soaring profits continued. Today's business community is desperate not only for solid, ethical leadership but also for spiritual statesmen.

Leadership: In the Church

Like every segment of society, the religious community has suffered from a leadership drought. Jesus warned his followers about false prophets who would rise up to lead the unwary astray (Matt. 24:11), but who could have anticipated the plethora of would-be spiritual leaders who have flooded the airwaves and descended upon churches with their books and prophecies, clamoring for followers? It is incomprehensible that well-educated professionals with lucrative jobs, upscale houses, and comfortable lifestyles would sell everything and abandon their families, friends, and reputations to follow a self-declared messiah such as Jim Jones or David Karesh.

It is even more amazing that sincere people would follow such delusional prophets to violent deaths for the sake of oblique causes. What turns people into sycophants who do the bidding of deluded, self-appointed messiahs? Could it be there is such an enormous vacuum of genuine leaders that would-be saviors always find a ready market of followers looking for someone to enhance the quality of their lives?

The modern church faces an array of challenges it must overcome if it is to thrive in the future. The following are three major issues the church must effectively address.

LACK OF EFFECTIVE LEADERSHIP

Modern society is displaying widespread and growing interest in spiritual issues. Amazingly, at a time of renewed societal interest in things spiritual, most American churches are plateaued or declining. According to George Barna, "The American church is dying due to a lack of strong leadership. In this time of unprecedented opportunity and plentiful resources, the church is actually losing influence. The primary reason is the lack of leadership. Nothing is more important than leadership."[23] The church has answers to the most pressing questions people are asking, yet society views the church with increasingly skeptical eyes. Tragically, church leaders are regularly being exposed for immorality or unethical conduct.

Burnout among ministers is widespread. Pastoral firings are commonplace. Today's pastors must deal with controversial dilemmas much more complex and divisive than clerics faced a generation ago. In a society addicted to entertainment and pleasure, the church faces stiff competition for holding congregants' attention. Churches require leaders who can not only overcome the enormous challenges but also attract new members and secure the necessary resources to finance an increasingly expensive organization. Though many theological seminaries are enjoying healthy enrollments, denominational leaders continue to bemoan the fact these schools are graduating so few leaders. Although the leadership shortage is universally acknowledged, there is little consensus on how to discover and develop them.

RELIGIOUS CONSUMERISM

In our consumer-oriented society, companies inundate us with every manner of promise and incentive. Churches also compete for our allegiance, expending enormous energy and resources to attract both believers and nonbelievers. The result is a smorgasbord of congregations offering something to satisfy every palate. In some churches sin or anything "negative" is never mentioned. Other churches strive to be politically correct, changing their doctrines with every shifting wind in society. Then there are the Hollywood-driven churches seizing every new entertainment fad in their crusade to be relevant.

World religions are growing in record numbers dotting the skyline with their enormous temples. Religious offerings are easily accessible on television, radio, and the Internet. If your current place of worship has offended, neglected, or bored you, a "new and better" religious experience is just down the street or on the next channel.

OPPOSITION

For centuries the Christian church has been preeminent in the Western world. Towns throughout Europe were dominated by cathedrals and church spires. If a public occasion called for a prayer, Americans would expect it to come from a minister in the Christian tradition. Those days are gone. In an ironic turnaround, now that American society values political correctness above all else, the Christian church is habitually ridiculed and subjected to flagrant public discrimination.

Atheists and those adamantly opposed to the Christian faith have become increasingly vocal and belligerent. Now it is *de rigeur* to condemn the church for being intolerant of alternative lifestyles or life choices. Church leaders who were once politely accepted in society are now just as likely to be met with ridicule and antagonism. Whereas once churches were involved in the community and their presence was expected, now the welcome mat has been decisively yanked from under the Christian community. For churches to enjoy success in an increasingly secularized culture, they need a different kind of leadership than that to which they have been accustomed.

Leadership: In the Home

Scripture has volumes to say about the leadership role of parents. It declares: "The one who lives with integrity is righteous; his children who come after him will be happy" (Prov. 20:7). Yet the Bible reveals the failings of numerous fathers among the saints. Samuel, one of God's greatest leaders in biblical times, failed miserably to raise his two sons to be godly men (1 Sam. 8:1–5). David was Israel's most successful monarch, but he neglected his children and suffered dearly for his error.

History reveals numerous people who were heralded as great leaders in politics, business, or the church; and yet they could not keep their own children from pain and rebellion. John Rockefeller, an oil tycoon, built one of the most powerful companies in the world, but he was estranged from his daughter Edith, and no power at his disposal could bring her back to him.[24]

Tragically, many people who are great leaders in public for whatever reason leave their problem-solving ability, people skills, and team-building instincts at the front door when they return home to their families. While this is not a book about parenting, it should be stated there is no greater leadership position you can hold than being a parent. Whether you see yourself as a leader or not, if you are a parent, you owe it to your children to learn to lead as effectively as possible.

Leadership: Secular or Spiritual?

In considering spiritual leadership, several key issues must be addressed. First, is there a difference between secular leadership and Christian leadership? Bookstores are capitalizing on the chronic thirst for improved leadership and management. Successful leaders in business, sports, politics, or any other field have written autobiographies detailing their story. The myriad of such volumes testifies to the mass of people eagerly gobbling up their advice hoping to gain from their wisdom or to adopt their methodology. The key issue for Christians is whether the principles that make people successful in sports, business, entertainment, or politics are equally valid when applied to issues within the kingdom of God. The pastor examines the leadership style of a successful football coach and wonders: *Could his formula help me effectively lead my church?* A church staff witnesses a crowd bursting through the gates at Disney World and speculates, *What are they doing that we could mimic to attract people to our church?*

A significant question for Christian leaders is: Do theories and practices found in secular writing and seminars equally apply to work done in God's kingdom? Many Christian leaders think so. The current generation of Christian leaders has immersed itself in cutting-edge leadership philosophy. Secular leadership pundits are regularly highlighted at Christian leadership conferences, and the broad acceptance of secular approaches by Christian leaders has spilled over to numerous Christian contexts. The shift in the traditional nomenclature from the pastor's study to the pastor's office is one consequence. In times past churches focused on the Great Commission. Today's congregations adopt mission statements. In earlier times churches spoke of building fellowship. Contemporary Christian leaders lead their people through team-building exercises. Churches used to disciple their people in evangelism. Today's churches apply mass-marketing techniques to penetrate their communities. Pastors are expected to act more like CEOs than shepherds; the pastor's office is located in the executive suite, next to the boardroom where the leadership team meets. Is this adoption of secular leadership methodology a sorely needed improvement for churches? Or is it woefully missing the mark—to the point of violating biblical principles? Many church leaders claim these innovations have resulted in dramatic growth in their congregations, including an impressive number of converts. Others decry such approaches as blatant theological and biblical compromise.

The trend toward a CEO model of ministry has changed the churches' evaluations of effective leadership. The pastor's performance is measured in terms of numbers of people, dollars, and buildings. The more of each, the more successful is the pastor. The godliness of a minister or the fervency of his prayer life may not be sufficient to satisfy a congregation looking to keep up with the church down the street. Likewise, Christian organizations seem willing to overlook significant character flaws, and even moral lapses, as long as their leader continues to produce.

The trend among many Christian leaders has been toward an almost indiscriminate and uncritical acceptance of secular leadership theory without measuring it against the timeless precepts of Scripture. When considering next steps, many church staffs are more likely to query, "Will it work?" than they are to ask, "Is it biblical?" This book will examine contemporary leadership principles in light of scriptural truth. It will become clear that many of the "modern" leadership theories currently being espoused are, in fact, biblical principles God has commanded throughout history. For example, secular leadership gurus are insisting on integrity as an essential characteristic for modern leaders. This should be nothing new for Christians. The Bible has maintained that as a leadership standard for over two millennia.

Paradoxically, concurrent with the churches' discovery of popular leadership axioms, secular writers have been discovering the timeless truths of Christianity. A partial explanation for this juxtaposition may be that many secular writers on leadership are Christians, or at least religious people. More fundamentally, this shift to Christian principles is because leadership experts are discovering that doing business in a Christian manner, regardless of whether one is a practicing Christian, is good for business. Earlier leadership theories assumed the best CEOs were larger than life, charismatic icons who stood aloof from those they led, barking out orders to be followed unquestioningly. In contrast, today's leadership experts are writing books that appear almost Christian. Book titles such as *Jesus CEO, Management Lessons of Jesus, Servant Leadership, Love and Profit, Leading with Soul, Moral*

Leadership, and *Encouraging the Heart* sound like they ought to be shelved in a Christian college, not in the office of a corporate CEO.

The Christian tenor of these books goes beyond their titles. It is common to read in secular leadership books that companies should make covenants with their people, that business leaders should love their people, that managers should be servant leaders, that leaders should show their feelings to their employees, that business leaders must have integrity and tell the truth, and interestingly, that leaders must strive for a higher purpose than merely making a profit. These principles appear to be more in keeping with the Sermon on the Mount than Harvard Business School. Is it not ironic that while secular writers are embracing Christian teachings with the fervency of first-century Christians, Christian leaders are feverishly jettisoning many of those same truths in an effort to become more contemporary?

God or King?

The willingness of God's people to barter their spiritual birthright to gain the supposed benefits of contemporary secular thinking is not unique to this generation. Centuries ago when Israel was a small, insignificant nation consisting of twelve loose-knit tribes surrounded by international superpowers, the people had Samuel as their spiritual guide and God as their king. But as Samuel grew old, his ungodly sons abused their leadership positions. The Israelites compared themselves to neighboring nations and envied their powerful armies, magnificent cities, and the glory of their monarchies. Rather than trusting God to win their battles, direct their economy, and establish laws for their land, the Hebrew people aspired to be like other nations with a king. They took their request to Samuel. In response Samuel gave them God's appraisal of where this pursuit for a king would lead them.

> Samuel told all the LORD's words to the people who were asking him for a king. He said, "These are the rights of the king who will rule over you: He will take your sons and put them to his use in his chariots, on his horses, or running in front of his chariots. He can appoint

them for his use as commanders of thousands or commanders of fifties, to plow his ground or reap his harvest, or to make his weapons of war or the equipment for his chariots. He can take your daughters to become perfumers, cooks, and bakers. He can take your best fields, vineyards, and olive orchards and give them to his servants. He can take a tenth of your grain and your vineyards and give them to his officials and servants. He can take your male servants, your female servants, your best young men, and your donkeys and use them for his work. He can take a tenth of your flocks, and you yourselves can become his servants. When that day comes, you will cry out because of the king you've chosen for yourselves, but the LORD won't answer you on that day. The people refused to listen to Samuel. "No!" they said. "We must have a king over us. Then we'll be like all the other nations: our king will judge us, go out before us, and fight our battles." Samuel listened to all the people's words and then repeated them to the LORD. "Listen to them," the LORD told Samuel. "Appoint a king for them." Then Samuel told the men of Israel, "Each of you, go back to your city." (1 Sam. 8:10–22)

The world measured a kingdom's success by its grand palaces and magnificent armies. The glittering trappings of such monarchies dazzled the Israelites. But citizenship in such a kingdom came with a stiff price. Sustaining a monarchy required oppressive taxes from its citizens. The Israelites wanted a royal army, but such a luxury would demand heavier taxation as well as a draft of Israelite citizens into the king's service. A monarchy could not function without a legion of servants. God could not have been any more forthcoming about the consequences of choosing worldly leadership over divine guidance. Yet the Israelites stubbornly persisted in their desire to be like everyone else, so God granted them a perfect specimen of a worldly leader. Saul was handsome and physically impressive, yet he was insecure and vain. He was decisive, sometimes making on-the-spot pronouncements—many of which had to be rescinded later because they were foolhardy (1 Sam. 14:24–46). He was a passionate man, but he was also prone to violent temper tantrums. Saul was a hands-on general who spent much of his time chasing after his own citizens. The Israelites clamored for a leader who would lead them by worldly principles. God gave them one, and the results were disastrous.

What went wrong? The problem was that the Israelites assumed that spiritual concerns such as righteous living and obedience to God belonged in the religious realm while the "practical" issues of doing battle with enemies, strengthening the economy, and unifying the country were secular matters. They forgot that God gave them their military victories, brought them prosperity, and created their nation. God was just as present on the battlefield as he was in the worship service. When the Israelites separated spiritual concerns from political and economic issues, their nation was brought to its knees.

Applying spiritual principles to business and political issues doesn't call for pastors to serve as military generals, nor does it require seminary professors to run the economy. God created people as spiritual beings. Every person, Christian and non-Christian alike, has spiritual concerns. God can use his servants in the marketplace to address those needs. God is also the author of human relationships. He has established laws concerning human interaction that have not changed with the passing of time. Violating God-ordained relationship principles in the workplace invites disaster. Jesus Christ is the Lord of all believers whether they are at church or at work. The kingdom of God is, in fact, the rule of God in every area of life, including the church, home, government, workplace, and neighborhood. To ignore these truths when entering the business world or political arena is to do so at one's peril.

Society's problem is not that it lacks aspirants for leadership offices. Society's great deficit is that it is woefully in need of people from all walks of life who understand how to be *spiritual* leaders. People who "get things done" are not enough. Adolph Hitler did that. The world needs professionals who know how to apply their faith in the boardroom, in the classroom, in the courtroom, and in the operating room. Jesus summed up this truth for every executive, politician, schoolteacher, lawyer, doctor, minister, and parent when he said: "But seek first the kingdom of God and His righteousness, and all these things will be provided for you" (Matt. 6:33).

Mike, the young CEO introduced at the beginning of this chapter, struggled to understand how to remain true to his Christian beliefs and still be effective in the business world. The truth, as Mike was discovering, is that one's calling as a Christian not only takes precedence over a career; it gives it direction. Moreover, a Christian's calling provides meaning and purpose to every area of life. Is it possible to seek God's kingdom first while succeeding in business or politics? Growing numbers of Christian leaders are proving it is. Books such as *Loving Monday* by John Beckett, *It Is Easier to Succeed Than to Fail* by Truett Cathy of Chick-fil-A, *From the Shop Floor to the Top Floor: Releasing the CEO Within* by Wes Cantrell, and *Character Is the Issue: How People with Integrity Can Revolutionize America* by former governor Mike Huckabee of Arkansas provide examples of Christians who have incorporated their Christianity into their business and politics. The business world has recognized these leaders and rewarded them for their efforts. The world sorely lacks political and business leaders who are steered by the Holy Spirit and not from the latest public opinion poll. Society is weary of those whose personal agendas push aside God's standards. Families crave husbands and wives, mothers and fathers who know how to apply biblical promises in their homes rather than bewildered men and women stumbling through the self-help section at the local bookstore.

Great Man or Group Theory

Thomas Carlyle, an early observer of leadership, wrote: "Universal history, the history of what man has accomplished in this world, is at the bottom the History of the Great Men who have worked there."[25] In perhaps the earliest leadership theory, The Great Man theory viewed history as simply the elongated biographies of great leaders.[26] Typical history books might imply that mankind merely plodded along in mundane existence until the next great leader arose. History is often divided into categories such as the period of Alexander the Great or Caesar or Napoleon. However, while this perspective of history has long appeared overly simplistic, in our egalitarian age it seems offensive to suggest that any leader, whether the CEO or senior minister, is any more crucial to the organization's success than the person occupying the lowest box on the organizational chart. Tim Irwin cites the maxim: "If the leader didn't come to work today, everything would probably still get done; but if the people didn't come to work today, nothing would get done."[27] There has been a tendency to minimize the leader's role as if his or her voice was just one among many. Today's organizations often choose to work in teams rather than the customary top-down system of control. Many churches have decided the laity can run the church without the need for designated leaders.

An Arab proverb says, "An army of sheep led by a lion would defeat an army of lions led by a sheep." While it is true a team is as strong as its weakest link, we would also affirm that organizations rarely rise above their leader. An ordinary leader will produce an ordinary team. Great leaders tend to develop great organizations. While this does not make followers any less valuable as people, the unique function of leaders should not be minimized. Moreover, while on any given day the people may accomplish more tasks than the leader will, the longer those people labor without the vision, guidance, and support of a leader, the actual work they accomplish will deteriorate in quality, volume, and relevance. Leaders do not do all the work or even most of it. But effective leaders act as indispensable catalysts to ensure the right work is done.

We contend that God designed humanity to accomplish his purposes with godly, effective leaders filling a crucial role. Could the Israelites have freed themselves from bondage apart from a God-called leader like Moses? Perhaps, but they had numerous years to do just that and did not succeed until God sent his servant to lead them. Could the Israelites have conquered Canaan apart from the steady leadership of Joshua? If we are to infer anything about God's chosen method of guiding his people, Scripture clearly points to his repeated enlistment and equipping of individuals to act in a leadership capacity.[28] Would the Greeks have conquered the known world apart from Alexander the Great's leadership? Would the nomadic Mongols have built an empire four times the size of Alexander's ultimately reaching twenty-eight million square kilometers of land mass if they had not been united and mobilized by

Ghengis Khan?[29] Jacob Burkhardt declared: "Great men are necessary for our life, in order that the movement of world history can free itself sporadically, by fits and starts, from obsolete ways of living and inconsequential talk."[30] When there are no obstacles or challenges for people to overcome, then leaders are unnecessary. A manager will suffice who organizes people's work schedules, oversees payroll, and gives annual performance reviews. But, when problems arise, calamity strikes, or dramatic changes must be made, the universal need for leaders becomes evident. Today's problems have reached unprecedented levels of complexity and difficulty. Consequently, we find ourselves in greater need of leaders than ever before.

Ambition

One troubling dimension of leadership for Christians is ambition. Should a devout Christian *aspire* to lead? Such intent seems to contradict Scripture's teachings on humility and servanthood. After all, didn't Jesus come to serve and not to be served (Matt. 20:28)? While history might suggest some people had leadership thrust upon them, when scrutinizing the lives of famous leaders, one almost inevitably discovers they had an underlying desire to do something significant with their lives.

As a young boy, Benjamin Disraeli copied a passage from Petrarch that said: "I desire to be known to posterity; if I cannot succeed, may I be known to my age, or at least to my friends."[31] Disraeli would often pretend to be the prime minister of England while relegating his hapless younger siblings to the benches of the Opposition. Andrew Jackson's biographer concluded of him: "Basically, he was a conservative and deliberate man whose ambition and determination to succeed conditioned everything he did."[32] Woodrow Wilson was the son of a Presbyterian minister. Once when his father was asked why his horse was better groomed than he was, he quipped: "That is because I care for my horse and my parishioners care for me."[33] Young Wilson took voice lessons and practiced his speeches in his father's empty church auditorium. He confessed, "I make frequent extemporaneous addresses to the empty benches of my father's church in order to get a mastery of easy and correct and elegant expression, in preparation for the future."[34] Horatio Nelson confessed, "Glory is my object and that alone."[35] Such ambition would lead him to gain sparkling victories over Napoleon's fleet in Egypt and at Trafalgar. Prior to Nelson's celebrated victory at the Nile, the fearless commander predicted, "before this time tomorrow, I shall have gained a peerage, or Westminster Abbey."[36] It is questionable whether these leaders would ever have achieved what they did without a driving ambition to succeed.

But the question remains, should Christians be ambitious? Clearly, if their goal is to achieve personal fame, recognition, or wealth, then it is selfish and unbecoming. But if their purpose is to invest their one life as wisely as possible for the advancement of God's purposes on earth, then ambition is a good and useful force in a leader's life. Malcome Davies suggests, "Human communities have always had a need for people with very strong drives to do tough jobs like leadership."[37] Saul of Tarsus received a heavenly vision that God intended him to take the gospel to the Gentiles (Acts 26:12–18). By the end of his life he could proclaim: "Therefore, King Agrippa, I was not disobedient to the heavenly vision" (Acts 26:19). William Wilberforce was animated as a young man to achieve fame and fortune for himself through politics. But after his conversion to Christianity, he became convinced God placed him on the earth for a divine purpose. He therefore concluded that he would not be successful unless he fulfilled his God-given assignment. He declared: "God almighty has set before me two great objects: the suppression of the slave trade and the reformation of manners."[38] By the end of his life, Wilberforce's breathtaking ambition was realized, and he led in the dismantling of a system that had enslaved thousands of innocent people. Would that every Christian were equally ambitious to accomplish God's purposes for their life!

Great Leaders or History?

One final issue to mention at the outset of this book is the historians' age-old debate of whether great leaders make history or if history produces great leaders. Clearly if times of crisis and challenge generally call for leaders, then periods of peace and prosperity do not set the stage for individuals to make a great contribution to humanity. General George Patton lamented, "In peace I am useless."[39] It is generally in tumultuous times that people make the greatest difference in their world. The greater the crisis, the greater is the opportunity for leaders to make a difference. Those who complain about their difficulties or shrink from crises prove they are not leaders regardless of whether they hold such an office. But people who recognize the opportunity history affords them and boldly accept the invitation will change their world.

The American Civil War provided a singular opportunity for Americans to rise to levels of leadership theretofore impossible. President James Buchanan led the nation prior to the war. Thoroughly trained and immensely experienced, he could have addressed his nation's greatest ills. But he failed. Arthur Schlesinger notes: "The greatest presidents in the scholar's rankings, Washington, Lincoln, and Franklin Roosevelt, were leaders who confronted and overcame the republic's greatest crises. Crisis widens presidential opportunities for bold and imaginative action. But it does not guarantee presidential greatness. The crisis of succession did not spur Buchanan or the crisis of depression spur Hoover to creative leadership. Their inadequacies in the face of crisis allowed Lincoln and the second Roosevelt to show the difference individuals make to history."[40] It has been said of Abraham Lincoln, "Without the march of events that led to the Civil War, Lincoln still would have been a good man, but most likely would never have been publicly recognized as a great man. It was history that gave him the opportunity to manifest his greatness, providing the stage that allowed him to shape and transform our national life."[41] Likewise it has been said of General Ulysses Grant: "Grant was a perfect family man. Had peace prevailed he would have lived out his days as a slightly rumpled shopkeeper in the upper Mississippi valley, indistinguishable from his friends and neighbors."[42] Occasionally, history provides the opportunity for ordinary people to do extraordinary things.

Conclusion

Modern history is once again calling upon men and women to rise up and fulfill their God-given destiny to impact their world. True spiritual leaders do not wring their hands and wistfully recount the better times of days gone by. Genuine leaders understand they have but one life to live and so they expend it with purpose and passion. God placed you on the earth at this particular crossroad in history. You live in a time of great challenges but enormous opportunity. May you live, and lead, well.

—————— Responding to This Material ——————

In response to the material presented in this chapter, take a few moments to respond to the following questions:

1. If you inherited a fortune, would you quit your job? Circle one.

    definitely   probably   probably not   definitely not

What does your response tell you about your present career? Are you working in the right field? Are you working out of a sense of calling?

2. How much is the rapid development of technology affecting you and your work? Very little   occasionally   daily   very much

Are you maximizing technology to its greatest effect? Are you keeping up with advances in your field? What could you do to enhance your use of technology to improve your work?

3. What are three ways globalization is affecting you and your work? Consider how it affects your:

- ✦ style of communication
- ✦ leadership style
- ✦ reward system
- ✦ hiring practices
- ✦ Christian influence on your workplace
- ✦ global opportunities

4. Do you see a clear demarcation between secular and sacred dimensions to leadership? List three to five Christian and secular leadership principles that are alike. What are two approaches that are clearly different?

5. How do you view the role of a leader in relationship to the group? On a scale of 1 to 10, how important is the leader to the health of your organization?

6. On a scale of 1 to 10, how ambitious are you? List the top five areas in which you are driven to succeed (be honest!). They might include: earning money, building a comfortable retirement, building a reputation, becoming CEO, making a contribution to society, glorifying God, proving myself to my father, etc.

7. Which do you feel is more important, great leaders or the chances of history? How would you describe the time of history you are living in? In what way is history currently presenting you an opportunity to make a significant contribution to your world?

Chapter Two

The Leader's Role:
What Leaders Do

L eadership is one of the most observed and least understood phenomena on earth," asserts James MacGregor Burns.[1] Voluminous material is published continuously on the subject of leadership, yet there appears to be no simple, universally accepted understanding of what leaders do. Unless they clearly understand their role, leaders as well as their followers are destined for confusion, frustration, and failure. Perhaps that is why so many modern leaders are voraciously consuming leadership materials and seminars. Nevertheless, leaders worry that despite their heroic efforts and incessant working hours, they are still missing the mark.

If you are a leader and you sense God wants to accomplish more through your life than you are presently experiencing, this book was written for you. We will survey the modern literature on the subject as well as evaluate current leadership theories in light of scriptural truth. We hope by reading this material you will gain a clear sense of your role as a spiritual leader and you will focus on accomplishing what God has called you to do.

What Is Leadership?

In their 1997 book *Leaders: Strategies for Taking Charge*, Warren Bennis and Burt Nanus reported there were more than 850 published definitions of leadership.[2] Hundreds more have been added since then. No wonder today's leaders are unsure how they measure up! Each definition seeks to contribute new insight to the understanding of leadership, and many of them do. The following is a sampling of the diversity of helpful definitions of leadership:

+ "Leadership is the process of persuasion or example by which an individual (or leadership team) induces a group to pursue objectives held by a leader or shared by the leader and his or her followers." John W. Gardner, *On Leadership*.[3]

+ "Leadership over human beings is exercised when persons with certain motives and purposes mobilize, in competition or conflict with others, institutional, political, psychological, and other resources so as to arouse, engage, and satisfy the motives of followers." James MacGregor Burns, *Leadership*.[4]

+ "Leadership is influence, the ability of one person to influence others." Oswald Sanders, *Spiritual Leadership*.[5]

+ "A Christian leader is someone who is called by God to lead; leads with and through Christ-like character; and demonstrates the functional competencies that permit effective leadership to take place." George Barna, *Leaders on Leadership*.[6]

+ "The central task of leadership is influencing God's people toward God's purposes." Robert Clinton, *The Making of a Leader*.[7]

+ "A person influencing people to accomplish a purpose." Pat MacMillan, *The Performance Factor*.[8]

Each of these definitions brings focus to the leader's role. Some are secular definitions that address general leadership principles but do not take God and his purposes into account. In this book we will use the term *spiritual leadership*. By that we mean both leaders of religious organizations and Christian business leaders guiding secular organizations. Spiritual leaders are people who seek to lead God's way, regardless of where they serve him. They are as essential in the marketplace as they are in the church.

John Gardner's definition employs the terms *persuasion* and *example* to indicate the means by which leaders move people toward their objectives. According to Gardner, leaders' persuasion is never enough unless accompanied by personal example. Leaders must not only deliver a message to their followers; they must incarnate it personally. Spiritual leaders would do well to heed Gardner's emphasis on persuasion and example. The opposite form of leadership would be bullying and using dictatorial methodology. However, this secular definition fails to take into account God's will and the guidance he provides leaders. Secular leaders lead people to achieve their goals or goals held by their followers. But this is not the focus of spiritual leaders. Spiritual leadership involves more than merely achieving objectives. People can accomplish all their goals and still miss God's will.

James Burns, a respected scholar in leadership theory and promoter of the transactional model of leadership, has wisely insisted that followers have a key role to play in the process of leadership. He acknowledges that all leaders are driven by particular motives. He also identifies the institutional, political, and psychological arenas in which leaders work. Furthermore, Burns notes that leaders seek to meet the needs of their followers through the transaction of leadership. This may involve helping followers identify their highest needs before enabling them to meet those needs. His observation brings to mind Harry Truman's maxim: "A leader is a man who has the ability to get other people to do what they don't want to do and like it." Nevertheless, while Burns's definition is beneficial to leaders, it also falls short of describing the role of spiritual leaders. While leaders do have motives, spiritual leaders are directed by the Holy Spirit, not by their own agendas. Their leadership is not always in the face of conflict or competition but sometimes simply in the midst of the forces of inertia. At times embracing the status quo is the greatest enemy to advancing Christian causes, and the leader's task is to keep people from growing complacent. Most importantly, spiritual leaders are not primarily driven by their effort to satisfy the goals and ambitions of the people they lead but those of the God they serve. Spiritual leaders must be spiritual statesmen and not merely politicians seeking to pacify their constituents.

Oswald Sanders, in his classic work *Spiritual Leadership*, suggests that leadership is influence. The term *influence* pervades current discussions of leadership. More recently, John Maxwell has done much to popularize this definition.[9] Sanders correctly asserts that people who make no difference in others' lives are not leaders. We concur that leaders must exert influence if they are to lead. Paul Hershey is more specific in his definition: "Leadership is an attempt to influence the behavior of another individual or group."[10]

Influence, however, is too broad a term to precisely describe the process of leadership. A prankster can call the local post office and claim to have placed a bomb on the premises. That is exerting influence. Yet forcing terrified employees to flee a building while the bomb squad methodically searches for explosives is certainly not leadership. Some well-meaning people in leadership positions believe creating a stir or "making things happen" is exercising leadership. In reality, however, all they are doing is exerting a negative influence. Robert Greenleaf observed that, rather than choosing to become true leaders, "too many settle for being critics and experts."[11] Becoming your organization's chief critic is not leadership. Denouncing the actions of others is not leadership. Merely exerting influence is not in itself leadership. You must evaluate the result of that influence. Ronald Heifetz suggests that describing leadership as "influence" confuses means with ends.[12]

Leadership occurs when you move people from where they are to where they ought to be. The result of leadership is that people are not in the same place they were before they were lead. While benefiting from the contribution of Sanders, today's leaders need to know how to exert influence according to God's will.

George Barna presents a useful definition of leadership from a Christian perspective. He emphasizes the three C's of call, character, and competencies as essential for effective leadership. If we were to add anything to this definition it might be the aspect of results. Leadership is ultimately measured not according to the leader's performance but on the leader's results. As Peter Drucker points out, "Popularity is not leadership. Results are."[13] While individuals may hold a leadership position, one could question whether that person has truly led until someone has followed, and more importantly, until God's purposes have been advanced. All the functional competencies may be for naught if followers remain where they are. It is also restrictive to try to quantify and qualify specific leadership traits. Although certain skills are common to most leaders, there is widespread debate about which skills are essential. The biblical record suggests God used people who didn't look or act like leaders in the traditional sense. Certain biblical characters greatly impacted their society but demonstrated few of the commonly recognized leadership competencies. Rather, God chose to use the weak to demonstrate his strength (Exod. 3–4; 1 Cor. 1:26–27; 2 Cor. 12:9–10).

Robert Clinton's definition encompasses the spiritual nature of leadership in that God's people are led toward God's purposes. Clinton wisely observes that God's purposes are the key to spiritual leadership. A leader's dreams and visions are not. We would add at least two dimensions to Clinton's definition. First, spiritual leaders can lead those who are not God's people as well as those who are. Christian leadership is not restricted to within church walls but is also effective in the public arena. Second, Clinton notes that leaders lead their people toward God's purposes. However, simply leading people toward an objective may not be adequate. While most leaders cannot achieve all of God's purposes for an organization in their lifetime, they should strive to accomplish everything God intended for the organization during their leadership tenure. Many leaders have left their organizations after serving less than two years. They often proclaim they moved their organization forward, yet nothing of lasting significance was accomplished. They are like the pastor whose church was continually losing members. Every time someone asked him how his church was doing, he would reply grimly, "I think we have turned a corner." The pastor said this so often people wondered if he was leading a maze or a church!

Just as Moses was not released from his followers when they disobeyed God and began a forty-year hiatus in the wilderness, so true leaders stay with their people until they have successfully achieved the purposes for which God called them to lead the organization in the first place. Moses himself remained faithful to God, yet God did not release him from his rebellious people. To abandon followers because they refuse to follow is to forsake the leader's sacred calling. Spiritual leaders know they must give an account of their leadership to God (2 Cor. 5:10–11); therefore, they are not satisfied with merely moving people *toward* the destination God has for them; they want to see God achieve his purposes through them for their generation.

We should acknowledge that sometimes people may pressure leaders to compromise what the leader knows is best for their people. Such was the case with Samuel and the peoples' desire for a king. However, God gave Samuel a specific release to accommodate the peoples' request. Nor did Samuel abandon the rebellious people. In other cases leaders may be fired as a result of their faithful efforts to lead their people. That scenario is much different from leaders abandoning their people. In this case leaders may have no choice but to step down from their leadership role. However, as Samuel declared, "As for me, I vow that I will not sin against the LORD by ceasing to pray for you" (1 Sam. 12:23).

A New Definition

A number of helpful definitions of leadership are available, but we believe true spiritual leadership can be defined in one concise statement:

> Spiritual leadership is moving
> people on to God's agenda.

This is a succinct definition, not as extensive as others, but we believe it encompasses what is at the heart of spiritual leadership. Several truths are inherent in this definition.

THE SPIRITUAL LEADER'S TASK

Spiritual leadership is not identical to leadership in general. While spiritual leadership involves many of the same principles as general leadership, it has certain distinctive qualities that must be understood and practiced if spiritual leaders are to be successful. The following are the distinctive elements of spiritual leadership implied in our definition.

1. *The spiritual leader's task is to move people.* This is influence. Once spiritual leaders understand God's will, they make every effort to move their followers, who have previously been promoting their own agendas, to pursue God's purposes. Until this happens, those in charge have not actually led. They may have exhorted, manipulated, bullied, or held an office, but they have not led unless their people have adjusted their lives to God's will. We prefer the word *move* over *influence* although both refer to impacting followers. The word *move* implies journeying to a destination. It is leaving where you are and relocating to a new position. The connotations of motion indicate a significant change has occurred. There are many ways to move people; subsequent chapters will examine methodology more closely. Gardner used the verb *induce.* Burns's term was *mobilize.* Moving people is not the same thing as driving or forcing people to do something. It is, as Gardner noted, a process of "persuasion and example" by which leaders cause their people to change their attitudes and behaviors and move forward to achieve God's purposes. When spiritual leaders have done their jobs, the people around them have encountered God and obeyed his will.

Of course not all influence is of the same magnitude. A national president who brings unity to a divided nation is a leader of influence. But so is the college student who encourages her Bible study group to take one Monday a month and minister at the nearby retirement home. Both have moved people from where they were to where God wanted them to be.

2. *Spiritual leaders use spiritual means.* Our definition assumes spiritual leaders use spiritual methods to move or influence people as opposed to practices that dishonor God. Spiritual leaders function within a paradox, for God calls them to do something that, in fact, only he can do. Spiritual leaders cannot produce spiritual change in people; only the Holy Spirit can do that. Yet through the Spirit, God often uses people to bring about spiritual growth in others. Moses experienced this paradox when God commissioned him to go to Egypt to free the Israelites from their oppressive bondage. God declared, "I have observed the misery of My people in Egypt, and have heard them crying out because of their oppressors, and I know about their sufferings. I have come down to rescue them from the power of the Egyptians and to bring them from that land to a good and spacious land" (Exod. 3:7–8). So far this sounded fine to Moses. God was going to do something only God could do. Then God added an unsettling instruction, "Therefore, go. I am sending you to Pharaoh so that you may lead My people, the Israelites, out of Egypt" (Exod. 3:10). That is the crux of spiritual leadership. Leaders seek to move people on to God's agenda, all the while being aware that only the Holy Spirit can ultimately accomplish the task.

3. *Spiritual leaders are accountable to God.* Spiritual leadership necessitates an acute sense of accountability (James 3:1). Just as a teacher has not taught until students have learned, leaders don't blame their people when they fail to follow. Leaders don't make excuses. They assume their responsibility is to move people to do God's will. Until they succeed in this, they have not fulfilled their role as leaders. Spiritual leadership is taking people from where they are to where God wants them to be. Because God's agenda drives spiritual leaders, it is God, and not the leader, who determines when his will has been accomplished (1 Sam. 15:13–24).

We must add that people may faithfully serve God in a leadership role and yet not fully move people to where they should be. Leadership also requires followership. For example, was Moses a failure as a leader because he failed to lead the Israelites into the Promised Land? Certainly, followers have a role to play in responding to God's will for their lives and organizations. Moses was faithful in his assignments. God's chastisement for him was not because he did not lead the people to their proper destination but because in the process of leading ungodly followers, his actions dishonored God (Num. 20:1–13).

4. *Spiritual leaders focus on people.* Leadership is fundamentally a people business! It is not merely about budgets or visions or strategies. It is about people. Spiritual leaders never lose sight of this fact. Richard Nixon was an introvert who did not enjoy being around people. He once observed of the presidency, "This would be an easy job if you didn't have to deal with people."[14] Nixon constantly sought seclusion and eventually limited his time to only four key advisors. Nixon did not exude personal warmth. At one point Nixon acquired a dog named King Timahoe to soften his public image. However, Timahoe would not approach the president even when his aides strung dog biscuits up to his desk.[15] True leaders enjoy people and make them better for having followed.

5. *Spiritual leaders influence all people, not just God's people.* An important truth that is often overlooked is that spiritual leaders can influence all people, not just Christians. God is on mission at the local factory or technology company as well as at the local church. His agenda applies in the marketplace as well as the meeting place. Although spiritual leaders will generally move God's people to achieve God's purposes, God can also use them to exert significant influence upon unbelievers. The biblical account of Joseph is a case in point. God intended to spare the Egyptians from a devastating seven-year famine and, through them, to provide food for other Middle Eastern people as well. Pharaoh did not follow the true God so God sent Joseph to advise him. Joseph interpreted God's warning so Pharaoh could mobilize the pagan nation to respond to God's activity. Building grain storage bins or developing a nationwide food distribution system may not seem like an overtly spiritual activity, but God used these mundane tasks to save thousands of peoples' lives, including Abraham's descendents. God did not choose to use the religious experts of the day. Instead, he guided an unbelieving society through Joseph, a God-fearing government official.

History is replete with examples of Christian men and women exerting spiritual leadership upon secular society. Certainly William Wilberforce had a major influence in his day. Many in the British parliament despised his openly evangelical convictions. At one point Lord Melbourne lamented, "Things have come to a pretty pass . . . when one should permit one's religion to invade public life."[16] Yet Wilberforce's biographer concluded that "no politician has ever used his faith to a greater result for all humanity."[17] We have been pleased to meet with government leaders who were studying this book in the state capitol building each week as they sought to become spiritual statesmen. James Monti has written: "It is a testimony to the awesome dignity that almighty God has bestowed on each human soul that just one man can exert such a marked and lasting influence on the course of human events—an influence for good or for evil."[18]

Christians in business, like those in politics, ought not to assume that spiritual leadership is purely the local minister's domain. Spiritual leadership occurs down the middle of everyday life. We regularly disciple Christian CEOs from corporate America. These business leaders want their faith to inform the way they guide their companies. These are influential people: they play golf with world leaders; they serve on prestigious boards; they supervise billions of dollars and thousands of employees. They make time to dialogue regularly with one another about how Christ affects the way they lead their companies. They are spiritual leaders as well as business leaders. Is this possible? Absolutely!

6. *Spiritual leaders work from God's agenda.* The greatest obstacle to effective spiritual leadership is when people pursue their own agendas rather than seeking God's will. God is working throughout the world to achieve his purposes and to advance his kingdom. His concern is not to fulfill leaders' dreams and goals or to build their kingdoms and careers. His purpose is to turn his people away from their self-centeredness and obsession with temporal, material concerns and to draw them into a relationship with himself so they are his instruments for accomplishing *his* purposes.

The Gospel of Luke provides a graphic contrast between peoples' agendas and God's. Jesus took Peter, James, and John with him up a mountain to experience a divine encounter. God the Father was unfolding his specific will for his Son. The Father brought Moses and Elijah to encourage Jesus for the enormous work of redemption he was about to accomplish. So sacred was that moment that Jesus radiated the glory of his divinity. Peter and his companions, however, had been sleeping. When they awoke and saw the magnificent scene unfolding, Peter spoke up: "Master, it's good for us to be here! Let us make three tabernacles: one for You, one for Moses, and one for Elijah" (Luke 9:33). Peter's first thought was to build something tangible to institutionalize the divine encounter. Peter, a natural leader, could already envision the ongoing ministry he and his friends would administer as a result of that encounter. However, the instant Peter began talking, the vision was removed, and only Jesus remained visible. Clearly Peter's plan was not God's agenda. The heavenly Father immediately rebuked Peter, saying, "'This is My Son, the Chosen One; listen to Him!'" (v. 35). Peter, because he was human, instinctively thought in temporal terms. He envisioned something he could control and manage. He wanted to move Jesus, Moses, Elijah, James, and John on to his agenda instead of seeking to understand God's will and adjusting his own life accordingly.

Peter's ignorance of spiritual ways is all too prevalent among today's spiritual leaders. Too often people assume that along with their role of leader comes the responsibility of determining what should be done. They develop aggressive goals. They imagine grandiose dreams. They cast grand visions. Then they pray and ask God to join them in their agenda and bless their efforts. That's not the spiritual leader's role. Spiritual leaders seek God's will, whether it is for their church, family, or corporation, and then they mobilize their people to pursue God's plan.

The key to spiritual leadership, then, is for leaders to understand God's will for them and their organizations. They then move people away from their own agendas and on to God's. It sounds simple enough, but the truth is that many Christian leaders fail to put this basic truth into practice. They allow trends and secular models of leadership to corrupt the straightforward model set forth by Jesus.

7. *Spiritual leaders hear from God.* When this book was first released, we were inundated with people who affirmed that the role of spiritual leaders was to move people on to God's agenda. The most common question to follow was, how do we know what God's agenda is? We discovered that many people, even pastors of churches, were disoriented to God's voice. We subsequently wrote the book *Hearing God's Voice* to help people recognize when the Holy Spirit was communicating with them.[19] Spiritual leaders cannot know God's agenda if they are disoriented to his voice. As with any facet of the Christian life, it always comes down to one thing. The most important thing spiritual leaders do is cultivate their relationship with God (John 15:5; Jer. 7:13).

Spiritual Leadership: Jesus as the Model

Even secular writers recognize Jesus as a compelling model of good leadership. He began a worldwide movement with a handful of ordinary men, and Christianity continues to grow and expand two thousand years later. Numerous scholars have attempted to explain Jesus' leadership style. Theorists have developed elaborate leadership systems and training models based on what they discovered as they examined Jesus' methods. Jesus' life is so profound and beyond our common experience we must continually reexamine it lest we assume Jesus operated merely by leadership theories we value today.

The enormous success of Jesus' movement was not because he developed a plan or cast a vision. He did neither. Rather, Jesus sought his Father's will. Jesus had an agenda for himself and his disciples, but the vision came from his Father. Some portray Jesus as a leader who first accepted the enormous assignment of redeeming a lost and corrupt world and then set out to figure out how to do it. At times leadership experts present Jesus as though he stood on a mountaintop overlooking Jerusalem musing to himself, "How am I going to gain a following and spread the gospel worldwide? Should I seek to convince the religious establishment? Should I preach to the masses? Should

I perform an impressive array of miracles? No, I'll invest myself in the lives of twelve men. I'll train them so thoroughly that after I am gone they will carry out my mission for me. As they invest in other leaders, they will multiply themselves, and hence they will expand my ministry until they have extended my kingdom throughout the world." This is clearly a misunderstanding of Jesus' ministry.

Some leadership development proponents observe that Jesus concentrated primarily on training twelve followers. They conclude this model of leadership must be the pattern for all spiritual leaders. While not depreciating the value of leadership development or the significance of small-group dynamics, leaders would be remiss to infer the methodology Jesus adopted is the key to spiritual leadership. It is not. The key to Jesus' leadership was his relationship with his Father.

Scripture indicates, "When the time came to completion, God sent His Son, born of a woman, born under the law" (Gal. 4:4). The redemptive plan had always belonged to the Father. Even as he expelled Adam and Eve from the garden of Eden after they sinned, the Father knew how he would ultimately redeem humanity. His plan involved developing a people for himself out of Abraham's descendants. It called for the law, introduced under Moses, to reveal sin's nature and its consequences. The Father's plan culminated in his Son's lowly birth, his excruciating crucifixion for sins he did not commit, his resurrection, and ultimately his ascension to the right hand of the Father. This plan was not the Son's. It was the Father's (John 3:16).

We must emphasize that planning or goal setting is not wrong. Organizations must have direction and order. The key is the *source* of those plans. Spiritual leaders seek God's guidance in discerning God's purposes for their organization. Then they mobilize their organizations to effectively accomplish what God assigns.

As a young man, Jesus "increased in wisdom and stature, and in favor with God and with people" (Luke 2:52). He developed his relationship with God the Father as well as with people. Since he knew the Father, Jesus recognized his voice and understood his will. Because he knew the Father's will, Jesus did not allow people's opinions to sidetrack him from his mission (Mark 1:37–38). The temptations in the wilderness were Satan's attempts to prevent Jesus from obeying the Father (Matt. 4; Luke 4:1–13). Satan approached Jesus with a proposition: "So, your assignment is to bring salvation to the people of the earth. That's a big job. Let me help you. Transform these stones into bread. If you feed the people they will follow you." Jesus refused, so Satan offered another suggestion: "Cast yourself from the top of the temple. When the angels save you, everyone will see the miracle, and they'll know you are God's Son. Then they will follow you." Again Jesus refused. Satan offered a final alternative: "Jesus, there's no point in fighting over the dominion of this earth. Bow down and worship me, and I will hand over all the people to you. Then you won't have to do battle with me and you can avoid the cross. Crucifixion is despicable and totally unnecessary for you to accomplish your goals." Once again Jesus refused to take a shortcut to carrying out his Father's will. This would not be the last time Jesus would have to resist such temptations (John 6:15; Matt. 12:38; 27:40).

Satan's overt temptations during this encounter are obvious. He tried to convince Jesus there was an easier way, with a lower personal cost. Second, he claimed God's way was not necessarily the only option in achieving desired goals. But there was also a more subtle temptation at work. Satan sought to persuade Jesus that saving the world was his job so he should develop a plan to get the job done. Satan was offering what appeared to be shortcuts to God's will, but they were traps that carried enormous consequences. Jesus, however, knew he was not commissioned to develop ministry goals or action plans. He was sent to follow the Father's plan. Jesus was not at liberty to negotiate with Satan over various approaches to redeeming humanity. The Father had already developed the plan. Jesus' own words say it best: "I assure you: The Son is not able to do anything on His own, but only what He sees the Father doing. For whatever the Father does, the Son also does these things in the same way. For the Father loves the Son and shows Him everything He is doing, and He will show Him greater works than these so that you will be amazed. . . . I can do nothing on My own, I judge only as I hear, and My judgment is righteous, because I do not seek My own will, but the will of Him who sent Me" (John 5:19–20, 30).

The setting was Bethesda, a healing pool in Jerusalem. Jesus was passing by on his way to attend a feast. As he walked past the pool, Jesus encountered a multitude of invalids surrounding the pool, each desperately hoping an angel might come and stir the waters. Tradition suggested the first person entering the pool when this happened would be cured. Among the crowd was a man who had been lame for thirty-eight years. Of all the people there that day, it appears Jesus chose to heal only this one person. When the religious leaders challenged Jesus' actions, he explained he was doing exactly what the Father showed him to do. Jesus cultivated such a close relationship with his Father he could recognize his Father's activity even in the midst of a large crowd. Whenever and wherever he saw his Father at work, Jesus immediately joined him.

Even choosing the twelve disciples was not Jesus' idea but his Father's. Scripture says Jesus spent an entire night praying before he singled out his disciples. "During those days He went out to the mountain to pray and spent all night in prayer to God. When daylight came, He summoned His disciples, and He hose 12 of them—He also named them apostles" (Luke 6:12–13).

This was a critical juncture in Jesus' ministry. It is significant that Scripture notes the length of time Jesus spent in prayer over this matter. Perhaps the Father spent time explaining the role of Judas to his Son during those intimate hours of prayer.

On the night of his crucifixion, Jesus reiterated that the Father had chosen the disciples. In what is commonly referred to as Jesus' high priestly prayer, he gave an account to his Father for all the Father one had given him. "I have revealed Your name to the men You gave Me from the world. They were Yours, You gave them to Me, and they have kept Your word. Now they know that all things You have given to me are from You" (John 17:6–7).

Jesus did not choose twelve disciples as a matter of strategy. Nor was twelve an optimum number Jesus calculated for pedagogical reasons. He had a dozen disciples for one reason only: that's how many his Father gave him. Would Jesus have included Judas if he were simply implementing a discipleship strategy designed to multiply his efforts? No, Judas was given to Jesus as a part of God the Father's redemptive plan.

According to Jesus, even the teaching he gave his disciples came from the Father (John 6:49–50; 14:10; 15:15; 17:8). If these twelve men were to develop into the leaders God wanted them to be, they would need the Father's instruction. Jesus understood he was to facilitate the relationship between his disciples and his Father. His task was to bring his disciples face-to-face with the Father so they, too, could develop an intimate relationship with him (John 14:8–11). When the twelve began to mature in their understanding of spiritual truths, they recognized Jesus as the Christ. Jesus knew this was not the result of his teaching methods but due to the Father's work in their lives. This truth is evident in Jesus' response when Peter confessed him as the Christ: "You are blessed because flesh and blood did not reveal this to you, but My Father in heaven" (Matt. 16:17).

Jesus was the wisest teacher of all time, yet he understood it was his Father's activity and not his own that was the impetus behind any breakthrough in his disciples' spiritual understanding. Even in that sacred moment when he fell on his face and pled with his Father to let the terrible cup of crucifixion pass from him, Jesus yielded himself entirely to his Father's will (Matt. 26:39). There was never any question about replacing or modifying the Father's plan with the Son's strategy.

Further evidence of Christ's complete dependence on his Father is the fact Jesus did not know when his own second coming would be: "Now concerning that day and hour no one knows—neither the angels in heaven, nor the Son—except the Father only" (Matt. 24:36).

Jesus came to fulfill his Father's plan of salvation. He spent each day looking to see what the Father would reveal about his will. When he observed the Father at work, Jesus adjusted his life to join him. When Jesus entered the city of Jericho, masses of people crowded along the streets trying to catch a glimpse of him. Jesus did not orchestrate that event. He did not strategize: "This is the last time I will pass through this city. What can I do to make the greatest impact on the crowd and see the most people accept the gospel?"

Rather, out of the intimate relationship Jesus had with his Father, when he spotted the diminutive Zacchaeus in a tree, he recognized the Father's activity in the despised tax collector's life and he invited Zacchaeus to spend time with him (Luke 19:1–10). Had Jesus entered the city planning to have lunch with the most notorious sinner of that region? No. He was only passing through Jericho on his way to Jerusalem. But as soon as he saw where the Father was working, Jesus immediately knew the agenda for his own ministry. Likewise, he trained his disciples to watch for God's activity rather than to set their own priorities. Even in the most arduous assignments, including the cross, Jesus accepted his Father's will unwaveringly. Jesus left his future, as well as his second coming, for the Father to determine. Jesus characterized his entire ministry with these words: "I can do nothing on My own" (John 5:30).

Conclusion

Jesus established the model for Christian leaders. It is not found in his "methodology." Rather, it is his absolute obedience to the Father's will. Current leadership theory suggests good leaders are also good followers and this is particularly true of spiritual leaders. Spiritual leaders understand God is their leader. If Jesus provides the model for spiritual leadership, then the key is not for leaders to develop visions and to set the direction for their organizations. The important thing is to obey and preserve everything the Father reveals to them of his will. The Father leads the leader. God has the vision of what he wants to do. God does not ask leaders to dream big dreams for him or to solve the problems confronting them with their own best thinking. He asks leaders to walk with him so intimately that when he reveals his agenda they immediately adjust their lives and their organizations to his will and the results bring glory to God. This is not the model many religious leaders, let alone business or government officials, follow today, but it encompasses what biblical leadership is all about.

Is it possible for God to guide leaders so their actions and even their words, are not theirs, but his? Yes. Does God have an agenda for what he wants to see happen in your workplace? Your home? He does. Our prayer should be that which Jesus instructed his disciples to pray: "Your kingdom come. Your will be done on earth as it is in heaven" (Matt. 6:10). If Christians around the world were suddenly to renounce their personal ambitions, their life plans and their aspirations and begin responding in radical obedience to everything God showed them, the world would be turned upside down. How do we know? Because that's what first-century Christians did and the world is still feeling the impact.

Responding to This Material

1. Write your own definition of "leadership."

2. What are the key words or concepts you feel are crucial to being an effective leader?

3. Analyze our definition of leadership. What is missing? What do you like?

4. Measure the results of your current leadership with the seven aspects of our definition. How does your leadership compare?

5. *Spiritual leaders move people.* Have you moved people to where they need to be? What is the evidence?

6. *Spiritual leaders use spiritual means.* Could your leadership style truly be described as *spiritual* leadership? How is the Holy Spirit making a practical difference in the way you lead?

7. *Spiritual leaders are accountable to God.* What is the evidence you lead with a profound awareness you must give an account to God for how you have led?

8. *Spiritual leaders focus on people.* Do you consider people you work with to be important? What is the evidence? Do people generally like you? If not, what might be the reason? How might God want you to adjust your leadership style so you are more effective in working with people? Daniel Goleman has

written much on emotional intelligence. You may want to read his book *Primal Leadership* or *Working with Emotional Intelligence*.

9. *Spiritual leaders work with all people, not just God's people.* List three people you have affected spiritually who are not Christians. How might God want to use you in your current position to move non-Christians on to God's agenda?

10. *Spiritual leaders work from God's agenda.* Where do your goals come from? Can you confidently say they originated from God or from your own thinking? Do you sense there should be more to your leadership than what you are currently planning to do? Recall a time you adjusted your agenda to God's agenda.

11. *Spiritual leaders hear from God.* Do you have difficulty hearing from God? If so, why do you think that might be? If you want to hear what God is saying to you, try reading books such as *Hearing God's Voice* or *Experiencing God*.

Chapter Three

The Leader's Preparation: How God Develops Leaders

The greatness of an organization is directly proportional to the greatness of its leader. It is rare for organizations to rise above their leaders. Giant organizations do not emerge under pygmy leaders. Therefore, the key to growing organizations is to develop their leaders. Leadership involves specific skills, but ultimately it is more about *being* than about *doing*. Leadership development is synonymous with personal development. As leaders grow personally, they increase their ability to lead. As they increase their capability to lead, they enlarge the capacity of their organization to grow. Therefore, the most crucial objective for any leader is personal growth.[1] As Max De Pree poignantly observes: "We are sentenced to live with who we become."[2]

The question is, how do people become leaders? Are certain people endowed with natural leadership ability? Are certain men and women born to lead, or is leadership a particular set of skills anyone can learn? Religious leaders are seeking answers to these questions. George Barna conducted a survey of senior pastors from across various denominations. When asked if they believed they had the spiritual gift of leadership, only 6 percent responded yes.[3] The fact that 94 percent of the senior pastors surveyed did not believe they were gifted to lead may explain the sense of desperation many church leaders express as they examine their ministry and its current effectiveness. Is there hope for those who realize they are not yet the leader they need to be for their organizations to thrive? We believe there is.

The Making of a Leader

INNATE QUALITIES

There is little doubt some people display an aptitude for leadership early in their lives. Observe the dynamics on any playground and it soon becomes apparent which children have innate leadership abilities. For some, influence comes from their size and strength. Being the strongest and largest children on the playground, other children instinctively show them deference. Others have keen imaginations enabling them to conceive new games and gather a following. Some children are naturally charismatic and quickly attract a crowd. Many world leaders demonstrated precipitant signs of leadership ability. As a boy, Napoleon Bonaparte organized intricate battles with his classmates. As a child, Winston Churchill staged elaborate battlefield maneuvers with fifteen hundred toy soldiers and became engrossed in politics. At the tender age of six, Warren Buffet was going door to door selling chewing gum. He would develop numerous businesses throughout his youth in an effort to become a millionaire.[4] Others provided early evidence of the negative orientation of their future leadership. When Genghis Khan was thirteen, he became so angry at his half brother Begter, he murdered him.[5] Benito Mussolini was expelled from school on two occasions for stabbing fellow students. Richard Nixon was so concerned about his academic standing as a student he broke into the dean's office to learn what his final grades were.[6]

An examination of the early lives of famous leaders usually reveals telltale signs they were predisposed to be leaders. Indeed, the next generation of great leaders is already developing, but today's adults may be too preoccupied to notice. If churches are concerned about future leaders, they would do well to nurture their children and teenagers. Any strategy for enlisting spiritual leaders must take into account those emerging leaders currently in their preteens. It is a church's folly to banish its young people to a youth building across the parking lot so their loud music doesn't disturb the adults' worship. Wise churches will explore leadership opportunities for their teenagers rather than waiting until they are adults to try to enlist them into service.

Jacob's son Joseph was destined to be a leader. God gave him dreams indicating he would one day be used mightily by God. More specifically, his dreams revealed he would lead his ten older brothers (Gen. 37:5–11). Even though this vision was not enthusiastically shared by Joseph's older siblings, years later they stood trembling before him after he became the highest ranking official in Egypt. Then they wished they had taken their baby brother's leadership potential more seriously.

Contemporary leadership writing reveals that most scholars believe leaders are both born and made. Certain factors outside peoples' control, such as size, looks, genius, and charisma contribute to their aptitude to lead. However, other leadership qualities within people's control, if developed, can significantly enhance their leadership ability. Dwight Eisenhower believed: "The one quality that can be developed by studious reflection and practice is the leadership of men."[7] The media often portrays a stereotype of leaders which sets them apart from ordinary people. They are presented as unusually gifted, intelligent, charismatic, physically imposing and attractive people. Based on this distorted representation, society might assume all great leaders have the eloquence of Martin Luther King Jr., the physical presence of George Washington, and the charisma of John F. Kennedy. This skewed image of leadership can lead to self-doubt on the part of would-be leaders. Reality, however, suggests most people can exercise leadership in some area of life if they are willing to grow personally and develop certain leadership skills.

In truth, most of history's famous leaders have been decidedly ordinary. Many of them were neither physically impressive nor academically gifted. Napoleon Bonaparte, though a giant military figure of the nineteenth century, stood only five-feet-six-inches tall. Queen Victoria was described by one of her guardians as a "short, vulgar looking child."[8] She stood less than five feet tall and complained that, "Everybody grows but me."[9] William Wilberforce was five-feet-three-inches and at one point in his illness-riddled life weighed only seventy-six pounds.[10] Joseph Stalin, terrorist dictator of the Soviet Union, was a man of diminutive size. When Harry Truman first met the five-foot-five-inch Stalin, Truman noted with surprise that Stalin was "a little bit of a squirt."[11] Conversely, other leaders gained added influence by their size. Charlemagne was powerful enough as a monarch to fashion modern Europe, but he also stood 6'3" making him one of the tallest men of his day.[12] John Adams suggested that George Washington was invariably asked to lead every national effort because at six feet four inches, he was always the tallest man in the room! One of his biographers noted: "His body did not just occupy space; it seemed to organize the space around it. He dominated a room not just with his size, but with an almost electric presence."[13]

While today's media presents modern leaders in designer clothes, with fashionable hairstyles and flattering makeovers, many of history's most effective leaders were not physically attractive or considered in any way outstanding when they were young. Abraham Lincoln, America's first modern president was subjected to abundant ridicule because of his irregular features. His homely face and gangly physique caused him to be extremely self-consciousness. At one point, Lincoln rejoined, "Someone accused me of being two-faced. If I were two-faced, would I wear the one I have?" Harry Truman, describing himself as a child, said he was "blind as a mole" and "something of a sissy." Winston Churchill's biographer concluded: "Sickly, an uncoordinated weakling with the pale fragile hands of a girl, speaking with a lisp and a slight stutter, he had been at the mercy of bullies. They beat him, ridiculed him, and pelted him with cricket balls. Trembling and humiliated, he hid in a nearby woods. This was hardly the stuff of which gladiators are made."[14] When family finances grew tight, Arthur Wellesley's parents withdrew him from school at Eton so his two more promising brothers could continue their education. This was not a glorious beginning for the man who would become the Duke of Wellington and Napoleon's nemesis at the Battle of Waterloo. George Marshall, the top American military commander of World War II, was an average student who did not even bother to apply to West Point. Warren Buffet's application to Harvard was rejected.[15] John Rockefeller and his brother were excluded from their class picture because their suits were considered too shabby for such an important photograph.[16] Eleanor Roosevelt has been described as "an unattractive, almost ugly duckling child who felt chronically inferior to other members of her family, was always fearful, and craved praise."[17]

Peter Senge, in his book *The Fifth Discipline* observed: "Most of the outstanding leaders I have worked with are neither tall nor especially handsome; they are often mediocre public speakers; they do not stand out in a crowd; they do not mesmerize an attending audience with their brilliance or eloquence. Rather, what distinguishes them is their clarity and persuasiveness of their ideas, the depth of their commitment, and their openness to continually learning more."[18] Peter Drucker concluded: "There seems to be little correlation between a man's effectiveness and his intelligence, his imagination, or his knowledge."[19]

LIFE EXPERIENCES

Clearly people's life experiences can dramatically affect the caliber of leaders they become. Something as basic as birth order can exert a profound impact on a leader's development. Firstborn children are more likely to lead because they are generally given more responsibility by their parents, and they often share a greater affiliation with adults than do their younger siblings. Their superiority in size, strength, and knowledge over their younger siblings gives them confidence and enables them to exercise leadership in their homes at an early age. Malcolm Gladwell points out that the month of the year people are born can exert a significant impact on whether they excel at sports and enter the professional ranks.[20]

Home Life. The influence of a leader's childhood home cannot be underrated as a major factor in leadership development. While some great leaders were nurtured in wholesome, supportive environments, many were not. Bill Gates grew up in an affluent, supportive home and was enrolled in one of the first schools in the nation to provide a computer class for its students.[21] However, a high percentage of famous leaders had to overcome major hardships during their formative years. Numerous well-known leaders lost a parent to death, usually their father, while they were still young. Stonewall Jackson's father was an irresponsible gambler who died of typhoid fever, leaving his son and daughter to be distributed among relatives after their mother remarried.[22] When Martin Luther King Jr. lost his grandmother, to whom he was very close, he became so distraught he threw himself out a second-story window in an apparent suicide attempt. Eleanor Roosevelt lost both parents by the age of ten, whereupon her grandmother raised her. Her extended family suffered alcoholism, adultery, child molestation, rape, and other vices, which left an indelible impression on the future first lady.

James MacGregor Burns noted that many famous leaders grew up in dysfunctional homes. Burns observed that often these leaders had a distant relationship with their fathers and an unusually close relationship with their mothers. Adolph Hitler was close to his mother but hated his father. Joseph Stalin and George Marshall were dearly loved by their mothers but beaten by their fathers. Winston Churchill was sent to a boarding school at age seven and, despite his pitiful pleading, was not visited by his preoccupied parents even when his father was attending meetings near Winston's school. His parents would take separate Christmas vacations from their son. Churchill's biographer later observed, "The neglect and lack of interest in him shown by his parents was remarkable, even by the standards of late Victorian and Edwardian days."[23] Gandhi loved his mother but felt he was partially responsible for his father's death. Martin Luther King Jr.'s father disciplined him with severe beatings.

Abraham Lincoln's father hired him out to hard labor in order to pay off his debts. Lincoln became so estranged from his father that he did not invite his family to his wedding. Later, Lincoln refused to visit his dying father or attend his funeral.

Woodrow Wilson's father constantly criticized him, never giving him his approval. Queen Elizabeth I's terrifying father, Henry VIII, had her mother, Anne Boleyn, beheaded on charges of adultery and once banished his daughter from his presence for an entire year.[24] Alexander the Great's father was assassinated while Alexander was a young man. Some historians speculate Alexander's mother orchestrated the murder. In an effort to instill in her son the price to be paid for freedom, Abigail Adams took her young son John Quincy to Bunker Hill on June 17, 1775 and made him watch as people he knew were killed in the desperate battle. Abigail constantly chided her son and urged him to "let your ambition be engaged to become eminent."[25] When his son struggled in his studies at Harvard, John Adams refused to allow him to return home for Christmas, claiming, "I could take no satisfaction in seeing you."[26]

John F. Kennedy had to compete with his brothers to win the approval of his highly ambitious father. Bill Clinton lost his father as an infant and then lived the next three years with his grandparents. Clinton's mother eventually married a man known for his alcoholism, gambling, and unfaithfulness. When his parents' marriage ended in divorce, Clinton had to testify in court concerning the abuse his mother suffered at the hands of his stepfather.

Growing up with an aloof, abusive, or absent paternal figure often inspired people to strive for greatness as a means of enhancing their battered self-esteem. Having failed to win the approval of their fathers, these people attempted to compensate by winning the devotion of large followings. The young Churchill idolized his parents even though they neglected him. Of his mother Churchill confessed: "She shone for me like the Evening Star. I loved her dearly—but at a distance. My nurse was my confidante."[27] Churchill later surmised when his father encouraged him to enter the military: "For years I thought my father with his experience and flair had discerned in me the qualities of military genius. But I was told later that he had only come to the conclusion that I was not clever enough to go to the Bar."[28] When Churchill's father died, he resigned himself to the fact "all my dreams of comradeship with him, of entering Parliament at his side and in his support, were ended. There remained for me only to pursue his aims and vindicate his memory."[29]

When Hannibal was nine years old, his father, Hamilcar conducted him to an altar. There he instructed his son to place his hands on the offerings and to swear an oath to be forever an enemy of Rome. That vow would lead to the death of hundreds of thousands of soldiers, the destruction of numerous cities, the downfall of an empire, and Hannibal's eventual suicide.[30] Some of the world's famous leaders were raised in homes where fear for their own safety was a constant reality. This motivated them to gain power as a way to control their environment and escape feelings of insecurity. Anger and bitterness motivated some children to seek influential positions as adults.

Winston Churchill, in writing about his famous ancestor John Churchill, observed: "It is said that famous men are usually the product of unhappy childhood. The stern compression of circumstances, the twinges of adversity, the spur of slights and taunts in early years, are needed to evoke that ruthless fixity of purpose and tenacious mother-wit without which great actions are seldom accomplished. Certainly little in the environment of the young John Churchill should have deprived him of this stimulus; and by various long-descending channels there centered in him martial and dangerous fires."[31]

Secular leaders were not the only ones shaped by difficult childhoods. Many religious leaders were profoundly influenced by their dysfunctional homes and turbulent upbringings. J. Frank Norris, the infamous pastor of First Baptist Church, Fort Worth, provides a classic example. Not only was Norris pastor of the Fort Worth congregation from 1909 until 1952; he also simultaneously led Temple Baptist Church in Detroit for fourteen years beginning in 1935. During that time, more than twenty-five thousand people joined his Texas and Michigan churches. Norris was a leading figure among fundamentalists. He published his own widely distributed paper, *The Fundamentalist*, and was considered a spellbinding preacher. Yet many people wondered why Norris experienced such a stormy ministry. His house and his church both burned down and in both cases Norris was accused of arson. He was constantly embroiled in controversy, haranguing everyone with whom he disagreed. He sued his own congregation. Norris even shot a man to death in his church office. To comprehend Norris's flamboyant and vindictive leadership style, one must consider his childhood. When Norris was a young boy his father, an alcoholic, beat him mercilessly. Two gang members showed up at the Norris home and began shooting at his father. The young boy charged the two ruffians with a knife. He was shot three times. Norris was raised in poverty and turmoil. He later recalled the shame of his childhood:

> I was about eight years old, one day I was standing on the porch of the public school in Columbiana, two boys came up, one was twelve and one fourteen, each one of them had on a nice suit of clothes, a nice overcoat. I had on a little cotton suit, no overcoat, and the coat was tight around me—these boys, sons of a banker—they came up, looked at me, and they said, "Your coat is too little"—well I knew it. Then one of them pointed his finger at me while all the boys gathered around and said, "Your daddy is a drunkard and mine is a banker." I turned and went into the school room, buried my face in my hands. . . . Mother said, as she put her tender arms around me, and brushed away my tears, "Son, it is all right, some day you are going to wear good clothes—some day you will make a man—some day God will use you."[32]

Norris's troublesome past compelled him to strive for success, yet it also drove him into destructive, egocentric patterns of behavior that marred much of what might have been a productive ministry.

Whether for good or bad, the influence of the childhood home in shaping leaders is inescapable. Nurturing, supportive families provide an environment conducive to healthy personal growth. A wholesome background can build a strong sense of self-esteem and effective people skills that enable people to become healthy leaders. Leaders born into dysfunctional homes may also rise to prominence, as Norris did, but their past can often hinder or sabotage their ongoing growth and success as leaders.

A significant number of well-known Christian leaders grew up in unhappy homes. By God's healing grace, many of these men and women developed into healthy, successful leaders. Others, however, have remained in bondage to their troublesome pasts (2 Cor. 10:1–10). These people emerge as adults with feelings of inferiority, inadequacy, and anger despite their outward success. Gary McIntosh and Samuel Rima in their book *Overcoming the Dark Side of Leadership* concluded that many current Christian leaders continue to be motivated, albeit subconsciously, by their dysfunctional pasts. McIntosh and Rima observe: "In almost every case, the factors that eventually undermine us are shadows of the ones that contribute to our success."[33] It bewilders society when seemingly brilliant leaders make foolish choices that destroy a lifetime of work and success. Books such as *Derailed: Five Lessons Learned from Catastrophic Failures of Leadership* by Tim Irwin, *How the Mighty Fall* by Jim Collins, and the less charitable *Why Smart People Can Be So Stupid* edited by Robert J. Sternberg grapple with this issue. One study of CEOs found that most CEOs had two or three "dark sides" that if managed well could bring great success but if left untended could bring their careers crashing down upon their heads.[34] Craig Johnson analyzed "toxic" leaders who engage in destructive behavior. He acknowledges many causes that lead people to act this way. He points out, "If we want to manage or master the dark forces inside us, we must first acknowledge that they exist."[35] Clearly intelligence or skills alone are inadequate to ensure success. Leaders also must be aware of the "dark side" lurking within them that has the potential at any moment to derail them.

It has been said, "If knowledge is power, then self knowledge is superpower."[36] One of the greatest limitations for today's spiritual leaders is their inability to understand and acknowledge how their past cripples their current effectiveness. They minimize their emotional and spiritual need so they do not seek the healing available to them in Christ. Instead, they press on, never examining what fuels their desire to be a leader. Some Christian leaders are motivated more by anger than by love. Others are so insecure they cannot tolerate disagreement from anyone. Or, desperate for approval, they surround themselves with sycophants who shower them with steady, uncensored praise. It is not only possible but sadly common for people to seek positions of spiritual authority as a means of personal edification rather than as an avenue to serve God. These are negative and destructive motives; yet many leaders today are driven, far more than they realize, by the scars of their past.

Failures. Failure is as universal as it is inevitable. As Spreitzer and Quinn observe, "Someone who never fails probably isn't stretching enough."[37] Conversely, Max De Pree notes: "Continual success probably means our bar is too low or our tape too short."[38] While people strive to avoid it, failure often exerts a powerful force in making leaders and appears to be a prerequisite for leadership greatness. Failure itself is not the issue; it is what failure produces that is determinative in leadership development. Failure will not destroy true leaders but will further develop their character and leadership skills. A high percentage of famous leaders suffered dramatic hardships and failures, especially during their early years. George Washington lost five out of the first seven major battles he fought as he led the hopelessly outnumbered and untrained revolutionary army against the British. After suffering a series of defeats, Washington concluded: "I have been upon the losing order ever since I entered the service."[39]

Winston Churchill endured financial ruin more than once, and his political career was seemingly aborted on several occasions. Perhaps it was Churchill's numerous failures that led him to define success as "going from failure to failure without loss of enthusiasm."

Abraham Lincoln's failures are well documented. He, too, suffered bankruptcy. In his first attempt at elected office, Lincoln placed eighth in a field of thirteen candidates. When he ran for president, ten states did not carry his name on the ballot, and he was burned in effigy in several of the Southern states. His biographer noted: "Fate seemed to take a curious delight in finding new ways to shatter his dreams."[40]

Ulysses S. Grant could not find a successful career until the Civil War began. He was drummed out of the army for his struggle with alcohol. Every business venture he attempted failed until he found himself peddling firewood on street corners and applying to work for his two younger brothers. When he volunteered to serve in the Union army, the officer in charge did not bother to speak to him. In desperation he exclaimed: "I must live, and my family must live. Perhaps I could serve the army by providing good bread for them."[41]

William Tecumseh Sherman suffered so many personal crises before the Civil War he concluded: "Every castle that I build is undermined and upset at the very moment I flatter myself of its completion, but the fact is I'm getting pretty well used to it."[42] When Sherman was given a command during the early stages of the war, he had a complete mental breakdown and asked to be relieved. His commanding officer judged him unfit for duty, and it was rumored Sherman had gone insane. He was reduced to the point of suicide. No one could have imagined he would reach the end of the war as one of its most celebrated generals.[43]

The Duke of Wellington experienced a military setback early in his career. The most his biographer could say was that "he had learned what not to do and that is always something."[44] Dwight Eisenhower lost his first major battle. Of that battle his biographer concluded: "Kasserine was Eisenhower's first real battle; taking it all in all, his performance was miserable."[45]

Harry Truman's life was full of setbacks. He and his father both incurred bankruptcy. West Point rejected his application. In fact, Truman experienced so many failures as a young man he once wrote to his sweetheart, Bess, "I can't possibly lose forever."[46] Truman was his party's fourth choice for senator. He was the underdog in every election he fought. He was so poor even after he was elected senator, he was forced to use a public health dentist and to occasionally sleep in his car while on the campaign trail.

Walt Disney went bankrupt and weathered numerous financial crises.[47] Even great religious leaders overcame their share of early failures. Bob Jones, president of Bob Jones University, pronounced the college-aged Billy Graham a failure to his face, telling him he was only destined to additional setbacks in the future.[48]

Crises. Events beyond a person's control can produce the same effect as failures. They can either crush an aspiring leader or develop the character and resolve within emerging leaders that enables them to reach greater heights in the future. Julius Caesar is suspected to have had epilepsy.[49] Teddy Roosevelt endured severe asthma as a child and was considered too frail and sickly to attend school. As a young man he lost both his beloved mother Mittie, to typhoid fever, and his loving wife Alice, to childbirth, on the same day, February 14, 1884. This left the future president so stunned and disoriented he wrote in his diary, "The light has gone out of my life."[50]

Robert E. Lee lost everything he owned, as well as numerous loved ones and friends, during the Civil War. Franklin Roosevelt, considered one of America's most successful twentieth-century presidents, contracted debilitating polio as an adult that left him in a wheelchair. (In surveys of historians judging American presidents based on ten leadership qualities, the top five have consistently been: Abraham Lincoln, Franklin Roosevelt, George Washington, Theodore Roosevelt, and Harry Truman). It has been said Franklin Roosevelt was able to transform his humiliations into triumphs. He allegedly quipped, "If you have spent six months on your back trying to move your little toe, nothing seems difficult."[51] John F. Kennedy constantly felt the painful effects of Addison's Disease and was administered last rites four times as an adult.[52] He continued to live "by complicated daily combinations of pills and injections." Mahatma Ghandi was imprisoned numerous times and survived several attempts on his life before he was assassinated. Martin Luther King Jr., an ardent admirer of Gandhi, had multiple threats against his life and was frequently imprisoned. According to one study cited by Howard Gardner, 60 percent of major British political leaders lost a parent in childhood.[53] Wise leaders do not become discouraged by crises but rather they build on them, knowing these experiences are likely catalysts for their greatest personal growth.

Personal Struggles. Surprisingly, perhaps, many of history's renowned leaders experienced difficulty in public speaking. Winston Churchill, famous for his eloquence, had a speech impediment as a boy. Theodore Roosevelt spoke with difficulty. Mahatma Ghandi was so fearful of public speaking that in his first attempt to represent a client as her lawyer he became tongue-tied in court. The humiliated attorney was forced to refund his fee and locate other counsel for his disgruntled client.[54] During Benjamin Disraeli's first speech in the House of Commons, people laughed at him mercilessly. He retorted, "I sit down now. But the time will come when you will hear me."[55] Thomas Jefferson disliked public speaking.[56]

D. L. Moody showed no early signs of developing into the forceful speaker he would later become. So meager was Moody's grammar and so sparse his Bible knowledge that when he requested membership in the Mount Vernon Congregational Church he was initially rejected. When the young Moody attempted to speak up during his church's prayer meeting, he noted it made adults "squirm their shoulders when I got up." Some of the adults complained that Moody did not know enough grammar to address the congregation, and he was asked to abstain from commenting.[57]

Many great leaders had their hearts broken as young people. Harry Truman was so painfully shy it took him five years to muster the courage to speak his first words to his future wife. Because of his family's misfortunes, it was not until Truman was thirty-five that he finally felt able to marry the girl of his dreams. His correspondence to Bess during their courtship reveals his obvious feelings of unworthiness for her hand.

Lincoln was also woefully inept around women and suffered painful rejection. When Lincoln first spied Mary Todd, his future wife, at a party he allegedly told her, "I want to dance with you in the worst way!" Mary later informed her cousin he certainly had![58] Winston Churchill had the first woman he ever cared for marry another man while two other women rejected his marriage proposal outright. Churchill eventually married Clementine when he was thirty-seven.

John Wesley, the famous English preacher, endured great frustration regarding a young woman while he was a missionary in America. As a result, he returned to England a brokenhearted, disillusioned, and unsuccessful missionary.

Roger Williams, the first Baptist pastor in America, fell into severe depression when his low social status prevented him from marrying the young lady he loved. The Duke of Wellington, George Washington, and Thomas Jefferson had their marriage proposals summarily rejected.

Young John Rockefeller fell in love with his family's household help, Melinda. However, her parents insisted they break off their relationship because they did not feel John showed any financial promise for the future.[59]

A young Billy Graham was devastated when Emily, the girl he loved, rejected his marriage proposal for another suitor who showed more promise for ministry. Graham remembered: "That woeful night in the spring of 1938 when she called it quits between us was Paradise Lost for me. In my despondency, I looked up Dr. Minder. . . . I wept out my misery to his understanding ears."[60]

Eleanor Roosevelt made the agonizing discovery that her husband Franklin was unfaithful. Historians have suggested that much of the energy and passion she later invested in social causes stemmed from an absence of fulfillment in her marriage. In each of these cases, it seems, early disappointment gave the aspiring leaders both a sense of humble reality and a renewed zeal to achieve something significant in their lives.

Success through Hardship. So many of history's famous leaders suffered major failures, crises, and disappointments that these traumas appear to be prerequisite for leadership success. If any conclusion can be drawn from the biographies of well-known leaders, it is that none enjoyed an easy path to greatness. It could in fact be argued that, had they avoided hardship, greatness would also have eluded them. Peter Koestenbaum notes: "Good times blind us. Bad times reveal truth to us."[61] It would be incorrect to conclude that hardship and failure always produce successful leaders, just as it would be simplistic to assume good leaders emerge only out of adversity. However, most people experience some form of hardship as well as a degree of success. The key to leadership development lies not in the experiences, whether good or bad, but in peoples' responses to those events. It has been said a tragedy is not an event but rather the interpretation of an event.[62]

When some people face hardship, they become bitter or fearful, and they quit trying. Others suffer similar trials but choose instead to redeem their suffering by learning from their misfortune and growing stronger from the experience. The distinguishing characteristic of successful leaders is they use their experiences as learning tools, and they gain renewed motivation from their failures. At one point in the Duke of Marlborough's career, he found himself cruelly ostracized and passed over for office by the ruling government. Yet Winston Churchill noted, "Few features in Marlborough's long life are more remarkable than the manner in which he steadily grew in weight and influence through the whole of the six years when he was banished from favour and office."[63] Of Ulysses Grant's tortuous years before the Civil War, his biographer claimed: "Every setback seemed to enhance his inner strength. Grant was not brilliant, his appearance was not striking, his personality did not shine. He was not visited with flashes of inspiration that animated Stonewall Jackson. He did not have Lee's Olympian presence. His mind lacked the subtleties of Lincoln's thought. Sometimes he blundered badly; often oversimplified; yet he saw his goals clearly and moved toward them relentlessly."[64]

Regarding Abraham Lincoln, Donald Phillips concluded: "Everything—failures as well as successes—became stepping stones to the presidency. In this sense, Lincoln's entire life prepared him for his future executive leadership role."[65] Leaders are not people who escape failure but people who overcome adversity. Their lives confirm the axiom: "A mistake is an event, the full benefit of which has not yet been turned to your advantage."[66]

Failure and personal crises will not disqualify you for leadership. However, failure to learn and grow from your mistakes and hardships may prevent you from developing into the leader God intended you to become. God can use adversity to build certain qualities such as humility, integrity, or faith deep within your character that could not be similarly fashioned through lives of comfort and success.

God's Work in Leaders' Lives

GOD GIVES HIS HOLY SPIRIT

Although childhood experiences, physical strength, failures, successes, and even birth order can impact general leadership abilities, there is an added dimension to the personal growth of a spiritual leader not found in secular leadership development. That is the active work of the Holy Spirit. Oswald Sanders notes: "There is no such thing as a self-made spiritual leader."[67] Spiritual ends require spiritual means and spiritual means come only by the Holy Spirit. The apostle Paul identified leadership as something the Holy Spirit enabled people to do (Rom. 12:8).

This truth is evident in God's message to Zerubbabel, the governor over Jerusalem, who oversaw the rebuilding of the temple after the Jewish exiles' return from Babylon. Zerubbabel undertook the daunting task of governing a region decimated by war and exile, as well as rebuilding a massive temple that lay in ruins. At this critical juncture, he received this message from God: "'Not by strength or by might, but by My Spirit,' says the LORD of Hosts" (Zech. 4:6). Zerubbabel may have thought his primary concerns were brick and mortar, finances, taxation, and the surrounding enemies. But the deluged governor learned an invaluable lesson: spiritual leaders require the Spirit to work in their lives even when it involves undertaking tasks that appear to be unspiritual. Erecting buildings, administering people, and raising money are all spiritual jobs when the Spirit is involved. Without the Spirit's presence, people may be leaders, but they are not spiritual leaders.

GOD DEVELOPS REQUIRED SKILLS

A current debate in leadership theory relates to dealing with leaders' strengths and weaknesses. Every person has both. The issue is on where should you focus. For years self-help experts promised to improve your weaknesses. While there were some success stories, many people grew frustrated at their lack of progress as they found themselves spending so much time working on their weaknesses their strengths deteriorated.

In their influential book *Now Discover Your Strengths*, Marcus Buckingham and Donald Clifton argue that focusing on improving one's weaknesses is a waste of time.[68] They cite a Gallup survey of 190,000 employees from 7,938 companies in which people were asked: "At work do you have the opportunity to do what you do best every day?"[69] They discovered that most people spend an inordinate amount of time dealing with their weaknesses so they never have the opportunity to thrive in areas of their strength. Moreover, those who work in areas of their strength are much more motivated and produce greater results than those who do not.[70] Buckingham and Clifton also note the higher up the corporate ladder people ascend, the less time they spend working in their areas of strength.[71] Their book provides numerous inventories to determine your strengths. The authors encourage people to avoid wasting time trying to improve or change their talents but to focus instead on where they excel.

This message has understandably become popular. Experienced leaders know they must hire to their weaknesses. Just as Walt Disney was the creative genius, so he wisely relied on his administratively oriented brother Roy to handle the financial side of operations.[72] Walt might never have produced *Snow White* or other classics had he assumed primary responsibility for administration. He applied his creative genius where he could make his unique contribution.

However, while the strengths approach to leadership has become extremely popular, it has also received serious critiques. Robert Kaiser suggests the problem with this theory is "when practiced with a single-minded focus, the strengths approach can become an exercise in self-indulgence."[73] In his book a series of writers offer critiques of the strengths-based approach. They cite Peter Drucker's observation that "most people think they know what they are good at; they are usually wrong."[74] The writers also point out this method can put the needs and comfort of individuals before the needs of the organization. Everyone wants to do what they are good at and what they enjoy. However, sometimes people are called upon to do things they are unskilled at doing. Continued success tends to cause people to lose their humility and to become less teachable.

Kaiser and Kaplan also warn of "lopsided leadership" which characterizes executives who refuse to develop new skills because they are committed to the talents that earned them their promotion into the executive office in the first place.[75] The problem is the skills they needed in lower management positions are often a detriment in upper management. Because these one-dimensional executives believe pounding everything with a hammer made them successful on the shop floor, the executive team they now lead is being pummeled by that same hammer. The writers also point out the reason CEOs derail is often because they worked at ninety miles per hour in the areas of their strengths but they never took time to address their weaknesses. Eventually they meet a temptation, crisis, or pressure point they are unprepared to handle, and their careers hit a brick wall.

How should spiritual leaders view their strengths and weaknesses? The life of Moses provides a telling example. Notice what Stephen said about him:

> So Moses was educated in all the wisdom of the Egyptians and was powerful in his speech and actions. As he was approaching the age of 40, he decided to visit his brothers, the Israelites. When he saw one of them being mistreated, he came to his rescue and avenged the oppressed man by striking down the Egyptian. He assumed his brothers would understand that God would give them deliverance through him, but they did not understand. (Acts 7:22–25)

No Israelite was better educated or skilled in leadership than Moses. He attended the best management schools in the country. He was mighty in word and deed. The problem was, he knew it. He also assumed everyone else recognized his leadership abilities. As a result Moses took matters into his own skillful hands, and the results were disastrous.

Fast-forward forty years. Moses has been leading sheep, not Israelites, for forty years. He has been in God's school of humility and shepherding for half his life. When God invited Moses to be his instrument to deliver the Israelites, listen to Moses' reply: "Who am I that I should go to Pharaoh and that I should bring the Israelites out of Egypt? . . . What if they won't believe me and will not obey me . . . Please, Lord, I have never been eloquent—either in the past or recently or since You have been speaking to Your servant—because I am slow and hesitant in speech" (Exod. 3:11; 4:1, 10).

What happened? Moses used to think he was a gifted leader. Forty years later he claims he can't speak or lead! Which was correct? Both.

Moses may certainly have feared his oratorical skills had declined over the forty years of talking to four-footed audiences. But more importantly, Moses came to view his skills from God's perspective. Accomplishing God's work was impossible without God's presence. Conversely Moses would learn that with every divine assignment also comes God's equipping. God would enable his servant to accomplish everything he commanded him to do. The key was not Moses' skills but Moses' surrender. A servant, wholly submitted to God's will is an awesome instrument in God's hand. Spiritual leaders do not restrict their work to what they feel they are good at doing. Had Moses done that, he would never have returned to Egypt. By that stage in his life, Moses had no passion for a deliverance ministry, nor did he see himself as gifted for that kind of work. He only returned to Egypt because God clearly told him to do so. In the process Moses witnessed God's working through his ordinary life to do some of the greatest miracles ever recorded in history (Deut. 34:11–12).

GOD DEVELOPS LEADERS THROUGH A PROCESS

God can bring character development and personal growth out of any situation. Whether he does so is conditional on people's willingness to submit to his will throughout the process. God is sovereign over every life, but those who yield their will to him will be shaped according to his purposes. When the Lord is developing someone, all of life is a school. No experience, good or bad, is wasted (Rom. 8:28). God doesn't squander people's time. He doesn't ignore their pain. He brings not only healing but growth out of even the worst experiences. Every relationship can be God's instrument to fashion a person's character. At times, through our most painful experiences, God does his greatest work. Perhaps this is why Seth Godin suggests: "If you're not uncomfortable in your work as a leader, it's almost certain you're not reaching your potential as a leader."[76] The world can offer its best theories on leadership and provide the most extensive training possible, but unless God sets the agenda for a leader's life, that person, though thoroughly educated, will not be an effective spiritual leader.

Robert Clinton wrote *The Making of a Leader* in which he put forth a six-stage model of how God develops leaders. Clinton believes God matures leaders over a lifetime. God uses relationships and events in peoples' lives as two primary means for growing them into leaders. The six stages of leadership development in Clinton's model are:

- Phase One: Sovereign Foundations
- Phase Two: Inner Life Growth
- Phase Three: Ministry Maturing
- Phase Four: Life Maturing
- Phase Five: Convergence
- Phase Six: Afterglow or Celebration

Clinton provides a helpful model that speaks directly to the development of spiritual leaders but which also has applications to leadership development in general.

Sovereign Foundations involve God's activity during people's formative years. Parental love, birth order, childhood illness, prosperity or poverty, loss of loved ones, and stability versus constant upheaval are factors over which children have no control. History demonstrates the way people respond to these factors determines much of their leadership potential.

Inner Life Growth is the period in which one's character and spiritual life develop. During this stage people experience conversion. With the indwelling presence of the Holy Spirit, they are no longer subject to the whims of fate but are in a position to be systematically transformed into men and women who think and act like Christ. Non-Christian leaders without the Holy Spirit are much more controlled by their pasts than those whose characters are shaped by the Holy Spirit working within them. Thus, people without the Holy Spirit will often have major areas of their character that remain underdeveloped.

During the *Ministry Maturing* phase people make their earliest attempts at spiritual leadership. They may volunteer to lead a church program, or they may venture to share their faith with someone. Through such experiences God teaches them more specifically what it means to be a spiritual leader. When people first attempt to exercise leadership, they often fail or experience frustration. As they develop leadership skills, as well as a résumé of experiences, people begin to understand their strengths and weakness. At this stage the focus is more on who leaders are than on what they do. What leaders learn from these early experiences will largely determine how they advance in leadership ability.

Throughout the *Life Maturing* years spiritual leaders begin to focus on their strengths and to find leadership opportunities in which they can be most effective. Whereas until this time God was working primarily *in* the leader, now God increasingly works *through* the leader. An experiential understanding of God matures at this time. Through significant life experiences God teaches people about life and relationships. Through the normal experiences of failure and success, criticism and praise, loyalty and betrayal, illness and loss, God matures people. Again, much depends on the leader's reaction to the life circumstances through which God brings them. Positive responses to these life events will guide individuals into a more mature level of leadership.

During the *Convergence* phase, people's ministry and life experiences converge into a specific job or responsibility for which they draw on all they have learned to achieve maximum effectiveness. This becomes the leader's signature role for which they are best known and in which they enjoy their greatest success.

Clinton's focus is on the development of spiritual leaders, but the general principles can apply to secular leaders as well. Both can experience the merging of their life and work experiences into a leadership role that successfully integrates all they have learned with who they have become. Many of history's most famous leaders did not assume their most influential roles until late in life. The Duke of Marlborough would lead a multinational force for ten years on the continent against superior French forces without losing a battle. Yet he did not lead a major army until he was fifty-two.[77] Winston Churchill did not become prime minister until he was a senior adult. He considered all his life experiences a preface to his role as British prime minister during World War II. Although Churchill failed many times and was severely criticized throughout his life, it appears his earlier years were a training ground for his great moment on the world stage as Hitler's chief antagonist. General George Marshall, the celebrated American military commander of World War II, was not promoted to general until the age of fifty-nine. He was sixty-seven when he developed the famous Marshall Plan that rebuilt postwar Europe. Harry Truman was sixty-seven when he became president. Pope John XXIII was seventy-seven when he was chosen to lead the Roman Catholic Church. Unfortunately, many people never reach convergence. Some leaders never find jobs or challenges that bring to fruition all they learned and experienced earlier in their lives. The full benefit of their past is never brought to bear on society's needs. The Holy Spirit will pull together all the experiences in Christians' lives to bring them to a deeper level of maturity. When leaders neglect the Holy Spirit's role in their lives, they never reach their full potential as spiritual leaders.

Afterglow or Celebration is a level of leadership Clinton claims even fewer people achieve. It comes after people have successfully led others for a significant period of time. For spiritual leaders this phase occurs after they have faithfully allowed God to accomplish his will for their lives as well as for their organizations. Successful spiritual leaders spend this final period of their lives celebrating and building upon the work God did in and through them. This is also a time for celebrated leaders to leverage their successes to exert a positive influence on society as well as to teach the next generation. Leaders in this sixth phase have nothing to prove. Others respect them not because of their position of influence, or even because they continue to lead or hold purse strings, but because of who they are and what they represent. It is not uncommon for great leaders to spend their later years associated with a school. Jonathan Edwards, renowned spiritual leader during the First Great Awakening, spent his final days as president of Princeton University. Charles Finney, the outstanding evangelist of the Second Great Awakening, became president of Oberlin College. Charles Spurgeon invested much time in developing the young pastors who trained in his college. Robert E. Lee spent his last years as president of Washington College developing a new generation of southern leaders. Dwight Eisenhower retired from the military to become the president of Columbia University. A true leader can expect to be sought out by people one day for the singular reason of what they represent. Just as the face of Moses used to glow after having been in the presence of God, so there will be unmistakable evidence that leaders in this stage have walked intimately and powerfully with God for many years. When people recognize that someone has walked with God in this manner, they will seek to be around them and to learn from their spiritual pilgrimage.

GOD GIVES THE ASSIGNMENT

People may become leaders by responding in a healthy manner to all they encounter in life, but they will not become spiritual leaders unless God calls them to the role and equips them for it. Secular leadership is something to which people can aspire. It can be achieved through sheer force of will. Spiritual leadership, on the other hand, is not a position for which one applies. Rather, it is assigned by God. God determines each person's assignment. Historically, God has chosen ordinary people who were not looking for a divine assignment. Nevertheless, God saw something in their hearts that led him to assign particular tasks. While there is nothing wrong with wanting to experience God working powerfully in one's life, those wishing for God to use them mightily should not covet leadership positions in God's kingdom (1 Tim. 3:1). They should seek God with all their hearts and wait upon his will. The greatest area of concern for spiritual leaders is their hearts. When God sees people living righteously, he may exercise his prerogative to show himself strong in their lives to accomplish his purposes (2 Chron. 16:9).

Biblical Example: Abraham

Abraham's life provides a thorough example of how God chooses ordinary people and turns them into effective spiritual leaders.[78]

ABRAHAM WAS AN ORDINARY PERSON

Abraham was born in Ur among the moon-worshipping Chaldeans. Abraham's agenda for his life was probably uncomplicated. He likely planned to live out his days raising his herds and flocks. His wife Sarah was unable to bear children, so parenthood would not factor into Abraham and Sarah's plans. God's agenda was radically different from Abraham's. God's plan for Abraham was not for him to live a settled life without children but that he become a nomadic patriarch who fathered a holy nation. His life would be a spiritual example to God's people for thousands of years. The Messiah would be Abraham's descendant. Abraham's life would prove to be a pivotal point in history. Generations of believers would find inspiration and eternal salvation because of his life. To say that God's plans dwarfed Abraham's plans would be an understatement. The key was not for God to bless Abraham's plans but for Abraham to discard his life goals in favor of God's will.

It is not surprising, since God had so much in store for Abraham, he took time to thoroughly prepare him. Spiritual leadership does not happen by accident. It occurs as God develops people's character as well as their relationship with him. Jim Collins notes: "'Most 'overnight success' stories are about twenty years in the making."[79] The characteristics God builds into spiritual leaders over time include wisdom, integrity, honesty, and moral purity. A proper relationship with God involves faith, obedience, and love for him. Although God often used people who appeared to be the least likely candidates for true leadership, the common denominator was these people had godly character, and they walked closely with him (1 Sam. 16:7). The larger God's assignment, the greater the character and the closer the relationship with God is required (Matt. 25:23).

ABRAHAM BUILT ON HIS HERITAGE

When God first spoke to Abraham and told him to leave his homeland in Ur, God had already used Abraham's father, Terah, to begin the process (Acts 7:2–4; Gen. 11:31–32). What God began with Abraham's father, he continued through Abraham's life and eventually completed through Abraham's descendants. Terah would only travel as far as Haran. His son would complete the family's odyssey to Canaan. Heritage can be a powerful factor in leadership. As in Abraham's case, God may begin a work in one generation and bring it to fruition in succeeding generations. God wanted Abraham to go to Canaan, so he also gave that desire to Abraham's father. God called a son to be a nomad so he initiated a restless spirit in his father.

ABRAHAM GREW THROUGH FAILURE

Many events in Abraham's life contributed to his character development. As a young man, he was not a paragon of faith, but gradually over many years he developed a mature and deep relationship with God. God used Abraham's failures to prepare him for leadership. For example, God specifically instructed Abraham to leave his family behind, but instead Abraham took Lot with him (Gen. 12:1, 4). This meant Abraham would have to separate from Lot later, taking the land Lot rejected (Gen. 13). Still later Abraham would find himself interceding with God on Lot's behalf, pleading for the wicked city of Sodom when God was about to destroy it (Gen. 18:16–33). Lot's descendents, the Moabites and the Ammonites, would cause tremendous grief to Abraham's descendants (Gen. 36–38). With one act of seemingly minor disobedience, Abraham inadvertently endangered the inheritance God wanted to give him and his descendants. Through this failure Abraham learned a valuable lesson regarding his modification of God's will. Abraham's mistake makes it clear that adding to God's will is as dangerous as rejecting it.

Why is it important to follow God's will exactly as it is and not try to add to it so it makes more sense to us? God's ways are not our ways (Isa. 55:8–9). It seems ridiculous for God to call a seventy-five-year-old man to have a child and then to spend twenty-five years preparing him for the child-rearing task.

Yet God had plans for Isaac far beyond what Abraham could have imagined. God intended for Isaac to be a patriarch for God's people. For such an assignment, Isaac required a godly, faithful father.

ABRAHAM BUILT SPIRITUAL LANDMARKS

Abraham's spiritual pilgrimage can be traced by examining the altars he built. Every time Abraham came to a milestone in his life, or when he learned something new about God, he built an altar. "The LORD appeared to Abram and said, 'I will give this land to your offspring.' So he built an altar there to the LORD who had appeared to him. From there he moved on to the hill country east of Bethel and pitched his tent, with Bethel on the west and Ai on the east. He built an altar to Yahweh and he called on the name of Yahweh" (Gen. 12:7–8).

Each altar provided a testimonial to Abraham's growth in understanding God's ways and also to his trust in God. For today's leaders spiritual markers provide a backdrop by which they can see where God has helped them mature in their relationship with him. God's current instructions are best understood in light of the knowledge of all he has done in a leader's life thus far.

When a severe famine swept across Canaan, Abraham took matters into his own hands and relocated to Egypt. Unfortunately, he did not consult the Lord either when he left for Egypt or when he arrived. No mention is made of Abraham's building an altar while he was in Egypt (Gen. 12:10–20). Whenever Abraham made decisions without consulting God, the results were disastrous.

ABRAHAM EXPERIENCED GOD'S REDEMPTION

In Scripture, God seldom intervened when people were about to make mistakes. Rather, he allowed them to fail but stood ready to redeem them. Many individuals, through the process of failure and redemption, saw God's character revealed in a deeper dimension than if God had simply stepped in to prevent them from making a mistake. If there is anything leaders must carefully evaluate and process, it is their mistakes. Through systematically reviewing setbacks and making the necessary adjustments to ensure the same errors are not repeated, leaders can derive great benefit.

Abraham, fearing Pharaoh would kill him to marry his wife, had Sarah lie about their marriage. This deception would cost Abraham and his descendants dearly. It was one event that happened in the fear of the moment. However, the lie indicated a flaw in Abraham's character. Abraham's falsehood revealed he had not yet learned to fully trust God. There was more work to be done in his life before he could be entrusted with rearing a patriarch. This shortcoming in Abraham's character would manifest itself again (Gen. 29). Tragically, his son Isaac would also lie about his wife when faced with a similar situation (Gen. 26:7), and Isaac's son Jacob would become a notorious deceiver. Character flaws, left unchecked in people's lives, can tenaciously reappear in subsequent generations (Exod. 34:7; Deut. 5:9). Nevertheless, God forgave Abraham and helped him grow in character until he became the model of faith for generations of God's people.

ABRAHAM LEARNED BY EXPERIENCE

Abraham's understanding of God was not theoretical. He didn't learn it from books. He discovered it through personal encounters with God. Each time God revealed a new facet of his character to Abraham; it was through experience. For example, God gave Abraham a brilliant victory over a superior army (Gen. 15:1). Thereafter, Abraham knew he could trust God as his shield. This was not because God said he could protect Abraham but because Abraham experienced God's protection firsthand. Spiritual leaders must make the connection between God's activity in their lives and God's character.

ABRAHAM WAS NOT ALLOWED TO TAKE SHORTCUTS

Abraham's life demonstrates that attaining spiritual maturity is a lifelong process. Spiritual leaders don't take shortcuts. Genesis 16 details a low point in Abraham's life. Despite the incredible promise God made to develop Abraham into the father of countless descendents, Sarah remained childless. Undoubtedly one of the most powerful instruments God uses in forging character is making people wait. At this crucial time of testing, Abraham heeded people's counsel instead of trusting God. His wife, Sarah, advised him to produce a child through her servant Hagar. This was a commonly accepted way to compensate for a woman's inability to bear children. It was worldly reasoning at its best, but it was not God's way. After ten years of waiting on God, Abraham's faith wavered, and he took matters into his own hands. Hagar produced a son, Ishmael, who would become the founder of the Arab nations. These people would eventually become Israel's fierce enemies. Thousands of years later people continue to suffer and die because Abraham chose to take a shortcut rather than trust God's word.

Abraham was one hundred years old when Isaac was born. He waited twenty-five years for God to fulfill his promise. Abraham learned a lesson about the difference between God's timing and people's timing: God is not only concerned with *what* is done but *when* and *how* something is accomplished. Each factor has the potential to bring him glory, and God will not share his glory (Isa. 42:8). God views events from an eternal perspective. People have a temporal vantage point. Spiritual leaders court disaster when they panic and assume they must take charge of their own future (1 Sam. 13:6–9). When spiritual leaders wait patiently on the Lord's timing, regardless of how long it takes, God always proves himself absolutely true to his word. Occasionally the time it takes God's promise to be realized can seem eternally long, but a promise fulfilled by God is always worth the wait. Some leaders would see more successes occur in their lives and organizations if they were willing to wait as long as necessary for God to accomplish his will in his time and in his way.

ABRAHAM DEMONSTRATED HIS FAITH

By the time Abraham was a centenarian, God developed him into a godly husband and father. Still God had greater plans for him. The Lord intended for Abraham to be more than a father to Isaac; he wanted him to be a perpetual paragon of faithfulness. For this, Abraham had to advance farther in his relationship with God than had his contemporaries. To develop great faith in God, Abraham was asked to make the most difficult decision of his life.

> After these things God tested Abraham and said to him, "Abraham!"
>
> "Here I am," he answered.
>
> "Take your son," He said, "your only son Isaac, whom you love, go to the land of Moriah, and offer him there as a burnt offering on one of the mountains I will tell you about."
>
> So Abraham got up early in the morning, saddled his donkey, and took with him two of his young men and his son Issac. He split wood for a burnt offering and set out to go to the place God had told him about. (Gen. 22:1–3)

There was no mistaking what God was asking. The question was, would Abraham obey? Most of the time the problem with Christian leaders is not that they don't know what God wants them to do. The issue is that they know only too well but they are unwilling to do it.

To modern readers God's command appears unusually cruel. But to Abraham it would not have seemed peculiar. Abraham lived in a land of fanatical idol worship. Idolaters, desperate to gain their god's favor, would sacrifice their firstborn children on altars. In essence God's command would prove whether or not Abraham was as committed to his God as the people around him were to theirs. If Abraham was to be father of the faithful, it would require of him a deeper faith in God than possessed by the average person. For Abraham to do extraordinary things, he would need a deep and unshakable relationship with God.

ABRAHAM OBEYED GOD

Through obedience people experience God working through their lives, and they learn more about God's character. In response to Abraham's obedience, God spared Isaac's life. Abraham named that place "the Lord will provide," for there he discovered the truth that when people give everything they have to God, God will provide all they need. Abraham's response reveals the caliber of man he became. Scripture testifies: "So Abraham got up early . . ." Abraham received the single most difficult assignment God had ever given and he obeyed without hesitation. In passing this test, Abraham not only went deeper in his relationship with God; he also demonstrated his readiness to be a great leader of God's people. "By Myself I have sworn," this is the LORD's declaration: "Because you have done this thing and have not withheld you only son, I will indeed bless you and make your offspring as numerous as the stars of the sky and the sand on the seashore. Your offspring will possess the gates of their enemies. And all the nations of the earth will be blessed by your offspring because you have obeyed My command" (Gen. 22:16–18). Abraham's obedience was far more crucial than he realized. Abraham came to understand his actions did not affect him alone, but the generations that would follow.

ABRAHAM BECAME GOD'S FRIEND

What was the result of God's close relationship with Abraham over the years? He became a godly man, the patriarch of a nation, and the father of the faithful. But God's activity in Abraham's life helped him become something more important than all of these things. Abraham became a friend of God (2 Chron. 20:7; Isa. 41:8). It is one thing to call God your friend. It is quite another for God to call you his friend. Abraham is the only person in the Old Testament described this way (see Exod. 33:11; John 15:14–15). Scripture indicates: "So the Scripture was fulfilled that says, Abraham believed God, and it was credited to him for righteousness, and he was called God's friend" (James 2:23).

Abraham was far from perfect. He made many mistakes. Yet his heart was open before God, and God chose to develop him into a man of faith. God didn't choose Abraham because of his leadership ability. He selected Abraham because of his heart. The key was not that Abraham attended all the best leadership seminars. It was that he came to know God, and he allowed God to transform him into a leader through his obedience. When people strive to have their hearts right before God, God promises to "show Himself strong" (2 Chron. 16:9).

Conclusion

God appoints leaders. People may apply for various leadership positions, but God is the one who ultimately determines which leadership roles they will have and which ones he will bless. Leadership development comes through character maturation because leadership is a character issue. Therefore, the first truth in leadership development is this: God's assignments are based on character—the greater the character, the larger the assignment (Luke 16:10). Before God will give leaders important assignments, he will build in them greater characters. No role is more important than that of a spiritual leader; therefore, God will first build a character that is capable of handling a significant assignment.

Character building can be a slow, sometimes painful process. But the person willing to allow God to complete the work will know the joy of being used by God. Even better, those who submit their lives to God's refining process will experience the profound joy that comes from knowing God in a deeply personal way.

Two factors determine the length of time required for God to develop character worthy of spiritual leadership—trust in God and obedience to God's will. God builds character through the ordinary experiences and crises of life. Character does not grow significantly while one attends a seminar or takes a course. Rather, God uses everyday events, both good and bad, to shape leaders. Often these events are situations beyond peoples' control—events requiring them to place their trust in God.

Significant character development occurs as God redeems people from their mistakes. God does not always intervene when people are determined to go in a harmful direction, but he is always available to restore them. Through the redemption process, they learn more about themselves and God. The best leaders know themselves well. God uses life's experiences to teach leaders what they are really like. Wise leaders allow God to make the most of their mistakes. Those willing to submit themselves to the Lord's leadership development process have the opportunity to accomplish God's purposes in their generation.

—————— Responding to This Material ——————

1. Consider how God worked in the lives of your ancestors (your parents, grandparents, and even your great-grandparents). Do you sense any common, multigenerational themes to his work in your family history? If so, what implications might this have for his calling on your life? What character traits might you need to be more intentional about passing along to your children and grandchildren to ensure this legacy continues?

2. Take an inventory of all the natural qualities God put into your life that enhance your leadership (such qualities as intelligence, stamina, gift for administration, etc.).

3. Make a second list of all your qualities you feel works against your effectiveness as a leader.

4. Review the two lists. What do you see? Do you have more positives or negatives? Would your spouse or colleagues come up with similar lists? Which list would have been longer for Moses? Abraham? Peter? James? John? Paul? What do you conclude after considering the previous questions?

5. Take a large piece of paper. Make a time line from your birth to the present. Identify all the formative influences and experiences in your life. Write the negative ones in red and the positives in black. Record the neutral factors in blue. Take your time and be thorough, the more detail the better. Once you are finished, analyze the formative experiences in your life. Are there more positives or negatives? Look at each negative experience. Beside each one, write anything you learned or any way you grew as a result. Do you see any experiences from which you have not drawn anything positive yet?

How might God want to use those events in your life? You may want to enlist a trusted friend or leadership coach to review your findings with you.

6. Where do you spend most of your time: working in your strengths or managing your weaknesses? What are some ways God might want to address your weakness? Do you need to enlist someone with differing strengths to work with you? Are there classes or training that would help you? Does God have you in a position where you must depend upon him in your weakness? If so, do you think he is in as much of a hurry as you are to move you out of that place of dependency upon him?

Chapter Four

The Leader's Vision: Where Do Leaders Get It, and How Do They Communicate It?

W hen it comes to vision, no statement is more frequently quoted (or misquoted) by Christians and non-Christians alike than King Solomon's observation: "Where there is no vision, the people perish" (Prov. 29:18 KJV). Scripture's timeless wisdom once again proves relevant to modern life. Leadership pundits claim vision is crucial for the obvious reason that if you can't see where you are going, you are unlikely to reach your destination. Vision serves as the North Star to help leaders keep their bearings as they move their people forward. Hence, any organization that lacks a clear vision risks becoming sidetracked and failing to accomplish its purpose.

Contemporary organizations are inundated with discussions, memos, meetings, seminars, retreats, presentations, and slogans about vision. Vision statements are in vogue. They are everywhere—on letterheads, business cards, posted in offices, and on brochures, billboards, and advertisements. Leaders spend extensive energy encouraging their people to buy in to their vision. Those who don't embrace the corporate vision are often forced out the door.

If vision is critical for organizations, it stands to reason leaders must be visionaries. Visionary leaders understand at least three fundamental issues: (1) the source of vision; (2) how vision inspires people; and (3) how leaders communicate vision.

Where Do Leaders Obtain Their Vision?

If great visions inspire great organizations, then it is imperative for leaders to develop the loftiest vision possible. Walt Disney had a broad vision—to make people happy—and he redefined the entertainment industry. Henry Ford sought to democratize the automobile, and the result was a prodigiously successful automotive empire. George Marshall's vision was to assemble the mightiest army in the world; he began with 200,000 enlisted men in 1939 and by 1945 had created a force of 8.3 million. Bill Gates envisioned "a computer on every desktop and Microsoft software in every computer."[1] That vision's success is legendary. When considering the examples of exceptional business leaders, people often feel pressured to develop grandiose visions that will likewise propel their organization to greatness. But where do leaders discover visions that inspire people and unite them to grand accomplishments? Visionaries may draw from many wells.

Because It's There

In 1924, George Leigh Mallory, a British schoolmaster and son of a British Lord, determined to ascend the as yet unconquered peak of Mount Everest. When a reporter asked why he intended to climb the formidable mountain, he replied: "Because it's there." On June 8, the thirty-eight-year-old father of three young children was last sighted trudging up Everest with his companion Andrew Irvine. Seventy-five years later, in 1999, an American climbing team discovered Mallory's perfectly preserved body. Mallory sacrificed his life in an attempt to accomplish an unnecessary goal.[2]

While it is one thing for people to risk their lives in pursuit of a dream, it is quite another for leaders to take their organizations on a misguided and needless quest merely because the opportunity presents itself. The only vision some leaders have for their organizations is to do what they have always done or to address the obstacles immediately before them. They do not ponder why they are taking a particular action. They do not consider long-term ramifications. They hardly consider their alternatives. They value action over reflection—or more precisely, reaction over reflection. They assume any response is better than standing still. Hence, when a challenge presents itself, they impulsively charge forward. Such leaders eventually collapse on the slopes of their mountains, their labors and sacrifices misspent.

Leaders who subscribe to this reactionary approach to vision can be identified by their track record. For example, they may instigate a new building program without considering the long-term cost or effect. Once the expense of the building project escalates and their people begin to grumble, these impetuous adventurers find themselves halfway up a mountain without the resources to complete the climb. Impulsive or reactionary leaders may also begin new programs or hire additional staff simply because opportunities arise. Christians often call these "open doors." Because an opportunity presents itself, they assume it must be God's will to move forward. This is an undiscerning approach to leadership. There is much more to determining God's will than merely assuming every open door is a divine invitation.

DUPLICATING SUCCESS

A popular means for modern leaders to find their vision is to copy previous success. They can do this in one of two ways: the first is by repeating their own achievements. The easiest course of action is often the one already taken, especially if it paid off. But sometimes success becomes the leader's greatest enemy. Consider the following scenario: suppose a congregation is concerned that it is not reaching people in the surrounding community. Church leaders call for members to spend the next two months earnestly praying and seeking God's guidance on how to evangelize people in their neighborhood. Much of the regular church programming is shifted to prayer meetings where people pray together in homes throughout the week. After two months the members gather to report what God said to them.

Someone points out that a large public park near the church has never been used for church ministry. Another church member senses God leading their church to hold a public Sunday service on the upcoming Labor Day weekend. The congregation senses that perhaps God is leading them to hold it in the nearby park. Then a church leader excitedly suggests offering a free barbeque lunch in the park after the service. Someone else knows a Christian band that might play a concert in the park that afternoon. A woman who works at a printing shop has been wondering how God might use her job for God's kingdom. Now she senses God wants her to design an invitation that can be sent to every home in the neighborhood inviting them to the service, barbeque, and concert. The whole congregation is abuzz with excitement as it becomes clear Christ is guiding his church.

That Sunday hundreds of people from the community attend the service. People stay for the concert and rave about the free barbeque. The following Sunday, more than one hundred new visitors attend the church. Everyone realizes the service in the park was the most successful ministry the church has ever undertaken.

The dilemma: what does the church do *next* Labor Day Sunday? You know what would happen. The service in the park would immediately become an annual event! Why? Because it was successful! But *why* was it successful? Was it because the church discovered the secret to reaching people in their neighborhood was offering free food or outdoor services? No. The key was the church sought God's guidance. They did what God led them to do, and God blessed their efforts. But here's a second question: would the church spend as much time praying about the second annual Labor Day church service as they did for the first one? Of course not. And why? Because they wouldn't feel the need now that they knew what "worked." Another annual event would be added to the church's calendar that was already cluttered with annual events from successful events from days gone by. Long after people forgot how and why the first outdoor service was initiated, the faithful folks would be setting up barbeque grills and passing out flyers for the thirty-seventh annual Labor Day service. When new members ask longtime members why the church holds an annual service in the park, the veteran congregants simply shrug their shoulders and say, "I don't know. We've always done it that way."

Max De Pree warns: "Success can close a mind faster than prejudice."[3] A leader may be reluctant to reject previously successful methods to lead in a new direction. It's too risky. Peter Drucker observed: "No one has much difficulty getting rid of the total failures. They liquidate themselves. Yesterday's successes, however, always linger on long beyond their productive life."[4] What is worse than past success is previous moderate success. Moderate success is lethal to organizations because it offers just enough progress to be enticing but not enough to significantly move the organization forward. It functions like an opiate, sedating leaders into assuming no major adjustments or reevaluations of strategy are required.

Christian organizations should note in the Scriptures and throughout history that God rarely worked the same way twice. God's activity was always unique to the people with whom he was dealing and the time in which he was working. God's activity cannot be reduced to a formula because God is more concerned about relating to his people than he is with a specific task or program. Churches erroneously assume that because God worked mightily in a particular way in the past, he will work in exactly the same way today. Many organizations are locked into routines not because they are effective today but because they were effective yesterday.

The only thing worse than copying your own prior success, is duplicating someone else's achievements. Adopting the current methods of others can be as impotent as recycling your own worn-out methods. In 1982 Tom Peters wrote the immensely popular book *In Search of Excellence*, in which he described how he examined America's best run companies.[5] He concluded that if other companies mimicked the same behaviors, they could experience similar success. Millions of businesspeople devoured the book and began copying everything the heralded companies were doing. CEOs of growing, profitable companies hit the speaking and writing circuit, and their material was gobbled up. In 1994, Jim Collins and Jerry Porras wrote *Built to Last* in which they studied companies that had demonstrated success for over one hundred years.[6] People began modeling their businesses on those findings. Then in 2001, Jim Collins came out with his best-selling book *Good to Great.*[7] The theme of all of these books was the same. Companies that had consistently grown and made healthy profits should be emulated. What was overlooked in the dizzying rush to copy the latest business fad was that many of the exemplary companies cited in the books were beginning to struggle and suffer decline. In a scathing critique Phil Rosenzweig wrote *The Halo Effect* which suggested that despite the authors' claims to have studied successful businesses scientifically, most of the research had been done backwards. If a company was enjoying growth and profits, the authors assumed it must be the result of good leadership and therefore should be emulated. Rosenzweig posited that increased sales and revenues did not necessarily indicate good leadership or a strong corporate culture. Jim Collins published a hastily written addendum entitled *How the Mighty Fall* to explain why leaders and companies he had extolled were beginning to struggle soon after the ink from *Good to Great* was dry. Rosenzweig concluded: "There is simply no formula that can guarantee success. . . . The answer to the question, 'What really works?' is simple: Nothing really works, at least not all the time."[8] Rosenzweig claimed businesspeople are constantly looking for "success stories" and will rush in a herd to duplicate whatever methods are being heralded as the next best thing.

One would think churches, which have the Bible as their standard and the Holy Spirit as their guide, would not succumb to adopting worldly standards of measuring success. But many church leaders assume if a church attracts large numbers, its methodology is effective and therefore should be copied. Questions of whether the methodology is biblical or God honoring are often handled with impatience. If a church develops an innovative way to enlist new members, other pastors jump on board and lead their people to do the same thing. Mimicking the successful strategies of others is enticing to some leaders because it eliminates the need to think reflectively. The vision for some pastors is no more complicated than enthusiastically pursuing the latest fad. Martin Luther King Jr. lamented the shortage of leaders willing to pay the price of prolonged, creative, problem-solving thinking. He concluded: "There is an almost universal quest for easy answers and half-baked solutions. Nothing pains some people more than having to think."[9]

When churches emulate other churches, it virtually eliminates the need for Christian leaders to cultivate an intimate relationship with God. God can certainly lead more than one congregation to use similar methods, but church leaders must not be seduced into thinking all their church needs is the latest seminar or popular book. When a pastor invests his energy chasing fads and attending every church growth seminar, his beleaguered staff knows as soon as he returns to the office, memos will be flying out his door announcing all the changes that will be taking place . . . at least until the next seminar. Such leaders devote too little time examining and evaluating the effectiveness of their own organizations and cultivating their relationship with the Head of the church while they focus an inordinate amount of time monitoring others' activities. Pity the people who follow such thoughtless leadership.

VANITY

Although not always readily apparent as a source of vision, vanity motivates many leaders. Some leaders base the goals of their organization on what will bring them the most personal success or praise. Business leaders may act more out of a desire to expand their reputations, advance their careers, or acquire wealth than out of concern for benefitting their companies. They want their legacy to be established as the architect of the XYZ acquisition or merger. Likewise religious leaders may lead their churches to build larger auditoriums or televise their services, not because they genuinely sense God's leadership to do so but to enhance their stature as preachers. Such egocentric leadership can be easily cloaked in statements about "glorifying God" and "reaching the lost." But in truth the organization's growth merely stokes the leader's pride. Countless organizations have crumbled under leaders who were motivated by vanity rather than vision.

A pastor wanted to build the largest church in his region so he modernized the services to attract young families. Then he led the congregation into a multimillion-dollar building program to have the largest, most attractive facility in the area. Those who raised questions were edged out of the church for resisting the pastor's authority. Many older members began leaving the church, uncomfortable with the direction of its ministry. With them went their money. The church no longer had the funds to service its enormous debt. When it became clear the pastor's vision was leading the church into ruin, he suddenly felt God calling him into an itinerate ministry, and he left his congregation to pay the bills for his grandiose and misguided vision. Tragically, this story could be retold countless times. Such churches are led by people more concerned with making a name for themselves than for glorifying God's name.

Napoleon Bonaparte was constantly involved in warfare as he led the French Empire's effort to conquer Europe. In defeat, Napoleon surmised, "If I had succeeded, I should have been the greatest man known to history."[10] There is no doubt that Napoleon made a name for himself, but it's questionable whether his soldiers would have willingly laid down their lives on Europe's battlefields had they known the primary cause was to secure their emperor's fame. Today many are called upon to give their best efforts on behalf of their organizations, but they do so with nagging doubts that their personal sacrifices are for no more noble purpose than furthering their leader's career.

NEED

A popular basis for developing vision is perceived needs. Need-based visions are established by surveying target groups to determine their desires. Businesses discover what people are seeking; then they develop a product to meet the expressed need. While this has long been a profitable practice for secular businesses, Christian organizations are increasingly favoring the need-based approach in determining their vision. Churches survey their communities to discover peoples' concerns. Then they compile, categorize, and prioritize the data. They set the church's agenda to correspond with the survey's results.

The advantage of the need-based approach is obvious. In the marketplace producers are assured consumers consider their product necessary. Organizations gain a sense of relevance when they are equipped to meet the expressed desires of the general public. Churches reap a similar benefit: those churches most in touch with their community's expressed needs are viewed as most relevant.

Using the expressed needs of a target audience to establish a vision is not a foolproof approach, however. Successful companies are not entirely market-driven. Rather, businesses sometimes drive the market. Many popular inventions and products came not from the expressed need of the public but from the creative innovation of an enterprising company. When Bill Gates began developing software, most people did not own a personal computer. When Henry Ford began manufacturing automobiles, most people did not own one. Milton Hershey owned one of the most profitable caramel-making companies in America. He sold it to Daniel LaFean because he believed chocolate would dominate the future candy market and he wanted to be at the industry's forefront, setting the trends not copying what others were doing.[11] Companies that merely respond to society's expressed needs find themselves in a large pool of similar companies, all competing for the same consumers. Innovative companies, however, look to the future to anticipate eventual needs, or they create a sense of need in the public. Then they position themselves to lead the industry in meeting the resulting demand. W. Chan Kim and Renee Mauborgne refer to this approach as "Blue Ocean Strategy." This tactic "challenges companies to break out of the red ocean of bloody competition by creating uncontested market space that makes the competition irrelevant."[12]

Need-inspired visions, while relevant to a point in the marketplace, are only one aspect of successful businesses. Religious organizations should be cautioned about basing their ministries solely on meeting the needs expressed in their community. While churches must be sensitive to peoples' concerns, a need expressed is not identical to a divine call.

Moreover, when churches survey their neighborhoods, they are generally talking with unregenerate people. People who are not born again cannot fully understand their spiritual needs. One church surveying its community found the greatest need expressed was for a bridge to be constructed to provide easier neighborhood access to the downtown. The church asked, and the people responded. But the church was left in the awkward position of having to confess it could not meet the desire voiced by the majority of the community.

Non-Christians may recognize the symptoms of evil in society, but they generally do not understand the root cause. For example, when parents run their families by worldly standards, their children may experiment with worldly temptations. The parents might assume what they need is a community center to keep their teenagers off the streets. In reality they need Christ as the head of their home and to raise their children using God's standard instead of the world's values. Need-based visions not only allow unregenerate people to set the agenda for churches, but they also tempt congregations to focus on symptoms rather than causes.

God's assignment for a church may not include meeting every need expressed in its neighborhood. God equips each church for particular assignments (1 Cor. 12:12–31). The congregation must discover its vision not by asking people's opinions but by seeking God's direction. Often need-based church visions cause Christians to neglect their relationship with the Head of the church as they focus their energies on tabulating surveys and responding to expressed needs. Jesus addressed this problem when Mary took a pound of costly perfume and poured it on his feet. She then humbly wiped Jesus' feet with her own hair. Judas was indignant. "Why wasn't this fragrant oil not sold for 300 denarii and given to poor people?" he asked. Jesus' response was pointed: "For you always have the poor with you, but you do not always have Me" (John 12:5, 8). A relationship with Jesus is always a higher priority than meeting people's temporal needs. Jesus did not base his actions on what people wanted but on where he saw his Father at work (Mark 1:23–39;

Luke 19:1–10; John 5:17, 19–20). If the Father was working with the multitude, that is where the Son invested himself. If the Father was bringing conviction to a lone sinner, that's where Jesus directed his efforts. If setting vision occurs by merely tabulating a door-to-door survey, a relationship with the heavenly Father is unnecessary.

While productivity is a necessary and desirable goal for businesses, even secular leadership pundits concede that profit cannot be the sole determining factor in business. Warren Bennis observed, "Too many Americans believe that the bottom line isn't everything, it's the only thing, and America is strangling on that lack of vision."[13] Bennis also noted, "It isn't either a bull or a bear market anymore, it's a pig market."[14]

Spiritual leaders should be motivated by the Holy Spirit. We work with Christian CEOs who, when they meet with world leaders, are not only able to transact multimillion-dollar deals but to also give a witness for Christ. Some Christian business leaders have found that God's agenda was for them to give Bibles to foreign business and political leaders or to invest company profits in providing community centers for underprivileged children. Many privately owned businesses are using a substantial portion of the profits to support orphanages or to provide food internationally, to fund translations of the Bible into foreign languages, or to sponsor missionaries or Christian disaster relief efforts. These CEOs realize that their talented staff members want a greater cause than a bottom line or market share. One CEO contributes a percentage of company profits into a fund so his staff can engage in community service and international trips to provide disaster relief as well as food and medicine to impoverished countries. This executive and many others have found that the need to make a profit to satisfy investors is not the sole vision driving their company. Using the business platform and leveraging their executive position to serve and glorify God provides a major impetus for their corporate vision.

AVAILABLE RESOURCES

The availability of resources alone should not induce vision. Some organizations gravitate toward certain activities or priorities because resources such as manpower, finances, and equipment are available. Church programs are often motivated in this manner.

+ A church is informed that its denomination is making copies of evangelistic DVDs available for distribution in the community. The church decides this offer is too good to pass up, and it orders one thousand DVDs. For the next four Saturdays, church members are enlisted to go door to door in their community to distribute them.

+ A church hosts several college-age missionaries each summer for the simple reason that a local campus ministry makes the students available to them each summer.

+ An international mission agency offers free literature if the church will conduct a mission fair so the church schedules one.

+ The denomination alerts the church that funds are available for starting a new congregation in the area so the missions committee begins surveying neighborhoods, seeking interest in a new church plant.

+ When an elderly member donates a grand piano to the church in memory of her deceased husband, the auditorium is rearranged, and the worship program is adjusted to accommodate the new instrument.

Churches eagerly avail themselves of every opportunity presenting itself, but in time they find themselves burdened by the weight of trying to make use of all the available resources. Rather than the resources serving the churches, they begin to drive the church's programming.

Such a reactionary response can also occur in the business world.

+ The head office makes sales incentives available so the branch manager decides to promote a competition among her salespeople, though this method goes against her personal views of team building.

+ A business experiences a profitable quarter so it purchases new equipment and hires additional personnel because the money is currently available.

Wise leaders do not allow the availability of resources to determine the direction of their organization. For one thing, such "gifts" generally come with strings attached. Accepting equipment, volunteers, or program funds may mean committing one's organization to a philosophy or direction that contradicts the leader's personal or corporate values.

Resources should undergird vision, not steer it. Leaders must first decide the vision for their organization and then marshal the necessary materials to achieve it. Unwise leaders thoughtlessly accept resources and then try to piece together a vision that uses the various supplies they accumulated. Christian leaders should especially understand that God will provide whatever resource is required to accomplish the tasks he assigns. Spiritual leaders begin with their divine assignment and then watch for the heavenly provision.

LEADER DRIVEN

Seth Godin wrote: "The secret of leadership is simple. Do what you believe in. Paint a picture of the future. Go there. People will follow."[15] Many people assume being a visionary leader involves personally developing a vision for one's organization. The imagery is of a solitary figure ascending a mountain seeking a vision with the combustibility to spark a significant movement among the people below. Such leaders assume vision casting is a responsibility they cannot delegate or share. Many well-known writers support leader-based vision development. Warren Bennis notes: "Just as no great painting has ever been created by a committee, no great vision has ever emerged from the herd."[16] While George Barna believes God gives vision to leaders, he notes: "God never gave a vision to a committee."[17] While most leaders know vision is important, understanding how to achieve vision is not a simple endeavor. Burt Nanus asks, "So where does a leader's vision come from? Vision is composed of one part foresight, one part insight, plenty of imagination and judgment, and often, a healthy dose of chutzpah."[18] Kouzes and Posner claim that visions "flow from the reservoir of our knowledge and experience."[19]

How do leaders generate it? They perceive a desirable future for their organization and then develop a plan to achieve it. This undertaking can place enormous pressure on leaders as they assume responsibility for interpreting the rapid global changes around them and peering into the future to determine the best approach forward.

What kind of leader is qualified for such a demanding task? People who have traveled extensively, read broadly, know a wide variety of people, and have stretched their thinking through education and a mosaic of life experiences have the raw materials to develop compelling and innovative visions. But the job doesn't end there. Once leaders develop a vision, they have the onerous task of selling it to their constituents.

Often leaders put their reputations and credibility on the line as they attempt to win support for their desired future. People who reject their visions are viewed as expressing a lack of trust and/or commitment. Leaders feel pressured to develop visions grand enough and compelling enough to induce people to want to "sign up." James C. Collins and Jerry I. Porras in their book *Built to Last*, discuss "Big Hairy Audacious Goals," or BHAGs.[20] These organizational goals are so large and challenging they inspire people to unite to achieve what seems impossible. Companies have embraced such goals, and the results have, on occasion, been impressive.

Many Christian leaders have adopted BHAGs with gusto. Yet at times there seems to be a vacuous quality to the rhetoric. They proclaim, "We need to dream big dreams for God," or, "We must set goals worthy of the mighty God we serve." This sounds exciting and may elicit a chorus of amens from the audience, but is it biblical? Isaiah 55:8–9 cautions: "'For My thoughts are not your thoughts, and your ways are not My ways.' This is the LORD's declaration. 'For as heaven is higher than the earth, so My ways are higher than your ways, and My thoughts than your thoughts.'"

The message is clear. A leader's best thinking will not build the kingdom of God. Why? Because people do not naturally think the way God does. The apostle Paul observed, "Where is the philosopher? Where is the scholar? Where is the debater of this age? Hasn't God made the world's wisdom foolish?" (1 Cor. 1:20). God has different priorities and values than we do. When people "think great thoughts for God" and "dream great dreams for God," the emphasis is on people rather than God. The danger is in believing that human reasoning can build God's kingdom. It cannot (John 15:5). Such an approach is self-centered, not God centered.

In the wilderness Satan tried to entice Jesus into using the world's methods to accomplish God's will (Matt. 4:1–11). Satan said in effect, "Provide free food, and you'll attract a large following. Perform dramatic miracles, and you'll win followers. Worship me, and you'll provide Christianity without a cross." Jesus readily saw through Satan's guise and recognized his reasoning as unscriptural. In fact, throughout his ministry, Jesus identified many commonly accepted values and methods as being contrary to God's ways. The world says aim for first place. Jesus said the last would be first. We idolize strength. Jesus said God demonstrates his strength through weakness. Large numbers impress us. Jesus chose a small group to be his disciples and often ignored the crowds to focus on individuals.

The world seeks happiness. Jesus said, "Those who mourn are blessed" (Matt. 5:4). Crowds are attracted to large, spectacular performances. Jesus said his kingdom would be like a tiny mustard seed. People do good deeds to win praise. Jesus said do your good deeds in secret. Slick marketing campaigns can draw an audience. Jesus said no one can come to him unless the Father draws them. Over and over again Jesus rejected human reasoning in favor of God's wisdom! Ephesians 3:20 says that Christ "is able to do above and beyond all that we ask or think according to the power that works in us." When you commit your organization to achieving your self-set goals, you rob your people of something greater. Even secular companies realize they need to strive for a vision that goes beyond any one person, including the CEO.[21]

How significant are our Big Hairy Audacious Goals when viewed in light of Ephesians 3:20? Can men or women impress God with their grandiose visions? Can leaders dream any dream worthy of God? Can even the most perceptive leader look into the future and determine the most desirable outcome for their organization? God remains unimpressed with leaders' grandiose schemes and dreams because he is able to do immeasurably more than mortals can imagine (Job 38–41). Spiritual leaders who develop their own visions, no matter how extensive, rather than understanding God's will, are settling for their best thinking instead of God's plans. It's a sure way to shortchange their followers.

A poignant series of events is found in the book of Luke that vividly exemplifies leader-based vision casting (Luke 9:10–17). As Jesus was teaching a multitude, the disciples could foresee impending disaster. Evening was approaching and there was no food. The twelve disciples may have caucused together to discuss options:

Peter: Can we afford to buy food for this crowd?

Judas: Not a chance. The treasury is empty.

John: Maybe there are people who brought food with them!

Andrew: No, I checked. There is just one boy with a few loaves and fishes.

After reviewing all their options and perhaps considering what other popular leaders were doing to feed their crowds and reviewing the latest literature on the subject, the disciples developed the best possible plan: send the crowd home. They approached Jesus and asked him to disperse the crowd (Luke 9:12). The disciples weren't being insensitive. This was the most logical solution. What if Jesus responded to them by saying: "Well as a matter of fact, I was intending to do something else. But you have worked so hard on your plan. You are asking me in unity, believing in faith I can grant your request. So perhaps I will do as you have asked and send the multitude home in an orderly, dignified manner." How do you suppose the disciples would have felt? They would have been elated with their "success"! They would have achieved their goal. But of course, it is possible to accomplish your goals and completely miss God's will.

Luke 9 is filled with similar events involving the disciples (vv. 28–36). As Jesus and the disciples made their way southward toward Jerusalem, they sought to pass through a Samaritan village (vv. 51–56). When they encountered a rude reception from the villagers, how did James and John respond? They asked Jesus if they could call fire down on their insolent heads!

What were these overzealous Sons of Thunder thinking? Perhaps this reveals racism on the brothers' part, for Jewish people and Samaritans had a mutually contemptuous relationship. Here was an opportunity to destroy an entire community of Samaritans! It is telling that James and John never suggested such a drastic response to the Pharisees, even after Jesus called them children of Satan (John 8:44).

The brothers may have had good motives. Perhaps they saw this as an opportunity for Jesus to demonstrate his power so that, in sacrificing one village, many others would come to believe. It could be they were acting out of misguided protectiveness. They would not stand for their Lord to be disrespected. Whatever their reasoning, Jesus rebuked them. Once again their best thinking was completely out of line with the Father's plan.

Acts 8:14–17 provides an interesting epilogue to this event. The gospel message began to spread rapidly out from Jerusalem. Word came back to the apostles that the Samaritans were receiving the gospel, so the Jerusalem church sent Peter and John to investigate. One can only imagine what went through John's mind as he entered Samaria this time. Perhaps he came upon the village he and James previously intended to destroy. But this time, rather than sending a deadly fire, the Holy Spirit filled the Samaritan believers. What a contrast. Human wisdom for that place would have wreaked total destruction. God's plan produced joyful deliverance. Instead of death the villagers received eternal life. There is perhaps no more graphic biblical depiction of the contrast between people's best thinking and God's way than this account. Just like James and John, every time leaders develop their own vision instead of seeking God's will, they are giving people their best thinking instead of God's. That is a poor exchange indeed.

VALUES/PURPOSES

A seventh source of vision for many organizations originates from their corporate values. Organizations determine their core values and then choose a direction that aligns with them. Rick Warren popularized this approach in his book *The Purpose Driven Church*.[22] The value of this approach is that it anchors the church's vision to its corporate values, thus keeping its activities linked to its priorities. We often hear leadership consultants share how they helped an organization discover its core values in order to develop a plan for the future. However, this approach has two shortcomings. First, values tend to be more restrictive than prescriptive. Knowing your purpose helps you understand what you should *not* be doing, but it often gives only general directions for what you *should* be doing. For example, if a church identifies world missions as one of its core values or purposes, then it may decide not to build an expensive new facility because that would divert funds that could otherwise support international mission activities. However, such a broad purpose does not guide the church to know if it should do mission work in Cambodia, Korea, or Kamchatka. Churches are therefore left to do what makes most sense to them. This leads to a second problem.

Values and purposes can become substitutes for God. It is fine to be values driven. It is better to be God driven. God's people are constantly moving one step away from an intimate walk with God. If leaders develop their own core values, then they are establishing the vision themselves. If God authored the purposes of a church, then the congregation should seek direction from the God who gave them their purposes and not merely settle for the purposes themselves. If every time God's people need direction they turn to their core values, then they have inadvertently found a substitute for God. The greatest dangers for apostasy are not departing from God to a distant shore but moving half a degree away from where God wants you to be. In Scripture an idol was anything you turned to or trusted in God that asked you to go to him for. When a purpose drives what you do, you no longer need to abide in an intimate relationship with Christ or hear his voice. You simply need a list of core values. Don't mistake what we are saying. Identifying core values is a good thing. They will hopefully honor God and reflect a desire to serve him. But Christ is the head of your church. Your core values are not!

One other related motivator for many leaders is their passion. Some leadership proponents suggest leaders should determine their talents and their passion, and in so doing they determine their calling. They argue if you understand the passion God has given you and you identify the gifts God placed in your life, then you can deduce the kinds of things God has prepared you to do.

The problem with this line of thinking is the lack of biblical support. Consider Moses herding sheep in the wilderness. Had he discovered his gifts and passions, he would never have returned to Egypt to deliver the Hebrews. But that was God's agenda. Second, it is tempting to assume God wants us to do things we enjoy and are good at doing. However, for God to accomplish his purposes, he may ask us to do things we do not consider enjoyable (he asked his Son to die on a cross), but they are necessary tasks for God's will to be fulfilled. It's great to be passionate about the work you do. However, spiritual leaders are driven by God, not their passion and talents.

GOD'S REVELATION

The previous seven sources of vision have one thing in common—they are generated by human thinking. The world functions by vision because it does not know God. God's people live by revelation. Proverbs 29:18, although widely quoted, is also often misapplied. The popular translation is, "Where there is no vision, the people perish" (KJV). A more accurate translation of the Hebrew is: "Without revelation people run wild." There is a significant difference between revelation and vision. Vision is something people produce. Revelation is something people receive. God must reveal his will if leaders are to know it. The secular world rejects God's will, so nonbelievers are left with one alternative—to project their own vision. Christians are called to a totally different agenda, which is set by God alone. Throughout this book when the term *vision* is used, it will not connote the popular idea of a leader-generated goal or dream. Instead, vision will refer to what God has revealed and promised about the future. The visions driving spiritual leaders must originate from God.

Life is far too complex to comprehend apart from God's revelation and guidance. Former Arkansas governor and presidential aspirant Mike Huckabee recognized this reality. Huckabee was a prominent pastor of a twenty-five-hundred-member church in Texarkana. By all accounts he was a successful spiritual leader, yet there was a restlessness in his soul. In talking with Henry Blackaby, Huckabee acknowledged that God clearly led him to resign his church and enter Arkansas politics. Later, while governor of Arkansas, Huckabee faced situations beyond his wisdom. Huckabee notes: "Being governor has led me to depend on faith with a new sense of urgency. I face situations every day that would be insurmountable without using the faith God has given me to make decisions."[23] Huckabee's career and leadership of his state were dependent in large part on God's revelation of his will. Is it possible for a governor to be led by God's revelation? Certainly!

John Beckett, CEO of R. W. Beckett Corporation, faced a crisis. An Arab oil embargo caused oil prices to double, dramatically affecting his company's sales of oil heating products. Beckett's competitors followed a predictable course, curtailing sales initiatives, laying off staff, and adopting a siege mentality. Beckett was part of a men's prayer group that regularly prayed for God's guidance for the company. As they sought God's will for the present situation, they all felt God was revealing to them that the embargo would be short-lived and the company should continue with its operations and even increase sales efforts. The group sensed God saying, "Take one day at a time, and let me lead." God's guidance, though completely contrary to generally accepted business logic, proved brilliant. The company emerged from the crisis stronger than ever and ready to be the undisputed leader in their industry. Vision was born out of the revelation of God, not a textbook approach to crisis management.[24]

When Christian leaders adopt the world's approach to vision rather than seeking God's revelation, they inadvertently assume God's responsibility. God is on mission to redeem humanity. He is the only one who knows how to do it. Leaders must understand, as Christ did, that their role is to seek the Father's will and to adjust their lives to him. Being proactive by nature, leaders often rush into action. As a result, they don't spend enough time seeking to hear clearly from God. Instead, they have a cursory moment of prayer and then begin making their plans. They seek out a few relevant Scriptures and hurry into the goal-setting phase, falsely confident that because they incorporated prayer and Scripture into their goal-setting process, their plans are "of God."

Asking God to bless your plans does not ensure what you develop is from him. Only God can reveal his plans, and he does so in his way, on his time schedule, and to whom he wishes. How often do Christian leaders claim to have received their vision from God when in fact they have simply dreamed up the most desirable future they could imagine and then prayed for God to bless their efforts? It is critical for leaders to walk closely with the Father so they are keenly aware of his revelation and are prepared to respond to his initiatives. The role of spiritual leaders is not to dream up dreams for God but to be the vanguard for their people in understanding God's revelation.

The way God leads his people is best understood by examining the Scriptures. God frequently revealed his plans in the form of a promise accompanied by vivid imagery. Thus, when God spoke, his people clearly knew what he planned to accomplish and could often describe God's coming activity in rich symbolism. For example, when God revealed to Noah what he intended to do in response to humanity's rampant sin, he gave Noah a clear picture of how he would do it: a terrible flood would consume and cover the earth (Gen. 6:17). Noah's ministry of preaching and constructing the ark was not driven by his vision of how he could best serve his community. Neither did Noah surmise the best possible future for his society. Noah's vision came from God's vow of an imminent flood. After the flood subsided, God made a promise to Noah. The symbol of God's promise was a rainbow (Gen. 9:12–13).

God also approached Abraham with a promise that not only would Abraham have a son in his old age, but God would produce through him a multitude of descendants who would bless every nation (Gen. 12:1–3). God provided several images to help Abraham grasp the enormity of the promise. Abraham's descendents would be as countless as dust particles (Gen. 13:16), as numerous as the stars (Gen. 15:5), as innumerable as the grains of sand on the seashore (Gen. 22:17). God's revelation to Abraham came as a promise, clothed in vivid imagery.

When God pledged to deliver the Israelites from their bondage in Egypt, he spoke of a land flowing with milk and honey, giving the downtrodden slaves an inspiring vision of comfort and prosperity (Exod. 3:8). The risen Christ promised his followers an eternal home in heaven, and he used the imagery of a groom coming for his bride and of a spectacular celebratory feast (Rev. 19:7–9). In the Bible, God often presented his promises with imagery that captivated people's imaginations.

An examination of God's promises, as seen through the Scriptures, makes two things obvious: (1) God's plans are impossible to achieve apart from him, and (2) God's promises are absolute. He does what he says he will do exactly the way he says he will do it. Spiritual leaders must resist the temptation to alter God's plan with their own thinking. Attempting to hurry the process or to adjust God's plan to make it more achievable are both signs of immature spiritual leadership. Spiritual leaders must remember that what God has promised, God will accomplish in his time and in his way (Isa. 46:9–11). The leader's job is to communicate God's promise to the people, not create the vision and then strive to enlist followers to buy in to it.

Sources of Vision

1. Because It's There
2. Duplicating Success
3. Vanity
4. Need
5. Available Resources
6. Leader Driven
7. Values/Purposes
8. God's Revelation

How Does Vision Inspire and Move People?

Great visions move people. John F. Kennedy's vision to place a man on the moon by the end of the decade mobilized a nation to accomplish the seemingly impossible. Martin Luther King Jr.'s "I have a dream" speech on the steps of the Lincoln Memorial before 250,000 people electrified his listeners and shook his nation. Burt Nanus claims, "There is no more powerful engine driving an organization toward excellence and long-range success than an attractive, worthwhile, and achievable vision of the future, widely shared."[25]

The challenge for leaders is to understand how vision motivates followers to do things they would not attempt otherwise. Vision statements are inadequate. Many an office cubicle has an aging poster tacked to the wall displaying the company vision statement. Such statements, generally decreed from the top down, have little effect on the staff's daily activities. Even when the leadership asks for input, this is often little more than an exercise wherein the administration guides people to a preestablished conclusion.

Many lofty vision statements carry no innate appeal to the people lower down in the organization. Companies can generate goals such as "5 percent gain in market share next year" or "10 percent less waste next year." These objectives may be worthwhile, but they carry no obvious personal benefit for those who do the work. Churches develop similar goals: "Ten percent increase in membership" or "reach the second phase of our capital campaign." In reality, visions consisting of numbers do not have the same impact as a vision involving vivid imagery. As James Champy said, "Numbers by themselves never mobilize anyone but an accountant."[26] Just as God used memorable images to symbolize his promises, so spiritual leaders should put into pictures the promise they believe God has given their organization.

If people are asked to give their best, they need and deserve a clear picture of the good that will result from their efforts. The benefit of imagery is that it helps people see the breadth of the vision. Why would employees or volunteers make great sacrifices on behalf of puny visions? At times leaders encourage their people to give their best, but they fail to spell out any clear, compelling benefit. When this happens, those laboring in support of the vision may perceive that their efforts are only benefitting the ones promoting the vision. People have the innate need to believe they are making a valuable contribution to society. George Bernard Shaw's poignant message rings true: "This is true joy in life, the being used up for a purpose recognized by yourself as a mighty one; the being a force of nature instead of a feverish, selfish little clod of ailments and grievances complaining that the world will not devote itself to making you happy. And also the only real tragedy in life is the being used by personally minded men for purposes which you recognize to be base."[27] Leaders who understand that life is too precious to waste make every effort to help their people see the meaning and significance of what they do. Every day people invest their lives in their jobs or in volunteer work. They want to believe their effort is not being squandered.

To the world a good vision is an image of something that is both desirable and attainable. One difference between worldly visions and God-given visions is that the latter are impossible to achieve apart from God. In this regard, Christian leaders have a tremendous advantage over secular leaders. People want to be a part of something significant. If it is clear God made a promise to a group of people, there should be little difficulty in enlisting their support. Leaders of Christian organizations must not assume that because people are doing "God's work," their efforts automatically bring them a sense of meaning and value. Many Christian organizations are merely trying to make payroll or to attract new members and as a result are cultivating disillusionment and bitterness in their ranks.

How Do Leaders Communicate Vision?

Leaders can spend a great deal of energy trying to persuade their people to "buy in" to their vision. This coercion is especially necessary when the vision does not come from God. In the Christian context the process of selling a vision is flawed. If a vision must be sold to others, it is not compelling and is probably not divinely inspired. Spiritual leaders don't sell vision; they share what God has revealed to them and trust the Holy Spirit to confirm the vision in the hearts of their people. Today Christian leaders often develop a vision and then demand the members either get on board or find another organization. In his best-selling book *Good to Great*, Jim Collins uses the analogy of having your people board a bus.[28] He claims if you have the right people on the bus, they will be prepared to go to any destination that appears reasonable. However, the implication is those who are uncertain or unwilling to go in the direction the bus is heading need to be gently, but firmly, removed. This analogy should be used with caution. Of course a staff member who consistently and stubbornly opposes every new initiative may well need to find a different organization with a different vision. However, in a church setting pastors are remiss to think every person voting "no" in the business meeting needs to be encouraged to find another church. After all, God adds members to the body (1 Cor. 12:18). At times the reason people do not embrace a vision is because they have not developed the maturity to recognize when God is leading.

A minister did not allow the church members to vote on an enormous building project because the staff worried the general membership lacked the spiritual maturity to make such an important decision. Ironically, that person's job was minister of discipleship. If leaders are going to share a vision, they are also obligated to ensure their people are prepared to properly respond to it. Spiritual leaders must also consider that if the Holy Spirit is not convincing people to move in a new direction, perhaps God is not the author of the vision. God will support what he authors.

Peter Senge observes that "90 percent of the time, what passes for commitment is compliance."[29] People may change their behavior in response to a leader's encouragement, but that doesn't mean they have altered their core values and beliefs. Values go deep—they will not be transformed by a memo or sales pitch—people either believe something or they don't. God's people either hear from God or they don't.

Establishing that the leader's role is not create or to sell the vision begs the question: what *is* the spiritual leader's role? It is to bear witness to what God says. Spiritual leaders must bring followers into a face-to-face encounter with God so they hear from him directly, not indirectly through their leader. Spiritual leaders may never convince their people they have heard from God personally, but once their people hear from God themselves, there will be no stopping them from participating in the work God is initiating. That is because the Holy Spirit will take the truth, as shared by the leader and confirm it in the peoples' hearts. The leader cannot convince people a particular direction is from God. This is the Holy Spirit's task.

As people grow in their relationship with God, they will hear from him themselves and want to follow him. No one will have to cajole them or entice them. Following God will be their natural heart response. The key to spiritual leadership is to encourage followers to grow in their relationship with the Lord. This cannot be done by talking about God or exhorting people to love God. It can only be achieved when leaders bring their people face-to-face with God and he communicates with them and convinces them he can be trusted.

Jim was an extremely frustrated pastor. He believed he knew what God wanted his church to do, but the people refused to follow his leadership. He asked whether we thought he should resign and find a group of people who were willing to follow God. Jim wanted to be involved in God's activity and his frustration was understandable as his people resisted his efforts to lead them forward. Nevertheless, we had to ask, "Jim, what is it about your leadership that your people are unwilling to follow?" The question caught him by surprise. He assumed the problem lay with his church members, not with his leadership. What became evident, however, was this passionate young pastor was not taking the time to help his people grow in their relationship with God. Jim was asking his church to follow a God they hardly knew.

Jim needed to worry less about the people's activity in the church and to concentrate instead on encouraging their walk with God. If their relationship with God grew strong, their obedience would follow. So often enthusiastic pastors urge their congregations to participate in church outreach events and mission activities, but they make no connection between these programs and God's activity. Jim was asking his busy people to give up their valuable time to support church programs. We encouraged him to present his church's activities in terms of God's activity in their midst rather than in terms of church programs to support or meetings to attend. The truth is, a church program never changed a life. Only God does that. Church ministries are nothing more than busywork unless God initiates them. As people see God at work around them and as they are encouraged to join him, they will demonstrate much more than compliance. They will enthusiastically participate in those activities they sense God is orchestrating.

People are willing to dramatically adjust their lives when they see God at work. We have observed people make enormous sacrifices in response to God's activity. Doctors have relinquished successful practices for the mission field because they sensed God leading them to do so. Successful businessmen have forfeited lucrative jobs that would transfer them to another city. Why? Because God was working so powerfully in their church they did not want to leave and miss out on what God was doing. If people are not following a vision, the problem may not lie with the people. For a vision to move people, the people must be convinced it is a promise from almighty God and not merely the dream of an ambitious leader. When people sense they are a part of something God is doing, there is no limit to what they will do or sacrifice.

COMMUNICATING VISION THROUGH SYMBOLS

Leaders communicate vision in at least two ways: by using symbols and by telling stories. As the saying goes, "A picture is worth a thousand words." Good symbols can be powerful vehicles for communicating the values and vision of organizations.

Mahatma Ghandi used compelling symbols to mobilize his followers in their quest to liberate India from British domination. Ghandi adopted the spinning wheel as a symbol of how people in India could pull themselves out of dire poverty. By making homespun products on their spinning wheels, the Indian people could become more economically self-sufficient, and they could simultaneously boycott British-made products. Ghandi used salt as a symbol of his people's desire for freedom. The British had a monopoly on salt in India and made it illegal for Indians to produce it for themselves. In response

Ghandi led the "salt march" beginning March 12, 1930. Hundreds of people traveled with him to the sea where he symbolically picked up dried salt on the beach. Salt became an electrifying symbol of freedom to the people of India.

Winston Churchill also knew how to use symbols. During England's bleakest moments in World War II, Churchill's upraised hand making the sign for victory became a rallying symbol for his demoralized nation. Word pictures can be powerful as well, such as when Franklin Roosevelt told the American people they had a "rendezvous with destiny."[30]

When Duncan Campbell, the great revivalist of the Hebrides in Scotland, was visiting Saskatoon, Canada, in 1969, he shared the vision God gave him. He described flames spreading across western Canada. The imagery of a great fire sweeping across the Canadian prairies was vivid, and two years later a revival did spread across western Canada, which originated in Saskatuan. When it came, many people recognized that the image God gave Campbell was being fulfilled.

Symbols can be a powerfully effective means of communicating vision. For example, a church might portray their church as a lighthouse in a sin-darkened community. Another church might visualize itself as a world mission strategy center while another sees itself as a hospital for spiritually sick people. Many people are visual thinkers and so symbols help them grasp the vision God has for their organization.

COMMUNICATING VISION THROUGH STORIES

A second effective way leaders relate what God is doing is through stories. Often when leaders see God's activity in their midst, they neglect to share it with their people. This robs the people of an exciting opportunity to experience God's powerful activity. People need help making the connection between their efforts for the organization and God's activity.

Leaders are wise to continually share stories—*true* stories of how God has worked in the past and how God is working at present. Leaders reflect on what God has done and consider what he is doing. They link those to what he has promised to do in the future. That is what Moses did with his followers.

The book of Deuteronomy is essentially a series of sermons in which Moses recounted to the Israelites what God had done for them so far. Joshua, Moses' successor, continued the tradition. In Joshua 24:3–13, the old warrior recalled what God did for his people over the years. God spoke through Joshua saying, "I took your father Abraham, . . . led him throughout the land of Canaan, . . . multiplied his descendents. . . . I gave the hill country of Seir to Esau. . . . I sent Moses and Aaron, . . . I plagued Egypt by what I did, . . . I brought you out. . . . I brought your fathers out. . . . I brought you to the land of the Amorites. . . . I handed them over to you. . . . I annihilated them. . . . I delivered you . . . I handed them over to you . . . I sent the hornet . . . I gave you a land." Incredible! Joshua recounted the entire history of the Israelites in story form, and hearing what God did motivated the people to move forward to see what he would do next.

In the same way Stephen justified his ministry by reciting the account of God's activity through the ages (Acts 7:1–53). When the apostle Paul explained his mission work among the Gentiles, he recounted the story of God's call and commissioning of his life. The Bible is essentially the story of how God has related to people throughout history. The telling of stories has always been an essential component to leading God's people.

Howard Gardner claims leaders are storytellers. But, he qualifies, "It is important that a leader be a good storyteller, but equally crucial that the leader embody that story in his or her life."[31] The leader is a symbol as well as a "keeper of the stories." It is said revival is spread on the wings of the testimonies of those whose lives have been changed in revival. The leader should be both the messenger and the message.

A story is a compelling method of communicating vision. Max De Pree says people are "defined" by their stories.[32] Graphs and charts can convey data and engage people's minds, but a story engages people's hearts and enlists their commitment. Leaders should regularly tell their people at least three kinds of stories.

1. *Stories from the past.* Leaders should share with their people as Moses and Joshua did, what God has done for them thus far (Ps. 111:3–4). Stories

about the foundational period of an organization or pivotal moments in its history reveal much about its values and culture. God's activity is never haphazard. He always builds on what he has done before. Winston Churchill claimed the farther one looked back in history, the farther into the future one could see. Based on that truth, Churchill said he wished Adolph Hitler would read British history so he would discover his fate.

2. *Stories from the present.* Leaders should also share current inspiring stories. What is God doing right now? Leaders should never assume their people will automatically make the connection between what is happening in their midst and God's activity. The leader's role is to help people make the connection.

3. *Stories pointing to the future.* Leaders should hold before the people glimpses of the future. The difference between secular storytelling and God-centered stories is their source. When Coca-Cola envisioned people all over the world drinking a Coca-Cola product or when Bill Gates envisioned personal computers worldwide using Microsoft products, the images were self-generated for the purpose of making profits and defeating the competition. When spiritual leaders direct attention toward the days to come, they are not simply describing a desirable future. They are relating what God has revealed he intends to do. For spiritual leaders all past, present, and future stories should come from God and be God centered.

AN ILLUSTRATION FROM RICHARD

Richard led a seminary in Canada for thirteen years. When he arrived, the school had many serious needs. Enrollment was small. Resources were scarce. Facilities were limited. Some of the school's constituents and donors were becoming hesitant in their support, wondering whether the school had a viable future. Richard sensed God wanted to use the school to impact Canada and the world for Christ, but he realized that if people were going to support the seminary, they needed to see God was actively at work there. Richard began to collect a repertoire of stories that demonstrated God's continuing involvement in the school.

During Richard's second year as president, exciting events unfolded. A man named Wilton Davis from Dallas, Texas, called to say his organization felt led by God to construct a new academic building for the seminary. Richard met with Wilton at a conference in Texas. Richard told him that constructing the building, with volunteer help, would cost well over a million dollars and the seminary did not have a dime to put into the project. Wilton smiled and said, "I believe God is in this." He mentioned a godly woman who, if she were willing, could contribute significant funds to launch the project. "But," Wilton exclaimed, "I have been trying to talk with her for over two years to see if she would help our organization, but I have never been able to cross paths with her." The two men prayed and then opened the door to leave the room. As the door swung open, it almost knocked over a woman walking down the hall. It was the woman Wilton had just mentioned. She did give generous support, and the project was completed debt free. During the construction project Richard had several occasions to relate this story to the trustees and seminary staff.

During the construction of the facility, several problems occurred that could have discouraged the many volunteers working at the seminary. When difficulties arose, it was crucial that everyone connected with the project be reminded God not only initiated the project but he was also sustaining it. One particular incident that reminded the volunteers of God's involvement occurred one day while they were attempting to hang trusses. A violent wind was blowing; its force was so powerful people had to hold on to their hats to keep them from blowing off and disappearing across the field. As the volunteers gathered to pray that morning, they knew their situation was serious. An expensive crane had been rented that was quickly consuming the meager building funds. To delay hanging the trusses would throw the entire schedule of volunteers into disarray. Everyone knew it would be too dangerous to place the trusses in such a fierce wind. At the close of the prayer time, the men stepped outside to an eerie calm. Not a trace of wind. For the next three days, while the trusses were hammered into place, there was no breeze. As the last two trusses were hung, the wind returned; and, as the last nails were hammered, the wind was back to full strength.

Richard told that story over and over again. It was more than just a story; it was dramatic evidence the work on the seminary was not something people were doing but something God initiated and would complete (Phil. 1:6). That made all the difference.

As the academic building was completed, God gave Richard a promise for the future. It took the form of a vivid mental picture: as people walked down the hallway of the academic building, they would pass by one classroom where students were studying at the college level, a second room where students were studying religious education at a master's level, a third classroom filled with students in the master of divinity program, and a conference room where students were doing doctoral work. Richard could have simply concluded, "The seminary needs to expand and diversify its academic programs," but what God gave him was an image that symbolized a promise. Richard shared this image many times and it became apparent God was revealing the same promise to others. Professors and staff would also share this vision with visitors to the seminary. One day this picture became a reality.

Leadership Is Communication

You cannot be a poor communicator and a good leader. Max De Pree observed: "I learned that if you are a leader and you're not sick and tired of communicating, you probably aren't doing a good enough job."[33] Spiritual leaders don't merely tell stories for the sake of storytelling. They rehearse what God has done, they relate what God is doing, and they share what God has promised to do. If the story is about God's activity and promises, the Holy Spirit will affirm its authenticity in people's hearts. People don't have to buy into a vision; they simply have to see that God is involved in the current opportunity. Leaders cannot grow weary of bearing witness to God's activity. Some stories need to be repeated often to ensure everyone in the organization, including newcomers, is familiar with them. Churches ought to have stories all the members know, that remind the congregation of God's ongoing activity in their midst. As the stories of God's activity are recounted, the people will recognize that God has led them thus far, he is currently leading them, and he has plans for their future.

With Vision Comes Accountability

Robert Quinn cautions: "When evaluating a vision, people watch the behavior of their leaders and quickly recognize if a leader lacks personal discipline and commitment."[34] If leaders are going to ask their people to sacrificially strive to achieve the organization's vision, they must model the behaviors they want evidenced in their people. When pastors announce a fund-raising campaign for a new building, the pastor must give sacrificially to it. If the business's vision is to be exemplary in customer service, the leader must be customer oriented.

Leaders who help their people receive a God-ordained vision should remain with those people and walk alongside them to help them fully respond to what God revealed. Some visions take years to come to fruition. However, when possible, leaders who guided their people to understand and embrace a vision ought to stay with those people until the vision has come to pass. Bill Bliss notes that leaders must ask whether the vision will continue to be applicable after they are gone. "If the answer is 'no,' rethink the vision."[35] If a vision originates from God, it shouldn't be rescinded every time a new leader appears on the scene.

Conclusion

Vision is crucial for an organization. Its source is God's revelation. God's revelation can often be stated as a promise and can be expressed through an image. When leaders successfully communicate vision to their people, it will be God who sets the agenda for the organization, not the leader, and the people will experience what God can do.

—————— **Responding to This Material** ——————

1. After a time of reflection, draw a picture of the vision you believe God gave you for your business, organization, church, or family. Don't worry if you are not a good artist! Keep the drawing somewhere you can easily refer to and modify as God gives you more details.

2. Identify three stories that clearly symbolize an important truth about your organization, family, church, or whatever you are leading. If you are not comfortable telling stories, *practice!* Write them out so the details are clear and concise. Don't give up until you can effectively tell stories.

3. Examine the eight sources of vision listed in this chapter. Which one have you been using to develop your vision? What adjustments do you sense God might want you to make in how you develop vision?

4. Are your life and leadership presently driven by a clear sense of direction or vision? Or are you simply taking one day at a time? You may want to find a weekend or day off and get away somewhere with your Bible and a notebook. Take all day to pray and read Scripture and ask the Lord to impress on your heart what he wants to do through you and those you lead.

5. Review what God has told you about your organization, church, and family. Have you stayed true in following through with the vision God revealed to you?

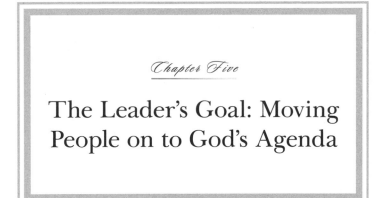

Chapter Five

The Leader's Goal: Moving People on to God's Agenda

When Mel Blackaby, the third son in our family, was a young seminary student, he was called to his first pastorate—a small, rural church in Texas. Soon after his arrival he was asked to conduct his first funeral. To his relief the service went fine. When it was time to drive to the cemetery for the graveside service, Mel was instructed to drive his car at the front of the procession, just behind a police car. Mel had not been to the cemetery, but he assumed the policeman would lead the way. The mourners moved slowly forward, forming a line of vehicles a mile long. When they came to an uncontrolled intersection, the policeman driving the lead car dutifully pulled over and, after waving the bewildered minister forward, stayed behind to direct traffic. Mel was leading dozens of cars on a solemn journey, but he had no clue where he was going! What should he do? As he tells it, "I drove as slowly as possible hoping someone would realize I didn't know where I was going and come to my rescue!"

Leaders acquiring a new position must ask, "Where should my organization go?" This question may seem simplistic, but it is amazing how many leaders become so enmeshed in the mundane aspects of the journey they lose sight of the destination. Or they have detailed plans of what they hope to achieve, but they fail to examine whether their objectives will lead them to where God wants them to be. If leaders do not clearly understand where their organization is and where it should be moving, they will be ineffective. The following are three of the most common, and perhaps most subtle, organizational goals that can disorient leaders to their true purpose.

Unworthy Goals

ACHIEVING RESULTS

What do people want to see happen when they choose a new leader? *Results.* In the marketplace effectiveness is based on sales and profit. The larger the market share, the greater the increase in sales; the more new products, or customers or stores, the more successful the leader is deemed to be. It is human nature to look for tangible measures of success. Even in religious circles people establish goals to measure their organization's progress. Churches evaluate their effectiveness by focusing on what they can count: number of occupied seats in the auditorium, number of dollars in the offering plate, number of ministries conducted throughout the week. Successful leaders must get things done. This demand for measurable results puts pressure on leaders to focus on quick accomplishments. What better way to appear successful than to set a goal and then meet it? According to Peter Drucker, a person hasn't led unless results have been produced.[1]

This results-oriented philosophy has compelled many leaders to arrive in their new leadership positions with lists of goals already in hand. Leaders often focus exclusively on achieving numerical results: increasing sales by 25 percent, constructing the building on budget, boosting attendance by 10 percent, cutting costs by 15 percent. When leaders achieve their goals, they are considered successful. But what about the price people pay when their leaders are driven to achieve results at all costs?

During the 1990s Al Dunlap was one of the most admired and hated CEOs in America. Investors liked him because he would slash costs, instigate massive layoffs, and defer maintenance costs, thereby driving up stock value. He would then find a buyer for his company and make a fortune for investors as well as himself. At Scott Paper, Dunlap, whose favorite personal nickname was "Chainsaw," laid off eleven thousand workers, greatly reduced the research budget, and eliminated gifts to charity. Stock prices rose 225 percent. When Kimberly Clark purchased his company, Dunlap earned $100 million by selling his stock options.[2] Dunlap achieved his numbers, but the lives and careers of thousands of former employees were devastated.

Secular writers recognize that organizational leadership involves far more than merely reaching goals. James Collins and Jerry Porras, in their book *Built to Last*, argue that great leaders do not establish goals and then mobilize their organizations to achieve them at all costs. Rather, they concentrate on building great organizations. Leaders can achieve their goals for a time but destroy their organizations in the process. However, organizations that focus on being healthy will regularly achieve their goals.

In the past organizations were generally built on the vision and goals of their leaders. Leaders made the plans; everyone else followed. But as Peter Senge contends in *The Fifth Discipline*: "It is no longer sufficient to have one person learning for the organization, a Ford, or a Sloan, or a Watson. It's just not possible any longer to 'figure it out' from the top and have everyone else following the orders of the 'grand strategist.' The organizations that will truly excel in the future will be the organizations that discover how to tap people's commitment and capacity to learn at all levels in an organization."[3]

Society has changed. Modern leaders cannot and should not do all the thinking for their organizations. New leaders cannot arrive at their organizations and begin imposing their preset goals and agenda. Rather, today's leaders must develop their personnel in order to build healthy organizations.

Max De Pree, former chairman of the board of Herman Miller, suggests that leadership is a "posture of indebtedness."[4] He claims followers have a right to ask these questions of their leaders:

+ What may I expect from you?
+ Can I achieve my own goals by following you?
+ Will I reach my potential by working with you?
+ Can I trust my future to you?
+ Have you bothered to prepare yourself for leadership?
+ Are you ready to be ruthlessly honest?
+ Do you have the self-confidence and trust to let me do my job?
+ What do you believe?[5]

People are no longer acquiescent followers. They have more options so they choose to follow leaders whose answers to the above questions best satisfy them.

If this is true for secular businesses, it is even more so for organizations that rely on volunteers. When there is no paycheck to motivate followers, what inspires people to invest their valuable time, money, and energy? Will they be galvanized to action by a list of objectives? The primary purpose of spiritual leaders is not to achieve their goals but to accomplish God's will. De Pree says, "Reaching goals is fine for an annual plan. Only reaching one's potential is fine for a life."[6] Leaders can achieve all their goals and yet miss God's will. Spiritual leaders do not use their people to achieve their ends; their people *are* the end.

According to De Pree, leaders should enter a "covenantal relationship" with those they lead. He describes this as a "shared commitment to ideas, to issues, to values, to goals, and to management processes. Words such as love, warmth, and personal chemistry are certainly pertinent. Covenantal relationships are open to influence. They fill deep needs and they enable work to provide meaning and fulfillment. Covenantal relationships reflect unity and grace and poise. They are an expression of a sacred nature of relationships."[7] De Pree described his desire for his company: "My goal for Herman Miller is that when people both inside and outside the company look at all of us, not as a corporation but as a group of people working intimately within a covenantal relationship, they'll say, 'Those folks were a gift to the spirit.'"[8]

Leaders who achieve their goals but whose people suffer and fall by the wayside in the process have failed. Using people to achieve organizational goals is the antithesis of spiritual leadership. Firing personnel can be a symptom of failed leadership. Occasionally, leaders may have no choice but to dismiss personnel, but too often letting people go is merely a more expedient way to achieve desired ends than investing time and energy to help employees develop to their potential. If a company meets its annual sales goal but three of its key management personnel lose their marriages because of the stress of the campaign, the leadership has failed. If a church succeeds in building a new worship center but hemorrhages members through bickering and infighting, the church has failed. If costs have been cut by 15 percent but loyal, long-term employees have been ruthlessly downsized as part of the effort, the success is tainted. In God's eyes *how* something is done is as important as *what* is done (Num. 20:1–13). The end does not justify the means. Getting results can make leaders look good. God's way magnifies his name.

PERFECTIONISM

"God expects the best!" "Nothing but excellence is good enough for God!" How often we hear these emphatic assertions, sincerely expressed by Christian leaders. They sound noble, yet there is a subtle danger inherent in the philosophy that everything done in an organization must always be done with excellence.

Indeed, God does have high expectations for his people. He commands us to be holy (1 Pet. 1:15–16). God wants his followers to be spiritually mature (Matt. 5:48). He expects people to give him their best (Mal. 1:6–14). God commands employees to work as if laboring for their Lord (Eph. 6:7). But leaders must be careful how they use the term *excellence*. If excellence is understood to mean perfection, then that is not God's standard. If excellence refers to doing things in a God-honoring manner, then leaders should strive for it. There is a difference between giving God *your* best and giving God *the* best. Excellence generally describes tasks and tasks are usually a means to an end. People are the end. Churches that concentrate more on culling the best talent rather than developing their people are overlooking what God considers most important.

The apostle Paul did not claim his purpose was to do everything perfectly. Instead, he declared his aim was to "proclaim Him, warning and teaching everyone with all wisdom, so that we may present everyone mature in Christ. I labor for this, striving with His strength that works powerfully in me" (Col. 1:28–29).

Paul focused on developing people. He sought to take them from their spiritual immaturity and bring them to spiritual maturity. His joy came from seeing those he led blossom into the people God intended for them to become. The approach of many modern Christian organizations is contrary to that of Paul.

Misguided Excellence. Suppose a church embarks on a quest for excellence. Church leaders examine the music program, and they discover several of the singers have less than excellent voices. These people are discreetly removed. Several teenagers were taking turns playing instruments on the worship team. An announcement is made that henceforth only adults will be playing during the Sunday services. It becomes apparent the pianist cannot master the more difficult musical pieces, so a professional accompanist is hired. When the volunteer running the sound equipment makes one too many mistakes, a sound technician is hired. When volunteers working with the youth seem unable to expand the youth program, staff is hired to replace them. As time passes, the standard of excellence is brought to bear on every aspect of church life. In each case, when people do not measure up, they are replaced with someone who meets the most demanding standards. Volunteer-led programs are gradually taken over by paid professionals with specialized training in their fields. As new people join the church and look for ways to serve, they notice a large professional staff conducts most of the church ministries. They also observe that only the most highly skilled people are called upon to serve because the church values, above all else, excellence. So knowing they are far from excellent themselves, they settle in to a comfortable seat and let the professionals serve them one excellent program after another. Church attendance may grow, but its people do not.

Perhaps it was this attitude that prompted the risen Christ to accuse the church at Laodicea: "Because you say, 'I'm rich; I have become wealthy, and need nothing,' and you don't know that you are wretched, pitiful, poor, blind, and naked" (Rev. 3:17). The primary goal of spiritual leadership is not excellence in the sense of doing things perfectly. Rather, it is taking people from where they are to where God wants them to be. There is a tension here, for leaders want to motivate their people to develop their talents for the glory of God. But to help people grow, leaders may have to allow them to make mistakes. Developing people to their potential is not tidy. Often church staff could do a better job than volunteers could. Allowing amateurs to attempt things may not always be efficient in the short term, but good leaders recognize the long-term benefits. Both the people in training and the organization benefit when their leaders value developing people over doing things perfectly. This phenomenon can be especially seen in small churches. It is easy for megachurches to proclaim "excellence" as the only standard worthy of God. After all, they have large staffs, huge budgets, spacious facilities, and state-of-the-art equipment. If "excellence" is understood to mean flawless, Broadway-styled productions, then the small, single-staffed, talent-challenged church might as well close its doors. If "excellence," however, involves following God's will and honoring him through their best efforts, any church can do that.

SIZE

The Western world is mesmerized by size. Leaders of the largest churches or companies are automatically viewed as experts. If a leader has grown a religious organization to a significant size, people interpret that as a clear sign of God's blessing. That may not be so.

In the business world, the primary attraction for consumers used to be the lowest cost. Eventually, giant low-cost stores swallowed up smaller businesses. Sociologists claim people today are often more concerned with service and convenience than merely cost. For modern shoppers time is often more precious than money. Smaller businesses that concentrate on service will play a key role in today's market. Bigger is not always better.

In the religious sector leaders who grow megachurches are treated as spiritual heroes. They are encouraged to write books chronicling their success and are regular presenters on the speaking circuit for church growth conferences. Even if these leaders fall into immorality, their congregations may be reluctant to dismiss them because it appears God has his hand of blessing upon them. People have asked, "If what our pastor did was so wrong, why has God blessed him so?" This question equates growth in numbers with God's blessing. That's not always the case. Certainly church growth is inevitable in a healthy congregation, as the book of Acts testifies. But it is also possible for a congregation to grow in numbers apart from God's blessing. There is a significant difference between drawing a crowd and building a church. Marketers can attract a crowd. They can't grow a church. Cults can lure a crowd. They can't build God's kingdom. If numerical growth is a sure sign of God's blessing, then some cults are enjoying God's blessing to a greater extent than many churches.

The misconception is based on peoples' assumption that God is as impressed with crowds as people are. He is not. The essence of Satan's temptations for Jesus was trying to convince him to draw a crowd rather than build a church (Matt. 4). When Jesus fed five thousand people, he became so popular the people wanted to forcibly make him their king. Jesus knew that, even though a multitude was following him, many of them did not believe. They were merely looking for a free lunch. So Jesus preached about the cost of discipleship. "From that moment many of His disciples turned back and no longer accompanied Him" (John 6:66). So vast was the exodus Jesus turned to the Twelve and asked if they intended to abandon him too (v. 67). Jesus was never enamored with crowds. In fact, he often sought to escape them (Mark 1:35–37).

Churches often use the world's methods to draw a crowd. A grand performance done with excellence, using high-tech sound equipment, professional lighting, eye-catching brochures, and charismatic leadership, can increase attendance. It will not, however, build a church. Only Christ can do that (Matt. 16:18). Does this mean churches should never compose attractive brochures or invest in quality sound and lighting equipment? No. But leaders must never shift their trust from the Head of the church to the tools of the world. They should not assume that because attendance is increasing, their church is healthy and pleasing to God. Leaders must continuously measure their success by God's standards; not by the world's.

Misguided Goals

1. Achieving Results
2. Perfectionism
3. Size

Worthy Goals

Assuming leaders do not succumb to misguided goals for their organizations, what should they strive for? There are at least three legitimate goals spiritual leaders ought to pursue regardless of whether they are leading a committee, a church, a family, or a corporation.

DEVELOPING PEOPLE

The ultimate goal of spiritual leadership is not to achieve numerical results, to accomplish tasks with perfection, or to grow for growth's sake. It is to take their people from where they are to where God wants them to be. God's primary concern for people is not results but relationship. Calling comes before vocation. There is a profound comment on this issue in Exodus

19:4: "You have seen what I did to the Egyptians and how I carried you on eagles' wings and brought you to Me."

At first glance this verse can appear confusing. We tend to assume God delivered the Israelites from Egypt so he could bring them into the Promised Land. But that is not what God said. The key for God was not Canaan. That was just the means God used to draw his people to himself. God's agenda was his people. The reason the Israelites spent forty years wandering in the wilderness was not that God could not bring them into Canaan. God kept them in the wilderness for forty years to establish a relationship of faith with them. The Promised Land was accessible, but the peoples' relationship with God was too immature. Unfortunately, once the Israelites entered Canaan, they came to view the land as an end in itself rather than a means to a divine relationship. As a result, God ultimately took their land away from them.

One of the issues regarding spiritual leadership is whether spiritual leaders can take people where they themselves have not been. That depends on one's definition of spiritual leadership. If spiritual leadership involves taking people to a location or completing a task, then leaders can lead people to places they have not been. But if the goal of spiritual leadership is a more intimate relationship with God, then leaders will never move their people beyond where they have gone themselves. Leaders can lead people to relocate their organization or build a building or grow in size without prior experience in these areas. But leaders cannot take their people into a relationship with Christ that goes any deeper than where they have gone themselves. Followers may grow spiritually *despite* spiritually immature leaders, but they will not grow because of them. Thus, spiritual leaders must continually be growing themselves if they are to take their people into a more mature relationship with Christ. Leaders will not lead their people to higher levels of prayer unless they have already ascended those heights themselves. Leaders will not guide others to greater levels of faith unless they have traveled the road to robust faith themselves.

A spiritual organization will reach its maximum potential only when every member knows how to hear clearly from God and is willing to respond in obedience. It is not enough for leaders to hear from God and then relay the message to the people as in Old Testament times. Today's believers must learn to recognize God's voice and understand for themselves what he is saying. When this happens, leaders will not need to sell their visions; they will simply share with their people what God said to them and then allow their people to seek divine confirmation themselves.

According to Max De Pree, the first responsibility of leaders is to "define reality" for their organizations.[9] Ronald Heifetz describes this as "getting on the balcony" in order to gain a clear view of the present situation.[10] Followers do not always understand the full implications of what their organization is experiencing. They may be so immersed in the minutia of their day-to-day routines they do not see the big picture. It is a spiritual leader's responsibility to keep the big picture in mind and to help their people understand God's activity in the midst of the daily challenges.

This truth can be seen in the way God walked with Moses. Scripture says, "He revealed His ways to Moses, His deeds to the people of Israel." The Israelites saw God's acts. How could they miss them? God sent ten horrendous plagues on Egypt. He parted the Red Sea and obliterated the Egyptian army. God fed an entire nation with manna from heaven and brought water out of a rock. The pressing question is: after all the people witnessed, why did they continually struggle to trust and obey God? It is because, although they saw God's *acts*, they never gained the higher perspective of God's *ways*. The ways of God reflect on who God is, not merely what God does. When God destroyed the mighty Egyptian army, the Israelites were certainly appreciative at that moment. But they never understood that the same God who destroyed the Egyptian army could just as easily annihilate Canaanite armies. So, despite all God did, the next time the Israelites faced a new challenge, they grew frightened and discouraged once again. Spiritual leaders must help their people see beyond God's acts to recognize the way God consistently works with his people, time and time again. To do this, spiritual leaders must develop their own understanding and recognition of God's activity in their midst.

A Ship Captain. A spiritual leader is like the captain of an eighteenth-century sailing ship. As the vessel approaches its destination the crew watches for the first sight of land. The veteran captain has sailed the seven seas, but his crew on the other hand is much less experienced. At one point a novice sailor excitedly cries out, "Land ho!" But all he has seen are vapors coming off the water from the hot sun. Presently, another sailor shouts that he has spotted land, but the "land" proves to be only a pod of whales. As the captain carefully gazes about the sea, he detects a familiar shape to the west. Although it is only a slight bump on the distant horizon, the captain knows it is land.

Why couldn't the crew see what the captain saw? Did the captain have better eyesight? No. The crew's eyes worked as well as the captain's, but their inexperience at sea confused them. What does the captain do with his sailors? Does he say: "Don't worry. Seeing where we are going is my duty as captain. I'll do all the watching and announce when we are near land"? Does he chastise his crew for being too blind to see what lay before them? No. The captain understands he has had many more years at sea so he helps them learn to discern if a distant shape is a rock or a whale or driftwood. He shows them how to scan the horizon and how to recognize when their eyes are playing tricks on them. Eventually the captain no longer needs to be on the deck watching for land because his crew has learned how to do it.

Spiritual leaders often have an advantage over those they lead. Leaders may have walked with God for many years so they recognize when the Spirit's still, small voice is speaking. They can tell when an opportunity has the mark of God upon it. But leaders do not assign themselves the task of always being the one to recognize God's activity. Instead, spiritual leaders understand people tend to be disoriented to God. So they teach them to know God better. Once the people learn to recognize God's voice and determine his leading, the organization will have enormous potential for serving God. Its effectiveness will not depend on one overworked leader always having to decide what God is guiding them to do. The group will all know how to hear from God and recognize his activity. When spiritual leaders have brought their people to this point, they have truly led.

Missions in Canada: A Personal Example from Henry Blackaby

When I was a pastor in Canada, my goal was not to set the direction for the congregation but to bring the people into an intimate relationship with Christ so he could lead the church and the people would follow. It was not an issue of selling a vision. I was helping the people learn how to hear God's voice. It wasn't easy. At first the people were disoriented to God's voice and his ways so they had difficulty recognizing his activity. Len Koster, the pastor of missions, would discover a group of people in a nearby town who prayed for several years for a church to be started in their community. Initially, our church members would immediately focus on our limited resources and the difficulties involved in providing a ministry to that location. As the people grew to know and trust God more, however, their receptivity to what God was doing greatly increased. After they walked with God and saw him work in people's lives and witnessed his miraculous provision to meet every need, the people grew eager to join in what they saw him doing next.

In subsequent situations, when Len Koster reported another community in need of a church, the Holy Spirit would confirm with the membership whether this was God's invitation for our church to join him in his work. The people no longer needed their pastor to explain everything to them. They now had a mature relationship with God themselves and the same ability to hear from God as their spiritual leader did. Had the church's success depended solely upon what I could see, the church would have been extremely limited. But when the membership began responding in faith and obedience to God's direction, the effectiveness of the church grew exponentially.

In churches we led, we always instituted a regular time of public sharing by the people. Often during an evening worship service or a prayer meeting, we would ask the people to tell what they observed God doing during that week. One person might recount an opportunity he had to minister to an inmate in the local prison. Another might report that when she volunteered in a local school, she sensed a hunger among the staff for spiritual guidance. The congregation would pray together to see if God was leading our church to respond to any of the needs reported by those who shared. Most of the ministries in our churches did not originate from suggestions by the pastoral staff, but rather they grew out of God's activity in and around the lives of our members. Of course, when the church staff is equipping the saints to respond to what God is inviting them to do, enlisting or motivating people to serve is rarely an issue.

The key is not for the pastor to constantly cast visions of what the church should do next. The objective is to bring the people into an intimate relationship with Christ so they know when he is speaking and guiding them as his body. Then Christ will use the church to impact the world.

Business leaders must understand their preeminent task is to equip their people to function at their God-given best and not simply to accomplish organizational goals. From a secular perspective Peter Senge calls this a "learning organization." That is, every member of the organization is responding to new opportunities and developing personal abilities so the organization is thinking, growing, and learning at every level, not just at the top. When employees are set free to respond to opportunities, the organization will be far more effective than if everything depends on the leader's creativity and ability.[11]

Spiritual leaders in the workplace must also understand their calling is first to please their heavenly Father, then to satisfy their board of directors and supervisors. It is appropriate to provide spiritual guidance and encouragement to employees as well as to clientele. CEOs have a responsibility to care for the spiritual well-being of their employees. This should include praying regularly for their salvation. It may also involve providing a Christian witness. One business leader prayed about how to make seeking God's kingdom a top priority at his workplace. God led him to start a Bible study at work. This proved to be one of the greatest challenges this executive faced during his eventful tenure at his publicly traded company. Yet through that Bible study, people encountered God in powerful ways.

Spiritual Leadership on the Job: A Personal Example from Richard Blackaby

I was leading a series of meetings at a church. During the Sunday evening service I challenged the people to watch throughout the next day to see what

God was doing in their workplaces. A businessman in attendance took the challenge to heart. On Monday morning he prayed for God to reveal his activity in his company. As he sat in the lunchroom over the noon hour, he noticed a man sitting alone eating his meal. The Holy Spirit prompted him to join the man though he didn't know the colleague well. He discovered his fellow employee was in crisis. His marriage was under great strain, and that morning he and his wife engaged in a bitter argument. The man decided that when he returned home that evening he would pack his bags and leave.

As this hurting man shared his plans, the Christian knew this was God's invitation for him to become involved. He was unsure how to help, but he felt his colleague would abandon his family if he were to go home after work. He invited his new friend to dinner that evening and asked if he would join him for the special meetings being held at his church. To his surprise his coworker agreed. That evening during the service, he silently prayed that God would work powerfully in his new friend's life and heal his broken relationship. After the service the two men had a long conversation in the parking lot, which resulted in the Christian businessman leading his associate to the Lord. Through tears the new convert pledged to go home and ask his wife to forgive him. God brought new life to a soul and helped a beleaguered husband and father begin the healing process in his family.

A Christian businessman asked God to reveal his agenda for his workplace. On that particular day God's will included: transforming an angry man, saving a marriage, and preserving a family. If this Christian man had not heard from God directly, none of that would have happened.

EQUIPPING OTHERS TO LEAD

Leaders lead followers. Great leaders lead leaders. One of the worst mistakes leaders commit is making themselves indispensable. Insecurity can drive people to hoard all the leadership initiatives so no one else appears as capable or as successful. At times leaders become so immersed in their own work they fail to develop other leaders. If some people were completely honest, they might confess they enjoy being in high demand. They covet the organizational limelight. However, whether by design or neglect, failing to develop leaders in an organization constitutes gross failure by the leader.

It has been said Napoleon's greatest failure at the Battle of Waterloo was not training his generals to think independently. When victory hung in the balance and Napoleon counted on Marshal Grouchy, with thirty-four thousand men and 108 guns, to engage the enemy, Grouchy remained immobilized. Felix Markham, Napoleon's biographer, comments: "Lacking initiative, authority and energy, Grouchy took refuge in a literal obedience to orders. But the orders he received from Napoleon were lacking in precision and too late."[12] Markham suggests, "Napoleon frequently criticized his Generals' mistakes, but he never made any systematic attempt to teach them his methods, or to form a Staff College. He relied entirely on himself."[13] Napoleon's failure to develop leaders cost him his empire.

Many famous leaders have failed in this critical leadership task. When Franklin Roosevelt won his fourth term as president in 1944, many suspected he would not live to see it through and that the presidency would fall to vice president Harry Truman. It was one of the most critical periods in American history: The world's first nuclear bomb was nearing completion, and an executive decision would soon be required to authorize its use. As the most devastating war in history drew to a close, Europe lay in ruins. The Allied powers would have to decide what to do with the defeated nations. The Soviet Union was now a superpower, spreading its communist tentacles around the world. No previous U.S. president ever confronted so many monumental decisions as Truman faced, yet Roosevelt never prepared him. In fact, Roosevelt met briefly with Truman only twice during the eighty-six days of his vice presidency. As it happened, Roosevelt did not live to finish his term, and he scarcely prepared Truman to succeed him. In that respect Roosevelt failed as a leader.

In contrast, General George Marshall kept a "black book" of all the soldiers he believed showed promise for future leadership. Whenever he encountered someone who demonstrated leadership ability, he added his name to the book. When a vacancy arose in the officer corps, he referred to his book where he found an ample supply of qualified candidates. This system enabled Marshall to develop a large military organization filled with talented and effective officers.

Many leaders work extremely hard at their jobs and enjoy remarkable success during their leadership tenure. But a test of great leaders is whether or not their organizations can function well upon their departure. This phenomenon can be clearly seen in the life of Samuel. Samuel was one of the godliest leaders in Israel's history. At the close of his leadership, no one with whom he had worked could find fault with him (1 Sam. 12:1–5). Nevertheless, Samuel ultimately failed as a leader, for he did not prepare a successor.

> When Samuel grew old, he appointed his sons as judges over Israel. His firstborn son's name was Joel and his second was Abijah. They were judges in Beer-sheba. However, his sons did not walk in his ways—they turned toward dishonest gain, took bribes, and perverted justice. So all the elders of Israel gathered together and went to Samuel at Ramah. They said to him, "Look, you are old, and your sons do not follow your example. Therefore, appoint a king to judge us the same as all the other nations have." (1 Sam. 8:1–5)

As long as the Israelites had the noble Samuel to guide them, they followed without protest. But when Samuel grew old and appointed his sons Joel and Abijah to replace him, the people resisted. Later generations have castigated the Israelites for rejecting God's leadership and demanding a king. The fact is the spiritual leaders available to them were so inferior they considered a secular king preferable. Had Samuel groomed an acceptable replacement, the people might not have clamored for a king. The people's failure stemmed from their leader's failure to do his job in developing effective leaders.

Unless leaders are intentional about investing in the development of people within their organization, it will not happen. There are at least four habits leaders must regularly practice if they are to produce a corps of emerging leaders.

1. *Leaders delegate.* This is often difficult. Leaders are generally skilled individuals who can do many things well. In addition, if they are perfectionists, as leaders often are, they will be tempted to undertake more than they should so things are "done right." The inherent danger, of course, is that the organization's growth is directly tied to the leader's available time and energy. Leaders are, by nature, decision makers. However, it is unwise for leaders to make all the decisions. Doing so impedes the growth of emerging leaders. As Peter Drucker suggests, "Effective executives do not make a great many decisions. They concentrate on the important ones."[14]

Deciding Not to Decide: A Personal Example from Richard Blackaby

When I became a seminary president, I had to make numerous decisions. So I made them. The seminary had a talented business manager, and she would regularly stop by my office to ask my opinion regarding various financial matters. Because I was the leader, I would make a decision, and she would promptly implement it. One day it dawned on me what was happening. The business manager had an MBA. She had dealt with these issues for years. I had not. Why was I making these decisions? When she approached me the next time, I asked her, "What do you think?" She was caught by surprise but readily gave her response. "Excellent idea!" I replied. "Let's do that!" And we did. Thereafter, she only came to me for a second opinion after she formulated her own solution. I began using this method with all my staff. At first I thought I was being a decisive leader, but in fact, by making decisions I didn't need to make, I was unknowingly fostering a corporate culture in which people came to me for approval for everything. The advantages to my new attitude were soon obvious. First, the most qualified personnel were now making the decisions. Second, the faculty and staff took ownership of their responsibilities. Third, I was free to spend more time focusing on those tasks and decisions that were exclusive to my leadership role.

2. *Leaders give people freedom to fail.* If leaders are going to develop other leaders, they must delegate. But when they do, they must refrain from interfering. Nothing demoralizes staff faster than leaders who constantly

meddle in their work. Once a task has been assigned, it must belong to that person. If leaders continually second-guess staff initiatives, their people will stop making decisions. Inevitably employees will propose ideas and methods that differ from what their leaders prefer. Leaders must weigh the value of having work done by others against the advantage of having everything done exactly like they would do it themselves.

Business history provides a famous example of the hazards when leaders interfere. Henry Ford gave his only son Edsel the responsibility for overseeing his automotive business. The younger Ford had innovative and practical ideas that would make the company more efficient in the face of growing competition. Yet as Edsel sought to implement his ideas, the elder Ford constantly countermanded his son's orders. Soon after Edsel became president, he initiated building an addition to the Hyde Park plant. After the ground was excavated for the new building's foundation, Henry intervened, claiming the building was unnecessary. Edsel succumbed and offered to have the opening covered up. His father insisted, however, that the pit remain for a time as a graphic example of his authority and his son's humiliation.[15] The relationship between father and son was irreparably damaged. Finally, Edsel's fragile health broke and the Ford Motor Company languished under the administrative quagmire.

Ford Sr. sacrificed the development of a promising leader to ensure operations were always handled the way he wanted them to be. Leaders whose people are reluctant to work for them or leaders who experience difficulty recruiting volunteers should consider whether this is because they have earned a reputation for meddling.

3. *Leaders recognize others' success.* A sure way to stifle staff initiative is to take the credit for something a subordinate did. Good leaders delegate. They resist interfering. Then, when the job is done, they reward those responsible. Kouzes and Posner argue that business leaders must regularly give their employees positive feedback if they want to obtain maximum performance. One of the greatest rewards leaders can give is recognition. Leaders ought to regularly praise their people for their accomplishments and acknowledge

their contributions. Staff gatherings and special occasions are opportunities to do this. Although few leaders deliberately steal credit, this can happen inadvertently. If leaders fail to point out employees' efforts, people assume the leader is responsible for the success. If leaders continually ignore or steal the credit for work their people have done, people will naturally grow reluctant to give their best effort. In reality, when the people are successful, so is the leader.

This need for affirmation and expressions of gratitude is especially acute in voluntary organizations. Volunteers don't receive year-end bonuses or increases in pay for their efforts. That's why leaders should be especially diligent and creative in expressing their appreciation. At times leaders can "spiritualize" the work done by volunteers with absurd statements such as, "They were doing it for the Lord. They don't need to be recognized." That may be so, but people want to know their sacrifice of time and energy is valued. Volunteers need to believe they are making a positive difference. The leader can assure them of this. By publicly recognizing and thanking them, leaders alert the organization that volunteers are indispensable and highly valued. Leaders will not regret having said thank you, but an attitude of ungratefulness will soon take its toll.

While Harry Truman was president, the White House kitchen staff baked him a birthday cake. After the meal Truman excused himself from the table and went to the kitchen to thank the cook. The staff could not remember a president entering the kitchen for any reason, let alone to say thank you.[16] On a much larger scale, after World War II, Truman's secretary of state, George Marshall, presented a seventeen-billion-dollar European Recovery Program plan designed to rebuild Europe and propel the United States into world prominence. Truman's advisors encouraged him to dub it the "Truman Plan," named after the president who approved it. Truman deferred, insisting it be called the "Marshall Plan" after the man who created it. Truman would often say, "It is remarkable how much could be accomplished when you don't mind who receives the credit."[17] Such self-effacing leadership endeared Truman to those who worked with him.

4. Leaders provide encouragement and support. Once leaders delegate tasks, they should avoid interfering. However, this does not mean they neglect their people. Every time leaders delegate, they do so with the clear understanding that ultimately, to use Truman's vernacular, "the buck stops here." Delegation is a hazardous, albeit necessary, leadership task. If the people are successful, they receive the credit. If they fail, leaders shoulder the responsibility. Warren Buffet suggests: "Praise by name, criticize by category."[18] Jim Collins claims great leaders use the "window and the mirror." When something goes right, they look out the window to find someone in the organization to assign the credit. When something goes wrong, leaders stand before the mirror and assume the blame.[19] Coaches of professional sports teams are well acquainted with this reality. If the team wins the championship, the athletes assume most of the credit and seek more lucrative contracts. But when the team performs poorly, the coach is usually the first person to be fired. Good leaders don't make excuses. They recognize their organization's performance will be viewed as equal to their own.

Weak leaders cast blame upon subordinates when things go wrong. It is an abdication of leadership for a CEO to arbitrarily fire management when the company has a bad year. It is a sign of deficient leadership when a pastor blames his people for the declining condition of his church.

When people fail in their assigned task, their poor performance might point to one or more possible problems. Perhaps the leader made a poor choice in assigning a job to an unqualified person. Maybe the leader did not provide enough support, training, or feedback. Sometimes problems can be traced to the leader's communication skills and how clearly the assignment was delineated. Of course there are times when individuals simply underperform despite all the help their leader provides. Nevertheless, astute leaders provide ample support to their people, giving them every reasonable opportunity to succeed.

During the crucial battle of Gettysburg, General Lee ordered General Longstreet to move his forces forward. Longstreet delayed. For many precious hours when the Confederate forces might have gained victory, Longstreet held his forces in check. When Lee finally prevailed upon his reluctant general to proceed, it was too late. The Union troops were now well entrenched and prepared to repel the Confederate attack. Consequently they won the war's decisive battle. Lee had every reason to castigate Longstreet for his insubordination. But he did not. Lee took full responsibility for the defeat. He knew that despite his deficiencies, Longstreet was his best available general and that to alienate or lose him at that juncture of the war would be devastating. More importantly, Lee understood that as the leader the onus fell on him to achieve results even when his officers did not do as he instructed.

People must know their leader will stand by them when they fail. Church members want the assurance that when their pastor gives them responsibility, he will also back them up if things become difficult. When leaders neglect to support their followers, everyone else grows anxious because they rightly assume their leader would abandon them too. When leaders come quickly to the aid of someone who is struggling, everyone rests assured that they will receive similar support.

The people Moses led failed miserably. Even Aaron, the high priest, shirked his responsibilities. Consequently, the Israelites were sentenced to spend the remainder of their days meandering across the desert, shut out of the Promised Land. Moses did not disobey God. He was faithful. Yet God did not release Moses from his people. He was their leader. If ever God's people needed leadership, it was during this demoralizing period. Moses spent the remaining forty years of his life wandering in the wilderness, not because of his own mistake but because of his followers' error. Too often leaders forsake their people when they fail. Leaders may justify their abandonment, claiming, "I had to leave that church because no one wanted to obey God." Or, "My company had too many problems!" The only valid reason for leaving one's leadership position is that God clearly guides you to do so.

GLORIFYING GOD

Spiritual leaders should have a third goal for their organizations, one which is the ultimate aspiration of any organization—to glorify God. You can glorify God through your leadership, regardless of whether you lead a Christian or a secular organization. Although one would assume Christian organizations would embrace this endeavor wholeheartedly, this is not always so. Christian organizations affirm their desire to exalt God, but they can get sidetracked in many subtle ways. Churches can become so preoccupied with growing in numbers or constructing buildings or administering programs they incorrectly assume everything they are doing honors God. Schools can become distracted by educational concerns and assume that academic respectability automatically honors God. When funding issues consume nonprofit organizations, they may compromise their standards to stay afloat. As the media eagerly points out, some Christian leaders are more concerned with developing their own name and financial portfolio than they are with honoring God's name. Pastors can wrongly believe God is honored when they build a new facility or they are called to a larger congregation. Businesspeople can incorrectly assume that by achieving worldly success they indirectly bring glory to God. God seeks to glorify himself by the way he works through people and organizations that believe and obey him. His focus is not glorifying people. Leaders' assignments and positions will change over time, but the objective of glorifying God must always be the driving force of their efforts.

In 1978, the Chrysler Corporation faced a seemingly insurmountable crisis. Having suffered millions of dollars in losses and facing the potential layoff of 150,000 employees, Chrysler was in dire straits. Enter Lee Iacocca. Chrysler hired him as president and his success is legendary. His name has become synonymous with dramatic corporate turnarounds. He wrote best-selling books and was considered as a presidential candidate. Iacocca received the glory. Jim Collins notes that after Iacocca became a celebrity, he spent an inordinate amount of time speaking on talk shows, making commercials, and promoting his autobiography. As a result, before he finally retired, Chrysler's stock fell 31 percent behind the general market.[20]

That is not the way spiritual leaders function. They seek to honor God through their personal lives as well as their business. Spiritual leaders cannot relentlessly pursue their own personal goals and glorify God at the same time. It is possible to bring an organization to the apex of success but dishonor God in the process. True spiritual leaders value glorifying God more than personal or organizational success.

John Beckett is board chairman of the Beckett Corporation, North America's leading producer of residential oil burners. He is a committed Christian who strives to apply his Christian faith in the marketplace. His business is not a Christian organization, but he operates it on Christian principles. How does he do this? He gives priority to the needs of his employees and their families. He provides generous maternity leaves. He is open about his Christian faith. The Beckett Corporation encourages younger employees to go back to school by providing tuition money. Beckett uses his business platform to support numerous Christian causes.

Beckett's company is so unusual it caught the national media's attention, and Peter Jennings of ABC News sent a news team to the Beckett Corporation to investigate the story. The newscast opened with this introduction written by Jennings: "Tonight we are going to concentrate on the growing tendency of business leaders in America to have their personal faith make an impact in their companies. In other words, they are using the Bible as a guide to business." When Beckett was asked on national television about his life's purpose, he responded, "My main mission is to know the will of God and do it."[21] The fact the Beckett Corporation is a secular organization has not hampered Beckett from using his business to exalt God.

Truett Cathy, well-known Christian businessman and founder of the fast food chain Chick-fil-A, maintained a long-standing policy that his stores remain closed on Sundays, even though Sunday is a high-volume day. Even when shopping malls in which Chick-fil-A leased space required stores to remain open on Sunday, Cathy did not budge. Whenever Sunday shoppers walk past a closed Chick-fil-A, they receive a testimony to the convictions of a Christian CEO. The company also sponsors employees' spouses to attend special company training events in exotic locations as a way to demonstrate that families are valued. The Cathys generously use company profits to support many charitable projects such as providing recreational experiences for children.

Numerous Christian businesspeople are choosing to glorify God through their jobs: car dealers give generous discounts and service to local ministers; CEOs provide prayer breakfasts at their annual meeting; executives hire chaplains to care for the personal needs of their employees. Bricklaying, electrical, and construction companies offer their services for free on the mission field in order to share Christ's love to people who have never heard the gospel. These business leaders raise their standard for God's glory right in the middle of the marketplace.

A Christian MVP: A Personal Example from Henry Blackaby

The sports world has enticed countless athletes and coaches to sacrifice their principles on the altar of worldly success. Yet Christian leaders know life holds a greater purpose than simply leading one's team to victory. I served as chaplain to the St. Louis Rams football team on the day they won the Super Bowl in January 2000. Kurt Warner, the Rams' quarterback, won the MVP of the league for the NFL that year. He would win the MVP of the Super Bowl before the day was done. The day of the game he met with me, and, along with many others, we fervently prayed that God would receive the glory for whatever occurred that day. Warner was interviewed after the game, and he reverently gave God the credit for his success. Warner developed a sports card he autographed and handed out to fans. It read: "The greatest day of my life had nothing to do with throwing forty TD passes in a season, being invited to the Pro Bowl, or being named NFL MVP. It was the day I asked Jesus into my heart. Now my life is dedicated to living out God's will and telling others about him." Christian leaders who impact their society understand that their first calling is not to be successful in the business world, or the sports arena, or the medical or legal profession but in God's kingdom (Matt. 6:33).

When Jesus was seeking twelve disciples, he bypassed the professional religious establishment and enlisted businesspeople, including two pairs of fishermen and a tax collector. He found people who understood how the world operated and who were unafraid of working in the middle of it. He chose people who spoke the language of the marketplace. God does nothing by accident. When God places someone in a leadership position, he has a purpose. A Christian's first calling is to honor God.

Glorifying God is not complicated. People do it when they reveal God's nature to the world around them. Leaders glorify God by accomplishing God's purposes and moving people on to his agenda. Accurately reflecting God's nature to others brings him glory. When Christians forgive others, people learn that God is one who forgives. When Christian leaders are patient with those who fail, people experience that God's nature is long-suffering. When Christian leaders live with integrity, people gain a glimpse of God's holiness. Many peoples' first impression of the true God may be reflected in the Christians who work alongside them each week.

God has a specific agenda for every person and organization. However, developing your people, equipping leaders, and, most importantly, glorifying God ought to be bedrock objectives of every leader.

Worthy Leadership Goals

1. Developing People
2. Equipping Others to Lead
3. Glorifying God

Responding to This Material

1. List the goals you have for your organization (be honest!). Prayerfully review them. Do you think God is pleased with them? Do you think the people you lead are excited about them?

2. Are you driven in your leadership more by the bottom line or by your concern for your people? What is the evidence?

3. What percentage of your time is spent investing in developing leaders? List the names of people in leadership positions today you personally invested time with in the past.

4. What are some advantages to someone who chose to work under your leadership?

5. How does the way you lead and treat your people bring glory to God?

6. What adjustments could you make in your leadership that would better encourage your people? How could your organization glorify God to a greater degree?

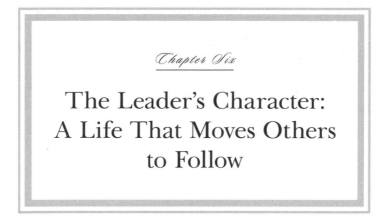

Chapter Six

The Leader's Character: A Life That Moves Others to Follow

For ten years the Duke of Marlborough led a tenuous coalition of Allied forces on the continent against the powerful armies of France. Yet, despite onerous political and military challenges, he never lost a battle. His admiring descendant, Winston Churchill, described his presence on the battlefield: "His appearance, his serenity, his piercing eye, his gestures, the tones of his voice—nay, the beat of his heart—diffused a harmony upon all around him. Every word he spoke was decisive. Victory often depended upon whether he rode half a mile this way or that."[1]

Influence is fundamental to a leader's role. It is not enough to know where people should go; leaders must have the capacity to move them to that place. Leaders such as the Duke of Marlborough, Alexander the Great, or Julius Caesar had the ability to inspire their followers to perform herculean tasks. Others, regardless of their leadership positions are unable to motivate people to follow.

People without followers are not leaders. We have encountered many frustrated people with noble aspirations and grandiose dreams but with no one prepared to support them or their vision. While the most powerful temptation spiritual leaders face is substituting their agenda for God's, their greatest frustration may be their inability to move people on to God's agenda.

In an attempt to enlist a following, many devote more energy to generating the appearance of a leader than developing the character required to lead. Someone who writes a book or earns a degree is too readily labeled an expert. Professional consultants provide "reputation management" to create the perception that people are qualified to lead. With the right kind of marketing, rhetoric, and makeover, people can generate a lot of hype, but they are only pseudo leaders. They have image but no substance.

Illegitimate Sources of Influence

Leaders move people in one direction or another. Spiritual leaders move people on to God's agenda. There are countless ways to exert an influence on others, but the following are three of the most common illegitimate ways people attempt to influence others.

POSITION

Previous generations associated authority and influence with position. Bosses were generally treated with respect, even if grudgingly, by virtue of their position. In spiritual matters people usually trusted their ministers and granted them respect as a matter of course. As a result, would-be leaders pursued positions of prominence to achieve the respect they craved. Each promotion up the corporate ladder rewarded ambitious executives with greater accolades from those on the rungs below. Each call to a larger, more prestigious church brought greater respect to the aspiring cleric.

The attempt to gain influence by way of position is inherently flawed. For one thing, this approach lends itself to flagrant abuses. A person can occupy an influential role without developing the corresponding character required to hold it. Individuals who use manipulative means to acquire powerful positions lack the integrity required to maintain peoples' respect over time. Moreover, insecure people who yearn for recognition and approval from others rarely find that their stations of authority fill the void in their lives. They inadvertently apply a worldly remedy to a spiritual problem. Both secular and religious organizations see countless men and women vainly attempting to satisfy their empty souls by garnering a following. Why are we shocked when prominent CEOs are caught in illegal activity or scandalized when a pastor commits adultery? It is because we falsely assume those in prominent positions have achieved their status based on sound character. Clearly this is not always the case.

It is sad but true that many Christian organizations as well as secular businesses are led by people who sought their office for the wrong reasons. These people assume the size of their ministry or corner office is directly correlated to their self-worth. Of course no position or title is exalted enough to satisfy someone whose self-worth depends on the job they hold. Oswald Sanders asked, "Should it not be the office that seeks the man, rather than the man the office?"[2]

Simply possessing a title does not guarantee respect. Today, more than ever before, respect must be earned. Due to the continuous barrage of media reports exposing scandalized executives, today's leaders face increased skepticism and scrutiny. This is the age of the "knowledge worker." Because of increased levels of education and training, people are not as impressed with titles and positions as were their less-educated predecessors. In previous generations the local minister was often the most educated person in the community. Today many church members have as much or more training and experience in their fields as ministers have in theirs. These educated church members have access to Bibles in numerous translations as well as software that holds more scriptural information than traditional ministers possessed in their entire libraries. No longer do congregations meekly accept the minister's theological pronouncements. People now have the knowledge and Internet search engines with which to critique and challenge their leaders' views.

Spiritual leadership is based on character and the working of the Holy Spirit. Without the Spirit's guiding, empowering presence, leaders may hold executive positions, but they are not spiritual leaders. Gaining a position as the pastor of a church or chairman of the elder board does not make one Spirit filled. Graduating from seminary does not transform students into spiritual leaders. Holding a leadership position in a Christian organization does not automatically provide God's anointing. Many misguided ministers assume people will follow them merely because they are the minister. Then, when the congregation resists their leadership, the disgruntled pastors denounce them as unspiritual. They resign and begin looking for a more "spiritually responsive" church. Some leaders, realizing that position alone doesn't automatically bring authority, will pursue influence over people by using force and instruments of coercion. Such insidious bullying produces even more disastrous consequences.

POWER

When Margaret Thatcher won a monumental third victory as prime minister of Great Britain during the 1980s, she seemed an invincible political force. But members of her party chafed under her leadership style. Ultimately her own colleagues, not the opposition, forced her resignation. Once people chose not to follow, the most successful British leader of her era could no longer lead.

Mao Tse-tung proclaimed, "Power comes out of the barrel of a gun."[3] He was unapologetic about using force to achieve his goals and consequently sent tens of millions of his own people to their deaths. However, even despots ultimately govern on the basis of their people's willingness to submit. The fall of communist governments such as the oppressive regime in Romania under Nicolae Ceausescu demonstrated that even the most repressive leaders can only sustain their power as long as they can induce sufficient numbers to follow. Communism was one of the most effective totalitarian systems in history, yet it could not withstand the popular will of the people once they refused to follow.

The business world cannot operate successfully over the long term with an authoritarian mind-set. The business world is full of examples of leaders who attempt to bully their staff, vendors, and even customers into submission. There was a time when dominant business leaders such as Henry Ford could intimidate labor movements and get away with statements such as, "Customers can have a car in any color they want, as long as it's black." That time is past. Max De Pree argues that business leaders must treat their top employees as volunteers.[4] Your best employees can generally find other employment if they don't like the way you treat them. One of the leading reasons employees consistently give for leaving their company is incompatibility with their boss. These people will remain with companies that function in harmony with their personal values. To impose authority upon such people is to risk losing valuable personnel to the competition.

Christian leaders also invite rebellion when they use force to achieve their goals. The my-way-or-the-highway approach fares no better in nonprofit organizations than in the marketplace. Some pastors exhibit Jekyll and Hyde personas. They are charming and cordial as long as church members submit to their authority. But when challenged, they become angry and lambaste anyone who dares oppose them. Others use the pulpit as a soapbox from which to castigate those who disagree with them. Some church leaders lobby for support from influential church members as if they were seeking to get a bill passed through Congress. Foolish is the pastor who ostracizes his detractors, treating them as wolves rather than as sheep in need of a shepherd. Ministers who attempt to strong-arm their opponents into submission will eventually find themselves either preaching to empty seats or searching the want ads. Incredibly, when this happens, many pastors stubbornly blame the people for refusing to follow their God-appointed leader. Spiritual dictatorship is one of the most oppressive forms of tyranny. It is one thing to dominate people because you have an organizational chart at your advantage. It is another to manipulate people because you claim to have God on your side.

Watchman Nee set forth the view that God delegates his authority to leaders. In his book *Spiritual Authority*, Nee argued that because God delegates his authority, "we do not obey man but God's authority in that man."[5] Nee maintained that followers' key responsibility was unquestioning obedience to their spiritual leaders. He concluded, "Henceforth authority alone is factual to me; reason and right and wrong no longer control my life."[6] Nee explained his position this way: "People will perhaps argue, 'What if the authority is wrong?' The answer is, If God dares to entrust His authority to men, then we can dare to obey. Whether the one in authority is right or wrong does not concern us, since he has to be responsible directly to God. The obedient needs only to obey; the Lord will not hold us responsible for any mistaken obedience, rather He will hold the delegated authority responsible for his erroneous act. Insubordination, however, is rebellion, and for this the one under authority must answer to God."[7]

It is easy to see how dictatorial leaders could abuse this teaching to justify an imperious leadership style. Cult groups and totalitarian governments demand absolute obedience to their leaders. They denounce independent thought. Nothing could be more unbiblical! Scripture instructs Christians to voluntarily submit to those in positions of authority because God has, in his sovereignty, allowed them to hold office (Rom. 13:1–2). But people are not to obey leaders blindly and unquestioningly simply because of their position. The Bible makes clear that all people must give an account to Christ for everything they do, regardless of who told them to do it (2 Cor. 5:10). Christ does not need a mediator to exercise his lordship over people. The Holy Spirit dwells within every believer, leaders and followers alike. When leaders claim God bypasses their followers and speaks directly to them, they greatly diminish God's work in believers' lives. God will tolerate no substitutes for a personal relationship with him. He relates to his followers directly. People who obey leaders as though they were responding to God are in danger of committing idolatry.

As we have seen, insecurity and a craving for affirmation drive some people to seek leadership positions. A telling sign of such leaders is their intolerance of those who challenge them. Insecure leaders find it much simpler to label their opponents as unspiritual or rebellious than to examine the truth of their critics' words. Sometimes people refuse to follow a leader's vision because they want to hear from God directly and not second-hand. Leaders who begrudge people the opportunity to seek God themselves and who do not actively teach their people how to hear God's voice have disqualified themselves as spiritual leaders.

PERSONALITY

As every child learns, there is usually more than one way to get what you want. If it doesn't come automatically (position) and if bullying doesn't work (power), you can always turn on the charm (personality). People often follow leaders merely because of their winsome personalities. A leader's popularity is not in itself bad, but it cannot be the only thing. Leaders must also demonstrate competence and a sense of direction. Seth Godin notes: "Being charismatic doesn't make you a leader. Being a leader makes you charismatic."[8] Countless businesses have been led to ruin by silver-tongued CEOs who were impressive but incompetent. Churches have blindly voted to follow their pastors into disastrous projects because they loved their leader, not because they heard from God. Numerous churches have ultimately dismissed their minister with this sad commentary: "We loved our pastor. He was a wonderful person. He just couldn't lead!" By itself, an engaging personality is insufficient to constitute spiritual leadership.

Collins and Porras, in their book *Built to Last*, concluded that the contention that "visionary companies require great and charismatic visionary leaders" is a myth. On the contrary, they determined "a charismatic visionary leader is absolutely *not required* for a visionary company and, in fact, can be detrimental to a company's long-term prospects."[9] Jim Collins, in his book *Good to Great*, asserted that the most successful CEOs demonstrated a "compelling modesty."[10] Great leaders build great organizations, not necessarily great reputations. When organizations are erected around a leader's personality, not only are they susceptible to the leader's weaknesses, but they also face an inevitable crisis when the leader departs. When a church plummets in attendance after its pastor leaves or a company's profits significantly decline after the CEO resigns, this may indicate the organization was built more on personality than on a healthy process or product.

This important principle is relevant for churches seeking pastors. Christ said he would build his church (Matt. 16:18). In order to thrive, churches do not require leaders who exude charm. Often pastor search committees erroneously look for a striking and charismatic spokesperson whose attractive appearance and charm will attract new members. They value charisma over consecration. But personality without purpose and charm without competence are recipes for disaster. Pastors who function more on personality than on true leadership qualities rarely stay in one place for long. They typically breeze into a church, preach through their meager repertoire of sermons, and then, as their winsome smile begins to wear thin, move on. They seldom accomplish anything of substance. They make a great first impression but rarely a lasting one.

There are numerous ways to exert influence on people. While some methods can initially appear effective, they are difficult to sustain, and they fail to glorify God or accomplish his purposes. However, there are certain sources of influence that not only exert a powerful influence on people; they also bring glory to God in the process. It is to these we now turn.

Illegitimate Sources of Influence

1. Position
2. Power
3. Personality

Legitimate Sources of Influence

Leaders influence people in two major ways. The first is by who they *are*, and the second is by what they *do*. Both can be powerful instruments to move people on to God's agenda. The rest of this chapter will examine the characteristics of leaders who motivate people to follow. The following chapter will examine what leaders do to move people to where God wants them to be.

GOD'S HAND

Of the many ways leaders can exert influence on others through their life, none is more powerful than when God affirms them before others (Ps. 80:17; 139:5). There are numerous biblical and historic examples of men and women whom God upheld as spiritual leaders.

Moses was arguably the greatest leader in the Old Testament. However, he could not attribute his success to his own leadership abilities, for he was not a naturally gifted leader. He was a poor public speaker (Exod. 4:10), inept at delegating (Exod. 18:13–27); and he had an anger problem which ultimately led him to commit murder (Exod. 32:19; Num. 20;9–13). Moses' accomplishments as a spiritual leader came from the depth of his relationship with God. Scripture indicates, "The LORD spoke with Moses face to face, just as a man speaks with his friend" (Exod. 33:11). The Israelites recognized Moses' close walk with God. Whenever Moses would return from a divine encounter, his face would glow with the glory of God (Exod. 34:29–35).

Because of his close walk with God, Moses was extremely humble (Num. 12:3). He was so demure that when Aaron and Miriam criticized him, the Lord came to his defense, rebuking his companions for their insolence (Num. 12:6–8).

Moses did not demand respect or act with a heavy hand. Surely that is why God chose to honor him (James 4:19). Moses could have appealed to his position of authority to silence his detractors, but he had no need to do that. God's methods of authenticating his leaders are far more convincing. Leaders who become preoccupied with defending themselves and their reputations display an acute lack of faith, for they do not trust God to vindicate them. Some people constantly enlist their friends and associates to promote them so they obtain prominent positions. True leaders don't do this. God's approval surpasses any honor people could bestow. Likewise, true leaders do not despair when people conspire against them. Those who are secure in their relationship with God know the antagonism of their fiercest foe cannot prevent them from achieving God's purposes (Rom. 8:31).

Joshua had plenty of reasons to feel insecure when God called him to lead the Israelites into Canaan.[11] He faced powerful, hostile enemy armies equipped with iron chariots and fortified cities. He succeeded Moses, the most esteemed and respected figure in Israelite history. No wonder God gave the following assurances, exhorting Joshua to have courage.

> No one will be able to stand against you as long as you live. I will be with you, just as I was with Moses. I will not leave you or forsake you. Be strong and courageous, for you will distribute the land I swore to their fathers to give them as an inheritance. Above all, be strong and very courageous to carefully observe the whole instruction My servant Moses commanded you. Do not turn from it to the right or the left, so that you will have success wherever you go. This book of instruction must not depart from your mouth; you are to recite it day and night so that you may carefully observe everything written in it. For then you will prosper and succeed in whatever you do. Haven't I commanded you: be strong and courageous? Do not be afraid or discouraged, for the Lord your God is with you wherever you go. (Josh. 1:5–9)

God did not encourage Joshua to draw confidence from his own strengths and abilities. Rather, God made abundantly clear that Joshua need not worry about his inadequacies because God was in control. Joshua could lead the Hebrew nation with absolute confidence, not in his own leadership skills but in the assurance of the Lord's presence.

The Israelites recognized who their true leader was. They pledged: "We will obey you, just as we obeyed Moses in everything. And may the LORD your God be with you, as He was with Moses" (Josh. 1:17). By this time the people had seen enough miracles to know they were not following a man but God.

More than anything else, people are looking for spiritual leaders who clearly demonstrate God's presence in their lives. There is no greater source of influence for spiritual leaders than the manifest presence of God.

True to his word, God worked mightily through Joshua. As the Israelites prepared to cross the Jordan River, God reaffirmed his promise to Joshua: "Today I will begin to exalt you in the sight of all Israel, so they will know that I will be with you just as I was with Moses" (Josh. 3:7). Leaders do not have to prove God is guiding them. God's presence is unmistakable. Whenever Joshua led the people into battle, God placed a crippling fear in the hearts of Israel's enemies (Josh. 2:11). When the Israelites fought, God caused the enemy to be routed (Josh. 23:10). God miraculously intervened so Joshua's army was victorious (Josh. 6:20; 10:13). Everyone could see that God supported Joshua and his army. Joshua had not embarked on a quest for military glory and fame. God gave it to him. Joshua's role was to live in obedience to God.

Samuel received God's promise: "I will honor those who honor Me, but those who despise Me will be disgraced" (1 Sam. 2:30). Eli the priest dishonored the Lord by the way he led his family and God rejected him. Conversely, "Samuel grew in stature and in favor with the LORD and with men" (1 Sam. 2:26).

God honored Samuel as long as Samuel honored him. Scripture reveals that "the LORD was with him and He fulfilled everything Samuel prophesied" (1 Sam. 3:19). God was the guarantor of every word Samuel spoke. That gave Samuel unmistakable authority. Like Joshua, Samuel refused to demand respect from people, and, like Joshua, he was greatly venerated.

Deborah served as a judge of God's people during a dangerous period in Israel's history. God bestowed such wisdom on her, people traveled great distances to seek her counsel. When Israel's enemies oppressed them, Deborah counseled Balak, the military commander, on how God would give victory. Despite this assurance Balak told Deborah: "If you will go with me, I will go. But if you will not go with me, I will not go" (Judg. 4:8). Deborah was not trained in military tactics, nor was she a valiant warrior, but Balak recognized God's hand on her life. He concluded that Deborah's presence in his army ensured God's presence.

Jesus exemplified the unpretentious life the heavenly Father honors in his servants. Despite the fact he was the only person in history with justifiable reason to exalt himself, being God's Son, he chose to live and die in humility. The Father continually affirmed his Son, as at Jesus' baptism, when God proclaimed: "This is My beloved Son. I take delight in Him!" (Matt. 3:17). Likewise, on the mount of transfiguration when Peter attempted to take charge of that sacred moment, the Father, not the Son, intervened: "This is My Son, the Chosen One; listen to Him!" (Luke 9:35).

Throughout Jesus' life, at his death, and finally through his resurrection, God the Father exalted his Son. Jesus never promoted himself, even when Satan tried to entice him to do so. This is the pattern of true spiritual leadership. When spiritual leaders pursue the praise and respect of others, they may achieve their goal, but they also have their reward in full. Those who seek God's affirmation receive a true and lasting honor. There is no comparison between the fleeting, fickle praise of people and the esteem of God.

Charles G. Finney was a nineteenth-century evangelist whose life demonstrated God's powerful presence. During a trip to New York Mills in 1826, Finney visited a cotton manufacturing plant where his brother-in-law was superintendent. As Finney passed through a spacious room in which many women were working at looms and spinning jennies, he noticed several young women watching him and speaking among themselves. As Finney approached them, they became more agitated. When Finney was about ten feet away, one woman sank to the ground and burst into tears. Soon others were sobbing, overcome with conviction of their sin in the presence of the visiting evangelist. The Spirit's outpouring spread rapidly throughout the building until the entire factory was singularly aware of God's presence. The owner, an unbeliever, realized something unusual was occurring, temporarily closed the plant and asked Finney to preach to his employees and tell them how they might find peace for their souls. Finney had not spoken to the laborers. He merely entered the factory. God's powerful presence in Finney's life was too overwhelming to ignore.[12]

When God exalts one of his servants, the world notices. The secular leader Abimilech and his military commander Phicol conceded to Abraham: "God is with you in everything you do" (Gen. 21:22). Regarding Oliver Cromwell during the English Civil War "It was observed that God was with him . . . and he began to be renowned."[13] When President George H. Bush ordered the commencement of the Persian Gulf War on January 16, 1991, he asked Billy Graham to sit with him at the White House as he received the initial battle reports. The U.S. Army was the best equipped army in the world. The president had some of the most brilliant military and diplomatic minds at his disposal, yet the commander in chief chose a spiritual leader upon whom God's hand was clearly evident as his companion during the tense moments of the war's outbreak.[14]

Spiritual leaders *must* determine if God is affirming their leadership. If God has his hand on a leader's life, there should be compelling evidence. For one, God will fulfill his promises to the leader. Leaders who continually present new plans and visions for the future but never see those dreams come to fruition demonstrate that God is not supporting the visions they espouse.

Second, when God affirms leaders, he vindicates their reputation over time. All leaders suffer criticism during the course of their work. Criticism is not necessarily a sign of poor leadership. It may stem from people resisting God rather than rejecting the leader. The way to tell the difference is that God will ultimately exculpate those who serve him.

A third sign of God's presence in a leader is changed lives. When someone leads in the Spirit's power, lives are transformed. People are moved to experience God in new dimensions. Leaders may entertain, impress, or even motivate people, but if their followers do not advance spiritually, their leadership emanates from their own talent and vision, not from God's powerful direction. Finally, the unmistakable mark of leaders who have God's powerful hand upon them is they demonstrate Christlike character.

Upon whom does Almighty God place his hand of affirmation? The key lies not in the leader but in God. Leaders can do nothing to guarantee God's blessing. All they can do is submit. Some spiritual leaders try to be more committed. What they need is to be more submitted. There is a significant difference between a personal determination to try harder and complete abandonment of one's self to God and his purposes. The former rests on human effort; the latter relies on divine sufficiency. The biographies of history's greatest spiritual leaders reveal specific divine encounters wherein these men and women yielded themselves to God at the deepest level of their lives. The more they came to know God, the more clearly they recognized their own limitations apart from God working through them (Phil. 4:13).

LEADING THROUGH SURRENDER

People do not choose to become spiritual leaders. Spiritual leadership flows out of a person's vibrant, intimate relationship with God. You cannot be a spiritual leader if you are not encountering God in profound, life-changing ways.

Charles Finney experienced a dramatic encounter with Christ that transformed his life and empowered him to be mightily used by God during the Second Great Awakening. So dramatic was Finney's experience with almighty God he thought he would die from the encounter.[15]

Dwight L. Moody was experiencing great success as the director of the YMCA in Chicago and served as pastor of a thriving church. He gathered a team of committed Christian leaders around him, including the gifted singer, Ira Sankey. By all appearances Moody was a successful minister. Then in June 1871, Mrs. Sarah Anne Cooke and Mrs. Hawxhurst sat in the front row during one of his meetings and prayed diligently throughout the service. When Moody asked the reason for their fervent intercession, they told him they sensed he needed the Spirit's power in his life and ministry. A change gradually took place in Moody. He confessed, "There came a great hunger into my soul. I did not know what it was. I began to cry out as I never did before. I really felt that I did not want to live if I could not have this power for service." Moody asked the two women to pray with him every Friday afternoon until he received the powerful anointing of the Holy Spirit.

While in New York City Moody finally yielded every part of his life and will to his Lord. Suddenly he experienced God's overwhelming presence in an unprecedented manner. Moody quickly found a place to be alone with God. "The room seemed ablaze with God. He dropped to the floor and lay bathing in the divine. Of this Communion, this mount of transfiguration," Moody said, "'I can say that God revealed Himself to me, and I had such an experience of His love that I had to ask Him to stay His hand.'"[16]

Not long afterward in England, Moody heard Henry Varley's challenging words: "Moody, the world has yet to see what God will do with a man fully consecrated to him." Moody was prepared to be that man and God used him to become the most prolific evangelist of the late-nineteenth century.

Billy Graham, at thirty years old, reached a crossroad in his life. His good friend and colleague Charles Templeton abandoned many of the beliefs he and Graham formerly shared. Although Graham was a successful college president and itinerant evangelist, the core of his life and ministry were shaken. If those closest to him were discarding their fidelity to the Bible and its teachings, was he naïve to continue trusting them?

> As that night wore on, my heart became heavily burdened. With the Los Angeles campaign galloping toward me, I had to have an answer. If I could not trust the Bible, I could not go on. I would have to quit the school presidency. I would have to leave pulpit evangelism. I was only thirty years of age. It was not too late to become a dairy farmer. But that night I believed with all my heart that the God who had saved my soul would never let go of me. . . . "O God! There are many things in this book I do not understand. There are many problems with it for which I have no solution. There are many seeming contradictions. There are some areas in it that do not seem to correlate with modern science. I can't answer some of the philosophical and psychological questions Chuck and others are raising." . . . At last the Holy

Spirit freed me to say it. "Father, I am going to accept this as Thy Word—by faith! I am going to allow faith to go beyond my intellectual questions and doubts, and I will believe this to be Your inspired Word." When I got up from my knees at Forest Home that August night, my eyes stung with tears. I sensed the presence and power of God as I had not sensed it in months. Not all my questions had been answered, but a major bridge had been crossed. In my heart and mind, I knew a spiritual battle in my soul had been fought and won.[17]

Shortly after this event Graham began his 1949 Los Angeles campaign which God used to propel him into international prominence. Before God elevated him, Graham yielded himself to a degree many of his colleagues were unwilling to do. The complete relinquishing of everything to Christ has been the turning point for many of history's greatest spiritual leaders.[18]

The common factor for Finney, Moody, and Graham was their total submission to God. They did not need to be more resolved to seek God's will; they had to be more yielded in faith to God, whatever his will was. Only then did a profound assurance of God's presence come. Their phenomenal success as spiritual leaders was not based on their superior oratorical abilities or management genius, but rather it came out of their absolute surrender to Christ. We are seeing this in the corporate world as well as in the church. God is working powerfully through a growing number of business leaders who are giving much more than lip service to Christ as the Lord over their lives. These men and women have humbly sought God's face, offering up every aspect of their considerable resources for God's use, and the results have been astounding. Many spiritual leaders never reach this depth of submission. Many make commitments; few offer absolute surrender.

INTEGRITY/HONESTY

Max De Pree observes "behavior is the highest form of expression."[19] When people's actions accurately mirror their beliefs and values, their life has integrity. For example, it is much easier to claim to believe in honesty than it is to be completely honest in every circumstance. Max De Pree adds: "Integrity in all things precedes all else. The open demonstration of integrity is essential; followers must be wholeheartedly convinced of their leader's integrity. For leaders, who live a public life, perceptions become a fact of life."[20] *Webster's* dictionary defines *integrity* as: "Adherence to moral and ethical principles; soundness of moral character. Honesty. The state of being whole, entire, or undiminished. A sound, unimpaired, or perfect condition."

Integrity demands consistency under every circumstance, including unguarded moments. If leaders are normally peaceable and well mannered but they throw temper tantrums when things go wrong, they lack integrity. If leaders are honest and moral in public but discard those standards in private, their lives lack integrity. When leaders have integrity, their followers always know what to expect.

It is said of Robert E. Lee that "however hot the blood in the chase and in the fight, Lee remained the Christian soldier."[21] During professional sporting events many high-profile athletes purporting to be Christians (and even some fans) have sacrificed their credibility through angry outbursts. After Tom Landry was fired as the head coach of the Dallas Cowboys, the sports media paid tribute to the well-known Christian coach. One commentator remembered interviewing Landry after the Cowboys suffered a humiliating defeat. Despite being embarrassed on the field that day, Landry answered every reporter's question with grace and dignity. At the close of the interview, as reporters were packing up their equipment, a newsman realized to his dismay that his camera had not properly recorded the interview. He had nothing for his station to broadcast that evening. In desperation the frantic reporter raced to catch Landry. When the weary coach heard the reporter's dilemma, he returned and completely refilmed the interview. As the reporter testified on national television during a tribute to Landry, he marveled at the Christian character of the man who acted with equal grace and dignity regardless of whether his team won or lost.

Integrity is best demonstrated during adversity. Anyone can demonstrate integrity if there is nothing to lose in doing so. Thomas More was consigned to the Tower of London because he refused to condone Henry VIII's divorce from Catherine of Aragon. Knowing a refusal to recant would cost him his life, More concluded: "It lieth not in my power but that they may devour me; but God being my good Lord, I will provide that they shall never deflower me."[22]

Kouzes and Posner, in extensive studies of employees from across America, asked people what they most valued and admired in their leaders. Over the years the trait that consistently topped the list was honesty— trumping vision, competence, accomplishments, and the ability to inspire others.[23] In an informal survey conducted for this book, various CEOs of major companies were asked what they looked for in a potential employee. Almost every one cited integrity as the number one qualification. John Beckett of the Beckett Corporation explained: "The chief trait I look for is integrity.... I believe if this trait is embraced and in place, other qualities such as honesty, diligence, and a good work ethic will follow."

The fact that honesty and integrity are mutually desired by both employers and employees comes as no surprise. Leadership is ultimately based on trust, and trust must have a foundation. Kouzes and Posner claim "credibility is the foundation of leadership. Period."[24] They add, "The ultimate test of leaders' credibility is whether they do what they say."[25] The business world is rife with dishonesty, yet great business leaders have understood that if people cannot trust your word, you will not be in business for long. J. P. Morgan has been derided for belonging to the Gilded Age's class of Robber Barons. Yet one who knew him claimed, "When he said a thing, and looked full at you as he said it, to doubt him was impossible."[26]

Christian leaders of all people ought to be known for their honesty. Yet many are not. Media coverage continually exposes high-profile religious leaders who deceived the public about their finances or moral lives. On a local level many ministers think nothing of embellishing the truth or misrepresenting the facts. When people see their leaders stretching the truth, they lose confidence in them. Followers cannot expect their leaders to be perfect, but they want them to be honest.

Scripture is filled with promises to the person of integrity:

> He stores up success for the upright; He is a shield for those who live with integrity. (Prov. 2:7)

> The one who lives with integrity lives securely, but whoever perverts his ways will be found out. (Prov. 10:9)

> Vindicate me, LORD, because I have lived with integrity and have trusted in the Lord without wavering. Test me, LORD, and try me; examine my heart and mind. (Ps. 26:1–2)

The Bible also uses the term "blameless" to describe people who live with integrity. The apostle Peter urged Christians, in light of Christ's second coming, to "make every effort to be found at peace with Him without spot or blemish" (2 Pet. 3:14).

A contentious topic is whether leaders who commit adultery can still guide their organizations effectively. Some argue one's personal life does not affect an individual's professional life. The issue, however, is not capability but integrity. If a man can deceive his wife and children, break a vow he made to God in the presence of witnesses, and knowingly betray the trust of those who love him, how can his organization trust him to always tell them the truth? People who prove themselves deceitful in one area of life are usually untrustworthy in others. Perhaps that is why when Warren Bennis and Burt Nanus surveyed sixty successful CEOs of major companies almost all of them were still married to their first spouse.[27] These leaders valued their commitments and were conducting their personal lives, as well as their business lives, with integrity.

Leaders with integrity possess the credibility to influence others. People without integrity may promote worthwhile causes yet fail to gain people's loyalty because their lives discredit the validity of their proposals. In evaluating Oliver Cromwell's personal life, John Milton observed: "He first acquired government of himself and over himself acquired the most signal victories, so that on the first day he took the field against the external enemy, he was a veteran in arms, consummately practiced in the toils and exigencies of war."[28] In evaluating leadership talent for his officer corps, Robert E. Lee surmised, "I cannot trust a man to control others who cannot control himself."[29]

Integrity alone is insufficient to ensure leadership success. Leaders must also be competent. Integrity may initially gain leaders the benefit of the doubt, but they must eventually demonstrate competence. Integrity is not automatic. Peter Kostenbaum suggests "leading is taking charge of your will—the innermost core of your humanity."[30] Integrity is a character trait leaders must consciously cultivate. Early in Billy Graham's ministry, he met with his associates during a crusade in Modesto, California. The notorious vices of well-known evangelists troubled them. They realized if they were careless they, too, could fall. Graham led his group to identify those issues most likely to destroy or hinder their ministry. Then they agreed on a list of principles they would strictly follow to ensure their integrity. Graham described this time as "a shared commitment to do all we could to uphold the Bible's standard of absolute integrity and purity for evangelists."[31] As a result of this early commitment, Billy Graham's evangelistic association became the foremost model of integrity for Christian organizations around the world. Integrity doesn't happen by accident. It occurs on purpose.

A SUCCESSFUL TRACK RECORD

Few things bring leaders more credibility than consistent, long-term success. The Duke of Marlborough led an international coalition for ten years despite enormous adversity. One reason people from diverse backgrounds readily followed him was because as his biographer notes: " he never fought a battle that he did not win, nor besiege a fortress he did not take. Amid all the chances and baffling accidents of war he produced victory with almost mechanical certainty."[32] Success is generally the telltale sign of good leadership and can also signify God's blessing. God promised Joshua he would be with him in every battle (Josh. 1:9). His army became invincible. Joshua's consistent victories were direct proof of God's blessing. Kouzes and Posner claim, "Having a winning track record is the surest way to be considered competent."[33]

Leaders cannot demand respect. They can only earn it. The problem with many would-be leaders is they want people's respect without first establishing a successful history. They are like the hopeful job applicant who commented on his application form, "Please don't misconstrue my fourteen jobs as 'job hopping.' I have never quit a job." People have the right to examine their leaders' record of achievement. If leaders failed in their two previous assignments, they should not be surprised when people hesitate to follow them. This is why younger leaders cannot expect the same degree of respect and authority given to veteran leaders. There are no substitutes for experience. "You cannot lead out of someone else's experience," Kouzes and Posner point out. "You can only lead out of your own."[34] John Beckett of the Beckett Corporation observes, "I am wary of 'potential' without a supporting track record."

A sincere young pastor serving in his first congregation was deeply concerned for a nearby town that had no church. He wanted to begin a mission church. Unfortunately, his people were unsupportive of his proposed project. No one volunteered to help. Several members openly questioned the wisdom of extending their ministry to another city when there were so many needs in their own church. The pastor was grieved because his people were unwilling to follow his leadership into this exciting new ministry. He asked what he should do to lead his people to embrace the Great Commission.

This scenario always creates an awkward situation. When people are discouraged, it seems unkind to point to their leadership as the primary problem. It is tempting to concur that the fault lies in their followers, the downturn in the economy, the unresponsive community, or the previous leader's mistakes. But to shift the blame elsewhere would not free this struggling leader from the shortcomings crippling his effectiveness. This minister sincerely wanted his church to extend God's kingdom, yet his own church was in dismal condition. The facilities desperately needed repair, the church was running a deficit, and there was a chronic shortage of Sunday school teachers. The pastor was wholly ineffective in addressing these problems. Members who saw their pastor struggling to organize and maintain one church had every reason to question whether he could effectively establish and maintain a second congregation. Further discussion revealed he was experiencing financial problems personally due to poor money-management skills and he had put on a great deal of weight under the stress. He began to see the problem was not with his congregation but with their leader. This pastor had not established a successful track record in his personal life or in his current leadership tasks, yet he was asking his people to trust his leadership in a major new venture. His people were wise to resist moving forward on his suggestion.

The above situation magnifies the need for small accomplishments. New leaders should be cautious in immediately undertaking large projects. Better first to prove themselves in smaller tasks that can be successfully completed in a relatively short time. When people experience a string of small victories, they will be more willing to attempt something larger. The best area to demonstrate small triumphs is in the leader's self-mastery.

Jesus told the story of three servants whose master entrusted them with large amounts of money. The first two servants invested their resources and doubled their value. The third person buried his assets and earned nothing for his master. Their master's response to the first two servants was: "Well done, good and faithful slave! You were faithful over a few things; I will put you in charge of many things" (Matt. 25:23). Jesus' parable illustrates two important truths. First, God expects a return on his investment in our lives. Second, those who prove themselves faithful with little will receive more from God. Conversely, those who squander the initial responsibilities God gives them will not be entrusted with additional ones. They may even lose the little they had. The problem is, too many people want to bypass the small assignments and get right to the big jobs—the ones with influence and prestige. But God doesn't work that way. He is sequential in developing leaders. When *he* believes you have been faithful in a little, *he* will entrust you with more.

Leaders who are frustrated that God is not blessing their zeal to do great things for him should examine their track record. Have they been faithful in small assignments? They should also be sure they are measuring success the way God does. "More" in God's economy does not necessarily mean greater amounts of people, money, or prestige. It may mean God entrusts them with a more difficult assignment, or greater suffering. God's Son received the greatest assignment ever given, and it culminated in a cross. Spiritual leadership is a progressive endeavor that depends on obedience. As God's servants obey him in each stage of their lives, no matter how humble the task, they will come to know God more intimately, and their faith will increase, giving them, step by step, what they need for the next assignment.

Eventually, through this pattern of obedience and growth, spiritual leaders will attain a higher degree of influence among those they lead. The evidence that God has honored leaders solidifies their credibility. On the other hand, leaders who use political means or attempt shortcuts to gain leadership positions have tenuous credibility. They may experience short-term success, but God will not honor them as leaders, and ultimately they will be discredited.

L. R. Scarborough, the second president of Southwestern Seminary in Fort Worth, was disconcerted at how many aspiring pastors were shamelessly pursuing prominent places of ministry. He issued this challenge: "If your place is not great enough to suit you, make it so. The minister who is unable to make a place great is too weak to hold a great one."[35] Leaders who fix their gaze on the horizon, hoping for something better rather than focusing on the tasks at hand, are unworthy to hold their current positions. Conversely, leaders who enthusiastically invest their energies into each new assignment God gives them will enjoy success where they are and they will develop the character God looks for in those to whom he grants larger assignments.

Spiritual leaders must understand what success means in God's kingdom, for it is not measured by the same standards the world uses. During the early years of the American Revolution, George Washington lost most battles he fought. But, considering the ragtag group of untrained, ill-equipped soldiers he was leading against the world's superpower, it was a major victory simply keeping his troops from starving or freezing to death. Sometimes a tactical retreat can be a success. Of Washington it has been said, "He was not a brilliant strategist or tactician, nor a gifted orator, not an intellectual. At several crucial moments he had shown marked indecisiveness. He had made serious mistakes in judgment. But experience had been his great teacher from boyhood, and in this his greatest test, he learned steadily from experience."[36] During World War II Dwight Eisenhower was given the coveted assignment of leading the Allied forces in the invasion of Europe. Eisenhower did not take shortcuts to arrive at that post. He spent years as a loyal subordinate to two of America's greatest military leaders: Douglas MacArthur and George Marshall. Eisenhower claimed: "My ambition in the Army was to make everybody I worked for regretful when I was ordered to other duty."[37] Consequently, he often worked eighteen-hour days and continually went the extra mile for his superiors. Because he was a faithful subordinate, he was eventually promoted to the top field command and ultimately to the presidency.[38]

God gauges success in terms of faithfulness, obedience, and growth. The definitive measure of leaders' success is whether they moved people from where they were to where God wanted them to be. This may be reflected in numbers or financial growth, but it is expressly seen in spiritual maturity.

Organizations seeking a new leader should critically examine candidates' track records. Prospective leaders may not have previously been a CEO, government leader, or a pastor of a large church; but if they are leaders, there will inevitably be evidence of leadership capacities. Emerging leaders may not yet have major accomplishments to their credit, but they should be accumulating a series of small successes. Perhaps they have demonstrated leadership capacity in sports or in volunteer organizations. Moreover, leaders generally accumulate promotions, raises, and greater responsibility in whatever jobs they hold, regardless of how menial, because their leadership qualities become evident. Success in previous, smaller ventures may indicate the emerging leader is now prepared for greater responsibility. This does not mean they never experience failure but they learn from their failures and continue to be effective in their roles. As Warren Bennis observes,

"Leaders, like anyone else, are the sum of all their experiences, but, unlike others, they amount to more than the sum, because they make more of their experiences."[39] Clive Jacobs sagely notes: "Good judgment is the result of experience. Experience is the result of bad judgment."[40] Experience is not the end factor; it is merely an avenue to reveal and develop character. It is character that enables people to lead. Spiritual leaders' personal growth is the accumulation of God's activity in their lives.

Leaders who are faithful in every assignment enjoy a tremendous sense of peace and confidence. An observer of General Robert E. Lee at the close of the American Civil War concluded, "It must have been the sense of having done his whole duty, and expended upon the cause every energy of his being, which enabled him to meet the approaching catastrophe with a calmness which seemed to those around him almost sublime."[41] Few rewards equal the joy of being able to look back over your faithful track record. When you have one as a leader, you will never lack followers.

PREPARATION

As Britain braced itself for a massive naval assault from Napoleon's fleet, Prime Minister Pitt turned to the one man he believed could assume command of the British forces and win a decisive victory—Horatio Nelson. When he asked Nelson if he could be ready in three day's time to take command of the British fleet, Nelson replied: "I am ready now."[42] Those who have left indelible marks on history have been prepared for their moment on the world stage. At the close of his autobiography, Billy Graham listed several things he would do differently if he could live his life over again. He said: "I have failed many times and I would do many things differently. For one thing, I would speak less and study more."[43] Billy Graham preached to more people and saw more conversions than any preacher in history, yet he acknowledged, had he been better prepared, God might have used his life to an even greater extent.

Preparation brings profound confidence to leaders. The most successful leaders were those who did their homework. It is said James Madison's great strength in committee was his prior preparation.[44] Winston Churchill read nine newspapers every morning over breakfast. He studied reports, refusing to have his staff digest information for him. Abraham Lincoln was so anxious to be informed of news during the Civil War he often personally visited the telegraph office to obtain the latest information as it came across the wires.

Harry Truman was not generally perceived as a brilliant man, but he was admired for always being prepared. When he took office at the death of Franklin Roosevelt on April 12, 1945, he faced an enormous task. He would meet with Joseph Stalin and Winston Churchill in July to discuss the world peace process and the postwar treatment of Germany and Japan. Truman was not in the earlier meetings with these two men, nor had his predecessor briefed him. Truman also had to confront the frightening reality of the atomic bomb. The decision of whether or not to use it now rested on his shoulders. Ultimately he would bear responsibility for each of these weighty decisions. Yet those who met with Truman found him to always be thoroughly prepared. He would fastidiously examine every document and briefing until he thoroughly understood the issues and was prepared to act. Truman became known for his decisiveness, but it was borne of meticulous preparation. Leaders can make momentous decisions with confidence if they are thoroughly prepared.

Many great leaders of the past were well versed in history. Queen Elizabeth I habitually set aside three hours a day to read history books.[45] Churchill was a historian so he was able to put his nation's conflict with Hitler into perspective. Napoleon was a voracious reader, especially of history. It has been said that "history was a goddess" to John F. Kennedy.[46] It behooves successful leaders to invest time in learning their organization's history to see how God has led to date. History is particularly important for spiritual leaders new to their churches or organizations. Incoming pastors are remiss to assume God arrives with them. God was there at the church's founding and he will be there when the pastor leaves. Wise pastors identify how God has led the congregation thus far and thereby gain perspective on how God is guiding at present.

Preparation for leadership also involves education and training. Many a zealous leader has charged off prematurely to positions of leadership. They disdainfully neglected opportunities to increase their education or skills then found themselves in conundrums that far exceeded their expertise. Leaders who make the effort to obtain proper training are not only better prepared for their leadership role; they also have greater credibility with those they lead. The writer of Proverbs extolled: "Do you see a man skilled in his work? He will stand in the presence of kings. He will not stand in the presence of unknown men" (Prov. 22:29). Too often leaders prematurely end their training because a job opportunity becomes available. By assuming "getting to the task at hand" is more important than thorough preparation, they enter their careers ill prepared for the inevitable challenges. Talented individuals often assume college has nothing more to offer them. However, as Albert Einstein noted, "The value of a college education is not the learning of many facts but the training of the mind to think."[47] There are of course notable exceptions such as William Randolph Hearst and Bill Gates who dropped out of prestigious universities such as Harvard and went on to great success.[48] However, emerging leaders who abort their educational preparation may be merely demonstrating a character that is not committed to finishing what they start or they lack a teachable spirit. The same men and women who do not carry through with their training often prove unable or unwilling to stick with difficult assignments later in their careers. The way people handle their preparation for leadership is a strong indicator of the kind of leaders they will eventually become.

Obviously not all learning comes through formal education, but a good education must not be discounted as an important means of preparation. The Old Testament leader who towers over the rest is Moses. But before Moses became a leader, he received a good education. He became a thinker, the systematic theologian of the Old Testament. Apart from Jesus there is no more influential leader in the New Testament than the apostle Paul. He, too, was a thinker, the systematic theologian of the New Testament. Paul studied under Gamaliel, who was considered one of the greatest minds of his day. Both Moses and Paul spent time learning how to think. This is the contribution formal education provides leaders.

In 1944, Leander McCormick-Goodheart, a recruiter for the Ford Motor Company, toured fifty universities across the United States to recruit the outstanding graduating student of each institution. At Lehigh University he met a young man named Lee Iacocca and offered him a position at Ford. This was a dream come true for Iacocca. His life's ambition was to work for Ford. Yet Iacocca asked if he could delay his employment for one year. He had the opportunity to earn a master's degree from Princeton University. Even though the ambitious Iacocca had the opportunity to launch his meteoric automaking career immediately upon graduation, he determined to be fully prepared for whatever opportunities might await him in the future. Spiritual leaders, especially those who will lead Christian organizations, are no less obligated to properly prepare themselves at the outset of their careers.

Howard Gardner, in his book *Leading Minds*, suggests there are both direct and indirect forms of leadership. Whereas Franklin Roosevelt, Winston Churchill, and Joseph Stalin wielded direct influence over others through their political power, thinkers such as Albert Einstein exercised indirect influence over people that in many ways was more profound and long-lasting. Thinkers lead with their minds. They cut new paths through traditional ways of thinking and solving problems. They envision new paradigms. They break through stereotypical, limiting traditions and offer fresh insights into organizational effectiveness.[49] In January 1931, Albert Einstein and his wife Elsa visited America. They were given a tour of the enormous telescope at Mount Wilson, California, by Edwin Hubble. When Elsa Einstein was informed that the massive equipment she was viewing was used to measure the scope and shape of the universe, Mrs. Einstein proudly retorted, "Well, my husband does that on the back of an old envelope."[50] While few if any mortals have the luxury of Einstein's mental capacity, effective leaders nonetheless use their cognitive skills to see possibilities and to discover solutions to problems others are unable to imagine. Effective leaders are not necessarily more brilliant than others. They simply learn to focus their attention on solving problems and seeing possibilities. Daniel Goleman notes, "Attention is our greatest resource."[51] While Goleman focuses on emotional intelligence, the reality is leaders influence what they give their attention to—whether people, problems, or the future. When leaders carefully reflect on past experiences (both successes and failures), they gain invaluable insight. As Michael and Deborah Jinkins point out: "We do not learn from our experience. We learn from disciplined reflection on experience."[52] It was said that Dwight Eisenhower's great strength lay in his "attention to detail, complemented by his intuitive knowledge of which detail to pay attention to."[53] People who thoughtfully analyze their situation, evaluate their leadership behavior, consider every possibility, and, most importantly, seek God's guidance, will regularly experience leadership success.

Thinkers have exerted the longest lasting influence on history. In fact, the time line of history can be divided according to the emergence of leaders who envisioned reality differently than people previously understood it. Historians mark the beginning of the Protestant Reformation from the time a lowly German monk named Martin Luther questioned the commonly accepted thinking about God and man. Likewise, his namesake, Martin Luther King Jr., dared to challenge the status quo of his generation.

Such significant leadership does not come about primarily by doing but by thinking. Society-shaking, world-changing, history-making thought is not produced by lackadaisical, idle minds. Warren Bennis laments that too many of today's leaders suffer from "celibacy of the intellect."[54] These are people of action who seldom stop to consider whether their behavior is appropriate or effective. The most effective leaders are those who prepare themselves physically, mentally, and spiritually for whatever God might assign them next.

HUMILITY

Thomas More was one of the most powerful leaders under Henry VIII. His king disliked having him far from his court and on several occasions paid a personal visit to his home. After one such visit More's son-in-law, William Roper, praised his father-in-law for his influence over the powerful monarch. More humbly replied: "I thank our Lord, son, I find his Grace my very good lord indeed, and I believe he doth as singularly favour me as any subject in his realm. Howbeit, son Roper, I may tell thee I have no cause to be proud thereof, for if my head could win him a castle in France . . . it should not fail to go."[55] More had an accurate view of himself and others, and as a result he did not allow his ego to blind him to reality.

In his book *Good to Great*, Jim Collins examined the characteristics of the most successful business leaders whom he labeled "Level 5 leaders." He found, perhaps surprisingly, that they were characterized by humility: "Level 5 leaders channel their ego needs away from themselves and into the larger goal of building a great company. It is not that Level 5 leaders have no ego or self-interest, indeed they are incredibly ambitious—but their ambition is first and foremost for the institution, not themselves."[56] In a later work Collins said companies that suffered a dramatic decline generally did so because of what he called, "hubris born of success."[57]

According to Collins, Level 5 leaders do not lack confidence, but they realize how tenuous their success is, and they recognize they are involved in a work far greater than themselves. Collins identifies Abraham Lincoln as one of America's few Level 5 presidents. In choosing his cabinet, Lincoln knew he was facing his nation's gravest hour. Unlike his predecessor, James Buchanan, who filled his cabinet with friends and supporters, Lincoln chose men who ran against him for his party's leadership and who, to a man, thought they were more suited to lead the nation than he. Yet Lincoln set his pride aside for the good of his nation. Lincoln explained: "We needed the strongest men of the party in the cabinet. . . . I looked the party over and concluded that these were the very strongest men. Then I had no right to deprive the country of their services."[58] Earlier, in Lincoln's career as a lawyer, he was snubbed by a prominent attorney named Edwin Stanton. In unconcealed disdain Stanton called Lincoln a "long armed ape" and shunned his services.[59] Later, when he was president, Lincoln needed a minister of war. Concluding that Stanton was the best available man, he enlisted him. General Ulysses S. Grant rose to become Lincoln's top field commander, not because he bore himself with the superiority commensurate to his position as a general but because of his humility in the midst of success. When Lincoln first brought Grant to Washington, the general did not impress people with his elegance or sophistication. Rather, his biographer claimed that "Grant's modesty captured the nation's imagination."[60] Both Lincoln and Grant possessed what Tim Irwin describes as "humble confidence."[61] Ironically, few things are as powerful as leaders who view themselves with an accurate and humble perspective.

COURAGE

Concerning the first Battle of Manassas, Lieutenant John Newton Lyle of the 4th Virginia later confessed, "I was scared. I said all the prayers I knew, even to 'Now I lay me down to sleep,' and threw in some shorter catechism and scripture for good measure." Then he spied Stonewall Jackson who "rode about in that shower of death as calmly as a farmer about his farm when the seasons are good." As Jackson rode along the lines of infantry his voice could be heard above the uproar saying, "'All's well, all's well' distinct and in tones as soothing as those of a mother to a frightened child. The repose of his face was of itself reassuring."[62] Benjamin Disraeli, the popular Victorian prime minister of Britain, mused near the end of his life: "You will find as you grow older . . . that courage is the rarest of all qualities to be found in public men."[63]

Great leaders demonstrate courage. Military leaders such as Hannibal, Alexander the Great, and Caesar were famous for their fearlessness in battle. Lord Nelson, the hero of Trafalgar, declared: "I am of the opinion the boldest measures are the safest."[64] But effective leaders also instill courage in their followers, as Franklin Roosevelt did in his now-famous exhortation to his nation: "The only thing we have to fear is fear itself."[65] During a World War II battle, General Patton came upon some officers who seemed more concerned about their personal safety than about leading their men. The bombastic general shouted, "Do you want to give your men the idea that the enemy is dangerous?"[66] At the battle of Princeton during the American Revolutionary War, the British routed the Philadelphia militia and began turning the tide of the battle. George Washington raced upon the fleeing revolutionary soldiers shouting, "Parade with us, brave fellows! . . . There is but a handful of the enemy and we will have them directly."[67] The courageous general personally led the bayonet charge, hat in hand, waving his troops forward to victory. Washington's courage is legendary. After one battle he famously mused: "I heard the bullets whistle, and believe me there is something charming in the sound."[68]

Courage is not an absence of fear. Courage is being frightened and yet doing the right thing anyway. The ancient Greeks understood courage was a foundational virtue. Without it, people might know what they should do but not resolve to do it. Seth Godin offers his own view of the famous Peter Principle. He claims, "In every organization everyone rises to the level at which they become paralyzed by fear."[69] When leaders reach a point where fear prevents them from acting, they and their organization stagnate. Some pastors know they should confront sinful behavior in their congregation, but they dread the repercussions. Some businesspeople lack the resolve to take a stand on moral principle because they fear for their career. The difference between great leaders and ordinary people is not necessarily that one knew what to do and the other did not. It is often that they both knew what should be done, but only one had the courage to act.

Conclusion

Whether you are a CEO, pastor, school administrator, parent, committee chairperson, or government official, you should periodically review your leadership performance. Ask yourself these questions: "Why are people following me? Is it because they are paid to do so? Is it because they can't find a better job? Is it because they believe it is their duty? Or do they see God's work and recognize his hand on my life? Do I have a track record of success? If my employees received more lucrative job offers, would they choose to remain with me? If a larger congregation providing more extensive programs were located near my church, would my people continue in my church? What motivates my people to follow?" Spiritual influence does not come automatically, haphazardly, or easily. It is not something upon which leaders can insist. It is something God must produce.

Legitimate Sources of Influence

1. God's Hand
2. Integrity
3. Successful Track Record
4. Preparation
5. Humility
6. Courage

───── Responding to This Material ─────

1. What character qualities do you possess that attract people to follow you? What character qualities do you have that hinders your leadership?

2. List the evidence that God's hand is on your leadership. If there is no manifest evidence, what ought you to do?

3. Are you known as a person of unimpeachable integrity? If so, what is the evidence? If not, why not?

4. Take a piece of paper and write out the leadership roles you have had. Beside each one, list a number between 1 and 10 with 10 being the highest, to rate the success of each of your roles and assignments. Then go back and review your track record. What does it suggest to you? Have you consistently been successful? Did you learn from earlier failures to become more successful later on? Or have you left a trail of repeated mistakes without any evidence of

growth? Regardless of what your record reveals, take some time with God to ask him what his evaluation of your leadership history is and what he wants to do now to make you a better leader.

5. Have you taken time to fully prepare yourself for your leadership role? Are there classes, books, or seminars you could take to improve your leadership? If so, why have you not availed yourself of them? What actions will you take to improve your skills in the near future?

6. Are you known as a person of humility? Is that a character quality you are pursuing? How might God help you develop humility in the coming days? Are you willing to cooperate in that work?

7. Are you a courageous person? Is there something in your life right now that you know you should do, but you have not? Is a lack of courage preventing you from taking steps God is asking you to take?

Chapter Seven

The Leader's Influence:
How Leaders Lead

When Horatio Nelson assumed command of the British fleet that would meet Napoleon's navy at Trafalgar, most of the British sailors had never served under him. Yet Nelson's reputation and the adoration of those who knew him were such that the mood of the seventeen thousand men dramatically changed upon realizing Nelson was among them. One of Nelson's former officers explained: "Lord Nelson was an admiral, every inch of him . . . yet never was a commander so enthusiastically loved by men of all ranks from the captain of the fleet to the youngest ship boy."[1] It is one thing to know where an organization should go. It is quite another to lead it there. For some people exerting influence comes naturally. They enter a room and immediately command peoples' attention and respect. People defer to them automatically, instinctively recognizing their inherent authority.

Conversely, some people aspire to lead but desperately struggle to gain a following. They do all they know to do to wield influence upon others but in vain. They grow increasingly frustrated because no one listens to them or values their insights and opinions. James MacGregor Burns poignantly observes: "Much of what passes as leadership—conspicuous position-taking without followers or follow through, posturing on various public stages, manipulation without general purpose, authoritarianism—is no more leadership than the behavior of small boys marching in front of a parade, who continue to strut along main street after the procession has turned down a side street toward the fairgrounds."[2]

The ability to influence others is an essential requirement for leadership. To quote Oswald Sanders: "Leadership is influence, the ability of one person to influence others."[3] The previous chapter outlined leadership qualities that generate respect from followers: God's hand upon leaders, integrity, a successful track record, preparation, humility, and courage. Leaders bring these qualities with them because of who they *are*. But what must leaders *do* to influence people? In other words, how do leaders lead?

When Horatio Nelson assumed command of the British fleet, his sailors cheered him because they knew of his past exploits. His leadership and daring were legendary. His reputation, however, was not enough. At a certain point the decorated admiral had to move his fleet into action to tackle the challenge looming before him. Leadership begins with *being* but ultimately results in *doing*. While one's credentials, reputation, past success, and bearing may all gain peoples' attention and initial respect, performance is what ultimately confirms people as true leaders.

A person, no matter how gifted or qualified, has not led unless people have followed. How do spiritual leaders accomplish this? Great leaders appear to do it instinctively. Alexander the Great led his band of soldiers to the end of the known world. Hannibal took his men on a thousand-mile, treacherous journey over the Alps and then fended off Roman legions in Italy for sixteen years. Martin Luther challenged the most powerful institution of his day and transformed the Western world. Martin Luther King Jr. led a group of disenfranchised people and transformed his society. While these leaders might not have been able to clearly articulate why people followed them, leaders can act in specific ways that greatly enhance their influence over others. The following are some of the major tools of spiritual influence.

Leaders Pray

Seth Godin, though not a Christian writer, notes: "Faith is the unstated component in the work of a leader. . . . Without faith, it's suicidal to be a leader."[4] Leaders must have faith in their cause as well as the likelihood of success, or else no one else will believe. Someone who is racked with worry and fear will not inspire others. Those leaders who believe change is possible align their conduct and conversations with their faith.

Spiritual leaders ultimately place their faith in God. They do this because they know God has called them and that whatever God begins he also completes (Phil. 1:6). Perhaps the clearest way leaders demonstrate their faith in God is through their prayer life. The leader's prayer life is critical for several reasons. First, nothing of eternal significance happens apart from God. Jesus declared: "You can do nothing without Me" (John 15:5). Leaders who neglect a close relationship with Christ will not achieve God's will through their organizations. It's that simple. Yet leaders often struggle to pray. They typically are doers, and many view prayer as a passive activity. We know a pastor who confessed: "It's fine to pray and ask God what he wants to do through your church. But I prefer to be proactive rather than reactive." May God have mercy on his church. Leaders are men and women of action. They are wired to obtain results. They are busy people with full schedules. Taking time to pray can appear to be wasting precious time. Prayerless leaders can keep full schedules only to discover later that despite their best efforts, little of eternal consequence occurred. Biblical praying can be the most challenging, exhausting, laborious, and yet rewarding thing leaders do.

Second, prayer is fundamental because to be a spiritual leader, one must be filled with the Holy Spirit. Leaders cannot fill themselves with the divine presence. Only God can do that (Eph. 5:18). While all Christians have the Holy Spirit's presence in their lives, the condition of being *filled* by the Holy

Spirit comes through concentrated, fervent, sanctified prayer. God's promise is: "You will seek Me and find Me when you search for Me with all your heart" (Jer. 29:13). Without the Spirit's activity, people may be leaders, but they are not spiritual leaders.

God's wisdom is a third reward for dedicated praying. God knows far more than the best-informed executive (Rom. 8:26–27; 1 Cor. 2:9). He sees the future. He knows the spiritual needs of the leader's staff. He is aware of what turn the economy will take. God knows what he wants to accomplish and how he intends to do it. God's invitation to leaders is, "Call to Me and I will answer you and tell you great and incomprehensible things you do not know" (Jer. 33:3). For leaders to have this relationship available to them and yet choose not to communicate with the one who offers to guide them is a gross dereliction of duty (Luke 18:1–8).

The fourth reason leaders pray is because God is all-powerful. He can do far more than even the most resourceful leaders. God's promise is open-ended: "Keep asking, and it will be given to you. Keep searching, and you will find. Keep knocking, and the door will be opened to you" (Matt. 7:7). If someone is angry with a leader, reconciliation might look impossible. But God can melt the hardest heart. Leaders can be stymied when people refuse to cooperate. But God can change people's attitudes. There are times when even the most powerful CEOs can do nothing but retreat to the privacy of the executive office, pray, and let God work. When Nancy Reagan was diagnosed with a malignant tumor and had to undergo a mastectomy, her husband Ronald, though he was president, realized that even the most powerful executive in the world has limits. Commenting on that day, Reagan confessed: "For all the powers of the president of the United States, there were some situations that made me feel helpless and very humble. All I could do was pray—and I did a lot of praying for Nancy during the next few weeks."[5] The stark truth is life is filled with situations that can only be overcome by God's power. The most powerful position leaders assume is when they kneel.

A fifth reason to pray is that prayer is the leader's foolproof remedy for stress. Leaders are intimately acquainted with pressure. Scripture encourages leaders to cast "all your care on Him, because He cares about you" (1 Pet. 5:7). Most leaders carry a heavy load of responsibility. It may be difficult to find someone with whom to share their concerns. Circumstances may dictate the need for complete confidentiality. But there is one who always stands ready to carry their burden. Christ said his yoke is easy and his burden is light (Matt. 11:28–30). Leaders who allow Christ to carry their emotional and spiritual loads are relieved of enormous pressure and can face the most arduous assignments with peace.

Finally, God reveals his agenda through prayer. Jesus modeled this truth (Mark 1:30–39). At the outset of his public ministry, when Jesus was staying in Peter and Andrew's home, crowds of sick and demon-possessed people came seeking healing. Jesus healed many people until late into the evening. Early the next morning Jesus rose to pray. The people wanted to keep Jesus in their city as the resident healer and they were reluctant to let him go. Had Jesus been a modern leader, he might have reasoned, "I am obviously having success here and receiving a good response from the people. Perhaps I should remain here for a while until my reputation is firmly established." Instead, Jesus sought his Father's will. As Jesus prayed that morning, the Father helped him understand what the crowd's agenda was, and he reaffirmed his will for his Son—to preach and teach in all the towns and villages and eventually to be crucified in Jerusalem. When the disciples found Jesus and told him the entire town was looking for him, Jesus responded, "Let's go to the neighboring villages" (v. 38). Jesus was in regular communion with the Father in prayer, so he was not sidetracked from his assignment.

More than any other single thing leaders do, their prayer life determines their effectiveness. If leaders spend enough time communing with God, the people they encounter will notice the difference. When pastors preach sermons, their people can soon tell whether or not they are speaking out of the overflow of their relationship with God. When leaders counsel others, the wisdom of their words will reveal whether or not they are filled with the Spirit. When leaders of Christian organizations conduct planning meetings with their staff, their people will recognize if the opening prayer is perfunctory or if it is a genuine plea for God to guide the planning process. The holiness of leaders' lives is a direct reflection of the time they spend with God. When spiritual leaders take their task of leading people seriously, they will be driven to their knees in prayer. They will recognize the magnitude of their responsibility. When the Israelites sinned against God and built a golden calf as an idol, God intended to punish them for their sin. But in one of the greatest intercessory prayers recorded in the Bible, Moses pleaded: "Oh, these people have committed a grave sin; they have made for themselves a god of gold for themselves. Now if You would only forgive their sin. But if not, please erase me from the book You have written" (Exod. 32:31–32; cf. Deut. 9:4–21).

What an incredible testimony to the integrity of a spiritual leader. Moses recognized his people's failure as being his failure because he was their leader. He could not stand by and watch them be destroyed even if they deserved it, so he earnestly interceded on their behalf.

When leaders come to the end of their own resources, they will discern that they can do nothing more for their people. Giving speeches will not fix the problem. Issuing memos will change nothing. Enlisting consultants will be futile. Some things can only be achieved through prayer (Ps. 50:15).

LEADING AN ORPHANAGE

George Mueller's name will forever be associated with effective prayer. Through fervent intercession Mueller established an orphanage in Bristol, England in the 1800s. Mueller saw that ministry grow to include the care of two thousand orphans in five orphanages. Mueller traveled over 200,000 miles to share the gospel in forty-two countries. In all that time he never once asked for money. He based his extensive ministry solely on prayer. Mueller also faithfully prayed for people's salvation. At one point in his life he observed:

> In November, 1844, I began to pray for the conversion of five individuals. I prayed every day without a single intermission, whether sick or in health, on land or at sea, and whatever the pressure of my engagements might be. Eighteen months elapsed before the

first of the five was converted. I thanked God and prayed on for the others. Five years elapsed and then the second was converted. I thanked God for the second and prayed on for the other three. Day by day I continued to pray for them, and six years passed before the third was converted. I thanked God for the three, and went on praying for the other two. These two remained unconverted. . . . The man to whom God in the riches of his grace has given tens of thousands of answers to prayer in the self-same hour or day in which they were offered has been praying day by day for nearly thirty-six years for the conversion of these individuals and yet they remain unconverted. But I hope in God, I pray on and look yet for the answer. They are not converted yet, but they will be.[6]

The last man accepted Christ as his Savior after Mueller's death, but each one did. Such was Mueller's trust in God and tenacity in prayer.

The executive office ought to be a prayer center from which fervent intercession emanates on behalf of those in the organization. As God in his grace responds to the leaders' prayers, things will occur that can only be attributed to God. People may not understand why certain dynamics are occurring in the workplace, but the leader will know.

Why Should Leaders Pray?

1. Prayer is essential.
2. Prayer brings the Spirit's filling.
3. Prayer brings God's wisdom.
4. Prayer accesses God's power.
5. Prayer relieves stress.
6. Prayer reveals God's agenda.

Leaders Work Hard

Few people have changed the world without working hard. Becoming a leader does not mean one has "made it" and is now exempt from strenuous effort. Rather, leaders dramatically influence the culture of their organizations through their work habits. What could discourage employees and volunteers any more than lazy leaders?

History's great leaders knew they could accomplish much throughout the day so they typically began their days at an early hour. Admiral Nelson commenced his day at five, walking the decks.[7] The Duke of Wellington's philosophy was that when it was time to "roll over" in bed it was time to "roll out."[8] He was fastidious about doing "the business of the day in the day."[9] U.S. presidents were often early risers. Martin Van Buren got up at 4:30.[10] John Quincy Adams normally rose between five and six.[11] Lyndon Johnson was a notoriously hard worker, rising at seven and often working until after midnight.[12] The reason some people achieve far more than others is that, quite simply, they work harder.

Leaders should set the example when it comes to work ethic. While the leaders' role prevents them from spending all their time laboring alongside their people on the shop floor, they can seek to encourage their followers by their personal example. Leaders should ask themselves, "If the people in my organization worked with the same intensity as I do, how productive would our organization be?"

This means if the pastor urges his members to volunteer at a workday at the church on Saturday, he is there in his work clothes, not in his study finishing off Sunday's sermon. If the store manager asks the clerks to stay an extra hour to do inventory, she is there counting too. A leadership position does not provide immunity from sacrifice; it actually provides occasions for greater effort.

The twelve men Jesus called to follow him were accustomed to long hours and hard work, but no one worked harder than Jesus. After Jesus fed the five thousand, he allowed his disciples to depart for a much-needed respite while he remained to disperse the multitude (Mark 6:45–46). On another occasion

Jesus ministered to the crowds until he was so exhausted even a raging storm could not awaken him as he slept in the back of a fishing boat (Luke 8:22–24). At other times Jesus would forgo meals so he could minister to people (John 4:31–34). Jesus taught his disciples not just with words but by example. Even when Jesus' disciples suffered persecution, they knew their Lord provided a model for suffering (Matt. 10:24–25).

Great military leaders understood there are times when they must lead their troops by example rather than exclusively by command. Hannibal, Caesar, Alexander the Great, and George Washington were known for charging to the front of their troops when their men began to waver and lose heart. When Caesar's legions were being overcome by the terrifying German warriors, Caesar raced to the front, calling out to his centurions by name.[13] George Washington miraculously survived many close calls from the enemy when he refused to retreat to safety while his men were under fire. When Alexander the Great was advancing upon an enemy city, his fatigued troops were reluctant to scale its walls. So Alexander climbed over the battlements and began fending off enemy soldiers. His chagrined troops frantically scaled the wall to rescue their zealous king. An enemy arrow seriously wounded Alexander, but his forces won another decisive victory. While his actions were unconventional for a commanding general, Alexander knew the power of motivating by example and such leadership inspired his men to conquer the known world.[14]

On May 28, 1970, Colonel Norman Schwarzkopf landed his command helicopter at the site where one of his companies inadvertently wandered into a minefield. As an injured soldier was being airlifted to base, a second soldier detonated a mine and began screaming out in pain, unable to escape the deathtrap. Realizing their peril, the rest of the unit panicked. Schwarzkopf assumed responsibility for the endangered troops and entered the minefield to rescue the traumatized soldier. Another mine was detonated twenty yards away, severely wounding a third soldier and injuring Schwarzkopf. Still Schwarzkopf managed to get both wounded men to safety. He clearly understood a truth that Jesus perfectly modeled: true leadership comes through personal sacrifice.[15]

A willingness to sacrifice gives leaders far more authority with their people than does their position on an organizational chart. Mahatma Ghandi's readiness to suffer for the sake of his cause gave him an international influence he would never have achieved by simply commanding his people to march into danger. Martin Luther King Jr.'s letter, written while he was unjustly confined in a Birmingham jail cell, gained the nation's attention. Nelson Mandela spent over twenty-seven years in the formidable prison on Robben Island before he was ultimately awarded the Nobel Prize and his nation's presidency. Corazon Aquino lived in exile with her husband, Benigno Aquino Jr., until he was assassinated upon his return to the Philippines. She ultimately ran for president of the Philippines against the corrupt dictator, Ferdinand Marcos, who presumably authorized her husband's murder. Despite numerous threats and a fraudulent election, Aquino ultimately mobilized the people to overthrow the government and institute a democratic process once again. Aquino would become the first democratically elected woman president and head of state in Asia and would be recognized by *Time* magazine as the Woman of the Year. History is replete with examples of leaders who enjoyed success only after enduring great suffering. Life offers few shortcuts to greatness.

If leaders want their people to arrive at work on time, they must set the standard for punctuality. If leaders want their people to go the extra mile, leaders must go two. If leaders need their people to work late to complete a project, their people should not see them exiting the parking lot promptly at quitting time. If leaders find their organizations filled with selfish, lazy employees, they must understand that each employee is ultimately a microcosm of the organizational culture and a reflection of its leader.

Astute leaders strive to model exemplary behavior before their people. This is not merely to impress people. It is because one of their greatest sources of influence is their example. Conscientious leaders ask themselves, "What do my people see when they watch me at work?"

Contemporary pastors must be particularly concerned about the model they exhibit. Society is often skeptical of the modern minister's work ethic.

Pastors have long endured the critique that they only work one day a week. As a result, ministers should maintain rigorous work habits and their people should know they are doing so. We know a pastor who was at home when the church treasurer stopped by his house near the end of the morning to have a check signed. To her surprise, she was greeted at the door by her disheveled and unshaven pastor. He was wearing an old pair of sweatpants and a ragged T-shirt. The treasurer was using the lunch hour from her secular job to carry out this task as a church volunteer. Could she be faulted for feeling slightly dismayed? Needless to say, the pastor's reputation as an early-rising, hardworking minister was jeopardized.

This leads to a special caution for leaders of Christian or charitable organizations. Leaders' work habits are particularly important in organizations that depend on volunteers. If volunteers are going to donate their time to an organization, they expect their leaders to work as hard as they do. We recall a church staff person who went home two hours early every Wednesday to make up for the time he would spend attending the prayer meeting that evening. He didn't lead the meeting, but his rationale was that, as a staff person, he *had* to attend. It is highly unlikely the accountants, secretaries, teachers, and storekeepers in his church left their jobs early to redeem the time they spent teaching children at the church on those same Wednesday evenings. If pastors want credibility with the businesspeople in their church who rise at six every morning to be at work downtown, then they must demonstrate they are equally diligent in their ministerial calling. When people perceive their leaders to be lazy, they will lose motivation to sacrifice for the organization themselves.

A related issue is dress code. Some ministers pride themselves on wearing jeans and a T-shirt during the week. While that may be fine in some circumstances, a minister who does not dress like the average professional may find he is not treated like other professionals either. Just as Christians are aware that a worldly lifestyle can discredit their Christian witness, so leaders know a careless lifestyle can diminish their credibility in their followers' eyes.

Warren Buffet notes: "A reputation is like fine china . . . expensive to acquire and easily broken."[16] As people observe their leaders, they draw conclusions about what they are like. Some pastors, when making conversation, talk more about their golf games than about God's kingdom. Some ministers are more excited about college football than about answered prayer. People will naturally conclude that whatever their leaders discuss most is what they consider important.

Leadership is hard work. There are no shortcuts. Some people look for easy paths to leadership. They want positions of influence, but they don't want to put time in the trenches. They are the ones who refuse to take a turn in the church nursery but are more than willing to run the preschool program. They are the ones with little Bible knowledge, yet they lobby to be Bible study leaders. They are the ones who seek jobs requiring minimum effort but provide the maximum pay. They revile sacrifice. They flee from hard work. They are dreamers who want others to pay the price for their aspirations. Such people are preeminently unqualified to be spiritual leaders.

Oswald Sanders observes, "If he is not willing to rise earlier and stay up later than others, to work harder and study more diligently than his contemporaries, he will not greatly impress his generation."[17] The reason there are not more great spiritual leaders today is because too few men and women are willing to pay the required price. Spiritual leaders serve the King of kings. The fruits of their work are eternal. Such a responsibility ought to compel them to always give their conscientious best.

Leaders Communicate Effectively

It has been said Abraham Lincoln's speaking went straight to the heart because it came from the heart.[18] On the day Lincoln delivered his Gettysburg Address, he was preceded by Edward Everett who was considered one of the most eloquent orators of that day. Everett's speech lasted over two hours. It was a masterful performance. Lincoln, however, sensed the mood of the moment and delivered his entire address in less than two minutes. Afterward,

Everett commented, "I should be glad . . . if I could flatter myself that I came as near to the central idea of the occasion, in two hours, as you did in two minutes."[19] Lincoln found words that vividly encapsulated the feeling of the moment and resonated with people for generations to come. Terry Pearce notes that authentic communication is a "continual dance between the heart and mind."[20] It is not enough to submit facts to people, however compelling they may be. Compelling leaders also touch peoples' hearts.

Howard Gardner, in *Leading Minds*, observed that most effective leaders exhibit "linguistic intelligence."[21] Not all leaders, however, are blessed with an equal mastery of communication skills. Harry Truman's biographer noted when Truman began making political speeches, "The most that could be said for his early speeches was they were brief."[22] While Thomas Jefferson used written words brilliantly, he hated public speaking. Jonathan Edwards, early in his ministry, preached his lengthy sermons from manuscripts that had to be held close to his face for him to read. Yet his sermon, "Sinners in the Hands of an Angry God," electrified his listeners and was a spark plug for the First Great Awakening.

Great leaders, while not always spellbinding orators, have found words that inspired and rallied their followers. It has been said of Winston Churchill that he "mobilized the English language and sent it into battle."[23] Churchill understood that choosing the right word was crucial to a leader's success. Such famous phrases as, "I have nothing to offer but blood, toil, tears, and sweat" became rallying points for his embattled nation. Yet, despite his obvious giftedness, Churchill's oratorical success came largely as a result of hard work. Churchill suffered from a speech impediment as a boy and labored at his craft before becoming an orator. At an early age he immersed himself in the English classics including Shakespeare and the King James Bible. Churchill's friend F. E. Smith once quipped, "Winston has spent the best years of his life writing impromptu speeches."[24] Churchill understood not all words are equally potent. Some words and phrases ignite people's passions and lodge themselves deeply into people's minds. Kennedy's "Ask not what your country can do for you" speech and Martin Luther King Jr.'s "I have a dream" speech both produced a powerful effect not only upon their audiences but also on generations who have heard them since.

Most leaders may not possess the eloquence of Churchill or Martin Luther King Jr., but they can still be effective communicators. The key to successful communication is lucidity, not verbosity. Ulysses S. Grant was not known for his oratory, but his communication to his officers was a model of clarity. When General Meade sought direction from Grant concerning his approach to the wily General Lee, Grant sent these orders: "Wherever Lee goes, there you will go also."[25] It was precisely such clear and concise communication that ultimately won the war.

Robert Greenleaf suggests this poignant self-check for speakers: "In saying what I have in mind will I really improve on the silence?"[26] Greenleaf also cautions, "From listening comes wisdom, from speaking comes repentance."[27] Leaders must be students of language, vocabulary, and communication. They should read Scripture, classic literature, history, and the writings of the world's great thinkers to expand the arsenal of words at their disposal. Public speakers, such as pastors, must beware of falling into verbal ruts lest their sermons become predictable and monotonous. A dynamic and active mind is better able to germinate fresh insights than a dull, lazy one. Conscientious leaders should also enlist trusted confidantes to evaluate and critique their communication skills. Many pastors have admitted that their loving, candid spouse has done more to enhance their speaking ability than their seminary preaching professor.

Effective leaders are sensitive to the nuances of their words. Jesus was adept at tailoring his words to his audiences. He called James, John, Peter, and Andrew "fishers of men." He spoke to rural audiences in terms of sowing, reaping, and harvest. While the use of buzzwords and marketplace clichés can bring a sense of contemporary relevance to an organization, the important thing to consider is the connotations of such words and phrases. For example, the word *team* is popular in contemporary management theory. Team-building exercises are in vogue, and many churches now use the words coaching or mentoring in place of the term *disciple*. Certainly the word *team* invokes positive connotations. The image of working together toward a common goal is appealing. Good coaches bring out the best in people. However, while several healthy qualities can be developed by participating in teams, spiritual leaders must be sensitive to unbiblical nuances attached to a word. The primary goal of teams is to win. Teams foster competition for positions; there are star players as well as benchwarmers. There are first and second strings as well as those who don't make the cut. For these reasons the word *team* conjures up negative images for some people. That is not to say the concept of teamwork is negative but rather to illustrate the importance of weighing one's words in light of the intended audience and the desire to adhere to biblical principles.

These cautions notwithstanding, spiritual leaders should gain confidence from the fact that when God entrusts assignments to leaders, he also equips them to communicate his message (Exod. 3:10–12; Isa. 6:5–7; Jer. 1:9). The key to effective communication is the Holy Spirit working in the leader's life. This does not negate the leader's obligation to develop linguistic skills. Nonetheless, the Spirit guides leaders to the right words through which to convey truths about the organization. Numerous studies have proven that one of the most effective forms of communication, as we mentioned earlier, is the story.[28] This is because stories speak to both the mind and the heart.

Howard Gardner suggests leaders tell several types of stories.[29] One type concerns the people themselves and helps answer the question, Who am I? People need to know their lives have relevance and they are meaningful contributors to the world around them. Leaders tell stories that give meaning to peoples' efforts and involvement in the organization. Sometimes leaders tell stories from their own lives to help others put their experiences into perspective.[30]

A second type of story pertains to the organization. Leaders explain the reason for the group's existence, perhaps also describing the vision of the organization's founders and chronicling the hardships they endured to make the organization what it is today. Leaders may also relate contemporary stories that describe ways the organization is currently making a positive difference.

Warren Bennis notes, "Leadership without perspective and point of view isn't leadership."[31] Leaders tell stories that address issues of value and meaning to help their people understand what is true, good, and important. Leaders also tell stories about culture, be it the culture of a church, a company, or a family. These stories identify the heroes and highlight what is considered valuable and noteworthy in that organization.

IVAH BATES: A PERSONAL EXAMPLE FROM HENRY BLACKABY

In our book *Experiencing God* we tell the story of Ivah Bates, an elderly widow who was a member of Faith Baptist Church in Saskatoon, Canada, while I was the pastor.[32] When our church began to sense God commissioning us to evangelize university students, Ivah came to see me. She was grieving because there was nothing she could do to help in this endeavor since she was advanced in years and in fragile health. I asked her to be the church's prayer warrior for college students. Whenever there was a Bible study or outreach activity on campus, Ivah was notified and she would pray. One day a college student named Wayne asked the church for prayer as he prepared to share his faith that week with his roommate Doug. The next Sunday Wayne walked to the front of the church with Doug to introduce him as a new believer in Christ. As I looked out over the congregation, I saw Ivah weeping with joy. She played a major role in reaching Doug for Christ, yet she never stepped foot on the campus. Over the years many students thanked Ivah for her role in helping them meet Christ.

I told this story and others like it to our church many times in subsequent years, and it always encouraged our people. What did the story convey? First, it addressed people's identity. Was it possible to be too young or too old, too rich or too poor for God to use them? Absolutely not! Did they have to possess the same skills or education as other people in the church to be valued or useful? No, *every* person was important in our church. The story also explained the way our organization functioned. When God commissioned us to do something, every member had a part to play and every role was important. There were no benchwarmers. There were no first and second string players.

Third, the story conveyed the church's values. Our congregation valued evangelism. Prayer was important. People's contributions were appreciated. Obedience to God was prized. Finally, the story explained the church's culture. Those who were faithful in prayer were heroes. People who shared their faith with others were heroes. Stories such as Ivah's answered so many of the questions people might have concerning our church that I told them often. When visitors to our church heard that story, they knew more about how we functioned than had they read our constitution and bylaws.

Leaders need to develop the habit of telling stories so their people learn to see God at work in their midst. It is the leaders' responsibility to clearly communicate God's activity to their people, for they often have the best vantage point from which to discern it. Pastors will see connections such as Ivah's prayers and Doug's salvation others might miss. Leaders who assume their people will automatically identify God's activity around them are shortchanging their followers.

With today's technology it is irresponsible for leaders to keep their people uninformed. Numerous forums for communication, many of them instantaneous, are easily accessible. That having been said, there is a danger in relying too much on technology. For decades technology has been overrated. Leaders should remember that nothing has yet been devised that has the impact of a face-to-face encounter. Leaders ought to seize every opportunity to speak directly to their people. Breakfast and lunch meetings with employees or volunteers as well as regularly scheduled staff meetings can build morale. Taking the time to walk about work areas speaking directly to people can communicate more than months of newsletters.

Admiral Nelson took it upon himself to personally dine with every captain under his command within three days of assuming command.[33] Alfred Sloan, the famed CEO of General Motors, used to visit between five and ten car dealers every day. He had a special train outfitted so he could travel quickly across the country to keep in touch with those in the field. Sam Walton, founder of Walmart, was famous for appearing at stores across the country unannounced to see how they were doing. Abraham Lincoln spent as much as 75 percent of his time receiving people in his office. Bennis and Nanus found the top CEOs in their studies spent 90 percent of their time with people.[34] Leaders who think they are too busy to be regularly listening to and communicating with their people are doomed to fail.

Leaders Serve

Perhaps the greatest Christian influence on leadership theory has been in the area of "servant leadership." Jesus' example has become the model not just for Christian leaders but also for secular leaders.[35] In all of literature there is no better example of servant leadership than that of Christ on the night of his crucifixion.

> Before the Passover Festival, Jesus knew that His hour had come to depart from this world to the Father. Having loved His own who were in the world, He loved them to the end.
>
> Now by the time of supper, the Devil had already put it into the heart of Judas, Simon Iscariot's son, to betray Him. Jesus knew that the Father had given every thing into His hands, that He had come from God, and that He was going back to God. So He got up from supper, laid aside His robe, took a towel, and tied it around Himself. Next, He poured water into a basin and began to wash His disciples' feet and to dry them with the towel tied around Him.
>
> He came to Simon Peter, who asked, "Lord, are You going to wash my feet?"
>
> Jesus answered him, "What I'm doing you don't understand now, but afterward you will know."
>
> "You will never wash my feet—ever!" Peter said to Him.
>
> Jesus replied, "If I don't wash you, you have no part with Me."
>
> Simon Peter said to Him, "Lord, not only my feet, but also my hands and my head."

"One who has bathed," Jesus told him, "doesn't need to wash anything except his feet, but he is completely clean. You are clean, but not all of you." For He knew who would betray Him. This is why He said, "You are not all clean."

When Jesus had washed their feet and put on His robe, He reclined again and said to them, "Do you know what I have done for you? You call Me Teacher and Lord. This is well said, for I am. So if I, your Lord and Teacher, have washed your feet, you also ought to wash one another's feet. For I have given you an example that you also should do just as I have done for you.

I assure you: A slave is not greater than his master, and a messenger is not greater than the one who sent him. If you know these things, you are blessed if you do them. (John 13:1–17)

Several keys to servant leadership are evident in this passage. First, it flows from the love leaders have for God and their people. Scripture says, "Having loved His own who were in the world, He loved them to the end" (John 13:1). Leaders cannot truly serve people they do not love. They may perform acts of service, but their followers will rightly perceive their actions as insincere and manipulative unless they are done out of genuine concern. Many leaders experience difficulty in this regard because they are unfamiliar with Christlike love. Many grew up in homes where love was in short supply. The result is performance-driven leaders who feel compelled to achieve at all costs, even if it means using or abusing others. Such men and women find it all but impossible to love those they lead. Yet it was the love Jesus showed his disciples (even Judas) that brought him undying loyalty from his followers.

Daniel Goleman suggests the higher in management someone rises, the more important that individual's emotional intelligence, or people skills, becomes.[36] When Kouzes and Posner studied the leadership traits of top CEOs, they found only one characteristic common to all of them: affection. These successful leaders cared for their people, and they wanted their people to like them in return.[37] Even well-paid, educated professionals will perform better when they believe their leader cares about them. In their book

First Break All the Rules: What the World's Greatest Managers Do Differently, Markus Buckingham and Curt Coffman ask, "Should you build close personal relationships with your employees, or does familiarity breed contempt?" To this the authors respond, "The most effective managers say yes, you should build personal relationships with your people, and no, familiarity does not breed contempt."[38]

In leadership, how something is done is often as important as what is done. When a company accomplishes its goals but decimates the lives of its members, it may win the battle but lose the war. Lee Iacocca guided Chrysler through an arduous time and achieved stellar results. But looking back over that period, the celebrated CEO observed: "But our struggle had its dark side. To cut expenses, we had to fire a lot of people. It's like a war: we won, but my son didn't come back. There was a lot of agony. People were getting destroyed, taking their kids out of college, drinking, getting divorced. Overall we preserved the company, but only at enormous personal expense for a great many human beings."[39]

During the 1990s "Chainsaw" Al Dunlop brutally overhauled companies he led to make a quick sale and a tidy profit. Here is John Byrne's description of working for Dunlop: "Working on the front lines of a company run by Al Dunlop was like being at war. The pressure was brutal. The hours exhausting, and the casualties high. . . . By sheer brutality, he began putting excruciating pressure on those who reported to him, who in turn passed that intimidation down the line. . . . People were told, explicitly and implicitly, that either they hit the number or another person would be found to do it for them. Their livelihood hung on making numbers that were not makeable."[40]

Ironically, while secular business grows increasingly aware of its responsibility to care for its people, many religious organizations remain oblivious to this need. Leaders come to Christian organizations filled with righteous zeal to see the Lord's work accomplished. Because they are striving to achieve God's purposes, they assume no price is too great. If downsizing an organization is required, they callously show long-term, loyal employees to the door in a manner that would shame secular business managers. If getting the job done calls for bullying and cajoling people into submission, these religious leaders pressure reluctant employees or church members. No matter how worthwhile a religious organization's goal, it is impossible to believe Jesus would lead in this manner. When leaders don't love their people, they are tempted to use them, to neglect them, and to discard them.

Leaders who are unable to love their people and unwilling to consider their needs are insecure in their own identity. Why could Jesus humble himself and wash his disciples' filthy feet? Scripture says, "Jesus knew that the Father had given everything into His hands, that He had come from God, and that He was going back to God" (John 13:3). Jesus was secure in his identity. His self-worth was not in jeopardy. He knew he was in the center of his Father's will. That made all the difference.

The second requirement for servant leadership is self-knowledge. Leaders must know and accept who they are. Insecure people worry about how others perceive them. They fear serving others may cause people to take advantage of them or to think less of them. Self-confident people are not enslaved by others' opinions. They are free to serve. President Harry Truman was one of the most unpretentious presidents in U.S. history. There was a buzzer on his desk that previous presidents used to summon aides to the oval office. Truman removed it. He refused to buzz people and insisted on going to the door to ask for them politely. During a special reception Truman held for Joseph Stalin and Winston Churchill, Sergeant Eugene List, an American soldier, prepared to play a special piece on the grand piano. When List asked for someone to turn the pages of music for him, Truman volunteered. Throughout the sergeant's brilliant performance, his commander in chief stood by his side turning pages for him. Later List wrote to his wife and marveled, "Imagine having the President of the United States turn pages for you! . . . But that's the kind of man the President is."[41] In recalling his leadership style Truman explained, "I tried never to forget who I was and where I'd come from and where I would go back to."[42] Truman's biographer concluded that because of the way he related to his staff, "The loyalty of those around Truman was total and would never falter. In years to come not one member of the Truman White House would ever speak or write scathingly of him or belittle him in any fashion."[43] Comfort with one's identity is mandatory for servant leaders.

Third, Christlike servant leaders must understand whom they serve. On the topic of servant leadership, there is some confusion about who leaders are actually serving. Spiritual leaders are not their people's servants; they are God's. The account of Jesus washing his disciples' feet is often cited in discussions of servant leadership, and rightly so. But Scripture only records a solitary account of Jesus doing this. Had Jesus been his disciples' servant, he would have washed their feet every evening. Had he been his disciples' servant, he would have granted Peter's request to be excluded from the foot washing. But Jesus was not giving his followers what they wanted; he was doing what his Father instructed him to do. Jesus' response to Peter, therefore, was, "If I don't wash you, you have no part with Me" (John 13:8). The disciples did not set the agenda for Jesus' ministry. The Father did. Jesus served his Father; not his disciples. Even as Jesus ministered to his disciples in this menial way, there was no question he was still their Lord.

When Jesus finished, he concluded, "For I have given you an example that you also should do just as I have done for you" (John 13:15). Jesus was not only attending to his disciples; he was teaching and demonstrating the ethos of his kingdom. Spiritual leaders' acts of service should be motivated and directed by the Holy Spirit. When leaders are unafraid to roll up their sleeves and help their people, they encourage a corporate culture which promotes mutual service. Servanthood breaks down barriers. Jesus' disciples needed to understand they were God's servants. God would call upon them to minister to one another. The Roman Empire would soon feel the tremendous impact of such love.

Leaders Maintain Positive Attitudes

During the battle of Shiloh, the conflict appeared to be going against the Union forces. A surgeon said to General Grant, "General, things are going decidedly against us." To which Grant replied, "Not at all sir. . . .

We're whipping them now!"[44] That evening a light drizzle began to fall. Colonel McPherson reported to Grant and asked, "Under this condition of affairs, what do you propose I do, sir? Shall I make preparations for retreat?" Grant immediately responded, "Retreat? . . . No. I propose to attack at daybreak and whip them."[45] A pessimistic leader is a contradiction in terms. Leaders, by virtue of their role, are obligated to nurture positive attitudes. Allan Leighton notes: "People don't enjoy following leaders whose appearance and demeanor give the impression that they're being led into the valley of death."[46]

Daniel Goleman suggests that leaders transmit their mood to those around them.[47] Leaders confident of success imbue that attitude throughout their organization. Negative leaders breed pessimistic organizations. Leaders who doubt success is possible and who fear the worst should immediately change their attitude or tender their resignation so a true leader can take their place. Some people in leadership positions assume they are simply being realistic when they expect the worst. The implication is positive leaders are being naive. However, true leaders understand that no matter how difficult the challenge before them, a group of people being led by the Holy Spirit can accomplish anything God asks them to (Rom. 8:31).

It is natural for people to grow discouraged in the midst of adversity, but a fundamental role of leaders is to maintain a positive attitude under every circumstance. When George Marshall became the U.S. secretary of state, he was informed spirits were low in the State Department. Marshall advised his staff, "Gentlemen, it is my experience an enlisted man may have a morale problem. An officer is expected to take care of his own morale."[48] If leaders cannot manage their own attitudes, they cannot be entrusted with the morale of others. When leaders believe anything is possible, their followers will come to believe that too. The Duke of Wellington claimed the effect of Napoleon's presence on his troops' morale was worth forty thousand men. It was said General Stonewall Jackson so inspired his troops that if soldiers in camp suddenly let out a yell, this could mean one of two things: either the beloved General Jackson just rode into camp, or someone spotted a rabbit. A biographer of Franklin Roosevelt said, "It was one of the constants of Roosevelt's adult life that he was often engaged in counteracting the pessimism of others, about polio, economic depression, and world war."[49] Winston Churchill has been similarly honored. Reportedly no one left his presence without being a braver man. Leaders inspire confidence, not fear or pessimism.

Good morale is intrinsically linked with a healthy sense of humor. De Pree suggests, "Joy is an essential ingredient of leadership. Leaders are obligated to provide it."[50] Joy was an inherent part of Jesus' ministry (John 15:11; 17:13). Abraham Lincoln reveled in telling humorous stories. Winston Churchill was famous for his quick wit. During World War I, Churchill lectured his officers in the trenches saying, "Laugh a little, and teach your men to laugh. . . . If you can't smile, grin. If you can't grin, keep out of the way until you can."[51] Churchill believed, "You cannot deal with the most serious things in the world unless you also understand the most amusing." Great leaders know when to laugh, and they know how to make others laugh. In 1984, Ronald Reagan was seeking re-election for a second term as United States president. Reagan was seventy-three years old and his opponents were deriding him for what they labeled the "senility factor." If elected, Reagan would be the oldest president in U.S. history. During a televised debate between Reagan and his opponent, former Vice President Walter Mondale, a reporter asked Reagan whether his age would be a handicap in the campaign. Reagan responded, "I am not going to exploit for political purposes my opponent's youth and inexperience."[52] Reagan's quick rejoinder even forced a chuckle out Mondale on national television and helped diffuse a potential land mine on his path back to the White House. While Reagan was serving his first term as president, John Hinckley Jr. shocked the nation by attempting to assassinate him as he left the Hilton Hotel in Washington, D.C. Reagan kept his humor even with a bullet lodged less than an inch from his heart. Upon seeing his wife, Nancy, after the shooting, Reagan quipped, "Honey, I forgot to duck."[53]

A good sense of humor is essential to effective leadership because leaders set the tone for their organizations. Upon Ronald Reagan's death, many reporters and former government officials reminisced about the Reagan White House. One staff member recalled that he could always tell when Reagan returned to the White House by the sound of laughter coming down the hallway as the president approached. Leaders with a healthy sense of humor help others keep perspective during tense situations. The ability to laugh, especially at themselves, reveals that circumstances do not ultimately control a leader's life. Thomas More kept his sense of humor even as he was laying his head on the executioner's block.[54] Spiritual leaders are driven internally by their character, convictions, and relationship to God. They are not sent into a dour mood whenever events are not to their liking.

It is far more pleasurable to work under a joyful leader than a pessimist. Spiritual leaders remain optimistic not only because it enhances morale and therefore their peoples' effectiveness but also because they know God. This is why they need to spend considerable time in the conscious presence of God. Only when they clearly understand who God is will they have gained a proper perspective of their situation (Isa. 40:12–31).

Everyone faces discouraging circumstances, but the Scriptures provide a vista for leaders to maintain or regain a positive attitude. Momentary setbacks are one thing, but many church leaders choose to dwell in the valley of despair. Incredibly some leaders actually pride themselves in being pessimists. They refer to their negative outlook as realism and privately consider it a sign of superior intelligence. After all, they detect problems and things to worry about the rank and file seem to miss. Some pastors, when their attendance dwindled and finances dried up, declared they knew their church could not possibly survive; they were staying only long enough to conduct the imminent funeral. One pastor concluded that since the last three churches he "led" all disbanded, God must have given him a ministry of helping churches shut down. He was serious. Such foolishness is an abomination to almighty God! These people desperately need a fresh encounter with the risen Lord so they will believe that, with God, all things are possible (Matt. 17:20; Luke 1:37). Henry's guiding life verse has been Daniel 3:17, "Our God whom we serve is able, . . . and he will . . ." (KJV).

We know of a small church that suffered years of decline. The remaining members were discouraged and ready to give up. Pastors came and went, but the church continued its downward spiral. The church facility was so neglected sections of it no longer met civic safety codes. Two-thirds of the facility was being rented to an ethnic congregation in order to generate desperately needed income. Pastors complained for years that the church's location made it almost impossible for visitors to find. Time after time ministers would grow frustrated with the church and the abysmal results and they would resign in discouragement. Rumor had it the church was actually demon possessed and this was the reason for its chronic failure. After many years in spiritual limbo, it appeared there was little left for the church to do but disband.

In a final act of desperation, the church called a young pastor fresh out of seminary. There was little to offer the minister and his young family by way of pay or benefits, but he agreed to come. The newly installed cleric refused to believe God was finished with the church or God was unable to use it to impact its community. He encouraged the people to pray. God began working. New people began visiting and joining the membership. Renovations were made to the facility. Revenues increased. A second staff person was added. A sense of excitement grew among the people that God was preparing their church for something special. The church's reputation in the community changed. It was no longer considered dead but became known as one of the most dynamic churches in the city.

What happened? The church continued to meet in the same facility in the same poor location. The pastor worked with the identical people previous ministers castigated. The surrounding community was just as hardened to the gospel as it ever was. Everything was the same except one fact.

The church now had a leader who believed that with God all things are possible, and he convinced his people to believe it too.

When Colonel Norman Schwarzkopf arrived to take command of his battalion in Vietnam, the outgoing commander met to brief him. This is how Schwarzkopf recalls the meeting:

"Come on back to my hooch," he said. "I need to talk to you a little." We drove about a mile to the battalion base camp, which was
at the bottom of a hill, and then walked to a little cabin halfway
up the hillside. On the table sat a bottle of Johnnie Walker Black
Label scotch. "This is for you," he said. "You're going to need it." I
was expecting a two- or three-hour discussion of the battalion, its
officers, its NCOs, its mission—but he only said, "Well, I hope
you do better than I did. I tried to lead as best I could, but this
is a lousy battalion. It's got lousy morale. It's got a lousy mission.
Good luck to you." With that he shook my hand and walked out.[55]

Schwarzkopf's predecessor was obviously not a leader. A true leader
would not have called his battalion lousy; he would have made it better. He
would not have accused his soldiers of lousy morale; he would have improved
their spirits. He would not have complained about the mission; he would have
accomplished and enlarged their assignment. This man pointed the finger of
blame at everyone and everything but himself. No wonder he failed.

In contrast, Schwarzkopf kept a positive attitude. It was not that he
overlooked his battalion's problems or shortcomings. He recognized them
better than his predecessor. By the time Schwarzkopf was finished with
his troops, morale was up and casualties were down. In fact, the Vietcong
concluded that a new, much tougher battalion had moved into the area and
replaced the previous, inept unit.

Norman Schwarzkopf gained worldwide attention for his handling of
the Gulf War. But throughout his career he succeeded in every task he was
given. His success was not based on easy assignments. Often he was given
difficult posts. Yet when others might have complained and cast blame, he
set out to improve each situation and to improve his unit. The reason he was
the chief of command during the Gulf War was because he built a career out
of strengthening whatever organization he was assigned to command. Great
leaders don't make excuses. They make things better. They are not unrealistic
or blind to the difficulties. They simply are not discouraged by them. They

never lose confidence that problems can be solved. They maintain a positive attitude. Great leaders don't blame their people for not being where they ought to be; they take them there. True leaders never lose faith that this is possible.

Leaders should pay close attention to their attitudes, for these serve as barometers to the condition of their hearts. When leaders become pessimistic, cynical, or critical, they need to evaluate the cause. They obviously need a fresh encounter with God. A wise practice for those in leadership roles is inviting some of their close friends and associates to help monitor their attitudes. Making oneself accountable to a small group of trusted people can ensure an unhealthy outlook is quelled before it harms both the leader and the organization.

Leaders Encourage Others

On August 2, 216 BC, an officer named Gisgo gazed upon eighty-seven thousand Roman soldiers preparing to attack him and his comrades. Seeing his commander, Hannibal, Gisgo expressed grave concern that the enormous Roman army spread before them dwarfed their own Carthaginian force. Hannibal, sensing his young lieutenant's trepidation, replied, "Yes, Gisgo, you are right. But there is one thing you may not have noticed. . . . Simply this; that in all that great number of men opposite there isn't a single one called Gisgo."[56] As Hannibal and his officers laughed together with Gisgo, the nearby troops noticed their commander's confidence in the face of the looming conflict and gained new zeal. The Battle of Cannae would feature one of the most brilliant military maneuvers in history, utterly destroying the Roman army and propelling Hannibal into legend.

Leaders do not become great by personally accomplishing impressive results but by motivating others to achieve notable victories. The world's finest leaders have known how to inspire their people to elevate their efforts to the highest levels. Leaders do this by encouraging their followers. While leaders must be internally motivated, followers are often less so. Followers can grow discouraged and fearful. This is when sagacious leaders find ways to bolster their peoples' spirits.

There are at least three primary ways to encourage followers. The first is through a leader's *presence*. It can be demoralizing to serve on the front lines while the officers are safely ensconced at the rear, far from danger. The best leaders find ways to be present with their people. Before the Normandy invasion, General Eisenhower visited twenty-six divisions, twenty-four airfields, and five ships to personally encourage his troops.[57] After every Union defeat, President Lincoln travelled to the front lines to support the troops.[58] Before a battle, the Duke of Marlborough passed down the ranks of his men, several thousand each day, until he had looked his men in the eye. He felt if he were to send them into battle, he owed it to them to have acknowledged them personally. Commanders such as Caesar and Hannibal suffered the same deprivations as their men. Robert E. Lee shared the same rations as his troops.[59]

When Admiral Nelson happened upon a young sailor who was terrified of climbing the masthead, he did not condemn the raw recruit or throw him in irons for cowardice. Rather, Nelson challenged him to a race to the top and then began playfully climbing in earnest. Throughout the ascent Nelson laughed and joked with the sailor, observing how climbing to the top was not nearly as frightening as some made it out to be.[60] Such encouragement of his men endeared him to them for life. Corporate executives should practice MBWA (management by walking around). Whether leaders can speak to every person on the shop floor is not as important as the fact they are occasionally *observed* walking the shop floor. Sam Walton was famous for appearing in the truck drivers' break room at four o'clock in the morning with a bag of doughnuts so he could question them about what they were seeing in the stores to which they made deliveries.[61] A common practice is for executives to hold regular breakfasts, lunches, or other roundtable meetings with those several organizational levels below them to get to know those employees and to discover how to make work more rewarding and productive for those employees. Executives who remain aloof in their corner office are deprived of valuable information and forego the opportunity to dramatically strengthen company morale.

A second way leaders encourage people is through their *words*. People need to be recognized as individuals and commended for their contributions. General Sherman could call five thousand of his men by their first name.[62] Henry Ford's biographer claimed the automaker could get his people to do anything for him by the way he spoke to them and inspired them.[63] Great generals understood that encouragement of their troops could make the difference between victory and defeat. Napoleon's dictum was, "Give me enough ribbon to place on the tunics of my soldier's and I can conquer the world."[64] During a pivotal moment in a battle, the Duke of Marlborough happened upon one of his generals beating a hasty retreat with his force of cavalry. Marlborough quickly rode up to them and commanded them to halt. Marlborough cried out, "Mr. ___, you are under a mistake; the enemy lies that way: You have nothing to do but to face him and the day is your own." With that the chagrined officer did an about-face and plunged his force back into the fray.[65] At the close of his illustrious career, the Duke of Wellington was asked if he had any regrets. His response: "Yes, I should have given more praise."[66]

Third, leaders encourage their people through personal *concern* for their welfare. Generals such as Caesar, Marlborough, Wellington, and Eisenhower were famous for procuring the best supplies available for their troops. It was said of Andrew Jackson when he was a general, "It was a mark of Jackson's leadership that he personally supervised the care of his men and concerned himself with every detail of their physical well-being. He had great pride in them, as he had in himself, and was extremely solicitous of their welfare. Over the years the men had come to know this, and they reciprocated with respect and devotion."[67] When General Andrew Jackson marched his men five hundred miles home, he turned over his three horses to transport those who were sick and he walked the entire distance with his men.[68] It was such care for those he led that made him one of the most popular leaders of his era.

Leaders Focus

One of leaders' most valuable tools is their attention. Leaders who accomplish much must focus on the critical issues at hand until they grasp them fully and discern the solution. Andrew Carnegie became enormously wealthy by following the mantra: "Put all your eggs in one basket and then watch that basket."[69] Those who knew Warren Buffet as a young man claimed that he "was a very focused person. He could focus like a spotlight, twenty-four hours a day almost, seven days a week."[70] Walt Disney was said to have "tremendous powers of concentration."[71] John Rockefeller once asked: "Do not many of us fail to achieve big things . . . fail because we lack concentration—the art of concentrating the mind on the thing to be done at the proper time and to the exclusion of everything else?"[72] While J. P. Morgan was not disposed to prolonged, systematic analysis, one of his contemporaries observed: "Morgan has one chief mental asset—a tremendous five minutes' concentration of thought."[73]

Today's leaders must learn to focus because modern problems, opportunities, and challenges are complex and not readily understood or easily dealt with. During the early 1870s, John Rockefeller visited a Standard Oil plant in New York City that filled and sealed five gallon barrels of kerosene for export. He noticed the workers applying forty drops of solder to each barrel. Rockefeller suggested they try thirty-eight drops. When a few cans leaked, he settled on thirty-nine drops per barrel. In the first year that one less drop saved the company $2,500. Over the ensuing years as exports multiplied, the oil man's keen attention saved his company a small fortune.[74] Focus enables leaders to accurately assess a situation. It was said of George Washington, "seeing things as they were, and not as he would wish them to be, was one of his salient strengths."[75]

The fact is, followers will look where the leader is looking. If problem solving is the leader's concern, the organization will zero in on solving its problems. If the leader's gaze is fixed on the vision, then the people will follow suit. That is why leaders must discern what is most important in their organization and refuse to be sidetracked by secondary matters. Thomas

Jefferson worked closely with George Washington and Benjamin Franklin during the formative years of the United States. He observed of those two men: "I never heard either of them speak ten minutes at a time nor to any but the main point which was to decide the question. . . . They laid their shoulders to the great points, knowing the little ones would follow of themselves."[76]

Effective leadership does not happen by chance. It occurs on purpose. Anyone can exercise certain leadership practices if he or she is serious about becoming an effective leader. Those who diligently follow these seven guidelines are well on their way to becoming influential spiritual leaders.

Leaders' Influence

1. Leaders Pray
2. Leaders Work Hard
3. Leaders Communicate Effectively
4. Leaders Serve
5. Leaders Maintain Positive Attitudes
6. Leaders Encourage Others
7. Leaders Focus

Leading a Movement

Leadership occurs at various levels. A mother who steers her children through the various developmental stages is leading. People may lead a committee at their church, a division in their company, a battalion in the army, or an arm of government. While all leadership has certain similarities, its scope can widely vary. Ordinary leaders lead followers. Great leaders lead leaders. Extraordinary leaders lead movements. With the global challenges facing society today, incremental changes are inadequate. Movements are required.

Movements are larger than one person or organization. They impact large numbers of people and cannot be controlled. Malcolm Gladwell popularized the concept of the "tipping point." He claims a tipping point is "the moment of critical mass, the threshold, the boiling point" where an idea, product, message, or behavior becomes a movement.[77] This is the point where an idea or behavior graduates from a local manifestation into something much larger. Max De Pree suggests, "A movement is a collective state of mind, a public and common understanding that the future can be created, not simply experienced or endured."[78] Movements do not grow incrementally but exponentially. They expand more rapidly than leaders can control. That is why to exert leadership in a movement one must be willing to surrender control. This phenomenon has been seen in the growth of secular industries such as automobiles and computers and in the colossal proliferation of the Internet and social networking. Divine movements such as spiritual awakenings have also spread rapidly across a nation, a continent, and the globe.

Spiritual awakenings are particularly explosive because they are animated not merely by human efforts but by the dynamic working of the Holy Spirit. In every large revival you can find leaders who were integrally involved, but it becomes clear that far more happened than can be explained by the efforts of talented leaders. In 1857, the North Dutch Church on Fulton Street in Manhattan enlisted Jeremiah Lanphier to lead the congregation's evangelistic efforts. The metropolis was filled with people whose faith in God was cold or nonexistent. After several failed attempts to impact the massive city, Lanphier announced a noon hour prayer meeting at the church on September 23, 1857. Only six people showed up. The second week twenty came, with forty attending the following week. In the fourth week there was a devastating crash of the financial markets. Businesses went bankrupt by the score, and thousands of people were thrown out of work. The prayer meetings were changed to daily events, and soon the North Dutch Church could not contain the crowds so the meetings spread to other locations. At one count dozens of prayer meetings were being held across Manhattan at the noon hour with thousands of people attending. Lanphier continued to be involved, but his name fades from the record as the revival movement spread across America and ultimately ignited similar revivals around the world, as far away as Great Britain and South Africa. Out of an American population at that time of thirty million people, one million were added to churches in America in one year. J. Edwin Orr, a leading authority on revivals, described this movement as "The Event of the Century."[79]

The problem, as De Pree notes, is that "movements tend to deteriorate into mere organizations."[80] Often a movement arises out of a general need sensed by a large number of people. People are motivated to make supreme efforts for the cause. There is a sense of unity and purpose among those involved in the effort. However, as more people join the campaign, efforts are made to administer and control it. Staff is hired, buildings are constructed, operations manuals become necessary, and the once dynamic, rapidly growing phenomenon is institutionalized. Its life ebbs away into bureaucracy.[81] Leaders by nature want to be in control. Most leaders think no further than administering an organization. Few think in terms of movements. The world is changed by movements, not incremental, planned growth. The world searches for the next movement in technology, philosophy, health, or entertainment. God is looking for someone through whom he can change the world (2 Chron. 16:9). Our day desperately calls for a fresh movement of God. The question is: Who will God choose through whom to launch it?

Stewardship of Influence

Influence is a powerful force in human affairs that carries tremendous responsibility. Therefore, a weighty issue for leaders is their management of influence. When people trust their leaders, they give them the benefit of the doubt. Such power can seduce leaders into using people to achieve their own ambitious ends. Influence used selfishly is nothing more than crass manipulation and political scheming. People need to know their leaders have their best interests at heart.

Leaders should realize that even when they say things casually, their people may take them seriously. Such was the case with David. David was camped outside Bethlehem with his men while a Philistine garrison occupied Bethlehem. In an unguarded moment, David remarked wistfully, "If only someone would bring me water to drink from the well at the city gate of Bethlehem!" (2 Sam. 23:15). Immediately, three of his loyal men set out for the well. David's friends fought their way through a contingent of Philistine soldiers until they reached the coveted water. When they returned with their prize, David was appalled at what he had done. By his selfish wish, three of his most loyal soldiers endangered their lives for something unnecessary. In that instance David was careless with his influence.

Are leaders' moral failures anyone's business but their own? A great deal of controversy surrounds this issue. Some contend (1) everyone fails at some point and (2) personal failure does not affect one's administrative skills and effectiveness. But when leaders experience moral failure, the repercussions are devastating. Leaders are symbols of their organizations. They are the repositories of their people's trust. When they prove untrustworthy, they shatter their peoples' faith and confidence. Leaders assume a higher level of accountability because there is more at stake if they fail. When God appoints spiritual leaders, he also holds them accountable for their influence (2 Cor. 5:9–11; James 3:1). Spiritual leaders should never accept new leadership positions without prayerful consideration. Modern society is reeling under the incessant scandals of leaders who abused their positions of influence. People trust leaders less than ever because so many of them have handled their positions irresponsibly. The good news is people today are eager to find someone who knows how to exert a positive influence on their lives. God gives spiritual leaders the ability and opportunity to do that. Few endeavors can bring the same level of joy and satisfaction than influencing people to achieve God's best for them and for their organization (2 Tim. 4:8).

─────────────── **Responding to This Material** ───────────────

1. Evaluate your prayer life. If God's blessing on your leadership were based solely on the quality of your prayer life, what results would you anticipate?

2. Evaluate your work ethic. Would you want everyone in your organization to follow your example? How do you think your people perceive your work habits?

3. Evaluate your communication skills. How might you improve them? Could you enlist a leadership coach? Could you review a recording of one of your sermons or presentations? Could you take a class in communication or speech? Good leaders never stop learning, especially in areas as critical as communication.

4. Do you have a reputation for serving those you lead, or are you known for demanding service from others? What is one thing you could begin doing to serve your people that would clearly demonstrate your concern for them?

5. Do you consider yourself a positive person or do you struggle with a negative attitude? Do people come away from meetings with you: encouraged, discouraged, or apathetic? Take an audit of your attitude. Ask your spouse and two close colleagues to observe your attitude for an entire week as you speak and lead. You might be surprised at what they notice. Don't assume you always come across as positive.

6. What are some practical things you could do to encourage those you lead? Make a list of at least five specific actions you can take. Don't just think in terms of what would encourage *you*. Consider the unique personality qualities of those you lead. How might you specifically encourage people so you speak the language they understand?

7. Are you focused? Take a moment to list all the issues you are currently concerned with as a leader. Evaluate that list. How long and diverse is it? Does it reflect someone who is focused? How might you narrow your attention to those issues that matter most?

8. Are you leading in a manner that could, by God's grace, expand into a movement? Have you set your sights high enough when considering what God might do through your life? Could it be God wants you to have an impact on his kingdom beyond the scope of what you have already considered?

9. Evaluate your stewardship of the influence God has granted you. Have you been faithful with what he has given you? Have you used your influence to bless others? Do you sense people are grateful for the influence you wield?

Chapter Eight

The Leader's Decision Making

I n the early morning of June 6, 1944, the top Allied commanders gathered around their leader. Five thousand ships were steaming toward the French coast. More than 156,000 soldiers were preparing to storm heavily fortified beaches. Thousands of these men would soon be killed. In the future, history would either record this event as one of military history's greatest debacles or one of its most magnificent maneuvers. Everything hinged on one person's decision. "OK, let's go." With that, General Dwight Eisenhower launched the Normandy Invasion, decisively turning the tide of World War II, and ensured his place in history.[1]

Decision making is a fundamental responsibility of leaders. People who are unwilling or unable to make decisions are incapable of leadership. Leaders may consult counselors, seek consensus, and gather information; but ultimately they make choices. Leaders who refuse to do so are abdicating their leadership responsibility. People rely upon leaders to make wise, timely decisions. The fear of making a wrong decision is the overriding impetus behind some people's leadership style. Such people become immobilized by fear of making a mistake. All decisions have ramifications, and leaders must have the fortitude to accept the consequences of their decisions.

In direct contrast to irresolute leaders are those who make decisions casually. They come to conclusions flippantly without giving serious consideration to possible outcomes. When a decision proves disastrous, they do an about-face, adding a second, equally reckless response to the first. Such foolhardy commitments, made in rapid succession, are often contradictory and create confused organizations with bewildered followers scrambling to and fro, uncertain which direction the organization is going. Decision making is critical to an organization's effectiveness. Choices must be made carefully because, as Peter Drucker observes, "Every decision is like surgery. It is an intervention into a system and therefore carries with it the risk of shock."[2]

When Leaders Make a Decision

A single determination holds the potential to significantly impact not only the organization but also those who work for it. It is therefore critical that leaders base their choices firmly on biblical principles that will protect them from mistakes. There are several guidelines spiritual leaders should follow when making decisions.

LEADERS SEEK THE HOLY SPIRIT'S GUIDANCE

The first choice leaders make in decision making is whether to rely on their own insights or on God's wisdom. People don't naturally do things God's way because they don't think like God does (Ps. 118:8). The world's method of decision making is to weigh the evidence, compare pros and cons, and then adopt the course of action that makes the most sense. When leaders make their choices in this manner, they can inadvertently lead their organization in the opposite direction of God's will (Prov. 14:12). God doesn't want people attempting to do what they think is best but what he knows is best. No amount of reasoning and intellectualizing will discover that; God himself must reveal it. The Holy Spirit reveals God's will through four primary avenues: prayer, Scripture, other believers, and circumstances. Our books *Hearing God's Voice* and *When God Speaks* cover these in detail, but for our purposes we will briefly summarize them.[3]

The Holy Spirit guides through prayer. Prayer is the leader's connection with the one who promised: "Call to Me and I will answer you and tell you great and incomprehensible things you do not know" (Jer. 33:3). The prayer described here is not the variety that is done in haste moments before a crucial decision must be made. Prayer should always be a leader's first course of action as they spend time daily asking God to guide them. Neglecting their prayer life is a foolhardy presumption by leaders who assume they already know God's agenda and who believe calling on God as a last resort is a legitimate function of leadership.

Leaders of Christian organizations are not the only ones God guides through prayer. God responds just as readily to the sincere entreaties of Christian business and political leaders. People tend to draw distinctions between secular and spiritual matters. God is not restrained by such artificial boundaries. He is as involved in the business world as he is in the church. God's wisdom applies as much to mergers, investments, and hiring personnel as it does to ecclesiastical matters. Decisions made in the political arena have far-reaching ramifications; God's guidance is critical. At times the marketplace can force leaders into situations where they face moral dilemmas with no readily apparent solutions. God will direct his people to solutions that achieve his purposes and honor him. At times profit motives dictate one course of action while the desire to glorify God suggests another. Prayer will guide leaders to a course of action that magnifies God while maintaining their integrity in the workplace. Prayerless leaders are like ship captains without compasses; they can make their best guess at which direction to go, but they have no assurance they are heading the right way. Prayer keeps leaders focused on the one absolutely consistent factor in their lives—God.

One of the grave realizations of many fallen leaders is that through the rigorous demands of leadership they neglected their relationship with God. Numerous brokenhearted men and women have testified that they became so consumed with fulfilling their official responsibilities they spent limited time with the Lord. After it was too late, these devastated leaders discovered that God does not promise to protect people from foolhardy decisions they make apart from his guidance. How tragic for leaders to be facing a major decision that desperately calls for God's wisdom, only to discover they have grown unfamiliar with God's voice. Even more painful is the reality that their spiritual lethargy has cost others as well.

Daniel had enormous government responsibilities, yet he habitually prayed three times a day. When his rivals used political intrigue to oust him from his position, Daniel faced imminent, mortal danger (Dan. 6). What he did in the next few hours meant life or death. Daniel prayed, as was his custom. Though the situation looked bleak, God faithfully guided and protected Daniel, and the godly government leader achieved even greater influence throughout the kingdom.

When Job entered a dark valley of tragedy, losing his children, his health, and everything he owned, that was not the time for him to hastily seek a closer relationship with God so he would have strength for his trials. During those tumultuous days either Job had a healthy relationship with God or he did not. When it appeared Abraham would lose his only son, when Hannah desperately longed for a child, and when David's son instigated a civil war, each of them sought solace from God, and their vibrant relationship with him sustained them.

The Holy Spirit guides through God's Word. God's Word is the plumb line for Christian living. When people give leaders advice, leaders compare their counsel with God's Word. When leaders sense God is saying something to them in prayer, they confirm it with what he says in his Word. The problem for many leaders is they are unfamiliar with the Bible. They don't know what it says so it doesn't guide them. They don't read it regularly so it doesn't influence their thinking. When a crucial decision is required, leaders have no alternative but to do what makes sense to them and hope it does not violate Scripture's teachings.

True spiritual leaders recognize their utter dependence on God so they regularly fill their heart and mind with his Word. When leaders immerse themselves in Scripture, they will start to think according to biblical principles. When a difficult situation suddenly arises, the Holy Spirit will bring relevant Scriptures to mind (John 14:26).

The Holy Spirit guides through other believers. It is said the difference between genius and stupidity is genius has its limits. The book of Proverbs candidly describes the enormity of suffering which results from foolish choices. Proverbs is also peppered with safeguards against commitments made apart from wise counsel: For example: "Without guidance, people fall, but with many counselors there is deliverance" (Prov. 11:14). "Plans fail when there is no counsel, but with many advisers they succeed" (Prov. 15:22). Leaders should: (1) recruit a variety of godly counselors; and (2) give their advisors the freedom to speak directly and candidly to them.

Enlisting advice can guard leaders against foolish decisions, but leaders should recognize that not all counselors provide equal value. Advisors must be selected carefully. Scripture advises seeking the guidance of several counselors, thus avoiding the trap of merely duplicating the mistakes of others. Because people have diverse expertise, leaders need advisors from various areas of specialization.

Warren Bennis observes that the downfall of President Richard Nixon occurred after he surrounded himself with clones of himself. He writes, "They couldn't tell him anything he didn't already know and so were useless to him."[4] Likewise, President James Buchanan was "intent on having his own way, surrounded by advisors who agreed with him."[5] As a result, he could not bring fresh perspectives and solutions to the most pressing issues of his day. Conversely, Abraham Lincoln sagely filled his cabinet with the strongest leaders available which guaranteed him a diverse pool from which to draw advice. The key to effective counselors is not that they agree with their leaders but that they tell their leaders things they would not otherwise know or recognize. John Gardner comments, "Pity the leader who is caught between unloving critics and uncritical lovers."[6] It is a dangerous trap when leaders let their egos hinder their effectiveness. In shielding themselves from any form of criticism, they also quarantine themselves from wise counselors who could offer much needed advice.

Leaders should enlist the best possible people to work with them and to advise them. These people must know how to think for themselves. They should possess expertise the leader lacks. They should have a consistently successful track record of demonstrating wisdom. They ought to be able to view situations from a different perspective than the leader. If, for example, a CEO is a rational, cognitive thinker who accepts guidance only from other rational, cognitive thinkers, the CEO will inevitably adopt what appears to be the most logical direction for the company. If, on the other hand, the leader also conscripts counselors who are affective thinkers, those counselors will be sensitive to interpersonal issues and will direct the leader away from actions that needlessly antagonize people.

While good leaders ensure they have varied perspectives available to them, the one common qualification for counselors should be a close walk with God. Advisors should demonstrate competence as well as a mature faith. Counselors who are disoriented to God can only offer their advice. Admittedly, it is not possible in every situation to enlist the guidance of fellow believers, especially in narrow fields of expertise. In such cases leaders should seek the counsel of colleagues who demonstrate honesty and integrity as well as wisdom.

Throughout history the best leaders have encouraged diversity in their organizations. Despite their forceful personalities, leaders such as Winston Churchill and Martin Luther King Jr. invited their personnel to be honest with them even if it meant voicing disagreement. Napoleon welcomed debate among his generals. Billy Graham developed a team in which each person was encouraged to honestly share their concerns. Of his teammate, Grady Wilson, Graham confessed: "He was my God-given balance wheel."[7] The evangelist wisely included people on his team who could compensate for his own shortcomings. Harry Truman liked to gather a variety of personalities around him who would provide diverse viewpoints for making decisions. Milton Hershey, founder of Hershey's chocolates, learned the value of honest feedback. During the 1890s, he hired his cousin, William Blair, to manage his caramel company. Blair was not intimidated by Hershey and often disagreed with the owner's suggestions. Eventually Blair resigned and Hershey hired someone who was more pliable to his ideas. The new manager's methods soon led the company to incur a $60,000 loss. The man was fired. Blair was rehired, and Hershey learned an expensive lesson.[8] Great leaders have become great by seeking out wise people and learning from their insights (Prov. 11:14).

Some leaders have suffered monumental disaster, not because there was no one to warn them but because they would listen only to those who told them what they wanted to hear. Often at the root of this problem is insecurity that cannot bear disapproval. The king of Judah had the prophet Jeremiah available to give him direct messages from God, but he refused to believe the prophet's warnings about his nation's perilous condition (Jer. 42–44). As a result, the stubborn monarch was eventually captured by the Babylonians, deprived of his children, blinded, and taken into captivity. Once leaders have carefully chosen their advisors and received guidance borne out by the Scriptures, they are foolish to ignore such counsel.

The Holy Spirit guides through circumstances. Leaders are never merely the victims of their circumstances. Wise leaders watch for God's activity in the midst of their experiences. Just as God speaks by his Holy Spirit through prayer, the Bible, and other believers, so God can send clear messages to leaders through their experiences. A chance encounter with someone at the airport, an unusual comment by a colleague, a surprise phone call are all viewed by leaders in light of what they have been praying about and reading in Scripture. Spiritual leaders astutely evaluate "coincidences" to see if these are God's answers to their prayers. Spiritual leaders are not discouraged by their circumstances; they are informed by them. Through circumstances and events in leaders' lives, God leads them forward in his will.

LEADERS STRIVE TO BE TEACHABLE

The Holy Spirit will reveal God's agenda to people who seek his guidance, but it is up to the leader to respond appropriately to the direction God provides. A major aspect of a leader's decision making is maintaining a teachable spirit. There is little reason for unteachable leaders to enlist wise counsel. Closed-minded leaders muzzle others from saying anything that appears to thwart their own designs. Leaders can stymie input by the way they ask questions. For example, "No one has a problem with this, do they?" is not a question; it is a statement. Another effective way to quench discussion is simply to do all the talking. When leaders spend all their time waxing eloquent about the virtues of their proposal, they are squelching any objections or divergent viewpoints. Leaders who want feedback will give ample opportunity for it. Leaders can also stifle feedback by a defensive posture. When someone raises a question or challenges an assumption, leaders must be careful not to immediately begin arguing their point or bristling into a stiff, angry posture. Defensive leaders learn nothing. Listening leaders constantly grow wiser. As the apostle James sagely cautioned, people should be "quick to hear, slow to speak, and slow to anger" (James 1:19). Leaders learn nothing by vehemently arguing their case. They already know their position. By listening they can gain new insights they had not previously considered. Even if a leader claims to want feedback, a defensive posture will nullify that statement. It is said that despite his strong personality, Winston Churchill received criticism meekly. No doubt he understood there was too much at stake for him to let his ego blind him to the best possible course of action.

Effective leaders encourage active, creative, energetic discussion among their staff.[9] When no one raises questions or suggestions, leaders should recognize they may have created an atmosphere where contributions are perceived as unwelcome. Leaders do not needlessly promote negative or divisive thinking, but they are careful not to inadvertently discourage critical feedback by the way they conduct their meetings. Kouzes and Posner encourage leaders to habitually ask for a second opinion. They cite studies which demonstrate that two-thirds of the time the second solution offered is preferable to the first option suggested.[10] If leaders want their organization to benefit from the collective wisdom available to them, they must create a culture where people feel free to contribute.

LEADERS MASTER THEIR HISTORY

One of the first things a new leader should do is study the history of the organization. This is important in any organization, but it is particularly crucial in the case of spiritual organizations such as churches and nonprofit organizations. New leaders are often enlisted to bring about needed change in an organization. However, wise leaders will resist the urge to immediately move their organizations in radically new directions before they understand how the institution arrived where it is today.

Biblical leaders functioned with a keen awareness of what God did before they arrived on the scene. Isaac knew the same God who was leading him had also instructed his father Abraham (Gen. 26:24). Jacob realized his God was also the God of Abraham and Isaac (Gen. 35:12). Joseph understood that God's activity in his life was building on what was already accomplished through his forefathers Abraham, Isaac, and Jacob (Gen. 48:15). When God commissioned Moses to deliver the Israelites, Moses understood he was simply fulfilling what God initiated through his ancestors (Exod. 3:15).

Biblical leaders repeatedly used spiritual benchmarks as the framework for their decisions. They knew God always builds on what he has done before. Unfortunately today's leaders often assume they unpack God's plan, along with their office furniture, when they arrive on the scene.

God has been unfolding his will since time began. Much history has preceded the leader's arrival at the organization. Leaders are remiss if they make decisions as if there were no track record or history to their organization.

As soon as possible new leaders should investigate God's previous activity in the church or institution to which they have been called. A new pastor should review the minutes of past business meetings to learn what the people sensed God leading them to do previously. Reading written histories of the church, as well as talking with longtime members provides a critical perspective, as well as assuring the people their new leader will not blithely discard all God has already accomplished. For various reasons pastors may feel they must immediately initiate sweeping changes. This is especially true when a pastor is called to a declining church and wants to generate renewed vibrancy. Sometimes new ministers seek to adopt an approach to ministry distinct from their predecessors, just to be different. They arrive with a comprehensive set of plans and directions for the church without considering how their agenda integrates with what God has already done. This is not to say God will not lead the congregation to make significant modifications under the new leadership. In fact, God may have called the new leader specifically to effect change. The church leader, however, should be cautious that any innovations are on God's agenda and that they are implemented for the correct reason and with the right spirit.

Many new leaders develop a subtle, unconscious need to prove they are as capable as their predecessors, especially in situations where they are replacing a more experienced and much-loved leader. People must diligently guard their hearts from pride-driven insecurity that motivates them to cancel good initiatives by previous leaders.

God is purposeful and progressive in the way he leads people and organizations. God does not rescind everything he said previously when a new leader is installed. Leaders come and go, but God's plans, purposes, and presence remain. Astute leaders understand their place in God's overall plan and are content to lead on God's agenda, setting aside any selfish or ungodly motives that may tempt them to "show what they can do."

The book *Experiencing God* discusses spiritual markers as a means of discerning God's leading.[11] By identifying instances of God's unmistakable guidance and reviewing God's activity, people can identify patterns and gain a sense of the direction in which God has been guiding. The practice of identifying spiritual markers can be applied to leading an organization as well. When making decisions and seeking direction for their organization, leaders should review their organization's history, taking careful note of every event they recognize as God's activity. This helps them recognize if a new decision is consistent with God's guidance in the past. Leaders have a greater assurance of making the right decision when they understand how God has led previously. If a decision seems out of line with what God has communicated to the organization thus far, leaders are prudent to reconsider.

LEADERS PLAN

Long-range planning is an essential role of leaders. Phil Rosenzweig cites strategy as one of leaders' primary roles.[12] Strategy, he says, is what distinguishes one organization from another. Planning also enables organizations to effectively mobilize their resources to achieve their goals and overcome anticipated challenges. But, as Rozenzeig admits, "Strategy always involves risk because we don't know how our choices will turn out."[13]

The key for spiritual leaders is the role God plays in their long-range plans. Many planning exercises for Christian organizations typically begin with prayer. Then the participants brainstorm, often falsely encouraging participants that "there is no such thing as a bad idea." Once the ideas have been expressed, organized, categorized, and prioritized, a long-range plan is formalized. A closing prayer asking for divine blessing on the plan generally ensues. For the next five or ten years, the plan becomes the guiding document for the organization.

This approach has several problems. For one, with the rapidity of change, long-range planning is fraught with danger. The landscape can alter so dramatically that apart from regular amendments, plans soon become obsolete. Second, the process described above assumes (falsely) that because the meeting opened in prayer, whatever plan was developed thereafter originated from God. In reality, Christian organizations often follow the same planning procedure secular organizations use except for the symbolic bookend prayers. While planning is obviously a necessity for any organization, God only obligates himself to bless, sustain, and bring to completion that which he initiates (Isa. 46:9–11). Christian organizations must be highly wary of becoming long-range, plan driven rather than God directed. Long-range plans are not sacrosanct. Almighty God has the right to alter or discard our best laid out plans any time he chooses.

LEADERS GIVE AN ACCOUNT TO GOD

The secular media has become something of a moral watchdog for public leaders and celebrities. Decades ago, those in the public eye enjoyed an unspoken relationship with the press that shielded their personal lives from public scrutiny. Not so today. Their moral failures are announced worldwide, including the lurid details. The fear of having every flaw exposed as well as twisted and misrepresented in an ugly way has discouraged many people from pursuing high-profile careers such as politics. Having your life laid bare can be disconcerting, even for those with nothing to hide.

Spiritual leaders are visible to the probing eyes of the media. In fact, the press takes delight in exposing the failures of Christians. But spiritual leaders need not shun public accountability. In fact, they should welcome it as a safeguard against the temptation to abuse their power and influence. They lead with integrity not only because they are accountable to public opinion and the judicial system but more importantly because they know God is observing and assessing their actions. Moreover, one day they will give an account to God for everything they have done (Job 7:17–18). The writer of Proverbs observes: "One turns from evil by the fear of the LORD" (Prov. 16:6).

The apostle Paul, one of the greatest saints in history, had a lengthy and impressive résumé. He started churches across the Roman Empire, shared his faith with kings, and performed miracles. He was a respected leader among Christians, and today his inspired writings compose a large portion of the New Testament. Yet even Paul knew his stature in God's kingdom did not exempt him from divine accountability. Paul said, "Therefore, whether we are at home or away, we make it our aim to be pleasing to Him. For we must all appear before the tribunal of Christ, so that each may be repaid for what he has done in the body, whether good or worthless. Therefore, because we know the fear of the Lord, we seek to persuade people. We are completely open before God, and I hope we are completely open to your consciences as well" (2 Cor. 5:9–11).

According to Paul, not only will unbelievers stand before Christ on judgment day; *everyone* will give an account. Paul enjoyed a close relationship with Christ, yet he knew the awesome God he served. Paul raised the dead back to life in the name of Christ, yet the thought of standing before the risen Christ and giving a thorough account of his actions made him tremble.

This sobering realization, far more than the fear of public exposure, should compel true spiritual leaders to act with integrity toward their peers, staff, families, and public. Leaders of Christian organizations who do not lead their organization to act in faith will eventually answer to God for their unbelief (Heb. 11:6). Christian CEOs who compromise their values will one day be required to explain their actions to the righteous, eternal judge. Spiritual leaders will be held accountable for what they should have done (James 4:17). This knowledge makes decision making a much graver matter for spiritual leaders than for those who believe they are only responsible to a governing board.

Guidelines for Decision Making

1. Leaders seek the Holy Spirit's guidance.
2. Leaders are teachable.
3. Leaders know their history.
4. Leaders plan.
5. Leaders are accountable to God.

After Leaders Make a Decision

As important as decision making is, it is only half of the process. Living with the decision is the other half. Some leaders find making plans and commitments easy. However, sticking with choices and accepting the consequences is difficult. The benefit of hastily made decisions is, of course, negated when those decisions are constantly being amended or discarded. The following are three guidelines for following through on decisions.

LEADERS ACCEPT THE CONSEQUENCES

Decision making would be much easier if there were no consequences, but of course every decision carries inevitable results. A good and timely decision can solidify a leader's successful reputation. A bad decision can overshadow many years of hard work, especially when left uncorrected. It is the potentially devastating or career-making effect of choices that makes decision making a central aspect of the leadership role.

Harry Truman has been called a great leader because he had the ability to decide. But more than that, he was willing to accept the consequences of his decisions. Truman's famous dictum, "The buck stops here," encapsulated his belief that leaders cannot shirk their responsibility to make decisions or shoulder their consequences.

This is the juncture where true leaders separate themselves from mere officeholders. When there are negative repercussions to leaders' decisions, they refuse to blame others. They do not make their subordinates shoulder the weight of negative outcomes for their decisions. True leaders accept the ramifications of their choices.

LEADERS ADMIT THEIR MISTAKES

Because leaders make so many decisions, they are particularly vulnerable to making mistakes. Moreover, the results of their actions are often magnified because of their public stature. Most mistakes are not terminal in nature, however, and they can provide beneficial opportunities for personal growth. Success is intoxicating and can easily blind leaders to their shortcomings. In contrast, mistakes expose leaders' inadequacies. Effective leaders are not successful because they never err in judgment but because they continually learn from their shortcomings. Mistakes made once can often be overcome and transformed into catalysts for personal growth and future success. The same mistakes, made repeatedly, are inexcusable.

J. P. Morgan's biographer noted: "To acknowledge defeat was foreign to his temperament. He was always loyal to his mistakes."[14] Mistakes are inevitable. True leaders understand and accept this fact. The only leaders who never make mistakes are those who don't attempt anything, which is a mistake. However, it is a travesty to refuse to acknowledge or grow from a failure. In fact, setbacks can often be opportunities in disguise. When leaders properly address their failures, their followers observe that though they are not perfect, they are honest. Honesty, not infallibility, has repeatedly been listed as the most important quality followers expect from leaders. Almighty God can bring good out of our worst experiences (Rom. 8:28). When spiritual leaders err, they need to begin by confessing it to God, seeking his forgiveness, and then moving forward in faith. Failure is not to be dreaded with paralyzing fear; it should be seen as a learning tool to be thoroughly analyzed so leaders are better prepared for similar situations in the future.

During a difficult time for the British army, the Duke of Wellington surmised he "lernt what not to do, and that is always something."[15] Moreover, admitting a mistake to followers is an opportunity for leaders to demonstrate how failures will be handled in their organization. If leaders readily admit their own errors, learn from them, and perform their job more effectively thereafter, then followers are reassured they, too, can make honest mistakes without being condemned. It bears repeating that failure is an event, not a character trait. Covering up or refusing to accept responsibility for failure is a character issue; making a mistake is not.

LEADERS STAND BY THEIR DECISIONS

If leaders are meticulous in their decision making, they ought not to waver once they commit. The confident ability to stand firmly behind a decision does not make a leader an unyielding tyrant. It is a characteristic of good leadership. Leaders who vacillate every time they encounter someone holding a different view are agonizing to follow because people never know when they will abruptly change direction again. Obviously, if circumstances alter significantly, or if leaders learn new information that reveals their present approach to be in error, they must adjust their decision, but these scenarios are usually the exception. More often, leaders who continually change their minds do so because they have no clear sense of direction or because they are seeking to please whomever they last spoke with. Such vacillations greatly damage organizations' morale and are often costly.

The best insurance against inconsistency is, of course, to be circumspect in making the correct decision in the first place. Christian leaders do not have to be indecisive if they learn how to know when God is speaking to them. Surprisingly, many spiritual leaders, despite all their rhetoric about hearing from God, do not know how to clearly understand God's assignment for their lives or organizations. Scripture provides the unmistakable pattern of God speaking to his people and guiding them in their decisions. Yet many leaders' behavior reveals that they do not believe God will specifically guide them. Some offer a token prayer and then compile a list of pros and cons from which to make their decision just like an unbeliever would do. Of course God has gifted leaders to be thinkers, but leaders must be cognizant that determining God's will is not a matter of compiling a list of pros and cons but rather of relating to a personal God who is more than willing to guide them.

Indecisiveness may reflect a people-pleasing tendency. Spiritual leaders move people with them in their decisions, but ultimately leaders are concerned with pleasing God, not people. There may be spiritually immature people in the organization. While leaders need to help these people grow personally, they should not allow them to set the pace for everyone else. Good leaders do not abandon their weaker members, but neither do they allow them to determine the agenda. Jesus didn't forsake Judas, but neither did he allow Judas to sidetrack him from his mission. When a mountain hike becomes too difficult for the children who are accompanying their parents, the adults do not abandon the children along the trail, but neither do they allow the children to lead the expedition. This fine balance of leadership often reveals the most skilled leaders.

Having a clear sense of direction for the organization will prevent leaders from pursuing fads. When leaders understand God's plans and purposes for their organizations, decision making becomes more straightforward. When a new opportunity arises, leaders ask, "Will this opportunity take us closer to where God is leading, or will it distract us?" When leaders have no God-given vision, one option can appear as attractive as another. Anyone can decide between good and bad options, but choosing between two seemingly good possibilities can be agonizing for leaders unless they know which one is consistent with the God-given vision. Leaders who are constantly waffling reveal that they do not know where they are going.

It takes courage to stand behind a decision in the face of resistance or opposition. Some leaders simply lack the fortitude to take a stand or to make unpopular decisions. Such leaders often delay, hoping a difficult issue will go away. Unfortunately, it is usually the opportunities and rarely the difficulties that vanish over time.

King Jehoshaphat was a godly king, ruling his small nation in a turbulent and dangerous time. When he was informed that the armies of the Moabites, Ammonites, and Meunites were preparing to attack Jerusalem, Jehoshaphat knew he lacked adequate resources to repel the invaders. The commonly accepted practice was to sue for peace and accept whatever terms his oppressors demanded. The king knew the wrong decision could cause the suffering and death of thousands of his subjects as well as the end of his rule and his life. Jehoshaphat turned to God for guidance.

He cried out, "'Our God, will You not judge them? For we are powerless before this vast number that comes to fight against us. We do not know what to do, but we look to You.' All Judah was standing before the LORD with their infants, their wives, and their children" (2 Chron. 20:12–13).

God spoke to the people through his prophet Jahaziel, saying, "Do not be afraid or discouraged because of this vast number, for the battle is not yours but God's" (2 Chron. 20:15). Jehoshaphat took courage from God's word. In an incredible move the king ordered the choir to lead the army out of the city into battle. Never before had a king given such an unorthodox command. The only basis for such an unusual plan of action was that God's Word to him gave him courage. When Jehoshaphat's forces came upon the enemy, they found they had turned on themselves and destroyed each other. Corpses of enemy soldiers were strewn across the land. The choir had already been singing praises to God. Now they redoubled their efforts!

We find ourselves back to the core principle of spiritual leadership: trusting God. Leaders who know what God has said and who have a clear sense of God's purpose for their organization can be steadfast in their leadership, regardless of whether everyone agrees with them. As long as God approves, they should proceed.

A time comes when leaders must decide to decide. After they have sought God's guidance and confirmed what God is saying through the Scriptures, through prayer, through the affirmation of other believers, and through an evaluation of their circumstances, after they have gathered all the pertinent information and consulted with trusted advisors, the time comes for leaders to make an informed, Spirit-led decision. Essential leadership skills include the ability to make a decision, to stick to it, to admit mistakes along the way, and finally to accept its consequences.

When Leaders Make a Decision

1. Leaders accept the consequences.
2. Leaders admit their mistakes.
3. Leaders stand by their decisions.

Improving Decision Making

Here are some steps leaders can take to strengthen their decision-making skills.

LEADERS EVALUATE THEIR DECISIONS

In 49 BC Julius Caesar stood at the Rubicon River preparing to make the most critical decision of his age. The Roman senate commanded him to resign his governorship of Gaul, relinquish command of his nine legions, and return to Rome where he would be arraigned before the courts and tried for his abuse of power. If Caesar refused and entered Italy with his army, civil war would ensue causing the deaths of thousands and the disruption of the known world. He observed: "To refrain from crossing will bring me misfortune; but to cross will bring misfortune to all men."[16] Caesar could not delude himself or others that he was standing on principle or defending a great cause. As the famous orator Cicero observed, "This cause lacks nothing but a cause."[17] Clearly Caesar was choosing to advance his personal interests even if it meant enormous cost to others. Caesar's legendary conclusion, "The die must be cast," incurred the death of many thousands, the destruction of the republic, extensive property loss, and ultimately his assassination. Every decision is attended with consequences, and therefore leaders must carefully evaluate the nature and the number of decisions they are making.

Leaders can convince themselves their decisions are based on their concern for others. Many a fallen corporate CEO has believed that by falsifying numbers on audits or spending company funds for personal use, they were making good and even noble decisions. Pastors have deluded themselves into assuming that expelling half their church membership or summarily firing loyal staff members was in the best interest of the church. Such leaders must carefully and honestly assess their decisions as well as the motive and spirit behind them.

One reason some leaders struggle is because they are bombarded by too many decisions. Leaders who are deluged with decisions are almost certainly taking responsibility for things they should be delegating. Effective leaders continually appraise the volume of their decisions and regularly give away routine work to others so they can concentrate on critical issues. Leaders should restrict themselves to making only the most important decisions.

LEADERS WALK CLOSELY WITH GOD

When spiritual leaders struggle to make decisions, they need to immediately examine their relationship with God. God is perfectly capable of communicating with them. If leaders are not hearing from God, they need to discern the reason. Do they really know how to recognize God's voice? One of the most difficult admissions for pastors and other spiritual leaders is that they struggle to know when God is speaking. Instead, many of these people simply take the direction that seems most logical to them and then pray for God to stop them if they are making a mistake. The most important thing leaders can do in such situations is to get alone with God in an unhurried, uninterrupted time until they clearly know God has spoken and what he wants them to do. Waiting on God is not a passive activity. It is one of the most strenuous, agonizing, faith-stretching times in a leader's life. Modern leaders have been socialized to think that unless they are constantly in motion they are unproductive. There is no reason to be embarrassed or apologetic about the need to retreat for an hour, a day, or longer to gain God's perspective on a matter. Seeking the mind of God at the front end of a decision can save leaders years of painful regret later (Ps. 19:13).

General Eisenhower sagely advised: "Make no mistakes in a hurry!"[18] He knew a careless decision could cost lives. He was willing to take the time to ensure his judgment was not compromised. In a similar vein Michael and Deborah Jinkins support the view you can always qualify a "no" but not a "yes."[19] They caution that if leaders feel pressured to decide before they are absolutely certain about the best policy, it is better to begin by saying "no" and then later to adjust their decision than to begin by saying "yes" and then try to add restrictions later.

The key to effective decision making is to recognize God's voice amid the din of leadership. King Rehoboam inherited an enviable position. He inherited the kingdom from his illustrious father Solomon, the wealthiest king in Israel's history. Immediately upon assuming the throne, however, Rehoboam faced a critical decision. The people asked him to reduce the oppressive tax rate his father levied. Rehoboam maintained two sets of counselors; one group consisted of ambitious young men like him. Wise counselors from his father's era comprised the other group. The young executives counseled toughness; the more experienced seers recommended leniency. Rehoboam listened to his peers and split his kingdom (1 Kings 12:1–17). One of the gravest blunders of any Israelite king occurred under a leader with not one but two sets of counselors. What went wrong? Why was Rehoboam susceptible to worldly, unwise counsel? Was it simply because he was young and prone to listen to youthful advisors? No. Scripture tells us why he failed: "Rehoboam did what was evil, because he did not determine in his heart to seek the LORD" (2 Chron. 12:14). Rehoboam was unfamiliar with God's ways because he did not make the effort to know God. When he was presented with godly, wise counsel that could have preserved his kingdom, he didn't recognize God's voice. When leaders are disoriented to God, all their decisions—political, business, and religious—are susceptible to poor advice.

LEADERS SEEK GOD'S VISION

Leaders may struggle to make decisions because they have no clear picture of where their organization is going. It's surprising how many leaders settle into managing the day-to-day operations of their organization with no comprehensible idea of where God is leading them. Every decision is a step toward a destination. It has been said that if you don't know where you are going, any path will take you there. A leader who is unable to identify the organization's purpose needs to stop and seek God's direction. There is no value in making great progress in the wrong direction.

When leaders have received God's vision for the future, they will gain a clear sense of direction on which to base decisions. Then options will eliminate themselves because they are obviously contrary to, or a deviation from, the organization's God-given destination.

LEADERS SEEK GOD'S WISDOM

Today's complex world is confusing enough to make anyone indecisive. Yet while the task of leadership has not become easier over time, God continues to provide the wisdom leaders need. When Solomon's father, King David, was approaching death, the kingdom was filled with political intrigue. Although David wanted Solomon to be his successor, Solomon's older half brother,

Adonijah, was maneuvering politically to gain influential supporters in his quest for the throne. Abiathar, the high priest, gave his support to Adonijah as did Joab, the army commander. Nevertheless, Solomon ultimately ascended the throne. Perhaps it was facing such powerful opponents that helped Solomon realize he needed supernatural wisdom. When God asked him what he desired, Solomon requested, not wealth, or a long life, or security, but wisdom (1 Kings 3:9).

The world has not grown less complicated since Solomon's time. Political intrigue is nothing new to God. God has been helping his people overcome aggressive lobbyists, deceit, bribes, false accusations, factions, and every manner of sinful behavior throughout history, and he stands ready to assist leaders today.

Decision making need not be an ominous task. God is willing to dispense the wisdom necessary for problem solving and making good choices. The book of Proverbs is filled with helpful advice to all people and specifically to leaders. With so much at stake in leaders' decisions, it is imperative they accept every resource God offers if they are to wisely and effectively lead their organizations to be on God's agenda.

Responding to This Material

1. List the last five major decisions you made in your leadership role. Reflect on their quality. Were they good decisions? Have you had to alter them? Do you regret any of them? Did you seek God's wisdom in all five of them?

2. How might you improve your decision making? Could you take more time in making important decisions? How might you seek God's wisdom in your decision making?

3. Evaluate the caliber of your counselors. Do you have advisors with integrity who feel free to tell you the truth? Do you have a variety of counselors with diverse areas of expertise? Who might you enlist as a counselor who would strengthen the quality of counsel available to you?

4. Evaluate the number of decisions you regularly make in your leadership role. Should you be making all of them? Which decisions could you delegate to someone else?

5. Do you have a clear sense of God's leading in your organization? If so, how does that help you make decisions? If not, take time to gain a sense of God's leading before you make your next important decision.

Chapter Nine

The Leader's Schedule:
Doing What's Important

T he longer Harry Truman served as president of the United States, the more time conscious he became. Over the years his aides noticed an increasing number of clocks on his desk in the oval office. Every time Truman sat at his desk, he faced a barrage of timepieces. With so many significant decisions to make, Truman knew, as do all great leaders, that time was a precious resource. Napoleon allegedly told his generals, "You can ask of me anything you wish except of my time." Leaders' effectiveness is commensurate with their ability to manage their time. Even the most gifted leaders will struggle if they squander it. Spiritual leaders understand God has granted them adequate time to accomplish any assignment he gives them. The key to successful leadership is not creating more time in one's life or packing more activities into one's day but staying on God's agenda.

Scientists used to proclaim that modern time-saving devices would produce large amounts of free time for people. Yet even as new time-saving gadgets are rolling off assembly lines, life seems to get busier and more stressful year by year. *U.S. News & World Report* noted that between 1977 and 1997 the average workweek of salaried Americans rose from forty-three to forty-seven hours. Americans were working two weeks longer each year than the notoriously hardworking Japanese—ten more than Europeans.[1]

Kouzes and Posner observed that the harried nature of the modern office means the average executive has only nine minutes of uninterrupted time to devote to any one item.[2] If that is true, executives must be diligent and proactive about how they spend those minutes. The term *time management* is misleading. Time will proceed second by second, minute by minute, hour by hour despite leaders' best efforts to administer it. What leaders can manage is *themselves*. Despite the pervasive and unrelenting pressures on their schedule, leaders ultimately choose what they will do with the time at their disposal.

The most inefficient and unproductive leaders have as much time as history-making, world-changing leaders. Each is constrained by the need for sleep, food, exercise, and family concerns. Everyone encounters financial issues, unforeseen circumstances, and daily pressures. The difference is wise leaders let God, not life's daily demands, determine their priorities. Unwise leaders succumb to extraneous pressures and enticements bombarding them so they don't accomplish what God intends for them. Spiritual leaders don't allow their busy lives or their numerous responsibilities to sidetrack them from God's agenda. Rather, they become the masters of their schedules through determined and conscientious effort.

Taking Control of Time

Peter Drucker offers helpful suggestions for leaders' time in his classic book *The Effective Executive*. He notes, "Effective executives, in my observation, do not start with their tasks. They start with their time."[3] It is not unusual for leaders to have more jobs to do than they have time to accomplish. This is business as usual. Earlier time management experts focused on how leaders could pack more activity into their days. Like business travelers sitting on their overstuffed suitcases attempting to cram in one more pair of pants, so earlier theory provided schemes to insert one more activity into an already crowded schedule. Leaders who subscribed to this approach were often able to attend more meetings, write more letters, and complete more projects. But like a house of cards, one activity that ran late, or one missed flight, or one day with the flu, and their intricately woven schedules came crashing down around them. Such leaders would arrive home having accomplished enormous amounts of work, but they would be exhausted and left wondering what difference their herculean efforts made in the grand scheme of things. Simply squeezing more tasks into a day is not the answer to an effective schedule. The key is doing the right things. An effective schedule is preferable to an efficient schedule. Leaders can avoid becoming slaves to their time by following several important practices.

LEADERS SUBJUGATE

Thomas More was once attending a Mass when Henry VIII sent word for him to report to him at once. When the king's chief minister did not come, additional messages were urgently sent. Finally, More sent word to his sovereign that he would come but only after he paid homage to a "higher king."[4] Leaders are surrounded by people's agendas in addition to their own plans. Everyone has priorities: the board of directors, the leader's family, employees, clients, and competitors. Governing agencies require certain commitments as do leaders' friends and churches. Each group is motivated differently. Employees' livelihoods are intrinsically linked with the leader's performance. Family members depend on them. Often people seek the leader's involvement to ensure a program or event is successful. Others know jobs will get done if the leader is involved.

There is no way to satisfy the desires of all the people who clamor for their time, so leaders must subjugate their schedule to God's will and invest themselves in those activities and projects most critical. Unlike people, God never assigns more than someone can handle. God never overbooks people.

He never drives his servants to the point of breakdown. He never burns people out. God never gives people tasks beyond the strength or ability he provides.

If this is true, why do so many people struggle with too much to do? Why are Christian leaders burning out from overwork and exhaustion? Is God responsible? No. When people become overwhelmed by their commitments and responsibilities, they are operating on their own priorities. Ministers of religion are particularly susceptible to assuming responsibility for things they should not. They do this because the Lord's work seems never to be finished. There is always another phone call to make, a Scripture passage to study, a hospitalized member to visit, a prayer to be offered. The key for overworked leaders is to examine each of their current responsibilities to determine whether they have inadvertently assumed responsibility for things God did not assign to them.

The apostle Paul instructed Christians: "Pay careful attention, then, to how you walk—not as unwise people but as wise—making the most of your time, because the days are evil. So don't be foolish, but understand what the Lord's will is" (Eph. 5:15–17). Jesus was the consummate leader. No one was ever in higher demand than he was. His disciples thought they knew how he should invest his time (Luke 9:12, 33; Mark 10:13, 37). Religious leaders had other designs for him (Matt. 12:38; Luke 13:14). The sick, the poor, and the hungry clamored for his attention (Mark 1:37; Luke 18:35–43; John 6:15). Jesus' family had notions about what he should do. Some people urged Jesus to remain with them and teach them. Others wanted to travel with him (Mark 5:18). Satan planned to divert Jesus from his Father's will. Jesus was besieged with opportunities to help people, and he had the power to make a difference in every situation. Only by keeping his Father's purposes continually before him could he focus on doing what was most important.

Why did Jesus rise early to pray? He understood that maintaining an intimate relationship with his Father was the single most important thing he could do. Why did Jesus occasionally escape the crowds to spend time teaching his disciples? He knew it was important to invest time training them. Why did Jesus associate with outcasts and sinners such as Zacchaeus and the Samaritan woman? He realized he was sent to heal those who needed a spiritual physician. Close friendships mattered to him, and he purposefully spent time with Mary, Martha, and Lazarus in Bethany. Out of Jesus' intimate relationship with his Father came the direction he needed for investing his time day by day.

Following Jesus as their model, when leaders understand God's will, parceling out their time becomes straightforward. If God confirms to a leader that she should remain with her current organization, she does not need to spend weeks in agonizing prayer just because a job offer lands in her lap. When God directs a leader to stay close to home because his teenager is going through a tumultuous time, he knows he should decline or postpone extended business trips for the time being. When leaders see God's activity and recognize it as his invitation to join him, decisions become clearer. When people do not understand God's will, their schedules careen out of control. Then every opportunity to take on another project is hard to reject because harried leaders are unsure of their priorities.

Spiritual leaders ask questions such as: "What is God's will? In light of his will, what is important? What is he asking me to do?" Leaders should first direct their time to the most important matters. If anything must be neglected, it should always be less critical activities. If leaders never take time to determine their God-given priorities, however, they will invariably spend inordinate amounts of time on projects extraneous to their main purpose.

LEADERS ELIMINATE

The higher you ascend in leadership, the more often you must say no. Greater numbers of opportunities are available to executive leaders so they must be more stringent in maintaining their priorities. General George Marshall's effectiveness as a leader of the American Army during World War II is attributed to his ability to prioritize. It has been said: "Marshall did not possess the intellectual brilliance of someone like Acheson, or the gift of eloquence, but he could distinguish what was important from what was unimportant, and this made him invaluable."[5] Executives' daily schedules primarily reveal two things: those activities they have chosen to do and those things they decide *not* to do.

Many leaders find saying no excruciating. Leaders are susceptible to the messiah complex. They may assume that only their involvement can guarantee an initiative's success so they immerse themselves in as many projects as possible. They dash from meeting to meeting and appointment to appointment, trying to ensure the success of every enterprise their organization undertakes. They must understand their success as leaders is not based on how much they personally accomplish but on how wisely they perform their leadership role. By spending the bulk of their time on less significant issues, leaders invariably neglect the weightier ones. A wise practice is to "sleep on it" before committing themselves to new responsibilities. What seemed possible or appealing at the moment can fade in importance once the big picture is considered.

Some leaders have difficulty saying no because their sense of self-worth compels them to be indispensable. They take pride in the fact they are in great demand and their calendars are brimming over. The busier they are, the more irreplaceable they feel. If they decline to serve on a committee, what if they are overlooked the next time board members are needed? What if not getting involved in a project means they won't be consulted on subsequent matters? So these overwhelmed zealots trudge from meeting to meeting complaining about their taxing workload, but they would have it no other way.

Good leaders graciously yet regularly say no to many of the opportunities presented to them. In fact, they reject far more than they accept. By declining to become involved in projects, these leaders are not belittling the activity as if it were beneath them to participate. Rather they are acknowledging they are human beings with limitations, and thus they must make choices with their time. Leaders who are deluged by their schedules may simply not know how to say no. It's that simple. God does not give people more than they can handle, but people are inclined to assume responsibility for things they should not be doing.

Overburdened leaders often have no idea how they became so busy. The condition crept up on them. The problem is leaders are often tempted to take on just one more task because doing so appears easier than saying no. The axiom, "If you want to get something done, ask a busy person" is true. Busy people may reason, "Well, I am already going to be at home working on these projects over the weekend. I guess I can squeeze this job in too." Responsibilities gradually pile up as leaders valiantly try to force one more job into their crowded lives. People with overwhelming schedules must ask themselves: "What items are currently on my calendar I should have declined or delegated?" Commitments can spring up like weeds in a garden. Small, isolated responsibilities undertaken out of a desire to please others can demand ever-increasing amounts of time until they have crowded out the rightful priorities. As leaders meet daily with God, he will set their priorities. Superfluous activity must be weeded out so those activities on God's agenda can flourish.

It is a wise practice for leaders to audit their commitments annually. They should ask, "Is it beneficial for me to serve on this committee for another year? Do I need to be responsible for this project again next year, or have I contributed all I can? What commitments did I fulfill last year that I do not need to assume this year?" By asking such questions, leaders prune their schedules of activities and responsibilities that are extrinsic to their primary purpose.

LEADERS CULTIVATE

John Jacob Astor, founder of the Astor fortune, counseled his son William: "The man who makes it the habit of his life to go to bed at nine o'clock usually gets rich. . . . It's all a matter of habit and good habits in America make any man rich."[6] Unfortunately, routine is to some leaders like eating spinach is to children—an unpleasant, albeit necessary, task. Some leaders go to great extremes to avoid being locked into routines. Yet wise leaders cultivate healthy routines to ensure their priorities are not overlooked. Drucker says routine "makes unskilled people without judgment capable of doing what it took near genius to do before."[7] Drucker also observes: "Effective executives do not race. They set an easy pace but keep going steadily."[8] Life is a marathon, not a sprint.

Routines ensure that leaders have scheduled their most important responsibilities into their calendars. Some leaders enjoy the exhilaration of spontaneity. They covet the freedom that comes from not being shackled to a daily timetable. But impetuous living can lead to enslavement. If you do not schedule your time, someone else will. Every phone call or person who stops by your office will determine your itinerary. Generally people who seize leaders' "free" time are not concerned with critical issues but peripheral matters. Better for leaders to personally identify their crucial tasks and secure those activities into their calendars rather than submitting themselves by default to the whims of the people around them. The latter is crisis management; the former is self-management.

Some people are wary of routines because they fear being stifled or falling into ruts. Routines, however, can be as unique as the individuals who employ them. Some perform better under stringent schedules. Churchill, for example, meticulously followed the same schedule every week, including a daily afternoon nap. Churchill observed by resting when he did, he could work late into the night going over reports and preparing for the next day in the quiet hours while others slept. By morning he was fully briefed and ready for the day's events. Churchill claimed that by following his unusual regimen he was far more productive than if he kept more conventional hours.

Many of history's greatest leaders were early risers. While others were still sleeping, they were previewing their day, reading reports, and plotting a course of action. This does not necessarily mean these leaders slept less than others. Rather, they arranged their schedule to be the most effective.

Jesus' life seemed to follow a different schedule every day, but he, too, was governed by routine. Scripture indicates Jesus habitually prayed late at night and early in the morning (Mark 1:35; Luke 6:12; 21:37; 22:39). Leaders must establish routines that fit their particular responsibilities as well as their health needs, but it is paramount for spiritual leaders to schedule regular and frequent times alone with God. To merely seize a few moments with God as opportunities present themselves is totally ineffective for busy leaders. Such opportunities rarely come. Spiritual leaders must follow Jesus' example and set times to regularly meet with God. Because Jesus made it his custom to spend time regularly with his Father, he was never caught off guard by the day's events, no matter how diverse they were. The Gospels never portray Jesus as being in a hurry or acting impatiently. There has never been a person with as many important things to accomplish as Jesus, yet he displayed serenity throughout his ministry. Why? He allowed the Father to set the agenda for his life.

The axiom says, "To fail to plan is to plan to fail." Those who neglect to schedule the important responsibilities of their lives into their routines invariably overlook them. Routine saves time. If leaders habitually spend time with God first thing in the morning, they don't waste time each morning considering what they should do first. Their schedule has already determined that. Leaders with routines are protected from trivial interruptions. When leaders plan regular meetings with their staff, they know those crucial encounters will not be preempted by less important activities.

Finally, routine protects leaders from becoming lopsided in their efforts. Some activities crave every moment of leaders' time. Leaders are naturally drawn to invest time in enjoyable endeavors while they tend to shun less fulfilling tasks. Only by carefully scheduling diverse activities into their schedules can leaders ensure they have covered the broad spectrum of their responsibilities.

There is one important qualifier in the matter of routine. Although routines can be extremely freeing, when abused, they can become unyielding taskmasters. Spiritual leaders understand God has the right to intervene in their schedule anytime he chooses. Leaders warily protect their schedules from those who want to usurp them, but they welcome God's intervention. Leaders impervious to God's insertion of his agenda into their calendars are in danger of making idols of their schedules. God is supreme over the most meticulous leader's regimen. Spiritual leaders often find that what might appear to be an interruption at first glance is, in fact, a divine invitation. Wise leaders remain vigilant to detect God's activity around them.

LEADERS DELEGATE

The quantity of work leaders can accomplish is in direct proportion to their ability to delegate work to others. Leaders who refuse to delegate limit their productivity to their own physical stamina, creativity, and intelligence. Leaders who assign tasks to others have unlimited production potential.

One of the best known biblical lessons on delegation occurred in the ministry of Moses. Moses was a national leader. His stature among his people was unparalleled. People knew Moses spoke face-to-face with God. Whenever there was a dispute, people naturally wanted him to settle the issue. What was the result? Long lines of people waited their turn with the esteemed leader (Exod. 18:13–26). From dusk until dawn, Moses dealt with issues that others could have processed for him. It was not until the wise intervention of his father-in-law, Jethro, that Moses appointed others to carry much of this responsibility. Thereafter, Moses only handled the most difficult cases and allowed others to adjudicate routine matters. Not only was Moses' administrative load greatly reduced, but the people received service in a much more timely and efficient manner. Furthermore, now other leaders took responsibility for the peoples' welfare. Moses' mistake was assuming that because he could do something, he should do it.

Leaders continually ask themselves, "Is this a task someone else could do?" Leaders take delight not in how much they are accomplishing but in how much those around them are getting done. Of course there are certain tasks leaders cannot delegate. Leaders have the responsibility to hear from God and to guide their organizations into his will. Leaders must ensure the right people are hired; the culture is safe, healthy, and productive; and the organization is focused on its mission. Therefore, they must delegate everything possible so they have time to focus on these crucial responsibilities. As a rule, if others *could* do tasks the leader is presently doing, they *should* do them.

The reasons leaders fail to delegate are legion. Some people are perfectionists who assume no one can do the job as well as they can. Others are task oriented and would rather complete the assignment themselves than take time to equip others to do it. Still others are uncomfortable asking people to do things; they find doing the job themselves less onerous than enlisting others. Then there are the leaders who are so disorganized that by the time they realize a deadline is approaching, it is too late to enlist someone to do the work. Whatever the reason for their reluctance, leaders must understand that mastering the art of delegation is preeminent among leadership skills.

LEADERS CONCENTRATE

Leaders who cannot focus will be enslaved to interruptions and fruitless diversions. Peter Drucker warns against dividing a leader's time into small segments. Drucker suggests most leadership tasks that can be done within fifteen minutes could often be delegated. Leaders deal with significant issues such as the organization's future and values as well as enlisting top personnel. These matters cannot be randomly plugged into fifteen-minute time slots. Leaders must allow themselves significant blocks of time to think through crucial issues. Leaders should insert one- to two-hour time slots in their schedules to focus intently and deeply on the critical issues facing their organization. The issues of the future are not comprehended after only ten minutes of consideration. Because of this, it behooves leaders to provide their staff with regular times of extended planning. Many organizations do not develop fresh, innovative, and revolutionary ideas because their leaders fail to budget sufficient time for their people to do so. Great insights don't come from rushed thinking.

The difference between managers and leaders can be seen here. Managers often become embroiled in the daily grind of keeping the organizational machinery functioning properly. Leaders must occasionally step back from the day-to-day operations to gain perspective on the broader issues such as the nature and future of their organizations.

Another key difference between leaders and managers is managers are responsible for *how* something is done; leaders must consider *why* it is being done and continually communicate this to followers. Secular writers argue that strategic thinking separates organizations that fail from those that thrive. Concerning organizations that fail, Stuart Wells comments: "How did these stumbles happen? They are not victims of excessive government regulation. They are not victims of unfair foreign competition. They are not victims of unions. These forms of corporate whining are rather tiresome. It is not their fate or their stars. What happened is quite simple and profound; they are outthought. While they stumbled, others thrived. They are victims of one thing—their own thought patterns."[9]

Leaders must also invest focused time with key employees and volunteers. While brief encounters with employees and volunteers can certainly be helpful in maintaining personal contact, they are most often symbolic and are not substitutes for quality one-on-one encounters. If leaders are to truly understand their people and convey their appreciation to them, they will occasionally need time slots of more than a few minutes. Leaders should regularly allot at least an hour at a time to invest in key personnel. Breakfast or lunch meetings are helpful in building relationships. Wise leaders divide their time into large enough segments that they can devote sufficient time to their tasks as well as to their people. Drucker concludes: "If there is any 'secret' of effectiveness, it is concentration. Effective executives do first things first and they do one thing at a time."[10] Executive leaders have generally been known for multitasking. Queen Elizabeth I could manually write one letter, dictate a second one, while answering a courtier's questions simultaneously.[11] Today's business leaders have been trained to multitask. Yet juggling several jobs simultaneously may allow leaders to accomplish a multiplicity of tasks but it is not conducive for in-depth thought or developing advanced strategy. It may, in fact, enable leaders to make more than one mistake at a time!

> ## Leaders Take Control of Their Time
>
> 1. Leaders subjugate.
> 2. Leaders eliminate.
> 3. Leaders cultivate.
> 4. Leaders delegate.
> 5. Leaders concentrate.

Leaders Make Time for What Is Important

Warren Bennis notes: "I often observe people in top positions doing the wrong things well."[12] The question for most leaders is not whether they are busy but whether they are busy doing the right things. Good activities subtly crowd out the important. Careless leaders may not notice that serious work has been displaced by less crucial matters. They will continue to go to work at the same time and feel harried throughout the day, but there will be an emptiness to their efforts, a sense of futility as these leaders wonder whether their activity is making a significant difference to their organization.

When it comes to schedules, leadership theory tends to swing from one extreme to the other. During an earlier generation, leaders often felt obligated to neglect their health and families to maintain their heavy workload. Even church leaders would neglect their families and personal needs in deference to their higher calling to serve God. Then, as executives lost their marriages and ministers saw their children abandon their faith, leaders reacted by claiming they needed to have "balance" in their lives. New time management tools were developed so busy leaders could ensure they were not spending too much time at the office and they were investing a balanced amount of time with their spouse, children, exercise, devotional life, and recreation.

The problem is balanced people don't change the world. People can become so obsessed with protecting their health and home life that they make little impact on their company, or church, or world. We are not suggesting leaders should ignore their families or their health. However, seeking a perfect balance where leaders never stay late at the office, never miss a Little League game, and never miss a day on the treadmill can become a monstrous taskmaster that robs leaders of their greatest impact.

It would be a stretch to say Jesus lived a balanced life. Yet he managed to accomplish everything his Father assigned (John 17:4). There were times Jesus was too busy to eat or sleep. Yet on other occasions he escaped to an isolated location to rest with his disciples (Matt. 14:13). The key for Jesus was his *focus*. In whatever activity his Father assigned him, Jesus was fully engaged and focused.

When leaders are at the office, they must turn their complete attention to the matters at hand. When meeting with a colleague for lunch, they must be wholly engaged in that meeting. When spending time with God in the morning, they must remove every distraction and give God their full and undivided attention. When going on vacation with their family or spending time with their spouse on their day off, leaders remain focused and guard themselves from business distractions.

Balance is difficult to achieve daily. It is better measured over a longer time period than a day or week. If you are focused on each task or encounter God gives you, God will ensure that your life and all of its commitments and relationships remain healthy. While leaders cannot ensure they give equal time to each priority of their life each day, there are at least five areas of life to which effective leaders fastidiously reserve adequate time.

Leaders Schedule Unhurried Time with God

Spiritual leaders understand if they neglect their relationship with God, they forfeit their spiritual authority. Time spent in God's presence is never wasted. Everything spiritual leaders do flows out of their divine relationship. The vision they have for their organization originates from God. Their daily agenda comes from God. God determines the organizational values. God guides the choice of personnel. Spiritual leaders who become disoriented to God imperil their organizations. Unfortunately, most leaders easily allow other activities to preempt time with God. Rather than spending unhurried, quality time with the heavenly Father, many leaders quickly skim a devotional book and then mutter a frantic prayer as they run to their first meeting. Many busy leaders are like the Royalist soldier, Sir Jacob Astley, who before the battle at Edgehill on October 23, 1642 recited the prayer of a pious warrior: "O Lord, if I forget Thee this day, do not Thou forget me."[13] God is not mocked. What people sow, they reap (Gal. 6:7). If leaders attempt to do things in their own strength and wisdom, they will achieve commiserate results. If leaders wait upon the Lord, they will experience what God can accomplish. Unfortunately, leaders generally have calendars bursting with appointments, and they are desperately trying to avoid falling behind. The leader's mind-set is crucial. If leaders look upon their time with God as little more than an opportunity to gain a pithy devotional thought, they will be tempted to forgo the experience in favor of expediency. But if they view their time as a crucial consultation with the Creator of the universe, they will diligently guard it, regardless of the day's demands.

King Saul's downfall occurred when he rushed ahead of God's agenda (1 Sam. 13:5–14). The Israelites were facing the hated Philistine army at Gilgal. The enemy gathered thirty thousand chariots and six thousand cavalry, together with a large contingent of infantry. God instructed Saul not to engage the enemy until Samuel arrived to offer a sacrifice to the Lord. Saul impatiently waited seven days and witnessed his situation rapidly deteriorating. His soldiers, terrified of their deadly enemy, were steadily deserting. Saul wanted God's protection and power for his army, but he was impatient to wait any longer, so he offered the sacrifice himself. Samuel immediately appeared and rebuked the presumptuous monarch. Saul won the battle that day, but his lack of patience would cost him his kingdom and ultimately his life.

Hindsight affords modern readers the luxury of criticizing Saul for his foolishness, but spiritual leaders would do well to learn from his mistake. Few spiritual leaders would openly question their need to spend time in prayer, but their lifestyle reveals they resent that daily time commitment. God does not reveal his truth on people's terms. Spiritual leaders must remain in prayer as long as necessary until they are certain they have heard from God.

One CEO complained that his schedule was so grueling he was too busy for unhurried time with the Lord. However he committed to try for the following month. A month later he jubilantly reported he kept rising earlier and earlier in the morning until he felt he had a satisfactory amount of time to spend, unhurried, with God. His alarm was going off at 4:30 each morning. He jubilantly reported God had given him specific and significant guidance that month, which had greatly helped him lead his company; and, for the first time, he led an employee to faith in Christ. He also discovered that by allowing God to prepare his life each morning, he was much more efficient throughout the remainder of the day. The key is not whether leaders spend some time with God but whether the time they spend is unhurried and allows time for all God wants to say (Isa. 64:4). Leaders must consider what God might say to them or do in their life, if they spent sufficient time listening to him.

LEADERS SCHEDULE REGULAR, QUALITY TIME WITH THEIR FAMILY

Abraham Lincoln sent his son Robert to boarding school and then to Harvard University. Robert wistfully recalled, "Any great intimacy between us became impossible. I scarcely had ten minutes quiet talk with him during his Presidency, on account of his constant devotion to business."[14] One of the strongest indictments of today's leaders is that in their quest to be successful in their jobs, they are failing their families. Tragically, Christian ministers often neglect their families under the misconception that serving the Lord requires them to do so.

Lee Iacocca, former CEO of Chrysler, challenged the assumption that the more responsibility leaders were given, the more their families invariably would suffer. He noted: "Some people think that the higher up you are in a corporation the more you have to neglect your family. Not at all! Actually it's the guys at the top who have the freedom and the flexibility to spend enough time with their wives and kids."[15]

Leaders often have more leeway in their schedules *if they will use it*. They must be creative. For example, pastors who are busy most evenings could arrange to be home some mornings to have breakfast with their families and take their children to school. They could arrange a special one-on-one lunch date with each child as well as with their spouse. The pressure on leaders often comes not from their organization but from themselves. These misguided leaders feel compelled to keep going into their office and working when they should be spending time at home. Such leaders must determine what is most important to them and then make the adjustments required to protect those priorities.

Wise leaders schedule regular, quality time with their families. They are intentional about spending replenishing times with their spouse. They record their children's special events on their calendars well in advance and then guard those times from any encroachment. They protect the privacy of their home and avoid bringing work home with them if possible. Wise leaders strive to spend mealtimes with their family and refuse to submit to the tyranny of the telephone (or television).

Despite Harry Truman's role as president of the United States, he never forgot what was most important to him. When Bess Truman was asked what she considered the most memorable aspect of her life, she replied: "Harry and I have been sweethearts and married for more than forty years—and no matter where I was, when I put out my hand Harry's was there to grasp it."[16] Even the presidency of the United States during some of the nation's most critical moments did not confuse Truman about what, and who, was most important in his life.

Perceptive leaders understand there are more important things in life than their jobs. When leaders interview for a new job, they ask probing questions of their prospective employer to determine what the company's stance is toward the family. People should be wary of companies promoting lifestyles that can destroy families. Spiritual leaders know that the career advancement they attain means nothing if their teenage son refuses to speak to them or their daughter becomes addicted to drugs. Many shrewd leaders have declined lucrative job offers that mandated increased travel because they knew their spouse and children needed their presence at home. Businesspeople have turned down promotions because they realized the increased responsibility would bring multiplied pressures that would erode their family life. Promotions that would unduly pressure a leader to compromise Christian convictions should also be avoided. Many things in life are more important than career advancement or wealth accumulation.

LEADERS SCHEDULE TIME FOR THEIR HEALTH

Some leaders live antithetical lives. They lead their organizations to become strong, healthy, and vibrant while at the same time they allow their own bodies to become overweight, out of shape, and run down. Dr. Richard Swenson, in his book *Margin: Restoring Emotional, Physical, Financial and Time Reserves to Overloaded Lives*, discusses a topic so simple it should be obvious to everyone: people have limits. When people live their lives to the edge of their capacity—whether it is in finances, time, sleep, or emotional health—they run great risks. Just like a car that is continually driven at full speed and improperly maintained, human bodies will break down if they are continually pushed to their limit.

Swenson, a medical doctor, developed the conviction that people must build room (margin) into their lives for unexpected crises or opportunities. His formula is: Power − Load = Margin.[17] If people deprive themselves of sleep on an ongoing basis, their bodies will suffer. No one can continually endure emotionally draining events without restoring their emotions through hobbies, friendships, vacations, or laughter. People who maximize their spending to the limit every month are inviting financial ruin when an unexpected expense occurs. Likewise, those who saturate their schedules, leaving no room for unforeseen interruptions, are setting themselves up for a crisis. Leaders who never allow time in their annual schedules for a relaxing vacation are racing toward an inevitable breakdown. Margin is the reserve amount of time, money, energy, and emotional strength people maintain to remain healthy.

Leaders habitually live marginless lives. They cannot bear to be idle or unproductive. Empty spots on their calendars jump out at them as ideal places to undertake new projects. God never planned it this way. Since the beginning of time, God has emphasized the need for rest (Gen. 2:2–3).

Jesus himself required restoration and solitude. After ministering to the crowds all day, Jesus and his disciples deliberately sought a respite (Mark 6:45). At the beginning of Jesus' final week on earth, he allowed his good friends Lazarus, Martha, and Mary to minister to him (John 12:1–3). On the climactic night of his arrest and crucifixion when he could have preached to the crowds one final time, Jesus chose an intimate supper with his close friends (Luke 22:7–13).

While history has generally been harsh on him, President Warren Harding sacrificed his health in fulfilling his leadership responsibilities. It was claimed Harding was carrying a load five times that of President McKinley and doing so by putting in fifteen-hour work days.[18] Harding died of an apoplexy stroke in 1923 at the age of fifty-seven.

During General Dwight Eisenhower's campaign in North Africa and Italy, his boss, General Marshall, became concerned that his dedicated lieutenant was wearing himself out. When Eisenhower was transferred to England, Marshall recommended he first return to the United States for two weeks to obtain some much needed rest. When Eisenhower claimed he did not have the time, Marshall replied: "I am not interested in the usual rejoinder that you can take it. It is of vast importance that you be fresh mentally, and you certainly will not be if you go straight from one great problem to another. Now come home and see your wife and trust somebody else for twenty minutes in England."[19] Eisenhower would go on to lead the greatest amphibious invasion in history and would need every ounce of energy his commander helped him preserve.

Taking time to care for one's health is a pragmatic issue. As Kouzes and Posner point out, "How can you squeeze in time to think about the future when you are too tired to think about what you're going to have for dinner?"[20] Overweight leaders tend to tire more easily. People who eat poorly, who don't get enough sleep, or who don't exercise become sick more frequently. Unhealthy people do not have the energy and strength to accomplish as much as healthy people. Leaders need not become obsessed with physical fitness, but those who ignore health issues are ultimately choosing to be less effective over time than they could be. People who fail to care for their health risk having their leadership come to a premature end.

Healthy leaders understand that a sense of humor is essential to emotional health. Leaders are ultimately responsible for the positive, upbeat spirit of their organization. If they want their followers to enjoy working with them, leaders must foster a sense of joy in the workplace. Daniel Goleman notes, "The most effective leaders, then, use humor more freely, even when things are tense, sending positive messages that shift the underlying emotional tone of the interaction."[21] Kouzes and Posner have given this an official acronym, LBFA—Leading by Fooling Around. They cite empirical evidence linking fun with productivity.[22] Seth Godin notes: "It turns out that the people who like their jobs the most are also the ones who are doing the best work, making the greatest impact, and changing the most."[23] As a result, Godin urges leaders: "Don't be boring."[24] It *is* possible to work hard, to be productive, and yet to have fun. Godin intones, "Instead of wondering when your next vacation is, maybe you ought to set up a life you don't need to escape from."[25] Leaders ought to enjoy going to work and so should those they lead (Prov. 15:13; 17:22).

LEADERS SCHEDULE TIME FOR PEOPLE

Successful leaders tend to enjoy people and are typically surrounded by them. Abraham Lincoln spent the majority of each day receiving people at the White House. Those who prefer to work alone, or who find it difficult to relate to others, may not be suited for leadership roles.

Those in prominent positions must remember that without followers they are not leaders. They may be administrators who run large organizations, but they are not leaders. To be a leader one must invest time in people. This can be difficult for those who face a multiplicity of tasks. They can easily be tempted to look upon their people as interruptions to their work rather than its essence. Whether they lead a small church or a large corporation, genuine leaders make time with people a high priority.

In *Encouraging the Heart*, Kouzes and Posner argue that wise business leaders recognize, encourage, and thank their people. The authors note that many times administrators know little about their employees' lives even after working with them for many years.[26] A popular leadership theory is the Pareto Principle, or the 20–80 Principle. This theory suggests that 20 percent of people in an organization generally produce 80 percent of the results. Advocates of this theory argue that 80 percent of a leader's time should therefore be invested in the 20 percent of the people who are doing 80 percent of the work.

The investment of a leader's time in certain people will produce far greater results than equivalent time invested in others. People who work hard for an organization and who are teachable deserve their leader's attention. When leaders invest in people who are motivated to learn, those people have the opportunity to excel and to reach their maximum potential. Marcus Buckingham and Curt Coffman suggest that leaders "spend the *most* time with their *most* productive employees. They invest in the best."[27] When people are achieving what God designed for them, they can inspire others in the organization to strive to do the same thing. Sometimes pastors vainly invest many hours trying to revive carnal or apathetic church members when they could help their church far more by discipling those members who are eager to mature in their faith.

Leaders ought never to allow the least motivated members of an organization to set the pace for the others. Rather, when leaders help teachable people achieve their best, others in the organization see what is possible and can know what is expected of them. Wise leaders also link growing and productive followers with those who need encouragement because the strength of any organization depends on whether every member is successfully doing his or her part (Eph. 4:16).

The biblical record demonstrates that there were times when Jesus delivered profound teaching to the multitudes. At other times, he took his twelve disciples aside and gave them divine instruction not offered to the crowds (Matt. 10; 13:10–17; Mark 7:17–23). There were other occasions when Jesus met with his inner circle of disciples—Peter, James, and John—and went still deeper in spiritual matters (Luke 9:28; Matt. 26:37–38). Jesus sometimes invested time in a solitary disciple (John 20:27; 21:15–19). Why would Jesus be selective with divine, life-changing truth? Some people were better prepared to receive his teaching and to act upon it than were others. By investing in small groups such as the twelve disciples, Jesus was preparing for the day when they would become powerful leaders themselves.

Many leaders have experienced the frustration of pouring large amounts of time into people, only to find those people unable or unwilling to change. Meanwhile, hardworking members of the organization were neglected while their leader vainly attempted to strengthen unmotivated, resistant individuals.

Pastors continually face this dilemma. Every church has chronically needy people. Such people consume numerous hours of their ministers' time because they require extensive counseling and encouragement. Yet their unhealthy attitudes and behavior often remain unchanged. Meanwhile, church members wanting to grow in their faith receive scant attention from their pastor because they do not complain or draw attention to themselves. Leaders who allow this to happen find themselves channeling their energy into the least responsive people in their organization while neglecting those who would flourish with minimal investment. When leaders allow their time to be monopolized by the weaker members, they limit their organizations.

As with most leadership principles, the Pareto Principle addresses the experience of many organizations; however, caution must be used in its application. There is a subtle danger in misapplying the 20–80 Principle. For spiritual leaders, people, not tasks, are central. The primary role of spiritual leaders is not to merely accomplish tasks but to take people from where they are to where God wants them to be. Fulfilling this mandate requires watching to see where God is working in people's lives and then joining him. When God is working in people's lives, it is their leaders' responsibility to invest time and energy into helping these people grow. Since only God knows whether a weak member will respond positively to their leader's attention, it is essential that God set the leader's agenda. Conscientious leaders strive to make every person they lead into a productive contributor. Leaders never give up on their people. They do, however, invest their time wisely between those who are growing and productive and those who are not.

Leaders Make Time for What Is Important

1. Leaders schedule unhurried time with God.
2. Leaders schedule regular, quality time with their families.
3. Leaders schedule time for their health.
4. Leaders schedule time for people.

Leaders Avoid Timewasters

John Rockefeller was fastidiously punctual for appointments. He declared, "A man has no right to occupy another man's time unnecessarily."[28] Spiritual leaders who have witnessed what God can accomplish with one hour of their time are reluctant to waste precious minutes. Those who can flippantly dissipate their time in idle conversation and unimportant matters clearly have little understanding of the value of their time.

Besides making the best use of time, spiritual leaders steer clear of time wasters. A host of discussions, activities, and meetings do nothing more than consume leaders' valuable time. Whenever leaders are seduced into investing time in the trivial, they have become disengaged from the essential. For example, Clay Shirky notes that Americans watch 200 billion hours of television each year.[29] He claims their is an enormous "Cognitive Surplus" that, if invested more wisely, could produce startling results. The list of time-consuming diversions is lengthy, but the following are some of the most notorious offenders.

TECHNOLOGY

Technology can enhance leaders' work exponentially and save hours of time. It can also be an insidious time stealer. Technology is advancing so rapidly, few people can keep up. So many time-saving programs and devices are becoming available it would take weeks just to read about them. Some people fritter away hours on their computers every day performing nonessential tasks. One problem is computers are instruments for work as well as for entertainment and some people struggle to differentiate between the two. The Internet can be a great source of information and communication, or it can become a black hole of people's valuable time. Social networking programs can enable rapid dissemination of information, or it can fritter away hours of precious time each week. Everyone knows at least one zealous Internet junkie who inundates them with quotes, jokes, feel-good stories, and late-breaking news about impending crises or the most current computer virus that *must* be shared with everyone on their contact list. Some leaders who have better things to do with their time waste hours of their day on their computer while their organization languish. Incorporating new technology is essential for organizations, but it is imperative leaders monitor the amount of time they spend investigating and experimenting with new products against the potential gains in time and efficiency. The key is not for leaders to shun technology; that would be shortsighted. Leaders seek to master technology without squandering valuable hours constantly investigating the latest cyber-trend.

LACK OF PERSONNEL

Leaders who understaff their organizations are ultimately forced to divert their precious time into secondary issues. Leaders cannot delegate to nonexistent people. A large percentage of activities that would take leaders fifteen minutes or less to accomplish could easily be handled by an assistant. Leaders seeking to build large blocks of time into their day for creative thinking, planning, and problem solving need to have people available to them who can handle administrative tasks. For a variety of reasons, some leaders prefer to type their own letters, make their own appointments, or arrange their own travel, even though an assistant could do these more efficiently. Effective leaders view every task in light of the question, Is this something someone else could do? Jobs constantly accumulate on leaders' desks; therefore, they must be continually giving tasks away. Technology can help reduce the need for additional personnel, but ultimately an understaffed organization puts undue pressure on everyone and limits the organization's growth potential. Leaders do not add staff haphazardly or without regard to budget constraints, but they do monitor their organization's optimum effectiveness and ensure that enough trained personnel are available to accomplish its mission.

IDLE CONVERSATION

Warren Buffet's biographer noted: "He never let people waste his time. If he added something to his schedule, he discarded something else. He never rushed. He always had time to work on business deals and he always had time for the people who mattered to him. His friends could pick up the phone and call him whenever they liked. He managed this by keeping his phone calls warmhearted and short. When he was ready to stop talking, the conversation simply died. The kind of friends he had didn't abuse the privilege."[30]

Idle conversation is an insidious time waster. It is also one of the most difficult to avoid because leaders do not want to leave the impression they are too busy to visit with their colleagues. In fact, most leaders enjoy their people and have a genuine desire to spend time with them. However, a conversation that begins at the lunchroom coffee pot can eventually consume an hour of a leader's day. A casual chat in the office hallway about the local sports team can erode a leader's valuable time. That is not to say leaders never have lengthy conversations with those in their organization. Sensitive leaders are always willing to discuss substantive matters. Perceptive leaders learn to detect when a colleague has an underlying issue that needs discussing or whether a conversation is going nowhere. Conversations can be profitable, informative, redemptive, and mutually encouraging. Or they can swallow up valuable blocks of time both parties could better spend elsewhere. Leaders must find the balance between touching base with people and becoming engaged in prolonged, frivolous discussions.

People who loiter around the workplace visiting with every passerby send the clear message they are not occupied with important matters. Leaders should be pleasant conversationalists, but they should be intentional in how they spend their day. Good leaders find appropriate moments to excuse themselves from idle conversations and return to their work. Efficient leaders are brief and succinct in their communication. Their memos are concise. They get to the point when they make phone calls. They make their words as well as their time count.

Excessive Hobbies

Hobbies give leaders a welcome and wholesome outlet to relieve stress and restore emotional health. They can also provide a fitness regimen. Leaders often use hobbies such as golf as a means to get to know clients or colleagues. However, when a hobby consumes a leader's time to the detriment of important relationships and activities, it ceases to serve its rightful function.

Hobbies can do double duty for leaders. If they enjoy golfing or jogging, they can invite a client or colleague to accompany them. Activities such as skiing, hiking, or camping are conducive to family outings combining relaxation and exercise with quality family time. The key is ensuring that doing one important thing doesn't inadvertently lead to neglecting another. If leaders have no hobbies or recreational interests, this means they have probably been working too hard and may not know how to relax. At the other end of the spectrum, some need to reevaluate the excessive amounts of time and money they spend on recreation and recognize the adverse effect their hobbies exert on their families, work, or other priorities. Like technology and conversation, hobbies have their advantages and disadvantages. It comes down to wise choices.

Disorganization

Being disorganized can be the undoing of even the best-intentioned leader. Leaders cannot afford to be disorganized because they stand to waste not only their own time but also the valuable time of their people and clients as well. We have already touched on a few areas that can fall victim to disorganization such as punctuality and time management. A skilled assistant is an invaluable resource in keeping a leader organized. An effective record-keeping system is a must so leaders don't waste time searching for information they have misplaced. Effective leaders provide an agenda in advance for those attending their meeting so participants arrive fully prepared to maximize the time. Skilled leaders deal with administrative matters only once. They read and respond to correspondence once, take action, and file it away. They don't waste time continually searching for misplaced correspondence in their in-box.

Leaders of Christian organizations are often among the most disorganized professionals. There is a reason for this: most entered the ministry because they loved God and people, not because they felt gifted to lead. They may abhor administration because it takes them away from doing what they love to do—spend time with people. If they devote most of their energy to what they know and enjoy, they fail to organize themselves or their people to address critical issues. These ministers can brighten up a life with a hospital visit, but they conduct painfully tedious meetings. They may be gifted evangelists, but they continually frustrate their followers because they are either unprepared or unaware of the issues facing their organization. Too often ministers grow needlessly weary and discouraged under an administrative load when help is just around the corner. Many qualified people would gladly assist them if only the leader would enlist them. Administration is a significant ministry (Rom. 12:8; 1 Cor. 12:28). Leaders who are not proficient administrators need to find a competent administrator or seek training in administration themselves.

If leaders will do what it takes to get organized, they can enjoy productive and rewarding leadership tenures. When people organize their overstuffed closets and get rid of clutter, they are usually amazed at how much space they have for their clothes. Getting organized holds a similar advantage for leaders. Once they arrange their time into manageable blocks and eliminate the superfluous, they find they have enough time in the day to accomplish all God is leading them to do.

Leaders Avoid Timewasters

1. Technology
2. Lack of Personnel
3. Idle Conversation
4. Excessive Hobbies
5. Disorganization

Leaders Invest Their Surplus Time Wisely

Why do some leaders accomplish far more than others? Why do some leaders see nothing of significance occur under their tenure, yet their successors witness a flurry of activity and progress? There are, of course, many reasons for this, but one key factor is how they use their surplus time. To busy leaders the idea of surplus time may seem like a dream. The truth is, however, most people have extra time; they simply don't recognize it as such. The effective leader seizes these pockets of time. The mediocre leader squanders them. Effective leaders adhere strictly to the Boy Scout motto: "Be prepared."

Most leaders know of books and articles that could greatly inform them and enrich their leadership. Some leaders find ways to stay current in their fields while others complain they never have time to read. Wise leaders seize unexpected free moments for reading. When meeting someone at a restaurant for a breakfast meeting, prepared leaders take a book with them. If they must wait fifteen minutes while their appointment is caught in traffic, they read a helpful chapter. Productive leaders know the person they are meeting at the airport may arrive late, so they prepare themselves for possible delays by taking reading material with them.

Margaret Truman, Harry Truman's daughter, could not recall a time she saw her father spending an idle moment without a book in his hand.

Enforced times of waiting, such as in a doctor's or dentist's office are good opportunities to review helpful material. Commercial flights offer several hours of mostly uninterrupted time during which a prepared person can accomplish a great deal. Noise reduction headphones are a worthwhile investment. Laptops and handheld devices are invaluable for such times. A prepared leader could respond to several e-mails and preview material for forthcoming meetings. Entire books can be read during business travel. Unprepared people are left to glance through the in-flight magazine, look at their watches, or gaze out the window. Over the course of a three-hour flight, the person who planned ahead may have read several chapters of a helpful book, answered e-mails, and reviewed her calendar. The unprepared leader has watched a third-rate in-flight movie and viewed the cloud cover over Nebraska.

Do not misunderstand the point. Sometimes catching an in-flight nap is the wisest thing to do because the leader needs to be fresh for an important meeting that evening. There will also be times when God prompts leaders to put down their book to share their faith with the person in the next seat. The objective is not to work constantly but to be intentional about the way you spend your time.

Some leaders have found a gold mine of valuable time when they redirect lost hours spent watching television into enriching reading, exercising, or family time. Leaders who spend large amounts of time commuting in their cars could occupy the time by praying (with their eyes open!) or listening to informative audio books, including the Bible or challenging sermons. If leaders creatively seize moments of enforced idleness, they will be pleasantly surprised to discover they do have time for important matters.

When Elton Trueblood, the prolific Christian author, was once visiting a theological seminary, a student asked him if he ever attended social clubs. He replied, "I have written books while others have attended clubs." While not devaluing people's involvement in social organizations, Trueblood was acknowledging he made choices about his time investments. Trueblood chose to write well and people continue to be blessed by his efforts decades later.

Conclusion

No one should determine leaders' schedules but themselves, as God guides them. They must understand God's will and, from that perspective, set their priorities. Doing so requires identifying the most important things in their lives and arranging their schedules so none of these priorities are neglected. Staying organized is a deliberate and ongoing process. An uncluttered schedule one month can deteriorate into a calendar filled with extraneous activities the next. Wise leaders regularly prune their schedules of unnecessary commitments. They learn to delegate and to say no. They redeem the time (Eph. 5:16). Great leaders want their lives to count so they use their time wisely.

———————— **Responding to This Material** ————————

1. On a scale of 1 to 10 with 10 being the highest, rate your effectiveness in using your time for the following:

_____ Study time

_____ Meeting times

_____ Office times

_____ Breakfast, lunch, and dinner meetings

_____ Days off

_____ Vacations

_____ Evenings at home

_____ Travel

_____ Intentionally building up, developing, or encouraging key staff

2. List the three biggest time wasters in your life. Jot down ways you can protect your time against them.

3. What are three ways you could reclaim pockets of wasted time in your schedule?

4. What are ways technology could help you save time?

5. How might you make better use of personnel to save time?

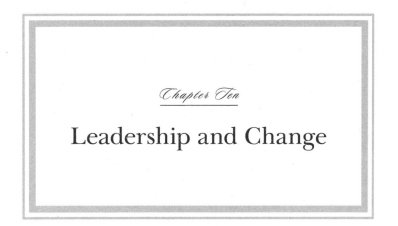

Chapter Ten

Leadership and Change

eadership would be much easier if everything remained the same. However, as John Kotter notes, "change is the function of leadership."[1] The question is whether leaders will successfully guide change or be summarily crushed by it. Leading change in today's organizations is not for the fainthearted. It calls for leaders' best thinking, fervent prayers, and profound wisdom. The reason change is so difficult is because people instinctively resist it. They do so for numerous reasons of which we will identify only a few:

1. *People are reluctant to make personal changes.* The dreaded King Henry VIII wore a gold medallion on a chain bearing the inscription: "I prefer to die rather than change my mind."[2] Of Henry's daughter, Queen Elizabeth, Sir Francis Bacon observed, "Her Majesty loveth peace. Next, she loveth not change."[3] Bringing about institutional change is difficult because to do so you must convince people to change. Robert Quinn notes, "Organizational change always begins with a personal change."[4] People must surrender some of their

previous attitudes, behaviors, positions, and comforts for their organization to advance. These are not easily relinquished or adjusted. Generally the reason people resist change so adamantly is not because they cannot stand to see their beloved institution altered but because they are unwilling to make personal adjustments on behalf of the organization.

2. *People find it difficult to keep pace with change.* Change today can be intimidating because it occurs so rapidly people feel unable to understand it or control it. Even techno geeks find it challenging to stay abreast of the latest communication devices and office tools. Even stellar companies such as those heralded by *In Search of Excellence, Built to Last,* and *Good to Great* can be identified as the best companies in the world in one book and already be languishing before the second edition is printed. Likewise, some churches would be completely relevant and in touch with their communities, if it were 1955. But time has passed them by, society changed, and the congregations didn't make timely, critical adjustments.

3. *People prefer the status quo.* We know of a church that had been declining for years as its white congregation became surrounded by a sea of Hispanic people who had moved into the neighborhood. The remaining church leaders met with the pastor of another Caucasian congregation located near them to seek advice. The pastor suggested one of three options: (1) they could hire a Hispanic pastor and intentionally transition their church to reflect the community; (2) they could give their building to a Hispanic congregation and then merge with his church to develop a stronger congregation; (3) they could do nothing and eventually die. Two weeks later the group's spokesman painfully reported they chose to die. Incredibly, the land is littered with organizations choosing to decline into irrelevance rather than adapt to the times. Claiming the Scriptures that speak of a "faithful remnant," these languishing churches prefer martyrdom over transformation. Likewise many once vibrant organizations enter a period of atrophy where they lose their zeal for growth, yet rather than adjust they hunker down for the inevitable end.

4. *People naively hope things will get better.* "Real politic" is seeing things the way they are and not the way you want them to be. As Michael and Deborah

Jinkins observe: ". . . idealism does not serve any leader well; it is a luxury the leader cannot afford."[5] Bossidy and Charan candidly conclude: "Most companies don't face reality very well."[6] Optimism has its place in leadership, but naïveté is another matter. Many organizations vainly assume that after the economic downturn is over, or the transitioning neighborhood stabilizes, or the summer season draws to a close, things will get better. But doing nothing is rarely an effective strategy.

5. *People do not see the need for change.* Some people have such a naturally positive outlook it is difficult for them to see what is wrong with their organization. Richard has a relative who, as a high school student, once received zero on a midterm exam. Attempting to look on the bright side, she shrugged her shoulders, smiled, and said, "Well, that's better than nothing!" Optimism detached from realism can inspire leaders to make claims such as, "Growth may have slowed, but at least we still have *some* growth!" While it would be foolish to push the panic button at every slight downturn in business, it is also foolhardy to wait until the barbarians are at the gate before sounding the alarm. Gordon Sullivan and Michael Harper in their book *Hope Is Not a Method* describe how, after the overwhelming victory of the Persian Gulf War, American Army leaders wisely realized it was imperative they reorganize.[7] These leaders recognized the growing trends in warfare would make much of their current methodology obsolete. It was imperative they transform the military so it was prepared for future challenges.

Leaders must not be content to merely focus on their organization's current effectiveness. They should be constantly watching for trends and indicators that suggest adjustments are required. A denominational leader in Australia told us his denomination enjoyed large surpluses for several years. His churches all had attractive facilities and, while not growing rapidly, were seeing incremental growth annually. However, the national census indicated the percentage of Australians who were regularly attending church was declining dramatically. He knew it would be foolish to pat himself on the back for his successful leadership while ignoring the reality his nation was racing to spiritual ruin. Wise leaders look at *all* the important indicators and not just the *positive* ones when determining if change is called for.

6. *People believe it is too difficult to mobilize their organization to change.* In many organizations people know reforms must be made, but the enormity of the task dissuades them from making the attempt. When Dietrich Bonhoeffer was fourteen, he announced his intention to become a minister and theologian. His father and older brothers were disconcerted that someone so bright would waste his life on "a poor, feeble, boring, petty bourgeois institution." Dietrich merely replied: "In that case I shall reform it!"[8]

Change provides the litmus test for true leaders. There is generally no shortage of volunteers when healthy organizations advertise for leaders. But genuine leaders are willing and even impassioned about guiding organizations to make necessary changes so they can thrive in the future. Despite the reluctance of many people to change, leaders must press forward if they are to successfully bring their organizations into the future. To implement organizational change spiritual leaders must do seven things.

Implement Organizational Change

SEEK GOD'S DIRECTION

People's lives are valuable. It is wrong to make them endure the discomfort of change unnecessarily. Some leaders want to initiate change in their organization for the wrong reasons. They may be motivated to legitimize their leadership by instituting comprehensive changes once they assume the executive office. Insecurity compels some to eradicate any sign of their predecessor. One pastor who followed a beloved, long-tenured minister felt oppressed by his predecessor's legacy. The picture of the former pastor in the church lobby, the veteran church staff, even the distinctive colors the previous leader chose for the auditorium communicated to the new pastor that he was not yet "in charge." Therefore, he systematically removed any trace of his predecessor. When none of this solved his issue, he suggested the church relocate and construct a new facility. The people rebelled, and he was forced to find a different congregation where the ghost of a beloved predecessor would not haunt him. An equally illegitimate motive is trying to build a legacy through enlarging and changing one's organization. When initiatives are launched to enhance the leader's reputation, career, or profits, people feel no obligation to embrace and support the leader's change efforts.

Truly spiritual leaders are driven by God's agenda. They seek his direction before launching changes. They know that their best intentioned efforts will fail to accomplish God's purposes if they are not divinely inspired and empowered. Leaders must heed Jesus' counsel to carefully consider the cost before undertaking major ventures (Luke 12:28–32). Change merely for change's sake can be disastrous for careless leaders. Before performing organizational surgery, leaders must be certain of the need and purpose of their efforts. Change always comes with a price. If leaders do not ensure their efforts are inspired, led and blessed by God, their people's sacrifices will be for naught.

DISCERN THE ORGANIZATIONAL CULTURE

Jinkins and Jinkins assert, "Leadership is always grounded in a particular time and place—in a particular culture."[9] Perhaps more bluntly, they acknowledge "leadership takes place in the crossfire of conflicting self-interests."[10] If there is any time leaders must be sensitive to organizational culture, it is when they attempt to initiate change. John Kotter defines *culture* as the "norms of behavior and shared values among a group of people."[11] Keith McFarland says corporate culture is "company character," which he defines as "values translated into action."[12] Corporate culture is "the way we do things around here." It is not necessarily always good, wholesome, effective, or Christian. It is simply the accepted way things get done in a particular organization.

Robert Quinn notes, "organizational cultures are not designed; they tend to evolve naturally."[13] Cultures involve values: what is considered important and what is rewarded. It encompasses power brokers: those whose approval is critical to getting something done. It includes traditions: the organizational memory of how things have been done and the organization's heroes. One does not change a culture by issuing a memo. A pastor may arbitrarily remove the pews from his antebellum church auditorium, but that does not mean he has changed peoples' views on how church is supposed to be conducted. Instituting change requires altering peoples' thinking and values, and that is not easily accomplished.

Some CEOs feel as if they are constantly stepping on land mines because every time they try to make needed changes they collide with a deeply entrenched corporate culture. A pastor who was called to a historic church in the South, steeped in tradition, was told the congregation wanted to attract young families and better evangelize its community. The pastor believed them and eagerly set about initiating the necessary changes. The people, however, instinctively resisted and thwarted his efforts. The church functioned so long in one manner the people could not bring themselves to alter the status quo. They genuinely wanted different results, but they were unwilling to make the necessary changes to achieve them.

King Josiah's story provides a classic biblical example of attempting to change culture. Josiah's father was the most wicked king ever to rule the kingdom of Judah. King Manasseh brought in the worst depravity and abominations of the idol-worshipping nations around Judah and forced them on his people. He built altars to Baal and encouraged the practices of spiritualists, soothsayers, and witches. He even built altars to pagan gods and placed them in the sacred temple. Manasseh ruthlessly put to death those who opposed him (2 Kings 21:1–18). Tragically, Manasseh also enjoyed the longest reign of any king—fifty-five years. For over half a century, the evil king encouraged the vilest depravities upon his society. Then his son Josiah ascended the throne at the age of eight. By then the people were unfamiliar with Scripture, and the temple was too filthy and cluttered to be used.

Josiah eventually implemented an extensive and aggressive reform. He tore down the altars and temples devoted to idols. He executed those who promoted idolatry and evil practices. He called his people to repent and return to God (2 Kings 22:1–25). There had never before been a king who turned to God with all of his heart like Josiah did (2 Kings 23:25). Nevertheless, God still judged the people. He declared that society had become so evil even a righteous king like Josiah with all the royal powers at his disposal could not transform that wicked culture (2 Kings 23:26–27). In fact, despite Josiah's heroic efforts, even his own sons and grandson embraced the wickedness he tried so hard to purge from the land (2 Kings 23:32, 37; 24:9). That is the power of culture. Even a king, encouraged by a prophet as righteous as Jeremiah, could not change the evil culture of his day, though he had the power to slay his opponents. Organizational culture should not be treated lightly.

Usually when people move from one organization to another, they take the cultural attitudes from the first place with them—at least to some degree. While it may enrich the new institution, there can be negative repercussions. For example, church planters who gather a core group of members to help launch a new congregation with a unique approach to ministry will inevitably have some of these members instinctively revert to their previous way of doing church. "Well, at my old church, we always did it this way" becomes their mantra. If people had a negative experience in their previous church, they may bring feelings of distrust and caution with them to the new church. Conversely, if they had an effective pastor at their last congregation, they'll have similar expectations of their new minister. Therefore it is important for leaders of new organizations to not only focus on the culture they are seeking to build but to also be alert to the cultures their people bring with them from their previous organizations. Michael Gerber goes so far as to encourage new companies to, when possible, hire people without previous experience so they can be trained from the outset to have the desired corporate values and not have their minds cluttered with management values and procedures from companies in which they previously worked.[14]

PROVIDE A CLEAR PICTURE OF THE DESIRED DESTINATION

Change is stressful so people must clearly understand why it is necessary. John Kotter describes *vision* as "a picture of the future with some implicit or explicit commentary on why people should strive to create that future."[15] Spiritual leaders do not create the vision; but, once God reveals it to them, they communicate it clearly, confidently, and compellingly to those they lead. God described the Promised Land as a place "flowing with milk and honey" (Exod. 3:8). Such picturesque language encapsulated implicit and tantalizing truths. *Flowing* implied abundance. It meant the land would be filled with well-fed cattle grazing peacefully. Honey was a luxury. It too symbolized abundance, not subsistent living. The contrast could not have been greater between the barren, parched desert the Israelites passed through and the land God promised to give them.

Kotter further suggests leaders should be able to effectively share the vision within five minutes.[16] Leaders rarely have time to make a sixty-minute presentation of the corporate vision so they must be able to describe the high points briefly and succinctly. Daniel Goleman argues people can and will change if they are given a compelling reason to do so.[17]

If leaders carefully consider their audience, they can frame the vision in a concise, compelling word picture that summarizes the vision so it specifically speaks to their people. For example, God burdens church leaders that they must make changes to effectually minister to young people. The senior adults may not respond when challenged to "broaden the demographic base" of their church or to "reach the next generation." But if the pastor meets with the senior members and describes what it will be like to see their grandchildren happily taking their seats next to them in the auditorium, they may be far more willing to make adjustments than church leaders think. Wise leaders help their people understand what it will look like after the changes have been made. Then their people will see the vision as attractive to them personally, and they may even grow impatient with the status quo.

CULTIVATE A SENSE OF URGENCY

Many organizations equate talking about change with implementing it. In fact, powerful forces of fear and complacency can lull organizations into an endless quagmire of meetings and debate rather than action. As a result, precious time and energy are squandered that could have been invested in critical change efforts. As Hannibal prepared his troops to engage the vastly larger Roman army, he exhorted his men: "Therefore no more words are wanted, but deeds"[18] Likewise, as John Adams described the lengthy debates and speeches by the American founding fathers, his wife Abigail urged him, "We have too many high sounding words and too few actions that correspond with them."[19] Enormous opportunities can sometimes be lost if people do not grasp the urgency of the hour and the necessity of quickly responding to the opportunity before them. As the saying goes: "Carpe Diem"—seize the day!

John Kotter suggests the single greatest error people have made when trying to effect change is they "did not create a high enough sense of urgency among enough people to set the stage for making a challenging leap into some new direction."[20] There are generally people in any organization who trust the leader and embrace change. Some may even see the need for action *before* the leader does. But others are uncomfortable with any level of change, and if it involves personal sacrifice, some people will naturally be reluctant to embrace it until it is absolutely necessary. Kotter suggests that leaders must help their people realize that remaining with the status quo will ultimately bring more discomfort than will launching out into the unknown.[21] Leaders may have to allow their people to come to grips with and feel the discomfort of remaining where they are. For example, some church members might not want to commence a new building program. Some members may not see the need. Others worry that changing the facility will be disruptive and costly. So the pastor allows the auditorium to fill to the brim each week, forcing longtime members to scramble to find a seat. The pastor relates stories from visitors who informed him they would not return because there was obviously no room for them. Wise leaders help their people experience the clear consequences of not embracing needed change. People must recognize that it is in their own best interest to make the necessary adjustments and that it is essential to respond in a timely fashion.

Leaders must be cognizant that just because *they* see something, it is not necessarily obvious to everyone else. Leaders have a unique vantage point and access to data the average person lacks. Much of the time, leadership is a matter of leaders describing the reality of the situation so others can grasp what they see. Whereas *managers* seek to relieve distress and to keep the existing machinery running smoothly by making small, incremental changes, *leaders* see the big picture and initiate uncomfortable periods of major change to ensure their organization continues to thrive in the future.

This is what God led Moses to do with the Israelites. When the Hebrews were unwilling to make the necessary changes to advance with God, Moses led them to experience the full weight of the status quo. Forty years of wilderness wandering made anything appear better than staying where they were. The Israelites previously thought they had options, such as returning to Egypt or settling down in the wilderness. But in time they realized how urgently they needed to advance into the Promised Land. Joshua inherited a people with a sense of urgency to obey God immediately no matter what he asked them to do. As a result, they became invincible.

ENLIST ADVOCATES

Because instituting change is no small feat, leaders must enlist others to champion the cause with them. This does not involve smoke-filled, back-room plotting and deal making. It does entail that leaders know their people's receptivity to change and current pain threshold. There is little point in leaders presenting a new idea to their people if they are going to be met with widespread resistance. Likewise, if key influencers in the organization are opposed to the initiative, leaders must first work to get those people on board before attempting to win over the people en masse. Too many times impassioned leaders have brought their careers to an abrupt end because they pushed changes on people who were unprepared to accept them. While it is important for leaders to be true to their values, a spiritual leader's primary role is to move people from where they are to where God wants them to be. Leaders who allow themselves to be cornered into a position where their people are rebelling against them or holding votes of confidence or seeking to fire them will be of no use to their organizations. As Stephen Sample advises: "It's fine to reveal, or even trumpet, your core values, but be careful about telling the world the exact location of the hill you're willing to die on."[22] Likewise Jinkins and Jinkins poignantly observe: "However inspiring martyrs may be, they do a poor job of leading organizations over the long haul."[23]

Some leaders see themselves as prophets who must bear an unwelcome message. When they proclaim what must be done, they are persecuted and even fired. Such leaders shuffle from post to post blithely assuming their calling is to deliver unpopular messages and to endure continual rejection. However noble this may appear, it is not leadership. Leaders do not merely deliver bad news and then grimly brace themselves for the fallout; they move people.

John Kotter recommends leaders develop a "sufficiently powerful guiding coalition."[24] If key leaders cannot be convinced of the need for change, the rank and file is unlikely to embrace it. Leaders want to avoid being a lone voice crying in the wilderness. Their credibility is always enhanced when respected colleagues stand with them and affirm the recommended actions. Leaders do this not to rule by oligarchy or to manipulate people, but as a way of convincing a growing number of people of the need for change and enlisting them to participate. Nevertheless, leaders must move their message outside their leadership team to the organization at large if they are to gain widespread acceptance and support. President Martin Van Buren noted:

> Those who have wrought great changes in the world never suc-
> ceeded by gaining over chiefs; but always by exciting the mul-
> titude. The first is the resource of intrigue and produces only
> secondary results, the second is the resort of genius and trans-
> forms the universe.[25]

One reason American presidents such as Abraham Lincoln and Franklin Roosevelt are rated highly as leaders is because they never advanced beyond where they knew the majority of people would follow. Lincoln did not enter the Civil War on a platform of emancipation. Many people in the north would not have supported that cause at the war's outset. Rather, Lincoln waited to announce emancipation until he knew public opinion was prepared to embrace it. His biographer noted: "Lincoln understood that the greatest challenge for a leader in a democratic society is to educate public opinion."[26] Lincoln observed, "Consequently he who molds public sentiment, goes deeper than he who enacts statutes or pronounces decisions."[27] Likewise, Franklin Roosevelt knew the United States would have to enter the war against Nazi Germany, but he also recognized the isolationist-minded populace was initially reluctant to take that step. To move the nation faster than it was prepared to go would ensure FDR a resounding electoral defeat, thereby consigning him to the sidelines where he could no longer exert effective leadership. Roosevelt gradually educated public sentiment and then advanced as far as the more enlightened mood would permit. His biographer notes, "He had begun the delicate and implacable process of moving ahead of opinion on foreign affairs, then retreating slightly and pulling opinion behind him before moving ahead of it again."[28] Roosevelt once quipped, "It's a terrible thing to look over your shoulder when you're trying to lead—and find no one there."[29] Wise leaders make sure they are bringing others with them when they advance.

In a classic leadership blunder, Moses failed to enlist support in advance of initiating a major change. While we should not speculate too far beyond what Scripture reveals, it appears Moses' change effort was scuttled by ten influential people who had not bought into the plan. Moses was asking people to leave their comfort zones and confront a powerful, well-entrenched enemy. They weren't happy in the wilderness, but the cost of moving forward seemed too great. So Moses selected one leader from each of the twelve tribes (Num. 13:2). These were Israel's key influencers. Of course, we know the story. Moses was not particularly skilled at working with other leaders (Exod. 18). In hindsight Moses should have first debriefed with these twelve spies to address any concerns before he asked them to present their report to the entire nation. Attempting to move forward before the majority of his key influencers were prepared to do so doomed Moses' plans.

Regardless of how talented leaders are, they cannot move their organizations forward without the help and cooperation of others. Hannibal was a brilliant general, but he also enjoyed the services of Maharbal, one of the finest cavalry commanders of that day.[30] Queen Elizabeth I enjoyed a long and prosperous reign, but she also had the loyal and astute Sir William Cecil at her disposal for over forty years. So dependant on him did Elizabeth become that she refused to allow him to retire, even when he grew feeble and deaf in his old age.[31] Caesar, Napoleon, Wellington, and Marlborough relied on trusted lieutenants who accomplished their commander's wishes. When leaders surround themselves with others who support the change initiative, they are much more likely to gain the trust of people at large and ultimately accomplish their goals.

PROVIDE SUPPORT

Implementing change calls for much more than inspired speeches. Leaders must also provide the needed resources to enable the accomplishment of the initiatives. They do this in five ways:

First, leaders provide ongoing encouragement for the change effort. They do so with their words, presence, and attention. Leaders make it clear to their people they will be walking with them throughout the endeavor. As Terry Pearce notes, "Your message needs your life, not merely your ideas."[32] Change is costly, and therefore leaders must consistently, enthusiastically, and intentionally encourage those involved in the process. To announce a change and then remain aloof from the process is to give your people unspoken permission to withhold their full investment as well. Encouragement can take the form of a rallying speech but also requires checking on progress, boosting sagging morale, and making whatever adjustments are necessary.

Second, leaders tell stories that undergird the change. Leaders tell stories about the reasons for the change, examples of those producing the change and stories about what the organization will be like once the change is complete. Stephen Denning, in his book *The Secret Language of Leadership: How Leaders Inspire Action Through Narrative*, suggests that stories can provide compelling impetus for organizational change.[33] Denning argues that many people think in stories and therefore stories can be more effective in arguing the need for change than an audiovisual presentation brimming with data. He notes, "If people think in narrative and make decisions in narrative, then talking to people in abstractions is akin to hammering the square pegs of analytical thought into the round holes in their brains."[34] Those who want to produce significant organizational change must think in terms of stories just as Jesus did in his parables.

Third, leaders equip the change efforts. Many an organizational effort has been thwarted because of inadequate staffing, budget, or attention. It demoralizes followers when a leader assigns them a task and then neglects to provide them with the necessary resources. Leaders must ensure those entrusted with implementing the change have access to the funds, personnel, or equipment required to complete the job. As Denning observes, "The fact is that leaders often underestimate what they are asking people to do when they propose basic change."[35] Astute leaders consider the cost of the effort and then allocate adequate resources to ensure it can be accomplished.

Fourth, leaders must also address naysayers. John Kotter identifies a group of people he labels the "Nonos" who relentlessly oppose change initiatives regardless of their merits.[36] These people are not merely skeptics who need to be convinced of the need for change. "Nonos" are people who are determined to resist change and will sabotage any new direction or endeavor. Leaders must not allow those stubbornly resisting change to set the organization's agenda. Leaders facing such opponents can be tempted to postpone the effort until they have achieved a broader consensus. Yet that is exactly what such opponents want as it allows them to hijack the process. When the rank and file observes leaders unwilling to challenge those who are trying to undermine them, they assume the proposed changes must not be critical, and they, too, withdraw their support.

An important issue in this regard is unanimity. While it is always good to have across-the-board support from a leadership team before moving forward, this is not always possible. Some leaders have delayed or discarded needed changes because they could not obtain a unanimous vote to proceed. While God can change people's hearts and bring unity to a leadership team, there are sometimes those determined to resist change at all costs. When such people are placed on a leadership team that values unanimity, they effectively control the entire process. Giving a veto to the least spiritual person on a leadership team can cause prolonged delays and frustration.

Opposition to reform is inevitable. Therefore leaders protect those who are supportive, and they refuse to allow opponents to set the agenda for their organization or derail its advance. When the majority is prepared to advance, it is the leader's responsibility to overcome obstacles and lead them forward.

John Kotter notes that short-term "wins" become especially important when facing critics.[37] Change resistors will constantly highlight the cost and negative consequences of change. Leaders therefore regularly herald the positive results as changes are being implemented. Leaders understand the power of momentum so they regularly highlight the small successes along the way in the change process.

Fifth, leaders reward those who produce change. Just as leaders challenge naysayers, they reward those who are paying the price to produce change. Change is costly, and if people are going to make sacrifices for the good of the organization, they deserve to be noticed, commended, and rewarded for their efforts. When leaders fail to support those making the changes or when they use them as scapegoats when criticisms come, it will not be long before leaders discover no one is willing to make sacrifices on their behalf.

FOLLOW THROUGH TO THE FINISH

Niccolo Machiavelli wryly observed, "The populace is by nature fickle; it is easy to persuade them of something, but difficult to confirm them in that persuasion."[38] Many a needed change effort has been scuttled because the leader did not follow through until the end. As Kotter notes, "While celebrating a win is fine, declaring the war won can be a catastrophe."[39] Moses led his people through ten devastating plagues in Egypt, the parting of the Red Sea, the destruction of the Egyptian Army, the defeat of the Amalekites, and the impartation of God's law from the top of the dreaded Mount Sinai. Yet Moses fell short of completing the ultimate goal: leading his people into the Promised Land. Effective leaders do not merely identify a vision for their organization or obtain a vote of approval from their leadership team or plead their cause to the rank and file; they stick with it until the change has been fully implemented and is now imbedded in the corporate culture. Bossidy and Charan argue that "execution" is the missing link to successful organizations. They note, "Too many leaders fool themselves into thinking their companies are well run."[40] Wise leaders recognize they have not been completely successful until the desired changes are clearly and fully implemented in their organization.

Conclusion

Through God's leading, effective leaders make organizations better. They take weak institutions and make them stronger. They lead unprofitable companies into profitability. They take declining churches and make them vibrant. They steer successful organizations and bring operational maturity to ensure continued excellence and expanded success. Change is not always easy. It has cost many leaders their jobs. Yet in the rapidly changing world in which leaders function, they must understand how to implement change in their organizations. They have no choice. They either change or perish. Leaders therefore must be prayerful, artful, wise, and skilled change agents.

To Bring about Change, Leaders

1. Seek God's direction.
2. Discern the organizational culture.
3. Provide a clear picture of the desired destination.
4. Cultivate a sense of urgency.
5. Enlist advocates.
6. Provide support.
7. Follow through to the finish.

—————————— **Responding to This Material** ——————————

1. What evidence do you have that the change efforts you've introduced to your organization are God inspired?

2. Evaluate the success of your last two attempts to change something in your organization. How did they go? Would you consider them successes? What could you have done better?

3. What is the greatest challenge you face in leading people to change? What steps can you take to overcome this challenge? Who will need to help you overcome this?

4. How good are you at guiding others through change? How might you provide more encouragement to those involved in the process?

5. How do you test the resistance to your change efforts to see if God is speaking to you through the opposition?

6. How is your track record of staying with it until the change has been fully implemented? What might you do to improve in this area?

Chapter Eleven

Building Effective Teams

I n 1860, storm clouds over the issue of slavery intensified in the United
States to the point a violent outburst appeared imminent. The new
Republican Party elected its first presidential candidate, the relatively
unknown Abraham Lincoln. In victory Lincoln defeated three men who were
eminently more qualified for the office than he was. William H. Seward,
a New York senator and a powerful orator, was the leading Republican.
Salmon P. Chase was the influential governor of Ohio, and Edward Bates the
leading statesman from Missouri. These ambitious men, along with Gideon
Welles, Montgomery Blair, and eventually Edward Stanton, would form
Lincoln's cabinet. Notes Doris Kearns Goodwin: "Every member of this
administration was better known, better educated, and more experienced in
public life than Lincoln. Their presence in the cabinet might have threatened
to eclipse the obscure prairie lawyer from Springfield."[1] Nevertheless, the
herculean effort of this unusual team during the nadir of American history

would save the Republic and earn Lincoln his reputation as America's first modern president.

Even the most outstanding leaders cannot accomplish significant tasks apart from the capable effort of others. A solitary leader is a contradiction in terms. History's most heralded leaders learned how to maximize the talents and sacrifices of others to multiply their efforts. The Duke of Wellington will be forever remembered as Napoleon's conqueror at Waterloo, but Wellington was successful due to the enormous sacrifices of his loyal lieutenants. At the close of the battle of Waterloo, rather than exuberantly celebrating his immortal victory, Wellington ate his dinner at a table set for many of his officers who would never return to dine with him again. Hours later Dr. John Hume arrived to give a preliminary report of the officers who had been wounded or killed during the titanic conflict:

> As I entered, he sat up, his face covered with the dust and sweat of the previous day, and extended his hand to me, which I took and held in mine, whilst I told him of Gordon's death, and of such casualties as had come to my knowledge. He was much affected. I felt the tears dropping fast upon my hand. And looking towards him, saw them chasing one another in furrows over his dusty cheeks. He brushed them away suddenly with his left hand, and said to me in a voice tremulous with emotion, "Well, thank God, I don't know what it is to lose a battle; but certainly nothing can be more painful than to gain one with the loss of so many of one's friends."[2]

Perhaps it was the staggering loss of his brave officers that led Wellington to conclude "next to a battle lost, the greatest misery is a battle gained."[3] While Wellington would attain his nation's highest honors and ultimately the prime minister's office, he always knew his glory and fame was purchased with the lives of many of Britain's finest young men.

Likewise, while Robert E. Lee was heralded as a daring and brilliant general, he relied heavily on Stonewall Jackson to gain some of his most brilliant victories. Of Jackson, Lee observed: "Such an executive officer . . . the sun never shone on. I have but to show him my design and I know that if it can be done, it will be done. No need for me to send or watch him. Straight as a needle to the pole he advances to the execution of my purpose."[4] When Lee learned that Jackson's left arm was amputated as a result of his wounds, Lee retorted, "He has lost his left arm, but I have lost my right arm."[5] Lee always maintained he could have won the decisive battle of Gettysburg had he still had Jackson to lead the advance.[6] The greatest leaders in history have recognized their dependence on others.

A leadership team is a reflection of its leader. Leaders who build crack leadership teams do the following six things.

Leaders Develop a Dynamic Culture

Whether you study the *esprit de corps* of victorious armies such as those under Alexander, Caesar, or Patton or analyze the corporate cultures of enormously successful companies in their prime such as Standard Oil or Microsoft, you will unearth vigor, confidence, and creativity that clearly set them apart from their opposition. Such a brilliant and upbeat collective disposition derives from a variety of sources, but when it is present, teams produce their greatest work.

Developing a dynamic, problem-solving, creative, and hardworking team begins by hiring the right people. Leman and Pentak observe: "Your people are your greatest competitive advantage."[7] Jim Collins qualifies: "The old adage, 'People are your most important asset' turns out to be wrong. People are *not* your most important asset. The *right* people are."[8] Leaders develop superior teams by intentionally hiring or enlisting the best people possible for their organizations. Edward Lawler III argues that companies ought to fire managers who "do not attract or retain the best employees."[9] Kevin McFarland suggests that successful companies "hired attitude and trained aptitude."[10] McFarland notes that when successful start-up companies interviewed potential employees, recruiters sought to unearth the applicant's character. Interviewers assumed "their [applicants] opinion of the world is also a confession of character."[11] McFarland concluded: "Breakthrough companies strive first to hire people of character and the performance tends to take care of itself."[12] The key to interviewing potential staff is not to ask them what they *would* do but what they *have* done. Anyone can proclaim what they would do in a hypothetical situation, but the most reliable way to predict future behavior is to discover what applicants did in previous situations. Likewise, those enlisting staff must seek to determine the aspirant's honesty. One way to discern this is to ask candidates to describe a time when they failed and what they did in response. If applicants cannot recall a previous failure, they are not being honest! By sharing a misstep, interviewees are demonstrating both honesty and humility, two important traits in new hires. Seth Godin concludes, "When you hire amazing people and give them freedom, they do amazing stuff."[13]

Challenging missions require carefully chosen teams. The book of Leviticus elucidates the high standard God maintains for those who serve him. When God chose to deliver the Israelites from the Midianites, he did not rely on large numbers but on a carefully selected team (Judg. 7). David was a great military leader, but he had a group of mighty men who were proven in battle to form the nucleus of his invincible army (2 Sam. 23:8–39). Leaders in the early church, such as overseers and deacons, had to meet a rigorous standard to be elected (1 Tim. 3:1–7, 8–13). Even Jesus, before he chose his twelve disciples, spent an entire night in prayer making sure he selected those his Father was giving him (Luke 6:12; John 17:6). These men were ordinary businesspeople, but their character allowed them to be fashioned into extraordinary apostles.

The greatest liability for many organizations is careless recruitment. Simply hiring the best person available is not always wise. It may be more prudent to delay filling a position until the right person is discovered. Many a chagrined leader has discovered it is better to endure a vacancy than to impatiently hire the wrong candidate. Jim Collins advises organizations not to hire people from the outside who do not know or embrace the corporate culture.[14] Collins' mantra is, "First who . . . then what."[15] The building blocks of outstanding organizations are excellent people. To attract such individuals, leaders must inspire greatness. Horace Walpole once commented to Sir William Pitt the Elder, "A minister that inspires great actions must be a great minister."[16] The reason some organizations fail to attract exceptional talent is their leadership is unexceptional. Godin observes: "The organizations of the future are filled with smart, fast, flexible people on mission. The thing is, that requires leadership."[17] Generally speaking, quality employees have numerous options before them, and salary/benefits are only one factor in choosing which organization to join. People want to invest their lives into something worthwhile. As Kouzes and Posner note, "People commit to causes, not plans. Commitment is fueled by what we cherish."[18] Leaders who promote mundane causes and provide ordinary management will entice average people.

Most importantly, leaders must go to great lengths if necessary to enlist the best people for their team. They may have to be aggressive in the salary package or working conditions they offer. They will need to provide a cause worth investing in as well as a job that challenges and rewards team members. Leaders may also have to overcome their own bias or preconceived methodology to enlist people with a fresh, creative approach.

John Rockefeller attributed the secret to his success to "my confidence in men and my ability to inspire their confidence in me."[19] At one point Rockefeller's Standard Oil lost a court case. Rockefeller immediately contacted the opposing attorney and said, "Mr. Kline . . . you have given us a good licking. Now I would like to have you come and work for me."[20] Likewise Abraham Lincoln recruited his former opponents and critics if he felt they were the best people for the job. As a result, these leaders developed unbeatable teams. The best leaders are always on the lookout for exceptional talent they can add to their ranks. Leaders who are not attracting outstanding talent must take a long, hard look in the mirror.

Leaders Maximize Diversity

Leaders are unwise to merely take on people who see and do things the same way they do. To thrive in a complex and diverse world, teams must have a wide spectrum of perspectives and skills at their disposal. Kouzes and Posner cite a study demonstrating that homogenous groups are more likely to reach incorrect conclusions when problem solving than are heterogeneous teams, and yet, despite their errors, they tend to be more confident of their conclusions.[21] Naturally, groups who view reality from the same vantage point will reach agreement far more quickly than diverse groups. Yet unanimity of opinion or reaching consensus is not necessarily a team's most important goal. What *is* crucial is determining the best solution. For that extensive discussion and even debate is needed. If this is to occur, leaders must intentionally recruit a multifaceted group to work with them. Christian organizations often mistake unity as the highest virtue. Yet if this means people are reluctant to raise questions or to challenge unproven assumptions, then organizations may maintain unity all the way to their ruin. Christian ministries have made enormous mistakes because no one wanted to appear divisive or negative when doing "the Lord's work." Yet unity is most evident when diverse people honestly and fearlessly share their concerns yet remain committed to their fellow team members and to the organizational goals.

Historically, the greatest teams have included a variety of strong personalities. Consider Jesus' twelve disciples: Outspoken Peter, always quick to get the discussion started, was balanced by young, tenderhearted John (John 13:24). The group included pessimistic Thomas (John 11:16; 20:24–28), approachable Andrew (John 6:8–9; 12:20–22), and the formerly despised tax collector Matthew (Mark 2:13–17). Simon the zealot was a rebel while Nathaniel was known for his integrity (John 1:47). God chose a motley team with whom to launch a movement that has continued for more than two thousand years.

Leading variegated teams requires a strong leader with superlative people skills. The Duke of Marlborough led a coalition of international forces for ten years on foreign soil against the world's superpower and yet managed to meld them into an unbeatable force. Much of Marlborough's success resulted from his ability to work with people. It was said that he could "refuse a favour with more grace than others could grant one."[22]

As leaders build their teams, there are at least three areas in which team members should exhibit diversity.

DIVERSITY OF PERSPECTIVE

A winning team intentionally assembled to include men and women as well as various personality types, ethnic groups, and educations will result in a diversity of perspectives. Hiring duplicates of yourself from your alma mater or creating a troupe of uniform thinkers may avoid dissension and strife, but as Ronald Heifetz notes: "Without conflicting frames of reference, the social system scrutinizes only limited features of its problematic environment. It operates at the mercy of its blind spots."[23] Today's organizations cannot afford blind spots.

An Illustration from Richard Blackaby

Richard learned an important lesson while he was leading a seminary. During faculty meetings one professor was always more reluctant than the others to jump on board with new proposals. This could be frustrating because numerous changes were needed and the constant questions about how the students, staff, and constituents would perceive the innovations seemed like needless hand-wringing. Then a personality inventory revealed that every faculty member but that one person had a cognitive, task-oriented disposition. The "hesitant" professor was an affective, people-oriented individual. Moreover, most of the faculty earned their doctorates at the same school (not surprisingly, that one professor studied elsewhere). The faculty was too homogenous. All the professors were brilliant people who knew how to think critically. Nevertheless, their similar perspectives produced a dangerously insular faculty. The one person who could have been viewed as "out of sync" with the team was actually a much needed cautionary voice in a room full of Type A personalities.

According to Patrick Lencioni, leadership team meetings that regularly proceed with unanimity and minimal discussion are unhealthy. In his books *Death by Meeting* and *The Five Dysfunctions of a Team*, he encourages teams to engage in vigorous debate over issues so every option and potential problem is uncovered and considered. This dynamic can be especially difficult for groups that experienced previous success together. David Dotlich and Peter Cairo warn: "Today, leaders must discipline themselves to look at problems and opportunities with a fresh eye. This is difficult because people naturally want to repeat an approach that worked in a similar situation. It is a challenge to consider an alternative to what brought you success in the past or to your current position in the present."[24] It is imperative to build diverse teams with fresh and varied perspectives that are not enslaved to the traditional and previously successful paradigms.

A leader with good people skills can foster and encourage vigorous discussion without losing control or condoning verbal assaults in the process. Bossidy and Charan note: "Only a leader can ask the tough questions that everyone needs to answer, then manage the process of debating the information and making the right trade-offs. . . . Only the leader can set the tone of the dialogue in the organization. Dialogue is the core of culture and the basic unit of work. How people talk to each other absolutely determines how well the organization will function."[25]

Leaders who want an effective team will avoid monopolizing the discussion during meetings. Rather, they will facilitate engaging, stimulating, comprehensive discussions that uncover a wide array of options and potential pitfalls in determining the best response to the challenge at hand. Leaders who see the entire battlefield are always at an advantage over those who have a limited perspective.

DIVERSITY OF SKILLS

Teams are designed to accomplish tasks. Pat MacMillan concludes, "No task, no team."[26] Unless an assignment is extremely focused and requires only a limited set of skills, effective teams must have a wide array of abilities at their disposal. Astute leaders fully develop and uses the skills and talents of their team members. A team of highly skilled personnel is a wasted resource if members are not called on to leverage their unique talents for the good of the organization. In that vein leaders should understand that a team member can shine in one setting and yet stumble in another.

William Pitt the Elder distinguished himself as a national leader while serving as Britain's minister of war during the Seven Years' War. However, later when he achieved the office of prime minister, "the great war minister was very quickly proved no minister for times of peace."[27] Pitt's decisive nature, while imperative during a crisis, led one critic to describe him as "in principle a friend to liberty, but in his temper a tyrant."[28] Pitt enjoyed center stage and insisted on having his way. He was not good at listening to the contrary views of others. His biographer concluded, "Pitt's public persona encouraged him to cultivate admiring deferential associates like Beckford, rather than the colleagues and allies who could aid constructive achievement."[29] In reality, Pitt was "utterly unable to bring out and benefit from the talents of others."[30] His success hinged on his own giftedness and energy and not on the collective skills and talents of his colleagues.

Likewise Oliver Cromwell was invincible when leading an army of Puritan soldiers into battle. However, according to his biographer:

> The tragedy of Oliver Cromwell as a statesman was that those qualities that had raised him in war, qualities so natural to his character, decision, speed and dash in a critical situation, the ability to strike and strike hard, could in the far more ambiguous sphere of politics turn to something quite else . . . The trouble was that these adaptive qualities were not only less attractive but even in the long term less effective. It was patience, management, reserve, and cunning which Milton's chief of men needed to bring about the victories of peace."[31]

General George Patton continually got himself in trouble off the battlefield. Before the Normandy invasion, General Eisenhower was under enormous pressure to demote Patton due to his continual gaffes. Yet Eisenhower recognized he needed Patton's military skills on the battlefield. Giving his chastened commander one last chance to redeem himself, Eisenhower said, "You owe us some victories. . . . Pay off and the world will deem me a wise man."[32] Patton did indeed use his offensive talents to gain victories for Eisenhower who was ultimately vaulted into the U.S. presidency. Leaders must be able to identify talent and rigorously apply the skills of their people to the utmost advantage.

DIVERSITY IN KNOWLEDGE

Knowledge is a crucial aspect of team selection. Leaders should enlist people who have expertise they lack themselves. If team members cannot tell their leaders something the leader doesn't already know, they are redundant. Modern leaders must lead knowledgeable workers. It is imperative, therefore, to create a culture which attracts outstanding knowledge workers and gives them the opportunity to thrive. Leaders must also be willing to heed the counsel of the experts they install around themselves. During the tumultuous and dangerous days after Julius Caesar's assassination, powerful and cunning figures such as Mark Antony, Brutus, Cicero, and Cassius were all vying for power over the empire. The teenaged Octavian, Caesar's acknowledged heir, had no military experience or political power and only limited understanding of political intrigue. It seemed inevitable that he would become another of Rome's political casualties. Yet, as his biographer noted, "he had that most essential of political talents, the ability to take good advice."[33] Ultimately that trait would lead the inexperienced Octavian to overcome his more experienced rivals and become Rome's first emperor.

Leaders Love Their People

Seth Godin suggests that people perform better when they enjoy their work.[34] People entrust their hopes, dreams, self-worth, and skills into their leader's hands. Employees who are neglected or exploited will never achieve the creative breakthroughs that emerge in a caring, stimulating, and supportive environment. Max De Pree suggests communities are far more productive than organizations.[35] The leader is responsible for fostering a sense of community. To this end, Bossidy and Charan suggest leaders should spend at least 40 percent of their time with their people.[36]

Jim Collins studied outstanding companies and found that people who worked in the best companies tended to make and keep lifelong friendships.[37] Team members, working toward a meaningful goal, feeling cared for by their leaders, will bond with their colaborers. Such concern by leaders must be real. A generic Christmas card or interoffice memo can never substitute for genuine concern by the leader.

During the Battle of the Nile, Admiral Nelson was struck down by a piece of shrapnel. When he was taken below deck for medical attention, the admiral waved the physician away saying, "No, I will take my turn with my brave fellows."[38] Such authentic humility and concern for his crew became legendary among Nelson's men and inspired them to herculean feats on his behalf. In 1915 the ship *Endurance* became entrapped in the ice floes off the Antarctic coast, and it sank. The captain, Ernest Shackleton, and his men survived nine months on the ice-packed seas. Then, taking two men with him, Shackleton sailed in a small boat through lethal weather for seven hundred miles to get help for his crew. In one of the greatest rescues in history, Shackleton managed to bring his crew home safely. His biographer noted: "No one seemed to doubt that Shackleton would save them all; and for him it was a responsibility on which he still seemed to thrive. It was almost as if he lived on a sense of being needed by his people."[39] Great leaders go to enormous lengths to care for their people.

Jesus described the difference between a hireling, a thief, and a good shepherd. He said hirelings abandon the sheep under their care at the first sign of difficulty (John 10:12–13). Thieves remain with the flock but only to profit at the sheep's expense (John 10:10). In contrast, the good shepherd "lays down his life for the sheep" (John 10:11). Effective leaders create an environment of trust and concern for those they work with.

Leaders Maintain Focus

Teams produce their best work when their mission is clear and their efforts are focused. Pat MacMillan argues: "The single most important ingredient in team success is a clear, common, compelling task. The power of a team flows out of each team member's alignment to its purpose."[40] Teams struggle when they lose sight of their goal. It is the leader's responsibility to keep the team centered on its mission.

Teams can become so enmeshed in doing good things they spend insufficient time on essential tasks. Organizations, no matter how dynamic they initially are, can easily lapse into bureaucracies in which policies, procedures, and meetings dominate people's efforts more than accomplishing their fundamental purpose. People all want to believe their work is crucial and requisite to the organization's success, but in reality bureaucracies employ most of their people in mundane or peripheral work while few people are allocated to the central mission or primary issues. Seth Godin points out, "Many people spend all their time trying to defend what they do."[41] Just because a staff person or a leader has a busy schedule does not entail they are doing work critical for their organization. Every team member has an opinion about what the organization's priorities should be. But effective teams stay riveted to their mandate. They relentlessly protect their priorities. Leaders keep their team focused and regularly delineate its objectives.

An inordinate amount of infighting is a red flag alerting the leader that the team has lost its focus. Vigorous debate is healthy. Constant arguing, personal attacks, and sabotage are debilitating. In 1957 John Diefenbaker led the Conservative Party of Canada to power for the first time in twenty-two years. The following year another election saw Diefenbaker reelected as prime minister when his Conservatives obliterated the Liberals, taking 208 seats to the Liberals' 49.[42] It was the largest electoral victory in Canadian history and it gave Diefenbaker a clear mandate to implement the many changes he vociferously demanded. The Canadian electorate saw "Dief the Chief" as their crusader for a new order. But Diefenbaker seemed more adept at seeking power than wielding it. He struggled to make decisions and often backpedaled on commitments his cabinet ministers assumed were in place. Because he was unable to manage his own cabinet, his ministers eventually rebelled against him. Seventeen of them departed his cabinet in the final ten months before his electoral defeat in 1963.[43] Despite Diefenbaker's impassioned speeches and debates in parliament, he was unceremoniously swept from power in 1963 by a population weary of rhetoric without corresponding action. The problem was not a matter of able personnel. Diefenbaker's colleagues were bright and talented. Rather the party's downfall was their leader's inability to keep his team focused and progressing in a singular direction.

A third symptom revealing a team has lost its focus is when members become obsessed with their own positions, pay, and perks rather than with the accomplishment of organizational goals. A desire for premier offices is nothing new. James and John sought the two most coveted positions in Jesus' kingdom (Mark 10:35–45). It is only natural for people to pursue the highest offices available and to be drawn to the largest salary. However, when people become consumed with accumulating impressive titles, larger offices, and executive benefits while remaining blithely unconcerned that their organization is routinely underperforming, they have lost sight of the purpose for their work.

Leaders Foster Healthy Communication

Movements that once were vigorous and flexible eventually become institutionalized, bureaucratized, and marginalized. Every institution, no matter how flat it may have begun, inevitably develops a hierarchy. In times past hierarchies were necessary because CEOs could not personally relate to a thousand employees. Busy leaders dealt with a limited number of direct reports, and those lieutenants were responsible for transmitting information down line to the rank and file. This approach bred numerous problems. For one, as Kouzes and Posner point out, "The higher up you go on the corporate ladder, the less likely it is leaders will ask for feedback. Leaders want to know how their subordinates are doing, but rarely seek feedback on their own performance."[44] The more steep and complex the hierarchy, the more diluted is the feedback ascending to the leader.

Likewise, when information trickles down from the top through numerous layers of bureaucracy, key pieces of information are frequently withheld. Middle managers may feel those lower down don't need as much information or they may want to retain an advantage by withholding facts. Warren Bennis calls hierarchies a "prosthesis for trust."[45] Information is power. The more information accessible to your team, the more empowered they become. Just as information drives modern organizations, so hierarchies and executive floor offices tend to dissipate organizational energy.

Modern leaders who are serious about providing real time information to team members have three primary tools available to them: technology, architecture, and meetings.

Technology. Computer networks make information available to staff even if they are dispersed globally. Agents in Hong Kong can access the company network to immediately gain pertinent information from Kansas City. Videoconferencing and numerous other communications technologies allow people to hold strategic meetings with people around the world. Electronic memos and webinars allow timely dissemination of information.

Architecture. The physical layout of an organization can do much to enhance or impede team effectiveness. Large executive offices far removed from the shop floor can cause far more separation than a short elevator ride might suggest. When Richard was seminary president, the entire faculty and staff were initially housed in one building. When a second, larger academic building was constructed, the faculty was moved to the new facility while the administrative office remained where it was. The two structures were joined by an attractive, windowed enclosed hallway and required only a short walk between buildings. Nevertheless, Richard began hearing rumblings from faculty members who felt out of touch with what was happening in the administrative building. The president and his administrative team were just as available as before, but the physical barrier of a hallway changed the team dynamics.

We know an architectural firm that highly valued teamwork and cross collaboration. To facilitate its values, a facility was designed so there were no offices—only cubicles in a large work area. Everyone worked together in one spacious room where information sharing and creative brainstorming were greatly enhanced. Even the president chose to move out of his corner office and into a cubicle so he could be more involved in his people's work. While this configuration would not work well for every organization, wise leaders nonetheless ensure their organization's facilities enhance teamwork and communication.

Meetings. Technology has reduced the necessity for the number of meetings required by organizations, but face-to-face encounters with staff continue to be needed. Leaders make use of a variety of settings to ensure their people are kept abreast of critical information. Regular team meetings, periodic staff retreats, even stand-up five-minute briefings at the beginning of the day can be useful in disseminating information. Meetings with staff over a meal as well as town hall meetings can be effective instruments in a leader's communication tool belt.

For teams to accomplish dynamic, creative, problem-solving work, they must have fast, reliable, crucial information; and the leader's role is to ensure they do.

Leaders Help Their People Grow

Most people want to believe their life makes a difference in their world. People want to do more than merely earn a living through their work. Why do some people accept lower pay or fewer perks to work in one place rather than opt for better remuneration at another organization? Because of less tangible but more important benefits such as joy and meaning derived from their work or because they feel they are contributing to a better society.

Jim Collins advises that leaders assign their best people to the biggest opportunities, not the biggest problems.[46] Furthermore, he suggests: "Managing your problems can only make you good, whereas building your opportunities is the only way to become great."[47] Wise leaders assign challenging tasks to their staff so they remain invigorated and so they grow personally and professionally. If your people do not grow under your leadership; you are not investing in them properly.

AN ILLUSTRATION FROM RICHARD

A large mission organization invited Richard's academic dean to consider moving to Europe to lead their extensive European efforts. The dean had joined the faculty as a professor but quickly demonstrated leadership ability and was promoted to the dean's office. The mission agency noted his excellence as a leader and considered him highly qualified for their position. He felt awkward seeking time off to investigate the job opportunity, but Richard assured him that (1) he was extremely talented so of course other agencies would covet his services; (2) Richard felt obligated to help staff members reach their maximum potential and in some cases it was understood they would have to move on to other organizations to do this; (3) Richard cared about his dean and would not want to stymie his career; (4) finally and most importantly, Richard trusted his dean's walk with God and knew he would act with integrity based on what he sensed God leading him to do. The dean did make the trip to Europe and to Richard's delight, did not sense God leading him to make the move. He continues to do an outstanding job at the seminary as of this writing.

Besides holding a genuine concern for their people, leaders also recognize that as their team member's capacity to lead increases, the organization's capacity to succeed also expands. Leaders are wise to maintain a healthy professional development budget and encourage their people to participate in seminars and programs that will enhance their professional growth.

If leaders are going to encourage personal and professional growth in their people, they will have to develop a high pain threshold for failure. By allowing team members to try and therefore sometimes fail, leaders can help their people process their mistakes and use them as stepping-stones toward personal growth.

Jesus gave ordinary fisherman the amazing opportunity to become his disciples and to change the world. Peter, one of those fishermen, had the additional opportunity to become the twelve apostles' chief spokesperson. Yet at a crucial moment, Peter denied his Lord. After that humiliating experience, Peter might well have concluded he lacked what it took to be a good leader. He returned to his fishing (John 21:3). Perhaps he was renouncing his earlier calling or at the very least he was attempting something he believed he could still do successfully. Yet despite fishing all night, Peter and his companions caught nothing. Another failure. What did Jesus do? First he allowed his discouraged followers to experience a success. He instructed them to cast their nets on the other side of the boat, and the catch was so immense they could not draw it in. Then Jesus entered a redemptive conversation with his chagrined disciple. Rather than asking Peter to proclaim his loyalty, as Peter had so confidently done earlier, Jesus asked him to affirm his love. Previously Peter wanted to impress others. Now Jesus got to the heart of the matter. By the time Jesus and Peter parted that day, Peter knew Jesus wasn't finished with him yet. He had a new assignment (John 21:15–17). Peter became a powerful leader in the early church, and we have no record of him ever denying his Lord again.

If modern organizations are to become great, they must develop their people and help them mature through their mistakes. There was a business unit leader at BP in the exploration and production business commissioned to develop and construct a challenging new $1.2 billon deepwater production platform. (Note: This was before the Deepwater Horizon tragedy in the Gulf in 2010). The timetable was tight, the technology challenging, and the overall success of the project was far from certain. This man took some calculated risks to deliver the project, but nonetheless, through a complex series of mistakes, overruns, and other issues (many beyond the immediate control of this leader), the project failed. The money was lost entirely. Shamed and embarrassed, the leader personally tendered his resignation to the CEO. The CEO responded: "You've got to be kidding me! I've just invested $1.2 billion in the training of one of my finest leaders, and now he wants to quit? Get out of my office and get back to work!" Because the leader lost credibility with his peers in E & P, the CEO wisely reassigned him to another division where he could start fresh. The executive succeeded in his new role and eventually made his way back to E & P where he experienced numerous successes in that stream of the business.

The most outstanding people will sign up and remain with leaders who bring out their best. A sure indication of a successful leader is the collective and consistent testimony of subordinates who are grateful for what they learned and how they grew while they worked under that leader.

Conclusion

Leaders can initiate personal growth all by themselves. But to change and grow organizations, leaders depend on other people. To launch a movement, leaders must interface with numerous people. Great leaders multiply their efforts by developing teams. A skilled team can accomplish far more than a talented individual. The key to success in today's complex, rapidly changing world is developing a diverse, skilled, flexible, and creative team with the freedom to grow, and fail, in pursuit of its mission. This must be one of a leader's top priorities.

Building Effective Teams

1. Leaders develop a dynamic culture.
2. Leaders maximize diversity.
3. Leaders love their people.
4. Leaders maintain focus.
5. Leaders foster healthy communication.
6. Leaders maximize their people.

————— **Responding to This Material** —————

1. What are you doing to enlist the best possible people to work with you?

2. Besides pay, what unique benefits do people receive for working on your team?

3. How frequently do you lose people from your staff or team? Have you analyzed the reasons people choose to leave working with you? If so, what did you discover?

4. List three specific things you could do to enhance the quality of your team process.

5. How are you treating your best people? Have you given them challenging work? Are you helping them to grow and to develop new skills and knowledge?

6. How often are your best people being offered executive positions in other organizations? Are you known for developing people into leaders?

Chapter Twelve

The Leader's Pitfalls: What Disqualifies Leaders?

Every year thousands of leaders shipwreck their careers, organizations, and families by making careless, foolish choices. The media parades a never-ending array of tarnished, discredited, and humiliated leaders before an increasingly disillusioned society. Why is it some leaders go from victory to victory, year after year, while others begin with great promise but eventually crash into oblivion? Certainly they did not begin their careers expecting to fail, but sadly their catastrophes can usually be traced to mistakes they could easily have avoided. A. B. Bruce observed: "One who knows his weaknesses may become strong even at the weak point; but he who knows not his weak points cannot be strong at any point."[1] This chapter examines ten of the most common pitfalls that cause spiritual leaders to fail.

Pride

Pride may be leaders' worst enemy, and it has caused the downfall of many. Pride is dangerous to unwary leaders because of its subversive nature. It can be couched in pious terms even while it brings out the worst in people. In his book *How the Mighty Fall,* Jim Collins points out hoe previously successful companies experienced dramatic downfalls after they allowed their success to lead to hubris.[2] Pride shows up in a variety of disguises, some of them obvious, others more subtle, but all of them lethal to leaders' effectiveness.

PRIDE DISORIENTS LEADERS

Pride blinds leaders to reality and causes them to view themselves in distorted proportions. Kouzes and Posner claim the most common reason for employees leaving their companies is their leaders gave limited praise and recognition for their efforts.[3] It is demoralizing for followers to labor on behalf of their organization only to have their leader minimize their efforts and hoard the accolades for themselves. Whereas authentic leaders shoulder the responsibility for their organization's poor performance, wise leaders enthusiastically acknowledge their people's efforts as critical to their organization's success. Leaders cannot always be as liberal as they would like with monetary rewards, but they should be generous with their honest praise and gratitude.

Leaders can be tempted to monopolize the credit for their organization's success as they seek the limelight. The writer of Proverbs urged: "Let another praise you, and not your own mouth—a stranger, and not your own lips" (Prov. 27:2). The fact is some leaders cannot wait for others' affirmation, so they blow their own horn, seizing opportunities in conversations and public gatherings to publicize their latest achievement.

Pride is an offensive trait in secular leaders, but it is even more repugnant in spiritual leaders. Pride causes Christian leaders to take the credit not only for what their people have done but also for what God has accomplished in their midst. God does not share his glory with anyone (Isa. 42:8). Spiritual leaders are God's servants, but some act as if God were their servant, obligated to answer their selfish prayers and to bless their grandiose schemes. When companies succeed financially, some executives attribute the success to their good business and management skills rather than citing God's guidance and protection. When spiritual leaders' organizations grow, pride can tempt them to credit their dynamic personality or their compelling vision or their marketing savvy. Thus they direct attention to themselves rather than to God. Political leaders must understand that presuming upon God's glory and sovereignty invites disaster.

Nebuchadnezzar, who was king of Babylon, possessed an overinflated ego. He learned humility the hard way: "As he was walking on the roof of the royal palace in Babylon, the king exclaimed, 'Is this not Babylon the Great that I have built by my vast power to be a royal residence and to display my majestic glory?' While the words were still in the king's mouth, a voice came from heaven: 'King Nebuchadnezzar, to you it is declared that the kingdom has departed from you'" (Dan. 4:29–31).

God rules over the world's nations, and he appoints rulers at his discretion. Political figures must recognize that, despite their political acumen or widespread popularity, they ultimately rule by God's consent. God abhors haughtiness (Prov. 6:16–17). When leaders continually cloak the successes of their organization in terms of what they have done, they are inviting God to humble them (Prov. 16:18). Leaders who fail to acknowledge God as the source of victory are leading people away from God and wrongfully causing their followers to misdirect their praise. Such leadership is contrary to biblical principles and will prove disastrous to churches, businesses, and ultimately to nations.

During the 1948 presidential campaign, Harry Truman was seeking reelection. The Republican candidate, Thomas E. Dewey, successful governor of New York, was the clear favorite. He had been elected governor by the largest margin in New York history, over 700,000 votes. Conversely, Dewey lost to the popular Franklin Roosevelt in the 1944 presidential election, but by the narrowest margin since 1916. Now he was supremely confident he could beat Truman, who was president only because Roosevelt died in office. The nation's top fifty political journalists were polled; all fifty predicted Dewey's victory. Twice as many reporters accompanied Dewey's campaign as followed the incumbent president's. Dewey brimmed with confidence.

He was disdainful of Truman, who did not attend college and who was painfully ordinary and uncultured compared to Dewey and Roosevelt. It was said of Dewey, he "was the only man who could strut sitting down."[4] Dewey was so confident in his ability and credentials he took his unassuming opponent for granted. The Chicago *Tribune* prematurely attributed Dewey the victory, running the front-page headline "Dewey Defeats Truman" the morning after the election before all the results were in. Then, in one of the greatest electoral upsets in American history, voters elected Truman over the heavily favored Dewey. The Dewey camp was shocked. The unthinkable had happened! Dewey overestimated himself and grossly underestimated his opponent. Truman's secretary of state, Dean Acheson, summarized the secret to Truman's success: He was "free of the greatest vice in a leader, his ego never came between him and his job."[5]

PRIDE MAKES LEADERS UNTEACHABLE

Pride closes minds. When leaders erroneously assume no one else could run their organization as well as they can and their pride convinces them they alone possess the qualities necessary for success, they become impervious to wise counsel. They grow impatient with those who do not readily accept their opinions, and in so doing, rob themselves of enormous opportunities.

King Ahab was a brilliant administrator and a capable military commander, except for one fatal flaw: he disdained godly counsel. When he proposed to the godly king Jehoshaphat that they combine their armies and attack the Arameans, Jehoshaphat suggested they first seek counsel. Ahab intended to rely upon his own cunning and military experience, but to placate his righteous colleague, he summoned his religious advisors. Zedekiah, the chief of Ahab's four hundred counselors, dutifully predicted what Ahab wanted to hear: complete victory. Dissatisfied, Jehoshaphat asked that Micaiah, the prophet of the Lord, be consulted. Ahab demurred, claiming, "I hate him, because he never prophecies good about me, but only disaster" (2 Chron. 18:7). Sure enough, Michaiah prophesied that Ahab's forces would be routed and Ahab slain. God, through his prophet, was duly warning Ahab that if he proceeded with his plans he would lose his life. Ahab's response? He threw the recalcitrant prophet in jail and marched off to battle. Ahab's pride deafened him to wise counsel and as a result he died an ignoble death on a meaningless battlefield (2 Chron. 18).

Pride's great victory is to turn otherwise successful leaders such as Ahab away from God's guidance. No matter how talented or smart a leader is, an unteachable spirit is the path to certain failure. In his book *Derailed: Five Lessons Learned from Catastrophic Failures of Leadership,* Tim Irwin studied the dramatic downfalls of successful CEOs.[6] Irwin noted: "Reality dictates that no matter how bright and capable a leader might be, the work of the organization must be accomplished by trusted colleagues. A leader's inference that he or she is primarily responsible for the organization's success demonstrates blatant hubris."[7] Leaders who have enjoyed spectacular success in the past can assume they are the experts and have nothing to learn from others. This makes them extremely vulnerable.

If there is any quality common to all effective spiritual leaders, it is a teachable spirit. The book of Proverbs assures us, "The fear of the LORD is the beginning of knowledge; fools despise wisdom and instruction. . . . For wisdom will enter your mind, and knowledge will delight your heart. Discretion will watch over you, and understanding will guard you" (Prov. 1:7; 2:10–11).

PRIDE CAUSES SELF-SUFFICIENCY

In his biography of Theodore Roosevelt, H. W. Brands commented on Roosevelt's early political efforts. He noted: "It wouldn't be the last time Roosevelt resisted someone who should have been an ally. Even at this early date he showed the egotism that would chronically compel him to denigrate almost anyone who competed with him for the limelight."[8] Historians claim Roosevelt was one of America's finest presidents, yet he had an unfortunate tendency to assume his causes were always right and just and those opposing him were corrupt and evil. Thus he alienated fellow politicians and supporters who would have naturally been his friends. His single-minded confidence in his own viewpoint contributed significantly to his defeat in a later reelection attempt.

History is rife with examples of people who were at the pinnacle of success one moment and tossed into the scrap heap of failures the next. Business leaders have been the toast of the town one day and scandalized by criminal charges the next. Coaches have won coach-of-the-year honors one year and been fired by mid-season the next. Pastors have stood at the helm of megachurches one week and forced to resign in shame the next. Politicians reached the apex of power one term and were cast out of office the next. After Winston Churchill was unceremoniously swept from office after World War II, the king offered to knight him. The chastened Churchill declined the offer claiming he could not accept a garter from the king when he had received the boot from the people. Leaders who allow a proud sense of self-sufficiency to blind them to their total dependence on God's grace and the support of their people will eventually be humbled (1 Sam. 13:13–14).

D. L. Moody clearly understood the source of his success. Upon meeting Moody, the evangelist known as Uncle Johnnie Vasser exclaimed, "How glad I am to see the man that God has used to win so many souls to Christ!" In response Moody stooped down and scooped up a handful of dirt. As he let the dust pour through his fingers, he confessed: "There's nothing more than that to D. L. Moody, except as God uses him!"[9] Despite Moody's international fame and massive audiences, he was mindful he owed everything to Christ.

Pride targets successful leaders, convincing them they have enough talent, wisdom, and charisma to achieve whatever they set their minds to do. Pride causes leaders to believe they can be lackadaisical in their obedience to God's Word. Max De Pree warns, "Leaders are fragile precisely at the point of their strengths, liable to fail at the height of their success."[10] Genuine spiritual leaders never take God's grace, blessing, and presence for granted. When they are enjoying their greatest achievements, they must be vigilant that pride doesn't cause them to fall. David Dotlich and Peter Cairo note, previous success can blind leaders: "We are not suggesting that leaders ignore their experiences. Rather, our suggestion is that they question them. People who are prisoners of experience repeat their actions and decisions with metronomic regularity."[11]

Napoleon's spectacular military success across Europe convinced him he could conquer Russia. Even though Russia presented a much different opponent than Napoleon previously faced, he was so confident of victory he did not research the climate or terrain before launching his massive invasion. As a result he neglected to prepare his soldiers for the lethal Russian winter. Napoleon, inflated by his prior successes, did not entertain the notion that he might not succeed in his next undertaking. His myopic arrogance cost tens of thousands of his soldiers their lives as Napoleon's empire began its steady decline. Many years later Adolph Hitler would be deceived by the same egotism and, having learned nothing from history, would thrust his forces into the identical Russian winter and suffer the same debacle Napoleon endured before him.

While riding on one's laurels can be dangerous for experienced leaders, young leaders can fall into the trap of self-reliance because experience has not yet taught them otherwise. Older leaders may particularly disdain the suggestions of younger, less-experienced colleagues, but such conceit can be costly.

Spiritual leaders must be especially careful not to presume upon God's blessings. A proud disposition is the counterpole of an intimate walk with God. Samson was a military man with enormous strength and more than enough power to defeat his enemies. His mistake was in taking that might for granted. Samson believed he could live any way he chose and still retain the robust strength God granted him. When he ignored God's clear instructions and neglected his relationship with the Lord, he was stripped of his power. When Samson set out to do in his own strength what he had always done before in God's, he suffered humiliating defeat (Judg. 16:15–21). Sagacious leaders recognize they can do nothing apart from their intimate relationship with Christ (John 15:5).

PRIDE LEADS TO A LOSS OF COMPASSION

Through the prophet Ezekiel, God castigated spiritual leaders who looked upon their followers as sheep to be fleeced rather than as a flock to shepherd (Ezek. 34:1–10). These would-be spiritual leaders led for profit rather than for service. Their people were being scattered and abused by others, yet their leaders' only concern was their own comfort and gain.

Spiritual leadership is a high calling and a God-given privilege. Leaders have the opportunity as well as the influence to enrich the lives of their followers. But when leaders lose the passion to contribute to their organization and begin to focus instead on what they can receive from it, they are no longer genuine leaders. They develop a sense of superiority that regards people as mere cogs in the organizational machinery. They see themselves as entitled to whatever they can siphon from their organization. L. Dennis Kozlowski is a prime example. As the CEO of Tyco, he used company funds to purchase expensive works of art, a six-thousand-dollar shower curtain, a fifteen-thousand-dollar umbrella stand, and half the cost of his wife's two-million-dollar birthday party.[12]

A sure sign that pride has taken root is when leaders lose compassion for those they are leading. When leaders become calloused to the hardships of their people, when they impose financial cutbacks and hardships upon their people but shower lucrative benefits upon themselves, they forfeit their prerogative to lead. Such was the case with Enron's CEO, Kenneth Lay, who was quietly selling off his stock in the doomed company while publicly encouraging his employees to purchase it. Leaders who become preoccupied with their own personal accomplishments and are oblivious to the contributions and needs of others are unworthy to lead. Pastors who remain unmoved when a church member is hurting or who are ambivalent when members fall by the wayside are abusing their role as spiritual leaders. They are like Nero, the Roman emperor who, according to legend, entertained himself with music while Rome burned, or like Marie Antoinette who, when told that French peasants had no bread to eat, purportedly responded, "Let them eat cake." History demonstrates that such insensitive leaders eventually meet their demise.

The apostle Paul, on the contrary, demonstrated exemplary compassion. Writing to the troubled church at Corinth, he stated: "There is the daily pressure on me: my care for all the churches. Who is weak, and I am not made to stumble, and I do not burn with indignation?" (2 Cor. 11:28–29). True leaders never lose sight of their responsibility to care for their followers.

PRIDE MAKES LEADERS VULNERABLE

It has been said of Julius Caesar, "His ego always occupied center stage."[13] While his self-confidence enabled him to accomplish herculean feats, it also led him to be careless and disdainful of danger. Despite repeated warnings to keep bodyguards due to perceived threats to his safety, he rebuffed his friends and advisors and, on the Ides of March, walked into Pompey's Theater where twenty-three senators rained dagger blows down upon him.

Leaders who allow pride to grow unchecked will eventually lose much— their relationships, their credibility, and ultimately their leadership position.

The writer of Proverbs sagely warns: "Pride comes before destruction, and an arrogant spirit before a fall" (Prov. 16:18). Likewise, Scripture reveals: "God resists the proud, but gives grace to the humble" (James 4:6). Jesus cautioned: "Everyone who exalts himself will be humbled, but the one who humbles himself will be exalted" (Luke 18:14). Proud people have God as their opponent. This ought to motivate even the vainest leaders to ponder their ways.

Sexual Sin

If pride is the most insidious pitfall of leaders, sexual sin is the most notorious. The media has meticulously chronicled the spectacular downfalls of leaders who succumbed to sexual temptation. Sexual sin has the heinous power to destroy a career, a family, and a reputation, all in one blow. With such lethal consequences one would think leaders would fastidiously avoid sexual temptations. Yet year after year society recoils under the continuous barrage of sexual scandals made public. This does not have to happen. Leaders can avoid this pitfall by proactively building safeguards into their lives.

SAFEGUARD 1: LEADERS MAKE THEMSELVES ACCOUNTABLE

The time to buy the smoke alarm is when you build the house, not after a fire starts. The time to enlist friends as partners in accountability is not when sexual temptation is already a raging inferno but before the first spark. Time after time disgraced leaders admit that although they were surrounded by people, they had no close friends with whom they were transparent. They rarely cite the lack of available people or the unwillingness of others to hold them accountable. Rather, they confess that once they strayed into sin, they deliberately avoided those who might ask tough questions and those who could help. Prudent leaders are proactive; they choose one or two trusted friends and give them permission to ask hard questions and to challenge their questionable behavior.

SAFEGUARD 2: LEADERS HEED THEIR OWN COUNSEL

In 2006, Ted Haggard, senior pastor of New Life Church and president of the National Association of Evangelicals, admitted to inappropriate sexual conduct as well as drug use. He regularly condemned the very sins he was committing himself. Leaders should listen to their own counsel. Most fallen ministers previously warned their church members about the dangers of sexual immorality. Moral failure does not result from lack of information on the part of the fallen. Spiritual leaders know full well what sexual sin is as well as its consequences. In fact, ministers may have counseled others who were caught in the web of adultery or other sexual transgressions, but they deceive themselves into believing their situation is different. They have usually witnessed firsthand the devastation of immorality, but their own sin blinds them to the reality that they, too, are headed for destruction (Prov. 14:12). Spiritual leaders must understand they are no more immune to moral failure than those they are leading. Therefore, as they share their wisdom with others, they should scrupulously apply it to their own lives.

SAFEGUARD 3: LEADERS CONSIDER THE CONSEQUENCES

Leaders carefully and regularly contemplate the consequences of committing sexual sin. They guard themselves from the attitude that they are exempt from the dangers that have derailed others. They reflect on the ugly reality of what their sin would do to their spouses, children, organizations, and how it would tarnish God's name. They remind themselves that one careless, selfish decision could cost them their job, reputation, friendships, and family, as well as severely damaging their relationship with God. Astute leaders ponder the horrific effects of sexual sin. Then, when they are tempted, they are armed with a graphic warning of sexual sin's deadly consequences and they are not unwitting victims of sin's treachery (Prov. 7:24–27).

SAFEGUARD 4: LEADERS DEVELOP HEALTHY HABITS

When Billy Graham learned that several fellow evangelists were committing sexual sins, he did not merely resolve to be careful; he built specific safeguards into his life and ministry to ensure he and his team avoided even the appearance of compromise. He made a commitment to never meet with, travel with, or eat alone with a woman other than his wife. He also developed a team of friends to monitor whether he was keeping this standard. While some considered his restrictions excessive, they shielded him from scandal for over half a century of high-profile, international ministry.[14]

Married leaders should enlist their spouses to help them develop protective habits, and they should *always* take the concerns and warnings of their spouse seriously. Leaders who cultivate a healthy marriage are less vulnerable to temptations. Some leaders who travel set up pictures of their spouse and children in their hotel room as a reminder of the loved ones they have waiting for them at home. Administrative assistants can ensure they avoid compromising positions with people of the opposite sex. Steps as pragmatic as installing windows in their office doors can help protect leaders against even the hint of impropriety. Likewise, leaders who desire to live holy lives also put safeguards in place to protect themselves from pornography. We know of many people who make it their habit never to turn on the television in hotel rooms so they are not tempted by the pornography the hotel makes available. Leaders are also wise to instill accountability over their computer so they are not tempted to surf the net and fill their minds with sinful images. Leaders with integrity will be proactive in guarding their hearts and minds.

SAFEGUARD 5: LEADERS MAINTAIN A HEALTHY, GROWING WALK WITH GOD

No matter how many intentional safeguards leaders establish, sexual temptation can sometimes ambush the unsuspecting leader. The most practical step leaders can take is to regularly pray that God would help them keep their lives above reproach. Leaders may be blindsided by unexpected events, but God never is. God in his grace will build a hedge of protection around leaders who earnestly desire moral purity. Leaders should also enlist the prayers of their spouses so they know that wherever they go and whatever they face, their spouse is interceding with God for them. Ultimately leaders are not the victims of sexual sin. They do not "fall" into sin. Rather, they reap what they sow (Gal. 6:7). Temptations will come, and leaders who neglect their relationship with God and fail to build protective habits into their lives will be vulnerable. Sexual sin is just as avoidable as it is devastating. Wise leaders heed the counsel of Proverbs that says, "The sensible one watches his steps" (Prov. 14:15).

Cynicism

Leadership is a people business and people invariably disappoint you. Anyone who has led for long has dealt with people who were dishonest, lazy, or incompetent. Leaders also inevitably face unfair criticism. At some point people will question leaders' motives and second-guess their decisions.

People who lead will also undergo failure. Any one of these experiences has the potential to harden leaders' hearts and make them cynical. But attitudes, unlike circumstances, are entirely within leaders' control. Leaders who surrender their positive attitude have resigned themselves to be mediocre at best.

If leaders always focus on their organization's problems and weaknesses, then their peoples' attention will invariably be drawn there too. When people concentrate on the negative, they lose the zeal and optimism required to overcome difficult challenges. Negative leaders spawn negative organizations. Cynical leaders cultivate clones of themselves. When leaders have no faith in their people, they prevent them from reaching their potential. Richard Nixon's biographer concluded: "He assumed the worst in people and he brought out the worst in them. He was too suspicious, his judgments were too harsh, too negative."[15] Leaders must not allow themselves to be consumed by a scornful spirit, for it will spill over onto everyone around them.

True leaders focus on that which is right and on what gives hope, not on what is wrong. Unfortunately, criticism or failure can make a leader skeptical about future success. After someone they trusted lied to them, leaders can question everyone's honesty. When one employee is lazy, they may suspect indolence in everyone who works for them. When a major project fails, leaders can be wary of taking further risks. Older leaders seem particularly susceptible to cynicism. Their youthful enthusiasm has worn off and what they consider "realism born of experience" may in essence be nothing more than a scornful attitude festering over time.

When leaders sense they are developing a pessimistic attitude, they must correct it immediately before it poisons their effectiveness and possibly even their health. Without question, a critical spirit in spiritual leaders reveals a heart distant from God. Only a conscious decision to return to God will save the leader from declining into contempt. It is crucial leaders guard their attitudes. Christian leaders serve the King of kings and therefore have every reason in the world to be positive and optimistic about the future.

Greed

A leadership position often brings material rewards. While a sizable income is not a sin, the relentless pursuit of one is. The allure of wealth has enticed many leaders to make foolish career decisions. The world maintains that the more money people make, the more successful they are. As a result, some people will sacrifice almost anything to achieve greater financial success. For some, money, position, and possessions are sure signs of success. Lee Iacocca sums this sentiment up well:

> I've never had any qualms about getting a high salary. I'm not a big spender, but I appreciate the achievement a high salary represents. Why does a guy want to be president? Does he enjoy it? Maybe, but it can make him old and tired. So why does he work so hard? So he can say, "Hey, I made it to the top. I accomplished something."[16]

Sadly, Iacocca tells how his efforts in climbing the corporate ladders at Ford and Chrysler took their toll on his beloved, frail wife, Mary. Mary's first heart attack came immediately after Iacocca was fired at Ford in a corporate power struggle. Iacocca notes: "On each of these occasions when her health failed her, it was following a period of great stress at Ford or Chrysler."[17] Iacocca achieved mammoth success that was the envy of CEOs around the world, but at what price?

The hunger for riches and possessions can destroy spiritual leaders. People valuing wealth above everything else will strive for jobs that pay more, regardless of whether they cause hardship to their families. Pastors can be lured to larger churches that pay higher salaries, even though their families were content in their smaller church setting. As one person asked, "Why does God always seem to call ministers to churches that pay more money and never to churches that pay less?"

Leaders who hunger for wealth can also be tempted to act unethical. Jim Bakker had his conscience dulled by the giddy financial heights he reached with his PTL organization. Bakker grew up in poverty and adversity and his success produced personal wealth he never dreamed possible. As his ministry thrived, he began to justify his increasingly lavish lifestyle, reasoning that he was the one who was largely responsible for PTL's success. He worked hard, and many people's lives were being changed positively because of his efforts, so didn't he deserve the material prosperity he was enjoying? Yet as the expenses of his organization escalated, Bakker was forced to devise increasingly creative ways to raise funds to maintain his dreams. In his all-consuming quest to raise more money, it was not difficult for him to cross ethical and even legal lines.[18]

Thankfully, many Christian leaders are resisting the temptation to automatically seek or accept positions simply because they offer a bigger paycheck. Christian leaders have learned money is not the most important thing in life. Obeying God's will is. At times business leaders have turned down lucrative job transfers because they became actively involved in ministry in their local church and they sensed God wanted them to remain where they were. Some pastors resist overtures from larger urban churches because they know God has uniquely prepared them for their rural congregation and their family is finding great joy in that lifestyle. Other leaders decline jobs requiring increased travel because they value time with their families. Wise leaders do not allow themselves to be enslaved to money but instead use their money to glorify God.

Alfred Sloan, the successful CEO of General Motors, made a fortune building his company and then spent the latter part of his life giving it away to worthy causes. Alfred Nobel, the inventor of dynamite, invested his fortune in the promotion of world peace and the advancement of science. The measure of a leader's success is not the size of their bank account but the quality and contribution of their lives.

Mental Laziness

In 1919, Henry Ford went to court in a libel suit he had leveled against the Chicago *Tribune*. The *Tribune's* lead attorney mercilessly cross-examined

Ford to reveal his meager education. The paper wanted to demonstrate that despite Ford's outspoken criticisms of government policy, he was in fact grossly uninformed and unread concerning the matters he was publicly criticizing. At one point Ford indignantly defended his ignorance of American history by claiming, "I could find a man in five minutes who could tell me about it."[19] As a prominent leader, Ford frequently publicized his opinions, but at times they were proven to be entirely unfounded.

Today's problems are not generally solved through brute strength or large amounts of money but by creative, inspired thinking. Problem solving is an essential function of leadership; therefore leaders cannot afford to become intellectually stagnant. Good leaders never stop learning. They seek the company of wise people. They read books and articles that stretch their thinking. They read the biographies of great leaders and thinkers and not merely the popular, predigested books flooding the market. They find authors who challenge their presuppositions and who bring fresh insights to their field. Ask effective leaders what they are currently reading, and they will readily cite something fresh off the shelf.

Spiritual leaders also allow the Holy Spirit to guide their thinking so it is based on God's timeless truths rather than on society's latest fad. Great leaders are always learning how to become better leaders. John Kotter observes, "Just as we don't realize the difference between a bank account earning seven percent versus four percent, we regularly underestimate the effects of learning differentials."[20]

A commitment to learn and to change produces a growing level of leadership competence. It is no longer enough to acquire an education in order to get a job. Additional learning is mandatory to keep a job. Earning a Ph.D. simply introduces someone to what they don't know. The reason some longtime employees are forced out of work has nothing to do with age. It has to do with a reluctance to learn. Methods that worked a decade ago may be ineffective today. Leaders who aren't continually growing will eventually find themselves obsolete. De Pree claims leaders respond to change by learning something.[21]

Leaders are not only readers; they are thinkers. True leaders take time to process the events around them. When a meeting goes poorly, they don't simply race off to their next appointment; rather, they take time to evaluate the unproductive meeting and consider a different tactic for next time. When personnel are struggling, good leaders do not arbitrarily fire them or grow agitated with them. Rather they take time to ponder root causes. Are they the right people for the job? Have they been properly trained and equipped? Have they been adequately informed? Are there factors beyond the employees' control? Leaders don't jump to conclusions. They process the facts and seek to determine the truth of their situation. When mature leaders receive praise or criticism, they do not accept or reject it out of hand; they contemplate what has been said so they continue to mature as leaders. Difficult circumstances can sometimes catch leaders by surprise, but once an adverse event has occurred, leaders seek to master the situation by careful, prayerful reflection.

Jesus helped his disciples grow as leaders by teaching them to process their circumstances. In Luke's Gospel, the twelve disciples are depicted as being unable to understand the events unfolding around them. Jesus gave them authority to cast out demons and to heal diseases (Luke 9:1) and the disciples experienced and witnessed incredible miracles as a result. When they returned to Jesus, they excitedly reported their success. Yet, shortly afterward, when faced with a multitude of hungry people, they surveyed the situation and instructed Jesus to "send the crowd away" because they could not possibly feed so many people (Luke 9:12). Had the disciples contemplated the power they saw demonstrated by Jesus thus far, they would have understood that feeding a multitude would not be difficult for him. Jesus miraculously fed the crowd, but the disciples did not process that event either. Mark 6:45 indicates that immediately after Jesus fed the five thousand, he sent his disciples in a boat across the Sea of Galilee to Bethsaida. When a storm arose, they were terrified. Why did they not trust Jesus in the storm after such obvious evidence of his divine power? Scripture indicates "they had not understood about the loaves. Instead, their hearts were hardened" (Mark 6:52). Because the disciples failed to process and learn from their earlier experiences, they were unprepared to face new challenges. Jesus rebuked them for being slow to understand the events and the teachings they were encountering (Luke 9:41).

How could the disciples witness incredible miracles and hear profound teaching and then panic on the next occasion to demonstrate faith? Their problem was they rushed from activity to activity. They did not yet know how to correlate their experiences with the nature and ways of God. Because they were not learning from their experiences, they continued to struggle. As Michael and Deborah Jinkins explain: "We do not learn from experience. We learn from disciplined reflection on experience."[22] Later, after Jesus ascended to heaven, the disciples learned to process their experiences. Once the disciples learned to do this, not even the fiercest opposition could discourage them from accomplishing God's will.

At the apex of D. L. Moody's success, he realized his mind had grown stagnant. He was leading enormously successful evangelistic campaigns in Great Britain and the United States, and he became one of the most famous religious leaders of his day, but he grew spiritually and intellectually malnourished. He was continually preaching, but he was not learning. Moody's biographer, John Pollock, notes, "At the moment of reaching a height of influence in the United States he stood in danger of spiritual insolvency."[23] Moody realized he had told people everything he knew, and he had nothing fresh to say. Moody confessed: "My lack of education has always been a great disadvantage to me. I shall suffer from it as long as I live."[24] Moody moved to Northfield and refused to accept major speaking engagements until he studied enough to gain fresh, new insights from God's Word to share with people. He set a rigid schedule that included six hours of study every morning. Even after he commenced traveling again, Moody carried a small library with him. He was determined that despite the press of people and responsibilities upon his time, he could not afford to stop learning if he was to be an effective spiritual leader. Likewise, Billy Graham noted as one of his regrets that he was too often improperly prepared for his speaking assignments. He confessed, "I have failed many times and I would do many things differently. For one thing, I would speak less and study more."[25]

Wise leaders continually learn from the events of their lives as well as from their studies. They take time after major events to process what happened and to learn from the experiences. Great leaders are thinkers. They are, to paraphrase Paul's words, transformed by the renewing of their minds (Rom. 12:2). They never stop learning or evaluating, so they never stop growing.

Oversensitivity

In 1874, Sam Andrews was becoming increasingly upset with his partner, John Rockefeller. Rockefeller's domineering personality and enormous ambition to build Standard Oil constantly overruled Andrews' desire for greater personal profits. One day Andrews reached his limit with Rockefeller and exclaimed, "I wish I was out of this business!" Rockefeller asked him his price. It was one million dollars. Rockefeller paid it to him the following day. Andrews boasted that someone had finally bested Rockefeller in business. Then Andrews learned Rockefeller turned right around and sold Andrews' former shares to William Vanderbilt for 1.3 million dollars. Andrews was incensed and claimed he was cheated. Rockefeller magnanimously offered to sell Andrews the same number of shares at the original price, but Andrews proudly refused. Historians estimate that by the 1930s Andrews' shares would have been worth over 900 million dollars. A biographer concluded: "This rash decision, motivated by pure pique and a bruised ego, kept him from becoming one of America's richest men."[26] People who cannot handle criticism or the strongly voiced opinions of others need not apply for leadership positions. Being criticized, second-guessed, and having one's motives questioned are unpleasant but inevitable aspects of leadership. Great leaders are not immune to criticism; in fact, the disparagement they receive is sometimes the most venomous. The reality is, it is impossible for leaders to avoid being censured. If leaders take decisive action, they are critiqued for being too reactionary. If they cautiously refrain from responding, they are chastised for indecisiveness. Faced with the prospect of criticism regardless of what they do, leaders must make a choice. Either they stop leading, or they do what they know is right and trust God to vindicate them.

Jonathan Edwards was one of the most brilliant thinkers of eighteenth-century America. As pastor of the prestigious Congregational church in Northampton, he was a leading figure during the First Great Awakening. Edwards' prolific writings were studied all over the Western world. Religious leaders such as George Whitefield, the most famous preacher of that era, traveled great distances to meet with Edwards and to discuss theological matters. Yet even a man of Edwards' impressive credentials was not exempt from censure. When Edwards sought assurance that his congregants experienced genuine conversion, a group of discontented church members took exception. They initiated a slanderous campaign against him that ultimately led to his dismissal from the church he made famous. Edwards assumed a modest pastorate in the small frontier town of Stockbridge.[27] One of the greatest theological minds and most devout pastors in American history was forced out of his church by the vehement criticism of malicious detractors.

If a leader receives ten words of support for every one word of criticism, which voice rings loudest? The critic's voice of course. Disapproval generally carries more weight than praise. Many leaders have resigned their positions despite widespread popularity because they grew weary of a handful of unrelenting fault finders. Sadly, leaders can allow the negativity of a few to abrogate the enthusiastic support of the majority.

Constructive criticism is good for leaders. They should not only receive such input graciously; they should invite those around them to give it. On the other hand, gossip and slander can quench the spirit of even the most stouthearted leader. Most leaders genuinely desire to do the right thing. They want to be liked and appreciated by their followers. When leaders' motives are routinely questioned or when their actions are misjudged, they lose their joy and are left wondering whether their calling is worth the pain. Whereas even the most loyal friends can be sporadic in their affirmation, opponents can be like a dripping faucet, relentlessly communicating their displeasure. One is reminded of Mark Twain's observation: "It takes your enemy and your friend, working together, to hurt you: the one to slander you, and the other to get the news to you."

How should leaders respond to unfounded rancor from hostile critics? First, they should honestly examine their hearts to be sure the criticism is without merit. This can hurt, but sensitive leaders can usually learn something, even when they are unfairly maligned. However, the old adage, "There is always a seed of truth in every criticism" is untrue. Some attacks are patently false and vindictive. We know sincere Christian leaders who have needlessly flagellated themselves seeking to discover the kernel of truth coming from unfair and cruel attacks. Leaders must face reproof with integrity before God and before people. True spiritual leaders know it is ultimately God's approval and not people's that matters most. When leaders know they have obeyed God, they set aside the desire to defend themselves. They find their security in God's affirmation. God promises: "'No weapon formed against you will succeed, and you will refute any accusion raised against you in court. This is the heritage of the LORD's servants and their righteousness is from Me.'" (Isa. 54:17). The wisdom of a right decision will prove itself over time. Wise leaders let God prove the purity of their motives and the wisdom of their actions.

Eventually Jonathan Edwards was exonerated before his critics. Some of his most vocal opponents confessed their sinfulness in attacking the godly minister.[28] Ultimately, Princeton University hired Edwards as its president. Historians have rated Edwards as one of the most influential Americans in the eighteenth century. History has nothing noteworthy to record about his former slanderers except their treachery. Oswald Sanders concluded: "Often the crowd does not recognize a leader until he has gone and then they build a monument for him with the stones they threw at him in life."[29]

The difference between statesmen and politicians is clearly seen here. Statesmen do what is right, regardless of the consequences. Politicians do what is popular. Spiritual leaders should strive to be statesmen who are more interested in doing the right thing than in attracting peoples' accolades.

Often the right thing to do is not the most popular, but spiritual statesmen do not allow detractors to deter them from God's will. Criticism has its most devastating effect upon the immature and the unsure. Leaders who clearly understand God's will do not waver when misguided or virulent opponents attempt to discourage them. Politicians may do what appeals to the majority, regardless of their private convictions. Statesmen take a stand for what is right though it costs them friends, supporters, and even their jobs. While leaders are always attempting to build consensus among followers, true spiritual leaders do not ultimately lead by consensus. A leader's decisions are not always based on a majority vote. Spiritual statesmen are not driven by what the majority think but by what God has said. True spiritual leaders fear God far more than they fear people (Prov. 1:7). Those who are motivated by a desire to avoid criticism are clearly unsuited for leadership. True spiritual leaders seek God's will, and then follow it unwaveringly.

While we were attending a large convention, a distinguished-looking middle-aged man approached us and told us his story: He was once a pastor, but some church members took exception to his leadership and doggedly attacked his character, family, and ethics. Their behavior crushed him, and he resigned his pastorate vowing never to work another day in Christian ministry. Shortly thereafter, a friend invited him to join a newly formed company as vice president and he accepted. The company flourished. The former pastor became a wealthy and respected executive vice president. Then the church he was attending studied the discipleship course *Experiencing God*. With a broad smile and tears in his eyes, he said, "God got a hold of me! I'm a pastor again!"

Spiritual leaders must keep criticism in perspective. Criticism will come and it will hurt, but it must not be allowed to derail leaders from God's call on their lives. Before yielding to the temptation to quit, leaders should revisit what they know God asked them to do. No amount of opposition or hardship or sacrifice is sufficient to cancel God's call. We have heard pastors say, "My family shouldn't have to put up with this!" Leaders must protect their families. But receiving criticism does not mean leaders are out of God's will. It may indicate the opposite. Jesus said, "'A slave is not greater than his master.' If they persecuted Me, they will also persecute you" (John 15:20). Leaders, and those they love, are much safer being criticized for remaining in God's will than when they receive praise while living outside it. Spiritual leaders would do well to help their families learn how to deal with opposition. Leaders who readily forfeit their calling in response to resistance do not clearly know God's will. When leaders know they are doing what God has asked, no amount of animosity will move them to do anything else.

Spiritual Lethargy

Leaders are generally driven people. Their role is to ensure things get done. Their enthusiasm to make things happen will tempt them to forgo the "passive" pursuit of spending time with God. Most spiritual leaders would list their relationship with God as number one on their priority list. At least that is where they know it should be. Yet with so many tasks to undertake and people to motivate, they inadvertently relegate their spiritual life to a place of unimportance in their schedule. Before an important meeting, it may seem more expedient to review their presentation than to make sure their heart is right before God. Lengthy reports requiring extensive reading may compel leaders to forgo reading their Bible "just this once." Christian ministers are no less susceptible to this mind-set. They are busy people, too. The danger for them to neglect their time with God is more subtle because their Bibles are open so often for sermon preparation, counseling, and other religious work. If they aren't careful, they'll view their Bibles as a tool for work rather than as the living Word of God. They'll begin substituting their public prayer life for their personal conversations with God. They'll be tempted to function on yesterday's walk with God.

Leaders who allow their daily commitments to crowd out their devotional life are severing their lifeline. No matter how much they accomplish, they will pay a price. Those they lead may get their best efforts but will miss the benefit of God working through their leader. The leader will not become the husband/wife/parent/son/daughter/friend God wants them to be. Their accomplishments will be, as the writer of Ecclesiastes says, "a pursuit of the wind" (Eccles. 1:14).

Spiritual leaders are not haphazard people. Just as they plan thoroughly for important meetings, they must also carefully schedule substantial time for listening to their Creator. First, they should consider how much time they set aside to spend with God. Is it enough? Is it rushed? Does that time slot face too many intrusions? Would a different time or setting be more conducive to quiet Bible study, reflection, and prayer? Would a varied approach to studying God's Word be beneficial? Perhaps a different Bible translation would give familiar verses a fresh sound and an added perspective. Perhaps the leader needs to use a devotional tool that will open up the Scriptures in new ways. Oswald Chambers' *My Utmost for His Highest* has been a favorite among spiritual leaders for many years. We have written two daily devotionals, *Experiencing God Day-by-Day* and *Discovering God's Daily Agenda*, which many have found helpful.[30] If they do not already do so, leaders should begin using a journal to record their daily spiritual pilgrimage. There is no substitute for an unhurried time with God.

Besides the immeasurable intrinsic value of knowing God personally, a strong relationship with God holds numerous advantages for leaders. They clearly know when God is speaking to them. When they begin to develop unhealthy habits, God redirects them, and his Spirit speaks forcefully to them to realign their priorities. God guides them through important decisions. Amid criticism and pressure to conform to worldly standards, God provides inner strength and resolve that enables them to stand firm in their convictions. Through a strong relationship with almighty God, leaders are strengthened, encouraged, convicted, and guided by God's Spirit so their efforts are not in vain.

Domestic Neglect

Theodore Roosevelt was once asked why he did not take a more active role in supervising his free-spirited daughter, Alice. Roosevelt purportedly replied,

"I can be president of the United States, or I can attend to Alice. I can't do both."[31] Such is the quandary of many leaders. When holding positions of influence and responsibility, leaders often struggle to balance their roles as a leader at work and at home. Billy Graham candidly relates a troubling event. He was entering the eighth week of his 1949 evangelistic campaign in Los Angeles. When Ruth Graham's sister and brother-in-law arrived for the final week of the crusade, they had a baby with them. Graham asked them whose child it was. It was his daughter Anne. Graham was away from home so long he did not recognize his own daughter. That night little Anne went to sleep crying not for her father or even her mother but for the aunt who was giving her primary care.[32] In concluding his autobiography, Graham confessed if he had his life to live over again he would travel less. Graham conceded that not every trip he took was necessary.[33] No one could fault Graham for his work ethic or evangelistic zeal, but every leader could learn from his dispiriting experience.

Nelson Mandela sacrificed everything he had to liberate his people from subjugation. Mandela eventually achieved his goal, won the Nobel Peace Prize, and was elected president of South Africa in the first election in which black voters participated. Yet Mandela also suffered two divorces and spent many years in prison without contact with his children. Mandela confessed that although he loved his wives, his work always came first, and his marriages dissolved as a result.

Ronald Reagan mediated international conflicts and made great strides in developing closer relations between the United States and the Soviet Union. Yet even his best diplomatic skills failed to appease his daughter, Patti, during his presidency. Graham, Mandela, and Reagan faced the enormous challenge of investing their lives in major causes and yet still fulfilling their responsibilities as husbands and fathers. Theirs were roles of national and international importance, yet they agonized over the same fundamental struggle every leader faces. Leaders must balance the responsibilities of their leadership role with their commitment to their families. Those who sacrifice their families may achieve great public success but suffer abysmal domestic failure.

John Adams played a prominent role in the liberation of the American colonies, but he could not free his son Charles from the demons that tormented him and would send him to an early grave.[34] John Rockefeller became the most successful businessman of his era, yet his daughter Edith refused to see him during the final years of his life.[35] Warren Buffet rose to become the wealthiest man in the world, yet his wife chose to live apart from him, and his children's marriages ended in divorce.[36] Cornelius Vanderbilt died as the wealthiest man in America but on his deathbed refused to see his son, Cornelius, who ultimately committed suicide.[37] Andrew Jackson was one of the most popular American presidents, but his wayward son quickly dissipated the vast estate his father left him.[38] Andrew Mellon, one of the wealthiest people of his era, went through a divorce and had a strained relationship with his children. After Mellon became fabulously wealthy, he asked a university professor whose position at the University of Pittsburgh he had endowed: "Duncan . . . are you happy at home?" to which Duncan replied: "Yes, Mr. Mellon . . . most happy." "Then you are a far richer man than I am," Mellon replied.[39]

Wise leaders strive to preserve their families in the midst of the pressures on their professional lives. Most leaders love their families, but many fail to apply the same prioritizing skills they use at work when relating to the most important people in their lives. Leaders must be proactive as they respond to their God-given responsibilities for their families. There is an exigent nature to leaders' families (Deut. 6:4–9). Their children represent the future generation of leaders. Emerging leaders at home have the potential to impact the world even more than their parents did. It is imperative for today's leaders to help their children develop as Christians and as the next generation of leaders.

Leaders should develop the habit of marking significant events such as birthdays, anniversaries, graduations, and special events on their calendars to prevent scheduling unnecessary commitments on those dates. When leaders travel, they should look for ways to bring family members with them. Technology offers numerous ways to stay in regular contact with one's family while traveling. As much as possible, leaders seek creative ways to make their jobs a blessing to their families instead of a rival for their attention. God is the family's greatest advocate; leaders who seek God's help will readily receive it.

Administrative Carelessness

Leaders are, by nature, visionaries. However, they may focus so much attention on the vision of where their organization is going they neglect to build the kind of organization that can arrive at its desired destination. They can be like a cross-country traveler who faithfully pours over the road map and knows exactly where he is going but doesn't bother to maintain the fuel and oil levels in his vehicle. Even when warning lights flicker on the control panel and strange noises emanate from under the hood, the traveler is absorbed in thoughts of what he will do once he arrives at his destination. Leaders can end up like this careless traveler, stranded and frustrated, far from where they want to be. Neglecting details can be disastrous for even the most enthusiastic leader.

Ultimately it is the leader's task to ensure the organization is capable of reaching its destination. Organizations are ultimately not about vision statements, constitutions, long-range plans, core values; they are about people. Therefore, while leaders are constantly delegating tasks, they are regularly monitoring attitudes, behaviors, effectiveness, and concerns to ensure that the organization is functioning at its optimum potential. There are at least four areas of administration to which leaders must give their attention if they are to experience sustained success. These are execution, culture, conflict, and communication.

Execution. Larry Bossidy and Ram Charan highlight the critical importance of execution in their influential book, *Execution: The Discipline of Getting Things Done.* They argue there is a huge gap between most organization's visions and their results.[40] Too many organizations boast compelling mission statements and produce attractive brochures detailing their corporate mission. But their results are abysmal. They lack execution.

Bossidy and Charan define *execution* as "a systematic process of rigorously discussing hows and whats, questioning, tenaciously following through, and ensuring accountability."[41] They identify this process as "a systematic way of exposing reality and acting on it."[42]

Leadership theory of late has strenuously emphasized vision. Leaders have focused on developing compelling visions and then enlisting people to embrace them. However, leaders often neglect to follow through to ensure the vision becomes a reality. Sometimes they begin formulating the next vision before the last one has been fully implemented. As Bossidy and Charan observe, "A leader who says 'I've got ten priorities' doesn't know what he's talking about."[43] Wise leaders do more than talk about change. They ensure that the organization is acting in alignment with its vision, and they hold people accountable for timely results. They never leave a meeting without reviewing what was decided, who is responsible for implementation, the due date for completion, and the system of accountability to ensure the work is completed on schedule.

Examine the vision God gave Moses, or Joshua, or Jesus; and it will be clear that these leaders were focused and determined to accomplish what God assigned them. When it was time for Jesus to go to Jerusalem to be crucified for humanity's sins, he "determined to journey" in the direction he was to go and *nothing* could stop Him (Luke 9:51).

Conflict Resolution. Effective leaders encourage vigorous debate and energetic dialogue among their people, but they do not allow animosity or bitter opposition to fester within the ranks.[44] A senior pastor had to discipline an associate because of his lax work ethic. After a heart-to-heart discussion about the matter, the pastor considered the matter settled. It wasn't. The chastised staff member began a covert campaign to erode confidence in the senior pastor. The pastor did not follow up with the associate. He did not document their discussion, nor did he inform other key leaders about the problem. And worse, he did not detect the shifting attitudes key church members began expressing toward him. Then one day a committee of influential church leaders made an unscheduled visit to the pastor's office and informed him his tenure had come to an end. Too often leaders discover the hard way that conflicts, left unattended, can fester or eventually erupt in their face.

One way to determine an organization's health is to measure how long it takes the top leader to become aware of a problem in the ranks. If issues are allowed to metastasize for weeks or months while the leader blithely concentrates on larger issues, there will eventually be a full-blown crisis. Capable leaders are known for their aggressive problem solving. Leadership positions are not for those who seek to avoid conflict at all costs. Insipid leaders will avoid people they know are unhappy or upset. Competent leaders will face problems head on. Few people enjoy addressing conflict, but experienced leaders know a seemingly minor snag neglected today can unravel the morale of the entire organization tomorrow. It is always better to address problems immediately and to resolve issues quickly. Spiritual leaders do not pursue "conflict management;" they strive for conflict *resolution*. While healthy organizations encourage a diversity of personalities and ideas, organizational vitality will wane in an atmosphere of constant discord. Alert leaders are quick to facilitate conflict resolution between personnel so valuable energy and time are not squandered on divisive and distracting issues.

Communication. Closely related to conflict resolution is the need for effective communication throughout the ranks of the organization. The leader is responsible for regularly communicating the direction the organization is going and its progress. It falls on the leader to clearly delineate the organization's values and to identify behaviors consistent with those beliefs. If leaders fail in this regard, the people who work with them cannot be faulted for inadvertently diverting the organization from its purpose.

Clear, timely communication is invaluable to successful organizations. Leaders who are out of touch with their people will one day be flabbergasted to find themselves alienated from their own organization. The loyalty they took for granted is illusory. The corporate values they assumed were jointly shared by followers will be summarily rejected. Their attempts to move the organization in a particular direction will be flatly resisted. Whenever the twelve disciples demonstrated a lack of understanding of their mission, methods, or values, Jesus quickly communicated truth to them.

One of the greatest hindrances to efficient communication in an organization can be the leader. Busy leaders can be so preoccupied with meetings and problems they neglect to inform their staff of important developments. Harried leaders can bring their organization to a grinding halt because they have not answered critical e-mails in a timely manner. The best leaders enhance the communication flow of their organization; they don't impede it. Leaders need to develop a reputation for dealing with important issues promptly and thoroughly. They use effective communication tools both personally and organizationally because good communication is a high priority.

Culture. The leader is the custodian of the corporate culture. That role cannot be delegated. The culture is often the embodiment of the leader. Richard Nixon was extremely suspicious and distrustful of others and quickly developed an environment of suspicion throughout his staff. Ronald Reagan was perpetually upbeat and confident, and his administration came to reflect his spirit. The two primary ways leaders affect culture is by actively participating in the hiring of key personnel and by vigorously ensuring the organization is aligned with its vision and operating according to its values.

Anyone who has led knows it does not take many negative or divisive people to poison an organization's morale. Combative or arrogant people generally have track records that reveal their attitudes. Leaders who hire or enlist these kinds of people eventually come to regret it. Jim Collins suggests that great organizations have been built by getting the right people "on the bus."[45] Wise leaders make this a top priority.

Attentive leaders regularly monitor the organizational culture. Some CEOs have mistakenly assumed that because of their rhetoric about teamwork, their company was team oriented. Yet the reality was the incentive programs the CEO initiated, which sent the top salespeople to exotic locations each year, created a cutthroat, competitive environment. A pastor may assume his congregation is missions minded because of his frequent mention of the

Great Commission. To his chagrin, however, he may encounter stiff resistance or even hostility when he recommends a ministry to an ethnic group in the community.

Effective leaders don't take the organizational culture for granted or assume it can be easily changed. Ignoring culture can be fatal to leadership careers.

Prolonged Position Holding

"It is better to leave them longing than loathing." Good public speakers know and follow this maxim. Skilled preachers recognize that if they haven't made their point after thirty minutes, they might as well send their parishioners home to their roast beef. Popular public speakers never abuse the privilege of a captive audience. On a much larger scale, wise leaders also know when the time has come to exit graciously and allow a new leader to step in. Some leaders have greatly diminished their contribution to their organizations by remaining in office long after their effectiveness was past.

Harry Truman observed that the prominent place people held in history had a lot to do with the timing of their death. Men such as Abraham Lincoln, John F. Kennedy, and Martin Luther King Jr. were immortalized as much, perhaps, by their dramatic, untimely deaths as by their significant contributions to society.

In his study of leaders, Howard Gardner observed, "Sooner or later, nearly all leaders outreach themselves and end up undermining their causes."[46] Gardner concluded, "Indeed, the greater the accomplishment of the leader; the greater the strain on the milieu, strong accomplishments breed strong reactions, and by and large, only those effective leaders who die at a young age are spared the disheartening sight of their accomplishments being severely challenged, if not wholly undone."[47]

The problem is that many leaders gradually come to see their identity as intrinsically linked to their position. They enjoy the respect and influence that comes with their position in their organization so they hesitate to yield their office to younger leaders, even when it becomes apparent a change is needed. Such leaders can become blinded to the reality they are no longer valuable contributors as they once were. Because they formerly experienced success, they assume they are still best suited for their job. Sadly, these leaders often negate much of the positive contribution they made to their organization in their early years because they refuse to make room for the next generation of leaders. Additionally, their personal reputations suffer decline precluding opportunities and invitations to new positions where they could actually perform well. It is pathetic to watch aging leaders who heroically led their organization to triumph in years past stubbornly refuse to vacate their office long after their abilities have waned.

Impotent leaders who refuse to retire from their positions may put forth grandiose statements about loyalty, but they are revealing a selfish character. They may genuinely want what is best for their organization, yet they are reluctant to relinquish the prestige, power, and financial benefits to which they are accustomed. Leaders with integrity recognize when they have made their most worthwhile contributions. Then they graciously hand over the reins of leadership to a new generation. How does a leader know when the time has come for a changing of the guard? God will guide leaders who seek his wisdom in this regard. Sometimes the performance of the organization gives a clear message. When an organization continually struggles, when it regularly loses to the competition, when no new ideas are being generated, when key personnel are leaving, when morale is chronically low, when there is no exciting anticipation for the future, something needs to change. Either the leader needs a dramatic turnaround, or the time has come for a new leader with different skills to take charge. We would add: When you find someone who could easily do your job, you must go to God and inquire if it is time for you to move on to your next assignment. Life is most fulfilling not when you are doing what others are waiting in line to do but when you are engaged in making your own unique contribution to society and God's kingdom.

Oswald Sanders observes: "Advance is held up for years by well-meaning but aging men who refuse to vacate an office and insist on holding the reins in their failing hands."[48] Dwight Eisenhower worried he would not recognize when his leadership abilities began to wane. He commented: "Normally the last person to recognize that a man's mental faculties are fading is the victim himself. . . . I have seen many a man 'hang on too long' under the definite impression that he had a great duty to perform and that no one else could adequately fill his particular position."[49]

Perhaps the classic biblical example of a leader who overstayed his mandate was King Hezekiah. Hezekiah was a good and righteous ruler of the nation of Judah. The Bible concludes of his reign, "Hezekiah trusted in the LORD God of Israel; not one of the kings of Judah was like him, either before or after him" (2 Kings 18:5). After ruling for fourteen years, Hezekiah contracted a terminal illness. The prophet Isaiah advised the king to get his house in order for it was God's will he should soon die. King Hezekiah wept bitterly and prayed for his life to be spared. God granted his request and promised him fifteen additional years of life.

Had Hezekiah accepted God's will, his period of leadership would have been unblemished. But during his extended tenure, he made two major blunders. When envoys visited him from Babylon, Hezekiah vainly showed them his kingdom's treasures. Such foolish indiscretion would come back to haunt his successors when the Babylonian armies returned to forcibly relieve Judah of its wealth. During the additional years God granted him, Hezekiah also had a son, Manasseh, but he failed to raise Manasseh to fear God. Upon Hezekiah's death, Manasseh ascended the throne and commenced the longest, most wicked reign in Judah's history. By the time Manasseh's rule ended, Judah's immorality and idolatry were so perverse and reached such intolerable levels God's judgment on the nation was irrevocable. By prolonging his leadership beyond what God ordained, Hezekiah planted the seeds for his nation's demise.

Theodore Roosevelt was an enigma to many Americans. Having been elected by one of the highest popular votes in American history, he believed he carried a strong mandate to lead his nation. However, he vowed not to hold office for more than two terms, so the popular president declined to run for a third term even though he could have most likely won. Instead, he strongly endorsed his associate and friend Howard Taft as the Republican candidate. It did not take long, however, for Roosevelt to become disenchanted with his successor. Taft did not govern as Roosevelt would have and Roosevelt found it increasingly difficult to deflect the attention he received from those who wanted him to seek office again. In the 1912 presidential election, Roosevelt ran as an Independent against both the Democratic candidate and incumbent president, Howard Taft. By running against his old party, Roosevelt divided the Republican vote. Despite the fact Roosevelt garnered more votes than Taft, he and Taft both lost to the Democratic candidate, Woodrow Wilson. The combined votes for Taft and Roosevelt would have beaten the Democratic ticket, but, divided, the Republicans lost their hold on the presidency. Roosevelt's major accomplishments in running were to hurt his good friend, divide his party, and bring his Republican party down to defeat for the first time in sixteen years. His refusal to shun public office and support the next generation of leaders produced disastrous results.

Older leaders often struggle to bless the emerging generation. Senior leaders can disparage their younger counterparts as too naïve or radical or inexperienced to conduct the important affairs of executive office. Veteran leaders see new and different techniques and misinterpret these as divergent values. In truth, while biblical principles and values never change, methods appropriate in one era may be obsolete, even counterproductive, in the next. Older leaders understand the next generation of leaders must develop its own leadership style. New leaders must seek God's direction for the organization just as their predecessors did. Senior leaders should become the greatest supporters of the emerging generation. They could become a valuable source of wisdom and experience if they fastidiously avoid meddling or criticizing their successors. Many aging leaders have lost the opportunity to advise the next generation because their criticism alienated their successors. This is an unfortunate way to end a productive career. How much better it would have been to generously express their affirmation and encouragement for the accomplishments of their younger colleagues.

Great leaders do not have to tenaciously cling to their positions of power. They know their influence transcends an office or title. George Washington has been described as a "veritable virtuoso of exits."[50] Washington could lay down his command of the army or the presidency because he knew his influence no longer depended on his position. Dwight Eisenhower chose to allow his performance and reputation to determine what positions he achieved. His biographer commented that in becoming president Eisenhower did not seek office, "but he so successfully managed his private life that, more so than any other candidate in American history, save only George Washington, the Presidency sought him."[51]

Leaders with integrity genuinely place the well-being of the organization before their own prestige. Spiritual leaders stand before God and ask whether their continued leadership in the organization is helpful or harmful. Leaders who truly care about their church or organization and its people may find it painful to acknowledge that the most helpful thing they can do is to step aside. Astute leaders read the organizational signs and recognize when it is time to leave. They look to God as the source of their contentment in life. They also realize that although they can retire from their career, they can never withdraw from their calling. Those leaders who have made a commitment to continually grow and learn have no need to keep a vice grip on their post because they know God has new challenges for them, and they are ready to embrace his next assignment.

Conclusion

Developing a healthy awareness of the pitfalls that can bring failure and disgrace to leaders is the first step to avoiding them. The second step is putting safeguards in place that will provide protection in times of temptation or indecision. Third, leaders should keep before them the continual reminder that (1) their organization is more about people than productivity; (2) they are not indispensable; and (3) the most effective, efficient thing they can do for their organization is to maintain a close, vibrant relationship with God.

Wise spiritual leaders are joining together all over the world to encourage and safeguard one another. Pastors are meeting to pray and to discuss ministry issues. Christian businesspeople are regularly convening Bible studies in the marketplace to discover how to be spiritual statesmen. We have written a resource, *God in the Marketplace: 45 Questions Fortune 500 CEOs Ask about Faith, Life, and Business.*[52] Our ministry, Blackaby Ministries International, developed a Spiritual Leadership Network at www.blackaby.org in which leaders from all walks of life can grow together and strengthen one another. More and more leaders are recognizing, with deliberate effort, good planning, and much prayer, they need not succumb to the pitfalls that could jeopardize their leadership and personal lives. Many Christian business groups such as Fellowship of Christian Companies International and C12 provide for Christian businesspeople to encourage one another to live out their faith in the marketplace. The Lord may lead you to gather a small group of believers to bolster one another as you live out your faith in the arena in which you lead. Groups should consist of three to five godly people with whom you feel free to be completely honest. Group members should be of the same gender. Here are some questions to consider both individually and as a part of your small-group discussion.

1. Do I pray regularly with at least one other leader?
2. Are there other leaders with whom I feel free to be candid about my personal struggles?
3. Who holds me accountable to follow through on what I know to be God's will?
4. What safeguards have I built around my relationship with my spouse? Are they sufficient to protect me from temptation?
5. How am I presently studying and applying God's Word to my life?
6. Have I built safeguards around my time with God so I regularly have unhurried time with him?

7. When was the last time I clearly heard God speaking to me? How did I respond to what he said?

8. Do I have people who are willing to challenge my actions when they think they are questionable?

9. Are the fruits of the Spirit growing in me (Gal. 5:22–23)? Am I becoming increasingly like Christ?

Leaders need not become victims of a pitfall. Take time to carefully reflect on these ten dangers as well as others and proactively take action today so you, your family, and your organization remains healthy and God honoring in the days ahead.

Responding to This Material

1. What are two ways pride could harm your life? How are you safeguarding against it?

2. List four things you do to protect yourself against even the appearance of sexual sin.

3. Do you tend toward optimism or cynicism? What are two things you could do to guard yourself against a negative spirit?

4. How are you vulnerable to greed? If you do not struggle with greed, what is the evidence? Are you overly concerned with pay and compensation? How easily can you give away money and possessions?

5. What are three things you are doing to remain mentally sharp? List the last three books you read. Evaluate them based on value, depth, and insight. Based on your intellectual appetite, what are you filling your mind with?

6. Are you overly sensitive to criticism and disagreement? Do you harbor grudges against those who oppose you? Do you allow critics to rob you of your joy? Is your leadership driven by avoiding criticism or by doing the right thing? What is the evidence?

7. List three things you are doing to keep your spiritual life vibrant and fresh. For example, do you use various Scripture translations? Devotional books? Devotional practices?

8. How are you guarding your domestic life? Does your family get the benefit of your best thinking, energy, and creativity? What are two or three things you could do that would enhance your family life?

9. On a scale of 1 to 10, rate your current administrative performance. Is your organization executing its goals into reality? What might you do to ensure your organization accomplishes what it sets out to do in a timely manner?

10. How long have you been in your current leadership position? Are there any signs it is time for you to move on to another assignment? What is the clear evidence God is continuing to use your life effectively where you are? Would you be able to leave if God told you to?

Chapter Thirteen

The Leader's Rewards

A. B. Bruce observed: "There is no certain work where there is an uncertain reward."[1] Knowing where the greatest rewards lay should motivate leaders to focus on actions necessary to achieve them. Much has been chronicled about leadership skills and responsibilities, but little has been delineated about leadership rewards. For those currently embroiled in the toil and stress of leading, reviewing their potential rewards can be encouraging. For leaders who feel unappreciated or taken for granted, a consideration of their rewards can generate renewed resolve. While leaders ought to fulfill their leadership responsibilities with noble intentions and not out of a desire for personal benefit, they should be aware their unique responsibility also comes with specific benefits.

While certain tangible rewards of leadership are well-known, not every prize is worthy of pursuit. Perhaps the most obvious benefit for holding a leadership position is monetary even though financial compensation should not be a leader's primary motivation. The fact those holding leadership positions usually garner higher pay than their subordinates has enticed countless people to aggressively pursue the highest office. However, many leaders have discovered that if the driving force behind their leadership aspirations is financial, the downside of leadership often outweigh the positives. Leadership always looks easier to those observing it from the outside! Those seeking a leadership position because of its perks and not out of a sense of divine call may discover that a stout bank balance does not compensate for the increased workload, pressures, and criticism that inevitably come.

Leadership brings a second, less measurable but equally enticing return—power. Leaders have greater freedom to control and change their environment. People pay attention to their opinions. The public enlists their involvement in projects and seeks their endorsement for major undertakings. For some this aspect of leadership is intoxicating. They are exhilarated when their views carry weight with people, and they welcome opportunities to express their thoughts to a wide audience. Nevertheless, such influence carries a price. Influence entails accountability. For this reason many find attaining a leadership position is relatively easy compared to the much harder task of maintaining it. The demands of influence including high expectations and increased responsibilities exact a higher price than some are willing to pay. Positional influence, unlike character and spiritual influence, is transitory because when the position ends, so does the influence.

A third transitory reward for leadership is prestige. Leaders are generally treated with respect. The world places a premium on status, but genuine leaders treat fame with caution. Esteem appeals to the ego. It can bring out the worst in people, and it is as fleeting as the morning mist. People who pursue leadership positions to achieve status may discover, to their dismay, that fame can be an albatross more than a reward. For along with prestige comes close scrutiny. Celebrities know only too well that in exchange for the public's adulation they forfeit their personal privacy. Over and over public personalities will, in the same interview, relate how they pursued fame and then they will chastise the adoring public for intruding into their privacy.

It can be unnerving, even to the most upright person, to have every move observed and evaluated. Prestige is therefore a third bittersweet reward for leadership.

The previous three ephemeral rewards: wealth, power, and fame are usually the goals of one-dimensional cartoon villains. There are, however, more noble benefits that make leadership efforts worthwhile. These rewards allow virtuous leaders to enjoy the fruit of their labors and to experience a deep sense of fulfillment. The following are three rewards leaders can anticipate when they lead according to God's standards.

The Reward of Heaven

At the end of his life, the apostle Paul said, "I have fought the good fight, I have finished the race, I have kept the faith. There is reserved for me in the future, the crown of righteousness, which the Lord, the righteous Judge, will give me on that day, and not only to me, but to all who have loved His appearing" (2 Tim. 4:7–8). Paul's words epitomize the highest reward spiritual leaders can attain: to receive God's affirmation and the satisfaction of fulfilling their high calling.

GOD'S AFFIRMATION

Heaven's rewards make gold watches, corner offices, and stock options pale in comparison. No other compensation could equal the joy resulting from knowing almighty God is pleased with you and what you have done with your life. To sense God's palpable affirmation and pleasure in this life and to anticipate eternal rewards that await you in the next is a prize of immeasurable value.

The Scriptures provide numerous examples of men and women with whom God was pleased. Job was a businessman whose righteousness on earth brought glory to God in heaven (Job 1:8; 2:3). Daniel was a government official whose conduct in the king's service earned him esteem in heaven's courts (Dan. 9:23). Elizabeth was a priest's wife who was "righteous in God's sight" and therefore found favor with God (Luke 1:6, 25). Likewise Mary was a young woman whose moral purity invoked God's praise (Luke 1:28). Jesus' life so pleased his heavenly Father the Father declared, "You are My beloved Son. I take delight in You" (Luke 3:22). Jesus promised his disciples that if their lives honored God, they too would be richly rewarded in this life as well as in heaven (Luke 18:28–30).

Despite their greatest accomplishments, non-Christians face death with apprehension and uncertainty. Winston Churchill was one of the twentieth century's most fearless leaders. He faced the full fury of Hitler's Nazi war machine without flinching. At one point he quipped: "I am ready to meet my Maker. Whether my Maker is ready to meet me is another question."[2] Yet despite his bravado, on his deathbed, at the threshold of eternity, Churchill's last words were: "There is no hope." The old warrior fought the fierce Pathans in India. He bravely charged with 310 cavalry into a mass of over three thousand enemy dervishes in Sudan. He had escaped captivity from the Boers in South Africa. He commanded British troops on the front lines during World War I. His apparent lack of fear for enemy bullets was mystifying. He once commented: "There is nothing more exhilarating than being shot at without result."[3] The only enemy he could not face resolutely was death.

Contrast Churchill's final moments with those of D. L. Moody. Shortly before his death at age sixty-two, Moody declared: "Some day you will read in the papers that Moody is dead. Don't you believe a word of it. At that moment I shall be more alive than I am now."[4] Four months later, as Moody lay dying, he said: "Earth recedes, heaven opens up before me! . . . If this is death, it is sweet. God is calling me and I must go. Don't call me back! . . . No pain, no valley, it's bliss."[5]

FULFILLING YOUR DIVINE CALLING

Having accomplished your personal goals and accumulated wealth can provide small comfort at life's terminus. Conversely, could there be any better satisfaction than having spent your life obeying God's call? Could there be any greater comfort than approaching death without fear, knowing you invested your life developing a relationship with the God of heaven? The highest reward is to know as the earth recedes, heaven welcomes you.

Scripture says of King David, "For David, after serving his own generation in God's plan, fell asleep, was buried with his fathers" (Acts 13:36). David was far from perfect, yet the Scriptures say God used him to accomplish his heavenly purposes. There is no more worthy ambition than to achieve God's will for one's life.

God calls some people to serve him in leadership roles (Eph. 4:11). For those people to do anything else would be to accept less than God's best for their life.

Paul's ambition was to follow God unwaveringly. Those who embrace God's purposes and diligently pursue them can echo the apostle, "I was not disobedient to the heavenly vision" (Acts 26:19). Achieving your life's maximum potential is enormously satisfying. At the close of Jesus' life, he prayed to his heavenly Father, "I have glorified You on the earth by completing the work You gave Me to do" (John 17:4). While Jesus hung on the cross at Calvary, about to breathe his last, he shouted in triumph, "It is finished!" (John 19:30). Jesus did not say, "I am finished." He had received the most difficult assignment ever given and he had faithfully obeyed to the end.

Leadership is a broad term that covers a wide spectrum of responsibility. Some are called to lead in smaller capacities. Others are assigned positions of great influence. Many are called to provide leadership in their home. No matter how grand or seemingly small an assignment appears, those called to lead will misspend their lives and squander their potential if they neglect to do so. Some people know God has called them to lead, but they are apprehensive. They are reluctant to leave the security of their present position. They fear the criticism that may come. They doubt their abilities, which means they question God's sufficiency. But if they will allow God to stretch them personally, he will lead them to do things they never dreamed possible. They will one day look back over their lives and marvel at what God accomplished through them. They will overcome any challenge and say, along with the apostle Paul: "But I count my life of no value to myself, so that I may finish my course and the ministry I received from the Lord Jesus" (Acts 20:24).

The Rewards of Relationships

The Roman emperor Tiberius cared nothing for his people's affection. He only desired their respect.[6] As a result, upon his death, public prayers were offered throughout the empire that his soul be tormented in hell.[7] In contrast, Dwight Eisenhower's biographer claimed that "nearly everyone who knew him liked him immensely."[8] Eisenhower was surrounded by a loyal cadre of companions who never sought to profit from their close proximity to their powerful friend.[9]

Effective leaders nurture and enjoy three major categories of relationships throughout their lives. These include their families, their colleagues, and their friends.

FAMILIES

The arena of leaders' greatest accomplishments ought to be their homes. After they have resigned from their formal leadership position, their families will remain. They should therefore be as purposeful in leading their loved ones as they are diligent in guiding their staff. If they are zealous in solving problems at work, they are even more earnest in problem solving at home. If they are known for their courteous and upbeat attitude at work, they are even more thoughtful with their family. If they are respectful of their coworkers, they go to even greater lengths to honor their spouse and children. Leaders who are consistently loving, patient, and kind whether at home or at work prove they are genuine spiritual leaders. Leaders can accomplish marvelous feats in the public eye and be praised as heroes. But the real champions are those who go home at day's end to a family who loves and respects them.

At the height of D. L. Moody's public success, he faced a personal crisis. His preaching ministry was enormously successful; he founded a thriving church, three schools, and a publishing house, yet he felt like a failure. His oldest son Will enrolled at Yale University and apparently rejected his parents' faith. In a letter to his wayward son, Moody wrote, "The thing that shames me most is that I am preaching to others and my son does not believe in the gospel I preach."[10] Moody's ministry success meant little to him if he failed those he loved the most. To Moody's great joy, Will eventually returned to Christ, joined his father in his ministry, and wrote his father's biography.[11]

True spiritual leaders move their families from where they are to where God wants them to be. Although they naturally enjoy seeing progress and growth in their organizations, they take even greater delight in fostering spiritual maturity in their families. God has clear principles for leading families (Deut. 6:4–9; Eph. 5:22–6:4). Those who unwaveringly follow biblical instructions will experience success in the most important arena of leadership—their home (Prov. 22:6). As a result, spiritual leaders will leave behind a "godly seed" to carry out God's purposes for generations afterward (Deut. 6:4–9; Mal. 2:11–15).

Family relationships have the potential to bring leaders their greatest joy and their deepest grief. Leaders who neglect their families in favor of achieving organizational goals may experience outward success but suffer abysmal failure in their home. Richard was leading a conference for pastors and at the close of one of the services, a handsome young man approached him in tears. He shared that five years earlier he took a half-dozen people and started a new church. Now, five years later, the church was flourishing, and attendance surpassed eight hundred people. From a church growth perspective, he was a resounding success. But through his tears he explained that when he was first considering starting the church, his wife pleaded with him not to do it. She warned: "I know what you're like. You're extremely driven. You'll give everything you have to grow your church and your family will lose you." The young pastor vehemently denied the possibility, for he prized his family. Through his tears this brokenhearted pastor admitted, "She was right! How did I ever get to this place?" Two weeks earlier his wife gently told him he could go his way with the church and she and the children would go theirs. He sacrificed his most precious human relationships for the sake of growing his church. In that moment of agonizing self-realization, this young man would gladly have forfeited all of his "success" to regain the close relationship he once enjoyed with his wife and children.

King David suffered similar anguish. As a general, king, and administrator, his leadership was unmatched. However, his remarkable accomplishments were tarnished by his failure as a domestic leader. David's wife Michal ridiculed him for publicly praising God (2 Sam. 6:20–23). David committed adultery with one of his friend's wives and initiated his murder (2 Sam. 11). David's son Amnon raped his half-sister Tamar (2 Sam. 13:1–22). David's son Absalom murdered Amnon and launched a civil war against his father (2 Sam. 15–18). Even while David lay upon his deathbed, his sons Adonijah and Solomon were plotting against each other for their father's throne (1 Kings 1:5–53). David's son Solomon, born out of his adulterous relationship, would prove susceptible to the influence of pagan women and allow his heart to turn away from the Lord during his reign (1 Kings 11:1–8). David's grandson Rehoboam foolishly listened to unwise counsel and saw the Davidic kingdom torn in two (1 Kings 12:1–15). David's inability to lead his family robbed him of much of the joy he should have experienced and ultimately nullified much of what he accomplished.

The rewards for intentional, godly leadership of one's family are directly proportional to the investment made. Leaders derive a rich dividend of joy and contentment when their families remain intact and serving God. Long after a task is done or a project is finished or even a career has ended, the leader's family will continue to provide a deep source of fulfillment. People who lead their families wisely can often set in motion a heritage of several generations who know how to lead their families as well as others effectively. What reward could equal seeing your children love and follow the same God they watched you serve during their childhood years? On several occasions we have been joined in a speaking assignment by one or both of Richard's sons, Mike and Daniel. They typically are the highlight! Having the next generation embrace our faith and our God is a reward beyond measure.

COLLEAGUES

Warren Buffet noted late in his career: "If you get to be my age in life and nobody thinks well of you, I don't care how big your bank account is, your life is a disaster."[12] Kouzes and Posner claim it is the "quality of our relationships that most determine whether our legacy will be ephemeral or lasting."[13] They also note that true leaders love the people they work with. They suggest if people don't want to be liked, "then they probably don't belong in leadership."[14]

Genuine leaders value people. They don't neglect them or manipulate them to accomplish their goals. One quality that characterized many of history's great leaders was the number of close, loyal friends they enjoyed. Having strong friendships among their colleagues is a leader's reward for investing in people's lives. Kouzes and Posner note: "A managerial myth says we can't get too close to our associates. We can't be friends with people at work. Well, set this myth aside."[15] Leaders cannot be successful if they do not invest in people. As leaders focus on people, friendships develop. You cannot care for people you work alongside for forty hours each week and not develop some level of friendship.

Leaders make their workplaces better. They enrich their colleagues' lives. When leaders invest themselves in the lives of those they work with, they leave a trail of grateful friends in their wake. Such leaders can return to former workplaces and find friends who still appreciate the contribution they made to their lives. As Kouzes and Posner note, people remember you for what you did for *them*, not for yourself.[16] Leaders who exploited people to accomplish their goals and who mortgaged their organizations to achieve personal success will be resented by those they eventually leave behind. Leaders embroiled in constant conflict with colleagues and who focused solely on personal advancement will not be missed.

Once people no longer hold positions of power and influence, they have an unobstructed view of who their true friends are. Those who failed to cultivate authentic friendships will find this time can be revealing and disheartening, but those who used their leadership to genuinely invest in people will find the experience supremely rewarding. Wise leaders realize they will not always hold their influential positions. Then those lackeys who merely courted their favor or sought their endorsements will no longer call on them. President Richard Nixon did not enjoy being around people. He intentionally scheduled staff Christmas parties for when he knew he would be out of town.[17] He jettisoned the few friends he did have out of political expediency. As a result, when Nixon unceremoniously left the White House, he found himself isolated, lonely, and shunned. One of the reasons some leaders tenaciously cling to their office is because they suspect their phones will stop ringing the moment they no longer control the organization's purse strings.

David certainly had a multifaceted character, but one obvious feature is he endeared himself to his friends. David and Jonathan's relationship is a model of devotion and loyalty. David gathered close friends around him throughout his life. The group of "mighty men" who accompanied him is legendary (1 Chron. 11:10–47). Even as David lay dying, his close friends continued to protect him and to strive to see his will was done.

The apostle Paul surrounded himself with colleagues many of whom became his close friends. Rarely do you hear of Paul working alone. Barnabas, Timothy, Titus, Luke, Silas, Epaphroditus, Priscilla, Aquila, and many others were dear to Paul.[18] The ability to attract so many high-caliber companions says much about Paul's character. Though Jesus was the Son of God and could have lived self-sufficiently, he too enjoyed close relationships with his associates (John 15:14). Few things provide more joy than good friends and leaders have the opportunity to make many over the course of their careers.

The responsibility of leadership can become overwhelming unless leaders are buttressed by supportive friendships. Friendship is an effective stress reliever. Being able to relax and share one's feelings with loyal companions is critical to a person's mental and emotional health. Leaders who insulate themselves from others and choose to bear their burdens single-handedly are destined for loneliness and burnout. Leaders, like everyone else, need friends, perhaps even more so in light of the weighty load they carry.

Some leaders have willingly forsaken relationships to achieve their goals. They alienate friends, colleagues, and family members. Some ambitious leaders use people as stepping-stones. Consequently, they leave a trail of embittered and resentful colleagues behind. By the end of their careers, they have little else but their work to occupy them. People are never the means to an end; they are the end. No matter how eager leaders may be to achieve their goals, they must always treat others with dignity and concern.

Samuel, the distinguished judge and prophet, maintained integrity in relating to those with whom he worked. As a result, when he neared the end of his tenure, he stood before the people he led and asked:

> "Here I am. Bring charges against me before the LORD and His anointed: Whose ox or donkey have I taken? Whom have I wronged or mistreated? From whose hand have I taken a bride to overlook something? I will return it to you."
>
> "You haven't wronged us, you haven't mistreated us, and you haven't taken anything from anyone's hand," they responded.
>
> He said to them, "The LORD is a witness against you, and His anointed is a witness today that you haven't found anything in my hand."
>
> "He is a witness," they said. (1 Sam. 12:3–5)

Samuel served as a leader for most of his life. Those he led saw him in every conceivable situation. He had numerous opportunities to mistreat people and to compromise his integrity. Nevertheless, at the close of his life, when he stood before his nation and asked if there was even one person whom he had mistreated, no one lodged a complaint. It truly is a rich reward to know God used your life to bring a blessing to your workplace.

FRIENDS

Leaders inevitably make friends among their colleagues because that is who they spend the bulk of their time with. However, healthy leaders will also cultivate friendships outside their work life. They do this for several reasons. For one, people need to be able to take their mind off work and to enjoy laughter and recreation with friends. Work-related friends tend to talk about office matters.

Second, effective leaders tend to surround themselves with a variety of friends. Companions can enrich people's lives, and each friendship makes a unique contribution. Some Christian businesspeople may find few if any of their colleagues are believers. They will therefore seek friendships from people in other companies or businesses. We work with CEOs of large companies. It has been wonderful to watch these busy executives take time to befriend and encourage one another to live out their Christian faith in the marketplace.

Friends can be developed in a wide variety of settings. A church can be filled with diverse, life-enriching friends. A Christian CEO of a large company may discover she thoroughly enjoys going skiing with friends from her church who are schoolteachers or attending an art class with a widow from her Bible study. Leaders can also develop unique friendships with people they meet while volunteering on nonprofit boards or while coaching their children's Little League teams. Leaders tend to be a blessing to their neighbors. Developing friendships with people of diverse ethnic groups provides fascinating opportunities to discover new foods, traditions, and cultures. Many Christian leaders have also found it enormously enriching and informative to befriend unbelievers not only for the opportunity to share Christ with them but also to learn from them and to enjoy their company.

It has been said of D. L. Moody, "One could not be downhearted or defeated in his presence."[19] People are naturally drawn to such people. Regardless of what organization or endeavor spiritual leaders involve themselves in, they naturally attract others to them because of their Christlike character and their genuine interest and concern for others. Over the course of a lifetime, such people accumulate a wide variety of friends.

Legacy

Andrew Mellon, one of the wealthiest and most influential men of the early twentieth century, mused that "every man wants to connect his life with something eternal."[20] Andrew Carnegie, perhaps the richest man of his day, came to believe "the man who dies thus rich dies disgraced."[21] He subsequently gave away the bulk of his wealth building libraries and numerous institutions across the country for the public good. Our lives on earth are brief. God has gifted leaders with abilities and influence that can change their world. Wise leaders want to leave a mark on their world that outlasts their transitory lives. So they strive to accomplish God's purposes in the place he has put them and with the time God grants them. Leaders can leave a legacy in three major areas. These are in their families, their work life, and God's kingdom.

FAMILY

John D. Rockefeller, the most affluent businessperson of his era, claimed, "My greatest fortune in life has been my son."[22] Abraham's legacy was entrenched because he was followed by Isaac, Jacob, and Joseph. Surprisingly, many well-known leaders did not bring up children who could effectively carry on their legacy. Moses chose Joshua, rather than his own son Gershom, to succeed him (Exod. 2:22). Joshua's sons played no prominent role in national affairs. History is filled with examples of people whose progeny carried on their legacy and those who did not. Presidents John Adams and George Bush Sr. had sons who followed them to the White House. Junius Morgan was succeeded by his son J. P. who was followed by his son Jack, thus enabling their financial institution to become one of the most powerful in the world. John Rockefeller passed his enormous wealth to his son, as did Cornelius Vanderbilt and John Jacob Astor, ensuring their ongoing legacy. While financial, artistic, or other secular legacies can bring glory to the founders and their descendents, spiritual legacies ultimately point people's attention to God. Billy Graham's children and grandchildren continue to lead his ministry and to preach the gospel around the world. Our family's spiritual legacy has been largely preserved through writing. Henry's father, Gerald Richard Blackaby, had several of his poems published.[23] Gerald's son Henry has had dozens of books published including the best known, *Experiencing God.* All five of Henry's children and his wife have been published, and now

Henry's two oldest grandsons, Mike and Daniel, have authored *When World's Collide*. Gerald Blackaby could never have imagined that as he was submitting poems to a publishing house in the 1920s that ninety years later his son, five grandchildren, and his great-grandchildren would be authoring books to the glory of God. What we begin in our lifetime can be seed that bears much more fruit in subsequent generations.

LIFE WORK

On his deathbed, Caesar Augustus claimed, "I found Rome built of clay; I leave it to you in marble."[24] People's success in life can largely be measured by the contribution they made to others. Some people live long lives but contribute nothing positive to those around them. Others may not become centenarians, but they leave their world changed. Winston Churchill noted, "History judges a man, not by his victories or defeats, but by their results."[25] Those who invest themselves solely in their own personal profit and comfort will inevitably lose everything they worked for at life's end while leaving behind no legacy. Those who labor to contribute something to humanity may not become wealthier than their colleagues, but they can take comfort in knowing they invested their lives profitably. John Adams participated in many of the landmark moments in the birth of the United States. After the issuing of the Declaration of Independence, Adams, who played a pivotal role, wrote to his wife Abigail: "When I consider the great events which are passed and those greater which are rapidly advancing and that I may have been instrumental of touching some springs, and turning some wheels, which have had and will have such effects, I feel an awe upon my mind which is not easily described."[26] Adams instinctively knew he had invested his life in something great.

William Wilberforce never achieved the highest political office, despite his brilliance and close proximity to power, yet he managed to eradicate his nation and the world of the legalized slave trade. Eric Metaxas concluded of Wilberforce:

> What Wilberforce vanquished was something even worse than slavery, something that was much more fundamental and can

hardly be seen from where we stand today: he vanquished the very mind-set that made slavery acceptable and allowed it to survive and thrive for a millennia. He destroyed an entire way of seeing the world, one that held sway from the beginning of history, and replaced it with another way of seeing the world. . . . Even though slavery continues to exist here and there, the idea that it is good is dead. . . . Because the entire mind-set that supported it is gone. Wilberforce overturned not just European civilization's view of slavery but its view of almost everything in the human sphere; and that is why it is nearly impossible to do justice to the enormity of his accomplishment: it is nothing less than a fundamental and important shift in human consciousness.[27]

Great leaders make the lives of others better. When longtime General Motors CEO Alfred Sloan retired, his employees spontaneously collected $1.5 million dollars and donated it to cancer research in his honor. It was a fitting tribute to their philanthropic leader who invested so much in them. On the contrary, Napoleon was a vain, ambitious leader. He lamented, "In this crowd of men I have made into kings, there is not one who is grateful, not one who has a heart, not one who loves me."[28] The manner in which people honor or ignore a leader's departure can often reflect the way the leader treated those who worked under them.

Spiritual leaders who invest in people will experience deep satisfaction when they see those individuals fulfill God's purposes for their lives. There is no greater experience for leaders than rejoicing with those who have matured in their faith as a result of their leader's faithfulness. Paul described the church he established in Philippi as his joy and his crown (Phil. 4:1). Leaders' joy is multiplied as younger associates follow their example and they in turn help others grow. D. L. Moody mightily impacted his generation by investing in people. The list of his friends and protégés reads like a Who's Who of Christian leaders of the late nineteenth century. Men such as F. B. Meyer, Ira Sankey, Philip Bliss, C. T. Studd, John R. Mott, Fleming Revell, S. D. Gordon, R. A. Torrey, Robert Speer, Wilbur Chapman, G. Campbell

Morgan, C. I. Scofield, Henry Drummond, and J. H. Moulton were just some of the hundreds of Christian leaders whose lives Moody impacted. At one point when his colleagues D. W. Whittle and Phillip Bliss were struggling to continue their evangelistic campaigns across the United States, Moody sent them funds and exhorted them, "If you have not got faith enough, launch out on the strength of my faith."[29] By the time Moody died in 1899, scores of dedicated Christian leaders in every sector of society looked to Moody as their mentor and encourager.

Another effective way leaders extend their influence is by investing in organizations. Jean Monnet observed, "Nothing is made without men; nothing lasts without institutions."[30] Robert Greenleaf noted: "The secret of institution building is to be able to weld a team of . . . people by lifting them up to grow taller than they would otherwise be."[31] Institutions can generally do more than individuals. One simple reason for this is they usually have a longer life span. D. L. Moody preached to more than one million people during his illustrious ministry, but his greatest impact was undoubtedly through the organizations left behind. Although he was not an educated man himself, he founded the Mount Hermon School for Boys and the Northfield Seminary for Girls. He established the Chicago Evangelization Society (later renamed the Moody Bible Institute), he developed the YMCA in Chicago and the Moody Church, and he began the Northfield Conferences from which sprang the Student Volunteer Movement. Through this movement hundreds of college graduates went out as missionaries around the world. Moody also played a role in founding the Fleming H. Revell publishing company as well as the Moody Press. These organizations continued to function effectively long after Moody's death. The Billy Graham Evangelistic Association and its rebroadcasts of the evangelist's sermons have seen more people experience salvation than occurred during Graham's crusade ministry. Leaders may exhaust themselves seeking to make an impact on society. However, those who invest in institutions can exert a continuing impact that extends long past their lifetime.

Leaders may not always know the full extent of their influence on people, but their impact upon an organization is more easily measured. Kouzes and Posner define *leadership success* as "leaving the area a better place than when you found it."[32] Leaders should expect that the organization they lead will one day be stronger because of their leadership. Mahatma Ghandi saw the day when his nation of India was liberated from Great Britain. After three decades of personal sacrifice, Nelson Mandela witnessed South Africa's first free election by black voters. Winston Churchill took a demoralized nation and led it to defeat the seemingly invincible German army. Leaders take great satisfaction in knowing when they leave an organization, it is stronger, more vibrant, robust, and effective than it was before they came.

Contributions to a Successor

One of the most important yet often overlooked responsibilities of leaders is preparing their organization for a successor. The Bible reveals God's pattern of working systematically through successive generations. God gave his people specific instructions concerning how they were to train and prepare the emerging generation of leaders (Deut. 6:6–9, 20–25). One of the primary reasons Scripture gives for God's disdain of divorce is that it disrupts the lives of the children God is preparing as "godly offspring" (Mal. 2:15–16). God's people always stand just one generation away from apostasy. For God's purposes to continue, each generation must embrace a fresh relationship of love for him and obedience to his Word. That is why true spiritual leaders are always investing in the next generation. It's no coincidence great spiritual leaders follow in the footsteps of outstanding spiritual leaders. Joshua succeeded the revered Moses and even surpassed his accomplishments. Elisha not only followed the mighty Elijah as prophet; he was given a double portion of Elijah's spirit (2 Kings 2:9–10). Jesus made this incredible statement to his disciples: "I assure you: The one who believes in Me will also do the works that I do. And he will do even greater works than these, because I am going to the Father" (John 14:12).

Often leaders do not carefully consider their replacement until they reach the end of their leadership term. However, when suddenly faced with leaving their office, they realize much of their work will have been in vain unless they are followed by a capable successor. Margaret Thatcher confronted this reality when she was forced from office as prime minister of Great Britain. When it became clear she must relinquish her office, she observed: "But there was one more duty I had to perform and that was to ensure that John Major was my successor. I wanted—perhaps I needed—to believe that he was the man to secure and safeguard my legacy and to take our policies forward."[33]

It is a grievous experience to laboriously build an organization only to watch it disintegrate under an ineffective successor. Former leaders have been forced to watch in horror as their successors subsequently dismantled everything they built.

True joy comes in knowing one's life work has been preserved and is continuing due to the leader's careful preparation of a successor. While Ronald Reagan was president, he met with Vice President George Bush every Thursday for lunch. Although American presidents historically neglected and marginalized their vice presidents, Reagan would review the week and the pressing issues they were facing with his associate. To Reagan's delight, Bush was elected president after Reagan's two terms came to an end. During Reagan's last moments in the Oval Office, he left a note for the new president on stationery with the heading, "Don't let the turkeys get you down." On it he wrote:

> Dear George,
>
> You'll have moments when you want to use this particular stationery. Well, go for it. George, I'll treasure the memories we share and wish you all the very best. You'll be in my prayers. God bless you and Barbara. I'll miss our Thursday lunches.
>
> Ron[34]

Reagan had the satisfaction of knowing his efforts would not come to an abrupt end at the close of his final term. While leaders cannot always choose their successors, they can prepare their organizations for the next leader and they can invest in emerging leaders who are prepared to take their place. Leaders always have an eye on the future and that entails preparing their organization for it.

KINGDOM OF GOD

John Rockefeller built Standard Oil to become the most powerful company in the world. However, after a remarkable forty-one-year history, on May 15, 1911, the U.S. Supreme Court ruled it must be dissolved.[35] J. P. Morgan and Company was America's most influential bank under the herculean influence of J. P. Morgan. However, after the Glass-Segal bill was passed by Congress in 1933, the prestigious bank was ordered to split into two entities, forming Morgan Stanley and losing the dominance it once enjoyed.[36] Some of America's most powerful and wealthy institutions have ultimately declined or even liquidated. While investing in institutions may allow leaders to extend their influence beyond their lifetime, only by channeling their energy into the kingdom of God can leaders elongate their influence into eternity.

Jesus made it clear what every leader's priority should be when he commanded: "Seek first the kingdom of God and His righteousness" (Matt. 6:33). A priceless reward awaits those who contribute to eternity. Those who lead Christian organizations know their personal investments will continue paying eternal dividends, but this command is also for people who lead secular organizations.

It has been our great pleasure to work with many leaders in the marketplace, military, education, and home who dedicated their lives to seeking first the kingdom of God (Matt. 6:33). Businesspeople have used their international travel to support mission causes. We know many who have provided Christian materials for people in prison or men and women serving in the military. Many of these leaders have served on the boards of Christian schools and ministries. Some have begun ministries to the poor and homeless or to orphans. Some volunteer to work with teenagers at their church or volunteer time at safe houses for battered women. These leaders recognize that long after the institutions they developed and the staffs they assembled have dissipated and dispersed, their investments in God's kingdom will last, and they will receive their reward in full (Matt. 25:31–46).

Conclusion

God is absolutely just and will reward those who seek him (Heb. 11:6). While spiritual leadership carries with it unique challenges and burdens, it is also accompanied by eternal rewards. If you have grown discouraged in your leadership role, take heart! God sees your sacrifice. He knows your pain. Even though people may never know all you did on their behalf, God does, and his reward is with him (Isa. 40:10).

Leadership Rewards

1. Heaven's Rewards
2. Relationships
3. Legacy

Responding to This Material

1. What have you found to be the most rewarding aspect of being a leader?

2. What unique ways has God already rewarded you for being a spiritual leader? Have you ever sensed God's pleasure on your life? If so, how did it feel?

3. List three relationships that have blessed your life as a leader. Have you viewed these as a "reward"?

4. List three things your leadership has accomplished that may outlast your life. How does that make you feel?

Final Challenge

In 69 BC Julius Caesar was serving as a quaestor in southern Spain conducting court proceedings. He came upon a monument to Alexander the Great near the temple of Hercules. He was troubled at the realization that at the age of thirty-one he had accomplished nothing noteworthy while at the same age Alexander had conquered the known world.[1] Of course the rest is history. Thomas Carlisle popularized the "great man" theory in which he claimed history was nothing more than the elongated biographies of great men. His emphasis on "great" and "men" has come under resounding criticism. However, one could say history has advanced as *people* have chosen to make a difference in their society and, at times, their world.

This life affords each person the opportunity to make their mark on their world. Every generation can affect the future by the way parents rear their children and the care leaders take to invest in the next generation. Occasional moments in history are characterized by significant change and transition. These eras provide enormous opportunities for people to step up and make a difference for good or ill. Franklin Roosevelt once said, "For each age is a dream that is dying, or one that is coming to birth."[2] We live in a time of enormous transition and change. Many of the formerly accepted values, worldviews, and religious beliefs are now fluid. Nations are being transformed. Economies are shifting dramatically on a global scale. Technology is outdating many skills, practices, methodologies, organizations, and careers. Globalization enables people in any location on the globe to impact the world.

Who will rise to make a difference in our day? Unquestionably, evil motivates men and women to spread death and destruction as far as they possibly can. Proponents of false religions and atheist philosophies are aggressively vying for dominance in popular thought. Evil dictators are willing and able to extinguish lives by the millions to perpetuate their power. We cannot afford to remain indifferent. Either we accept God's invitation to step out and affect our environment, or we become victims of those who are pushing their own agendas. Henry Wadsworth Longfellow said, "In this world, a man must either be anvil or hammer." God is looking to develop men and women into his divinely empowered instruments to impact today's culture.

History has seen numerous individuals who believed their lives were destined to make a difference in the world. For example, Queen Elizabeth I concluded her life was spared as a youth in order to lead her people as an adult. Others hoped for a moment in history when they might have the opportunity to accomplish something noteworthy. In 1832 Abraham Lincoln confessed: "Every man is said to have his peculiar ambition. . . . I have no other so great as that of being truly esteemed of my fellow men, by rendering myself worthy of their esteem. How far I shall succeed in gratifying this ambition, is yet to be developed."[3] History provided Lincoln the chance to change society, and he seized it. Likewise, Winston Churchill tried all his life to make a contribution to history and yet was continually thwarted until the darkest moments in Britain's history when he was already a senior citizen. But his moment eventually came.

The enormous global challenges in our day provide unprecedented opportunities for motivated people to make a positive impact on the world. True leaders are not intimidated by changing or turbulent times, for those are the days when they are needed most. Today's problems of spiritual hunger, domestic breakdown, hunger, poverty, disease, war, terrorism, crime, and disillusionment are omnipresent. The challenges of world religions, cults, materialism, and militant atheism are epidemic.

Yet history has repeatedly demonstrated that society's worst mobilizes leaders to make their greatest contributions. Globalization and technology provide Christians unprecedented opportunities to extend God's kingdom. History waits to see whom God will raise up to mightily impact the world today.

Perhaps you have never had the ambition to change your society. Or perhaps you tried to lead in the past and you failed. Don't be discouraged! As you read this book, God's Spirit may have convicted you to step up and be counted as a genuine spiritual leader. Don't limit what God will do through you. We can testify that God is more than able to accomplish his divine purposes through your life.

We have been tremendously encouraged by the exciting stories we have heard since the first edition of this book. God has used ordinary men and women to accomplish incredible things worldwide in the marketplace, churches, nonprofit organizations, governments, schools, and homes. We pray God has stirred your heart and is preparing you for the great work he intends to do through you. Keep your eyes on him and trust him to do amazing things through your life to change your world (Josh. 1:9).

Notes

CHAPTER 1

1. *USA Today*, March 18, 2009, Online Poll, http://www.weather.com/common/onlinepoll/results/travel_daily.html?dailytraveler_d183.

2. David McCullough, *John Adams* (New York: Simon and Schuster, 2001; Touchstone ed., 2002), 23.

3. Thomas Paine, *Common Sense, Rights of Man, and Other Essential Writings of Thomas Paine* (New York: Signet Classics, 2003), 71.

4. James Canton, *The Extreme Future: The Top Trends that Will Reshape the World for the Next 5, 10, and 20 Years* (New York: Dutton Publishing, 2006), 4.

5. Phil Rosenzweig, *The Halo Effect . . . and the Eight Other Business Delusions That Deceive Managers* (New York: Simon and Schuster, 2007; Free Press Edition, 2009), 146–49.

6. Brade Szollose, *Liquid Leadership: From Woodstock to Wikipedia— Multigenerational Ideas that Are Changing the Way We Run Things* (Austin, TX: Greenleaf Book Group Press, 2011), 59.

7. Gordon R. Sullivan and Michael V. Harper, *Hope Is Not a Method: What Business Leaders Can Learn from America's Army* (New York: Broadway Books, 1997), 48.

8. Thom Rainer and Jess Rainer, *The Millennials: Connecting to America's Largest Generation* (Nashville, TN: B&H Publishing Group, 2011), 8.

9. Szollose, *Liquid Leadership*, 4.

10. Craig E. Johnson, *Meeting the Ethical Challenges of Leadership: Casting Light or Shadow*, 3rd ed. (Los Angeles: Sage Publications, 2009), 304.

11. Thomas L. Friedman, *The World Is Flat: A Brief History of the Twenty-First Century* (New York: Farrar, Straus and Giroux, 2005; rev. ed., 2006).

12. Ibid., 10.

13. Quoted in Johnson, *Meeting the Ethical Challenges of Leadership*, 304.

14. Ibid., 316.

15. For an extensive discussion of this challenge, see Joel Kurtzman, *Common Purpose: How Great Leaders Get Organizations to Achieve the Extraordinary* (San Francisco: Jossey-Bass, 2010).

16. Warren Bennis, *Why Leaders Can't Lead* (San Francisco: Jossey-Bass, 1989), 36.

17. Ibid., 33.

18. Charles Handy, *The Age of Paradox* (Boston: Harvard Business School Press, 1995), 36.

19. Daniel Goleman, *Working with Emotional Intelligence* (New York: Bantam Books, 1998), 58.

20. Robert K. Greenleaf, *Servant Leadership* (New York: Paulist Press, 1977), 156.

21. See http://www.usatoday.com/money/industries/retail/2007-01-03-hd-nardelli_x.htm.

22. See http://money.cnn.com/2005/02/09/technology/hp_fiorina.

23. George Barna, *Leaders on Leadership* (Ventura: Regal Books, 1997), 18.

24. Ron Chernow, *Titan: The Life of John D. Rockefeller* (New York: Vintage Books, 1998; 2nd ed., 2004), 607.

25. Thomas Carlyle, *On Heroes, Hero-Worship and the Heroic in History* (London: Collins' Clear-Type Press, 1842), 7.

26. For a thorough overview of leadership theories, see Joseph C. Rost, *Leadership for the Twenty-First Century* (Westport, CT: Praeger Publishers, 1991; Paperback ed., 1993).

27. Tim Irwin, *Derailed: Five Lessons Learned from Catastrophic Failures of Leadership* (Nashville: Thomas Nelson, 2009), 138.

28. For an extensive look at how God raised up a leader to accomplish his purposes, see Henry and Richard Blackaby, *Called to Be God's Leader: Lessons from the Life of Joshua* (Nashville: Thomas Nelson, 2004).

29. John Man, *Genghis Khan: Life, Death, and Resurrection* (New York: Thomas Dunne Books, 2004), 260.

30. Quoted in Christian Meier, *Caesar* (Berlin: Severin and Siedler, 1982; English ed., London: Fontana Press, 1996), 336.

31. Christopher Hibbert, *Disraeli: A Personal History* (New York: HarperCollins, 2004), 11.

32. Robert V. Remini, *The Life of Andrew Jackson* (New York: Harper and Row, 1988; Perennial Classics ed., 2001), 12.

33. H. W. Brands, *Woodrow Wilson* in The American Presidents (New York: Times Books, 2003), 5.

34. Ibid., 10.

35. Tom Pocock, *Horatio Nelson* (London: Brockhampton Press, 1987), 158.

36. Ibid., 161.

37. Malcom R. Davies, "Unlocking the Value of Exceptional Personalities" in *The Perils of Accentuating the Positive*, Robert B. Kaiser, ed. (Tulsa: Hogan Press, 2009), 143.

38. Eric Metaxas, *Amazing Grace: William Wilberforce and the Heroic Campaign to End Slavery* (San Francisco: HarperCollins, 2007), 85.

39. D. A. Lande, *I Was with Patton: First Person Accounts of WW II in George S. Patton's Command* (St. Paul, MN: MBI Publishing Company, 2002), 297.

40. Quoted in Jean H. Baker, *James Buchanan* in The American Presidents (New York: Times Books, 2004), xviii.

41. Doris Kearns Goodwin, *Team of Rivals: The Political Genius of Abraham Lincoln* (New York: Simon and Schuster, 2005), xix.

42. Jean Edward Smith, *Grant* (New York: Simon and Schuster, 2001; Touchstone ed., 2002).

CHAPTER 2

1. James MacGregor Burns, *Leadership* (New York: Harper Torchbooks, 1978), 2.

2. Warren Bennis and Burt Nanus, *Leaders: Strategies for Taking Charge* (New York: HarperCollins, 1997), 4.

3. John Gardner, *On Leadership* (New York: The Free Press, 1990), 1.

4. Burns, *Leadership*, 18.

5. Oswald Sanders, *Spiritual Leadership* (Chicago: Moody Press, 1967; reprint ed., 1994), 31.

6. George Barna, *Leaders on Leadership* (Ventura, CA: Regal Books, 1997), 25.

7. Robert Clinton, *The Making of a Leader* (Colorado Springs: NavPress, 1988), 203.

8. Pat MacMillan, *The Performance Factor: Unlocking the Secrets of Teamwork* (Nashville: B&H Publishing Group, 2001), 94.

9. John Maxwell, *Developing the Leader within You* (Nashville: Thomas Nelson, 1993), 1.

10. Paul Hershey, *The Situational Leader* (Escondido, CA: Center for Leadership Studies, 1984; reprint ed., 1992), 16.

11. Robert K. Greenleaf, *Servant Leadership* (New York: Paulist Press, 1977), 45.

12. Ronald A. Heifetz, *Leadership without Easy Answers* (Cambridge, MA: Belknap Press, 1994), 18.

13. Peter F. Drucker, foreword in *The Leader of the Future*, ed. by Francis Hasselbein, Marshall Goldsmith, and Richard Beckhard (San Francisco: Jossey-Bass, 1996), vii.

14. Richard Reeves, *President Nixon: Alone in the White House* (New York: Simon and Schuster, 2001; Touchstone ed., 2002), 326.

15. Ibid., 35.

16. Metaxas, *Amazing Grace*, xix.

17. Ibid., xvii.

18. James Monti, *The King's Good Servant but God's First* (San Francisco: Ignatius Press, 1997).

19. Henry Blackaby and Richard Blackaby, *Hearing God's Voice* (Nashville: B&H Publishing Group, 2002).

CHAPTER 3

1. For a treatment of this, see Richard Blackaby, *Unlimiting God: Increasing Your Capacity to Experience the Divine* (Colorado Springs: Multnomah Publishers, 2008).

2. Max De Pree, *Leading without Power: Finding Hope in Serving Community* (San Francisco: Jossey-Bass, 1997), 32.

3. George Barna, *Today's Pastors* (Ventura, CA: Regal Books, 1983), 122, 125.

4. Alice Schroeder, *The Snowball: Warren Buffet and the Business of Life* (New York: Bantam Books, 2008), 59.

5. Man, *Genghis Khan*, 74.

6. Laurie Nadel, *The Great Streams of History: A Biography of Richard M. Nixon* (New York: Macmillan, 1991), 18.

7. Stephen Ambrose, *Eisenhower: Soldier and President* (New York: Simon and Schuster, 1990; Touchstone ed., 1991), 81.

8. Elizabeth Longford, *Victoria* (London: Wiedenfeld and Nicolson, 1964; Abacus ed., 2000), 30.

9. Ibid., 72.

10. Metaxas, *Amazing Grace*, 3.

11. David McCullough, *Truman* (New York: Simon and Schuster, 1992; Touchstone ed., 1993), 417.

12. Alexander Barbero, *Charlemagne: Father of a Continent*, trans. Allan Cameron (Berkeley: University of California Press, 2004), 118.

13. Joseph J. Ellis, *Founding Brothers: The Revolutionary Generation* (New York: Random House, 2000; Vintage Books ed., 2002), 124.

14. William Manchester, *Winston Spencer Churchill: The Last Lion, Visions of Glory 1874–1932* (New York: Dell Publishing, 1983), 17.

15. Schroeder, *The Snowball*, 126.

16. Chernow, *Titan*, 34.

17. Howard Gardner, *Leading Minds: An Anatomy of Leadership* (New York: Basic Books, 1995), 186.

18. Peter Senge, *The Fifth Discipline: The Art and Practice of the Learning Organization* (New York: Currency Doubleday, 1994), 359.

19. Peter Drucker, *The Effective Executive* (New York: HarperBusiness, 1996), 525.

20. Malcolm Gladwell, *Outliers: The Story of Success* (New York: Little, Brown and Company, 2008), 15–34.

21. James Wallace and Jim Erickson, *Hard Drive: Bill Gates and the Making of the Making of the Microsoft Empire* (New York: HarperCollins, 1992; HarperBusiness ed., 1993), 21.

22. Byron Farwell, *Stonewall: A Biography of General Thomas J. Jackson* (New York: W. W. Norton, 1992; Norton ed., 1993), 5–6.

23. Manchester, *Winston Spencer Churchill: The Last Lion, Visions of Glory 1874–1932*, 117.

24. Alison Weir, *Elizabeth the Queen* (London: Jonathan Cape, 1998; Pimlico ed., 1999), 13.

25. Robert V. Remini, *John Quincy Adams* in The American Presidents (New York: Times Books, 2002), 9.

26. Ibid., 62.

27. Winston S. Churchill, *My Early Life* (Glasgow: Fontana Books, 1930; reprint ed., 1963), 13.

28. Ibid., 27.

29. Ibid., 70.

30. Leonard Cottrell, *Hannibal: Enemy of Rome* (London: Evans Brothers, 1960; Da Capo Press ed., 1992), 10–11.

31. Winston S. Churchill, *Marlborough: His Life and Times, Book One* (London: George G. Harrap, 1933; University of Chicago Press ed., 2002), 33.

32. Homer G. Ritchie, *The Life and Legend of J. Frank Norris: The Fighting Parson* (Fort Worth: Homer G. Ritchie, 1991), 22–23.

33. Gary L. McIntosh and Samuel D. Rima, *Overcoming the Dark Side of Leadership* (Grand Rapids: Baker Books, 1997), 22.

34. Quoted in Malcom R. Davies, "Unlocking the Value of Exceptional Personalities," 146.

35. Johnson, *Meeting the Ethical Challenges of Leadership*, 4.

36. William A. Gentry and Craig T. Chappelow, "Managerial Derailment: Weakness That Can Be Fixed" in *The Perils of Accentuating the Positive*, Robert B. Kaiser, ed. (Tulsa: Hogan Press, 2009), 107.

37. Gretchen M. Spreitzer and Robert E. Quinn, *A Company of Leaders: Five Disciplines for Unleashing the Power in Your Workforce* (San Francisco: Jossey-Bass, 2001), 121.

38. De Pree, *Leading without Power*, 67.

39. Willard Sterne Randall, *George Washington: A Life* (New York: Henry Holt and Co., 1997), 143.

40. Goodwin, *Team of Rivals*, 173.

41. Smith, *Grant*, 107.

42. Lee Kennett, *Sherman: A Soldier's Life* (New York: HarperCollins, 2001; Perennial ed., 2002), 38.

43. Ibid., 140–52.

44. Holmes, 32.

45. Ambrose, *Eisenhower*, 94.

46. David McCullough, *Truman* (New York: Simon & Schuster, 1992; Touchstone ed., 1993), 99.

47. Neal Gabler, *Walt Disney: The Triumph of the American Imagination* (New York: Alfred A. Knopf, 2006), 405.

48. Billy Graham, *Just As I Am* (New York: HarperCollins, 1997; Harper Paperbacks ed., 1998), 48.

49. Meier, *Caesar*, 423.

50. H. W. Brands, *TR: The Last Romantic* (New York: Basic Books, 1997), 162–63.

51. Conrad Black, *Franklin Delano Roosevelt: Champion of Freedom* (New York: Public Affairs, 2003), 368, 1,130.

52. Richard Reeves, *President Kennedy: Profile of Power* (New York: Simon and Schuster, 1993; Touchstone ed., 1994), 24.

53. Gardner, *Leading Minds*, 37.

54. Calvin Kytle, *Ghandi: Soldier of Nonviolence* (Washington, DC: Seven Locks Press, 1969), 43.

55. Hibbert, *Disraeli*, 109.

56. R. B. Bernstein, *Thomas Jefferson* (New York: Oxford University Press, 2003), 16.

57. John Pollock, *Moody* (Grand Rapids: Baker Books, 1963), 31.

58. Goodwin, *Team of Rivals*, 7.

59. Chernow, *Titan*, 42.

60. Graham, *Just As I Am*, 62.

61. Peter Koestenbaum, *Leadership: The Inner Side of Greatness* (San Francisco: Jossey-Bass, 2002), 2.

62. Michael and Deborah Bradshaw Jinkins, *The Character of Leadership: Politcal Realism and Public Virtue in Nonprofit Organizations* (San Francisco: Jossey-Bass, 1998), 122.

63. Churchill, *Marlborough, Book One*, 430.

64. Smith, *Grant*, 15.

65. Donald T. Phillips, *Lincoln on Leadership: Executive Strategies for Tough Times* (New York: Warner Books, 1992), 109.

66. Senge, *The Fifth Discipline*, 154.

67. Sanders, *Spiritual Leadership*, 33.

68. Marcus Buckingham and Donald O. Clifton, *Now Discover Your Strengths* (New York: The Free Press, 2001).

69. Ibid., 5.

70. Ibid.

71. Ibid., 6.

72. Gabler, *Walt Disney*, 25, 44.

73. Robert B. Kaiser, "The Rest of What You Need to Know about Strengths-Based Development" in *The Perils of Accentuating the Positive*, Robert B. Kaiser, ed. (Tulsa: Hogan Press, 2009), 4.

74. Quoted in Robert B. Kaiser and Robert E. Kaplan, "When Strengths Run Amok" in *The Perils of Accentuating the Positive* (Tulsa: Hogan Press, 2009), 59.

75. Ibid., 68.

76. Seth Godin, *Tribes: We Need You to Lead Us* (New York: Portfolio, 2008), 55.

77. Churchill, *Marlborough, Book One*, 80.

78. For a more extensive study, see Henry Blackaby, *Called to Be God's Friend: How God Shapes Those He Loves* (Nashville: Thomas Nelson, 1999).

79. Jim Collins, *How the Mighty Fall: And Why Some Companies Never Give In* (New York: HarperCollins, 2009), 94.

Chapter 4

1. James Wallace and Jim Erickson, *Hard Drive: Bill Gates and the Making of the Microsoft Empire* (New York: HarperCollins 1992; Harper business ed., 1993), 153.

2. See http://www.answers.com/topic/george-mallory.

3. Max De Pree, *Leadership Jazz* (New York: Dell Publishing, 1992), 47.

4. Peter Drucker, *The Effective Executive* in *The Executive in Action* (New York: HarperBusiness, 1996), 628.

5. Thomas J. Peters and Robert H. Waterman Jr., *In Search of Excellence: Lessons from America's Best Run Companies* (New York: HarperCollins, 1982; HaprerBusiness ed., 2004).

6. James C. Collins and Jerry I. Porras, *Built to Last: Successful Habits of Visionary Companies* (New York: HaperCollins, 1994; Paperback ed., 1997).

7. Jim Collins, *Good to Great: Why Some Companies Make the Leap . . . and Others Don't* (New York: HarperCollins, 2001).

8. Rosenzweig, *The Halo Effect*, 156, 158.

9. Donald T. Phillips, *Martin Luther King Jr. on Leadership: Inspiration and Wisdom for Challenging Times* (New York: Warner Books, 1999), 185.

10. Felix Markham, *Napoleon* (New York: New American Library, 1963), 264.

11. Michael D'Antonio, *Hershey: Milton S. Hershey's Extraordinary Life of Wealth, Empire, and Utopian Dreams* (New York: Simon and Schuster, 2006; paperback ed., 2007), 89–90.

12. W. Chan Kim and Renee Mauborgne, *Blue Ocean Strategy: How to Create Uncontested Market Space and Make the Competition Irrelevant* (Boston: Harvard Business School Press, 2005), x.

13. Warren Bennis, *On Becoming a Leader* (Reading, MA: Addison-Wesley, 1989), 22.

14. Warren Bennis, *Why Leaders Can't Lead* (San Francisco: Jossey-Bass, 1989), 178.

15. Seth Godin, *Tribes: We Need You to Lead Us* (New York: Penguin Books, 2008), 108.

16. Bennis, *On Becoming a Leader*, 178.

17. George Barna, *Turning Vision into Action* (Ventura, CA.: Venture Books, 1996), 75.

18. Burt Nanus, *Visionary Leadership* (San Francisco: Jossey-Bass, 1992), 34.

19. James M. Kouzes and Barry Z. Posner, *The Leadership Challenge* (San Francisco: Jossey Bass, 1995), 109.

20. James C. Collins and Jerry I. Porass, *Built to Last*, 91–114.

21. Keith R. McFarland, *The Breakthrough Company: How Everyday Companies Become Extraordinary Performers* (New York: Crown Publishing, 2008), 31.

22. Rick Warren, *The Purpose Driven Church* (Grand Rapids: Zondervan, 1995), 95–152.

23. Mike Huckabee, *Character Is the Issue* (Nashville: B&H Publishing Group, 1997), 105–6.

24. See John Beckett, *Loving Monday: Succeeding in Business without Selling Your Soul* (Downers Grove: InterVarsity, 1998).

25. Nanus, *Visionary Leadership*, 3.

26. James Champy, *Reengineering Management: The Mandate for New Leadership* (New York: HarperBusiness, 1995), 55.

27. George Bernard Shaw, *Man and Superman* (Baltimore: Penguin Books, 1903), xxxii.

28. Collins, *Good to Great*, 42.

29. Peter Senge, *The Fifth Discipline*, 218.

30. Black, *Roosevelt*, 385.

31. Howard Gardner, *Leading Minds*, ix.

32. De Pree, *Leading Without Power*, 24.

33. De Pree, *Leadership Jazz*, 100.

34. Robert Quinn, *Deep Change: Discovering the Leader Within* (San Francisco: Jossey-Bass, 1996), 125.

35. William G. Bliss, *Leadership Lessons from the Book: Applying Biblical Lessons for Today's Leader* (Anderson, SC: NIN Publishing, 2009), 10.

CHAPTER 5

1. Peter F. Drucker, foreword to *The Leader of the Future*, ed. Francis Hasselbein, Marshall Goldsmith, and Richard Beckhard (San Francisco: Jossey-Bass, 1996), xii.

2. Johnson, *Meeting the Ethical Challenges of Leadership*, 95.

3. Peter Senge, *The Fifth Discipline: The Art and Practice of the Learning Organization* (New York: Currency Doubleday, 1990; Paperback ed., 1994), 4.

4. Max De Pree, *Leadership Jazz* (New York: Dell Publishing 1992), 23.

5. Ibid., 24.

6. Ibid., 91.

7. Max De Pree, *Leadership Is an Art* (New York: Dell Publishing, 1989), 60.

8. Ibid., 62.

9. Ibid., 11.

10. Heifetz, *Leadership without Easy Answers*, 252.

11. Liz, Wiseman, Multipliers: *How the Best Leaders Make Everyone Smarter* (New York: HarperBusiness, 2010).

12. Markham, *Napoleon*, 233.

13. Ibid., 143.

14. Drucker, *The Effective Executive*, 637.

15. Steven Watts, *The Peoples' Tycoon: Henry Ford and the American Century* (New York: Random House, 2005; Vintage Books ed., 2006), 361.

16. McCullough, *Truman*, 387.

17. Ibid., 564.

18. Schroeder, *The Snowball*, 21.

19. Collins, *Good to Great*, 34–35.

20. Ibid., 29.

21. Beckett, *Loving Monday*, 22–23.

CHAPTER 6

1. Churchill, *Marlborough, Book One*, 571.

2. Sanders, *Spiritual Leadership*, 11.

3. Jung Chang and Jon Halliday, *Mao: The Unknown Story* (New York: Alfred A. Knopf, 2005), 49–50.

4. Max De Pree, *Leadership Is an Art* (New York: Dell Publishing, 1989), 28.

5. Watchman Nee, *Spiritual Authority* (New York: Christian Fellowship Publishers, 1972), 12.

6. Ibid., 97.

7. Ibid., 71.

8. Godin, *Tribes*, 127.

9. Collins and Porass, *Built to Last*, 7.

10. Collins, *Good to Great*, 27.

11. For a more extensive study of Joshua's leadership, see Henry Blackaby and Richard Blackaby, *Called to Be God's Leader*.

12. Charles G. Finney, *The Autobiography of Charles Finney*, ed. Helen Wessel (Minneapolis: Bethany House, 1977), 124–25.

13. Antonia Fraser, *Cromwell* (New York: Grove Press, 1973), 119.

14. Billy Graham, *Just as I Am*, 692–95.

15. Finney, *Autobiography*, 21–22.

16. Pollock, *Moody*, 89.

17. Graham, *Just As I Am*, 163–64.

18. For inspiring reading on this subject, see V. Raymond Edman, *They Found the Secret* (Grand Rapids: Zondervan, 1960; Reprint ed., 1984); Wesley L. Duewel, *Ablaze for God* (Grand Rapids: Francis Asbury, 1989); Andrew Murray, *Absolute Surrender* (Chicago: Moody, n.d).

19. De Pree, *Leading without Power*, 72.

20. De Pree, Leadership Jazz, 10.

21. H W. Crocker, *Robert E. Lee on Leadership: Executive Lessons in Character, Courage, and Vision* (Rocklin, CA: Forum Publishing, 1999), 34.

22. Monti, *The King's Good Servant but God's First*, 312.

23. Kouzes and Posner, *The Leadership Challenge*, 21.

24. James M. Kouzes and Barry Z. Posner, *Encouraging the Heart: A Leader's Guide to Rewarding and Recognizing Others* (San Francisco: Jossey-Bass, 1999), 131.

25. James M. Kouzes and Barry Z. Posner, *Credibility: How Leaders Gain and Lose It, Why People Demand It* (San Francisco: Jossey-Bass, 1993), 185.

26. Ron Chernow, *The House of Morgan* (New York: Grove Press, 1990), 52.

27. Bennis and Nanus, *Leaders: Strategies for Taking Charge*, 24.

28. Fraser, *Cromwell*, 87.

29. Douglas Southall Freeman, *Lee* (New York: Charles Scribner's Sons, 1934; Touchstone ed., 1997), 510.

30. Peter Koestenbaum, *Leadership: The Inner Side of Greatness* (San Francisco: Jossey-Bass, 2002), 6.

31. Graham, *Just As I Am*, 150.

32. Churchill, *Marlborough, Book One*, 15.

33. Kouzes and Posner, *Credibility*, 17.

34. Kouzes and Posner, *Encouraging the Heart*, 145.

35. L. R. Scarborough, *With Christ after the Lost* (Nashville: Broadman, 1952), 79.

36. David McCullough, *1776* (New York: Simon and Schuster, 2005), 293.

37. Ambrose, *Eisenhower*, 54.

38. Only Washington, Grant, and Eisenhower have held both the top American military and civil posts.

39. Bennis, *Why Leaders Can't Lead*, 40.

40. Quoted in Allan Leighton, *On Leadership: Practical Wisdom from the People Who Know* (London: Random House Business Books, 2007), 157.

41. Crocker, *Robert E. Lee on Leadership*, 147.

42. Pocock, *Horatio Nelson*, 312.

43. Graham, *Just As I Am*, 852.

44. Garry Will, *James Madison* in The American Presidents (New York: Times Books, 2002), Arthur Schlesinger, ed., 17.

45. Weir, *Elizabeth the Queen*, 14.

46. Reeves, *President Kennedy*, 261.

47. Walter Isaacson, *Einstein: His Life and Universe* (New York: Simon and Schuster, 2007), 299.

48. David Nasaw, *The Chief: The Life of William Randolph Hearst* (Boston: Houghton Mifflin, 2000; Mariner Book ed., 2001), 49; Wallace and Erikson, *Hard Drive*, 110.

49. See also Howard Gardner, *Five Minds for the Future* (Boston: Harvard Business School Press, 2007).

50. Isaacson, *Einstein*, 354.

51. Goleman, *Working with Emotional Intelligence*, 61.

52. Jinkins and Bradshaw Jinkins, *The Character of Leadership*, 165.

53. Ambrose, *Eisenhower*, 202.

54. Bennis, *Why Leaders Can't Lead*, 48.

55. Monti, *The King's Good Servant*, 275–76.

56. Collins, *Good to Great*, 21.

57. Collins, *How the Mighty Fall*, 27–44.

58. Goodwin, *Team of Rivals*, 319.

59. Ibid., 174.

60. Smith, *Grant*, 294.

61. Irwin, *Derailed*, 144.

62. Farwell, *Stonewall*, 179.

63. Hibbert, *Disraeli*, 343.

64. Pocock, *Horatio Nelson*, 233.

65. Black, *Roosevelt*, 270.

66. Lande, *I Was with Patton*, 185.

67. Randall, *George Washington*, 329.

68. Ibid., 96.

69. Godin, *Tribes*, 44.

CHAPTER 7

1. Pocock, *Horatio Nelson*, 317–18.

2. Burns, *Leadership*, 427.

3. Sanders, *Spiritual Leadership*, 31.

4. Godin, *Tribes*, 79–80.

5. Ronald Reagan, Ronald Reagan: An American Life (New York: Pocket Books, 1990), 693–94.

6. Basil Miller, *George Muller: The Man of Faith*, 3rd ed. (Grand Rapids: Zondervan: 1941), 145–46.

7. Pocock, *Horatio Nelson*, 297.

8. Holmes, *Wellington*, 86.

9. Ibid.

10. Ted Widmer, *Martin Van Buren* in The American Presidents, Arthur Schlesinger, ed. (New York: Times Books, 2005), 42.

11. Remini, *John Quincy Adams*, 77.

12. Robert Dallek, *Lyndon B. Johnson: Portrait of a President* (New York: Oxford University Press, 2005), 29.

13. Meier, *Caesar*, 249.

14. J. R. Hamilton, *Alexander the Great* (Pittsburgh: University of Pittsburgh Press, 1973), 120.

15. Norman H. Schwarzkopf and Peter Petre, *It Doesn't Take a Hero* (New York: Bantam Books, 1992), 169–72.

16. Schroeder, *The Snowball*, 485.

17. Sanders, *Spiritual Leadership*, 180.

18. Goodwin, *Team of Rivals*, 165.

19. Ibid., 586.

20. Terry Pearce, *Leading Out Loud: Inspiring Change through Authentic Communication* (San Francisco: Jossey-Bass, 2003), 35.

21. Gardner, *Leading Minds*, 34.

22. McCullough, *Truman*, 162.

23. Steven F. Hayward, *Churchill on Leadership: Executive Success in the Face of Adversity* (Rocklin, CA: Forum, 1997), 98.

24. Manchester, *Winston Spencer Churchill: The Last Lion, Visions of Glory 1874–1932*, 32.

25. Smith, *Grant*, 298.

26. Greenleaf, *Servant Leadership*, 17.

27. Ibid., 300.

28. Pearce, *Leading Out Loud*, 60–62; Kouzes and Posner, *The Leadership Challenge*, 98–101.

29. Gardner, *Leading Minds*, 41–65.

30. Pearce, *Leading Out Loud*, 63.

31. Warren Bennis, *On Becoming a Leader*, 122.

32. Henry and Richard Blackaby and Claude V. King, *Experiencing God: Knowing and Doing the Will of God* (Nashville: Lifeway Press, 2007), 199.

33. Pocock, *Horatio Nelson*, 319.

34. Bennis and Nanus, *Leaders: Strategies for Taking Charge*, 52.

35. Two examples of this are: C. Gene Wilkes, *Jesus on Leadership: Discovering the Secrets of Servant Leadership* (Wheaton, IL: Tyndale House Publishers, 1998); and Ken Blanchard and Phil Hodges, *Lead like Jesus: Lessons from the Greatest Leadership Role Model of All Time* (Nashville: Thomas Nelson, 2005).

36. Goleman, *Working with Emotional Intelligence*, 33.

37. Kouzes and Posner, *Encouraging the Heart*, 9.

38. Marcus Buckingham and Curt Coffman, *First, Break All the Rules: What the World's Greatest Managers Do Differently* (New York: Simon & Schuster, 1999), 202.

39. Lee Iacocca, *Iacocca: An Autobiography* (Toronto: Bantam Books, 1984), 230.

40. John Byrne, *Chainsaw: The Notorious Career of Al Dunlop in the Era of Profit-at-Any Price* (New York: HarperCollins, 1999), 153–54.

41. McCullough, *Truman*, 427–28.

42. Ibid., 927.

43. Ibid., 559.

44. Smith, *Grant*, 200.

45. Ibid.

46. Leighton, *On Leadership*, 272.

47. Daniel Goleman, *Primal Leadership: Realizing the Power of Emotional Intelligence* (Boston: Harvard Business School Press, 2002), 7–9.

48. Ed Cray, *General of the Army: George C. Marshall, Soldier and Statesman* (New York: Cooper Square Press, 1990; Reprint ed., 2000), 591.

49. Black, *Franklin Delano Roosevelt*, 649.

50. De Pree, *Leadership Is an Art*, 146.

51. Manchester, *Winston Spencer Churchill: The Last Lion, Visions of Glory 1874–1932*, 591.

52. Reagan, *Ronald Reagan: An American Life*, 329.

53. Ibid., 260.

54. Monti, *The King's Good Servant*, 449.

55. Schwarzkopf and Petre, *It Doesn't Take a Hero*, 152.

56. Cottrell, *Hannibal*, 138.

57. Ambrose, *Eisenhower*, 129.

58. Goodwin, *Team of Rivals*, 663.

59. Freeman, *Lee*, 364.

60. Pocock, *Horatio Nelson*, 64.

61. Sam Walton, *Sam Walton: Made in America* (New York: Doubleday, 1992; Bantam Books ed., 1993), 267.

62. Kennett, *Sherman*, 100.

63. Watts, *The Peoples' Tycoon*, 117.

64. Quoted in Cray, *General of the Army*, 459.

65. Churchill, *Marlborough, Book One*, 862.

66. Holmes, *The Iron Duke*, 251.

67. Remini, *Andrew Jackson*, 63.

68. Ibid., 67.

69. Peter Krass, *Carnegie* (Hoboken, NJ: John Wiley and Sons, 2002), 114.

70. Schroeder, *The Snowball*, 148.

71. Gabler, *Walt Disney*, 208.

72. Chernow, *Titan*, 174.

73. Ron Chernow, *The House of Morgan*, 55.

74. Chernow, *Titan*, 180–81.

75. McCullough, *1776*, 40.

76. Randall, *George Washington*, 194.

77. Malcolm Gladwell, *The Tipping Point: How Little Things Can Make a Big Difference* (London: Little, Brown, 2000; Abacus ed., 2006), 7, 12.

78. De Pree, *Leading without Power*, 22.

79. J. Edwin Orr, *The Event of the Century: The 1857–1858 Awakening* (Wheaton, IL: International Awakening Press, 1989).

80. Ibid., 28.

81. See our discussion on "corporate hindrances to revival," "counterfeits to revival," and why revivals come to an end in Henry and Richard Blackaby and Claude

King, *Fresh Encounter: God's Pattern for Spiritual Awakening* (Nashville: B&H Publishing Group, 2009).

CHAPTER 8

1. Ambrose, *Eisenhower*, 139.

2. Peter Drucker, *The Effective Executive* in *The Executive in Action* (New York: HarperBusiness, 1996), 679.

3. Henry Blackaby and Richard Blackaby, *Hearing God's Voice: When God Speaks: How to Recognize God's Voice and Respond In Obedience* (Nashville: LifeWay Press, 1995).

4. Warren Bennis, *Why Leaders Can't Lead*, 92.

5. Baker, *James Buchanan*, 79.

6. Gardner, *On Leadership*, 135.

7. Graham, *Just As I Am*, 281.

8. D'Antonio, *Hershey*, 73.

9. Two helpful books on this subject are by Patrick Lencioni, *Death by Meeting* (San Francisco: Jossey-Bass, 2004); and *The Five Dysfunctions of a Team* (San Francisco: Jossey-Bass, 2002).

10. Kouzes and Posner, The Leadership Challenge, 85.

11. Blackaby, Blackaby, and King, *Experiencing God*, 193–96.

12. Rosenzweig, *The Halo Effect*, 144.

13. Ibid., 145.

14. Chernow, *The House of Morgan*, 141.

15. Holmes, *Wellington*, 32.

16. Meier, *Caesar*, 3.

17. Ibid., 5.

18. Ambrose, *Eisenhower*, 278.

19. Jinkins and Jinkins, *The Character of Leadership*, 137.

CHAPTER 9

1. James Lardner, "World-class Workaholics," *U.S. News & World Report*, December 20, 1999.

2. Kouzes and Posner, *The Leadership Challenge*, 250.

3. Drucker, "The Effective Executive," 549.

4. Monti, *The King's Good Servant*, 64.

5. McCullough, *Truman*, 533.

6. Lucy Kavaler, *The Astors: A Family Chronicle of Pomp and Power* (New York: Dodd, Mead and Company, 1966; Reprint ed., Lincoln, NE: iUniverse.com, 2000), 31.

7. Drucker, *The Effective Executive*, 565.

8. Ibid., 627.

9. Stuart Wells, *Choosing the Future: The Power of Strategic Thinking* (Woburn, MA: Butterworth-Heinemann, 1998), 4.

10. Drucker, *The Effective Executive*, 624.

11. Weir, *Elizabeth the Queen*, 227.

12. Bennis, *Why Leaders Can't Lead*, 18.

13. Fraser, *Cromwell*, 96.

14. Goodwin, *Team of Rivals*, 541.

15. Iacocca, *Iacocca: An Autobiography*, 288–89.

16. McCullough, *Truman*, 564.

17. Richard A. Swenson, *Margin: Restoring Emotional, Physical, Financial, and Time Reserves to Overloaded Lives* (Colorado Springs: NavPress, 1992), 92.

18. John W. Dean, *Warren G. Harding* in The American Presidents, Arthur M. Schlesinger, ed. (New York: Times Books, 2004), 147–52.

19. Ambrose, *Eisenhower*, 118.

20. James M. Kouzes and Barry Z. Posner, *A Leader's Legacy* (San Francisco: Jossey-Bass, 2006), 101.

21. Goleman, *Primal Leadership*, 35.

22. Kouzes and Posner, *The Leadership Challenge*, 300, 309.

23. Godin, *Tribes*, 11.

24. Ibid., 31.

25. Ibid., 101.

26. Kouzes and Posner, *Encouraging the Heart*, 91–93.

27. Buckingham and Coffman, *First Break All the Rules*, 153.

28. Chernow, *Titan*, 173.

29. Schroeder, *The Snowball*, 730.

CHAPTER 10

1. John Kotter, *What Leaders Really Do*, 59.

2. Alison Weir, *Henry VIII: King and Court* (London: Jonathan Cape, 2001; Pimlico ed., 2002), 355.

3. Weir, *Elizabeth the Queen*, 224.

4. Robert E. Quinn, *Deep Change*, 156.

5. Jinkins and Jinkins, *The Character of Leadership*, 2.

6. Larry Bossidy and Ram Charan, *Execution: The Discipline of Getting Things Done* (New York: Crown Business, 2002), 22.

7. Sullivan and Harper, *Hope Is Not a Method*, 5.

8. Geffrey B. Kelly and F. Burton Nelson, *The Cost of Moral Leadership: The Spirituality of Dietrich Bonhoeffer* (Grand Rapids: William B. Eerdmans, 2003), 5–6.

9. Jinkins and Jinkins, *The Character of Leadership*, 62.

10. Ibid., 15.

11. John Kotter, *Leading Change* (Boston: Harvard Business School Press, 1996), 148.

12. McFarland, *The Breakthrough Company*, 97.

13. Quinn, *Deep Change*, 99.

14. See Michael E. Gerber, *The E Myth Revisited: Why Most Small Businesses Don't Work and What to Do About It*, 3rd ed. (New York: HarperCollins, 1995).

15. Kotter, *Leading Change*, 68.

16. Kotter, *What Leaders Really Do*, 82.

17. Goleman, *Primal Leadership*, 245.

18. Cottrell, *Hannibal: Enemy of Rome*, 133.

19. McCullough, *John Adams*, 21.

20. John P. Kotter, *A Sense of Urgency* (Boston: Harvard Business Press, 2008), viii.

21. Kotter, *What Leaders Really Do*, 78.

22. Stephen B. Sample, *The Contrarian's Guide to Leadership* (San Francisco: Jossey-Bass, 2002), 112.

23. Jinkins and Jinkins, *The Character of Leadership*, 33.

24. Kotter, *Leading Change*, 51–66.

25. Widmer, *Martin Van Buren*, 72.

26. Goodwin, *Team of Rivals*, 206.

27. Ibid.

28. Black, *Roosevelt*, 427.

29. Ibid.

30. Cottrell, *Hannibal*, 26.

31. Weir, *Elizabeth the Queen*, 18, 436.

32. Pearce, *Leading Out Loud*, 35.

33. Stephen Denning, *The Secret Language of Leadership: How Leaders Inspire Action Through Narrative* (San Francisco: John Wiley and Sons, 2007), 114, 162.

34. Ibid., 213.

35. Ibid., 86.

36. Kotter, *A Sense of Urgency*, 145–68.

37. Kotter, *Leading Change*, 123.

38. Niccolo Machiavelli, *The Prince* (New York: Penguin Books, 1961; Reprint ed. 1999), 19.

39. Kotter, *What Leaders Really Do*, 88.

40. Bossidy and Charan, *Execution*, 4.

CHAPTER 11

1. Goodwin, *Team of Rivals*, xvi.

2. Holmes, *Wellington*, 250.

3. Ibid., 254.

4. Freeman, *Lee*, 292.

5. Farwell, *Stonewall*, 521.

6. Freeman, *Lee*, 347.

7. Kevin Leman and William Pentak, *The Way of the Shepherd: 7 Ancient Secrets to Managing Productive People* (Grand Rapids: Zondervan, 2004), 26.

8. Collins, *Good to Great*, 13.

9. Edward E. Lawler III, "The Era of Human Capital Has Finally Arrived" in *The Future of Leadership*, Warren Bennis, Gretchen M. Spreitzer, and Thomas G. Cummings, eds. (San Francisco: Jossey-Bass, 2001), 19.

10. McFarland, *The Breakthrough Company*, 105.

11. Ibid., 104.

12. Ibid., 105.

13. Godin, *Tribes*, 98.

14. Collins, *Good to Great*, 31.

15. Ibid., 13.

16. Marie Peters, *The Elder Pitt* (London: Longman, 1998), 236.

17. Godin, *Tribes*, 41.

18. Kouzes and Posner, *A Leader's Legacy*, 90.

19. Chernow, *Titan*, 223.

20. Ibid., 213.

21. Kouzes and Posner, *A Leader's Legacy*, 68.

22. Churchill, *Marlborough*, vol. 2, 265.

23. Heifetz, *Leadership without Easy Answers*, 33.

24. David L. Dotlich and Peter C. Cairo, *Unnatural Leadership: Going against Intuition and Experience to Develop Ten New Leadership Instincts* (San Francisco: Jossey-Bass, 2002), 17.

25. Bossidy and Charan, *Execution*, 25.

26. MacMillan, *The Performance Factor*, 59.

27. Peters, *The Elder Pitt*, 172.

28. Ibid., 242.

29. Ibid.

30. Ibid.

31. Fraser, *Cromwell*, 423.

32. Ambrose, *Eisenhower*, 132.

33. Anthony Everitt, *Augustus: The Life of Rome's First Emperor* (New York: Random House, 2006), 64.

34. Godin, *Tribes*, 11.

35. De Pree, *Leading without Power*, 109.

36. Bossidy and Charan, *Execution*, 118.

37. Collins, *Good to Great*, 62.

38. Pocock, *Horatio Nelson*, 165.

39. Roland Huntford, *Shackleton* (New York: Carroll and Graf Publishers, 1985; reprint ed., 2000), 494.

40. MacMillan, *The Performance Factor*, 35.

41. Godin, *Tribes*, 32.

42. Edgar McInnis, *Canada: A Political and Social History*, 3rd ed. (Toronto: Holt, Rinehart and Winston of Canada, 1969), 632.

43. Peter C. Newman, *Renegade in Power: The Diefenbaker Years* (Toronto: McClelland and Stewart, 1963; Power Reporting ed., 1989), 13.

44. Kouzes and Posner, *A Leader's Legacy*, 28.

45. Thomas A. Stewart, "Trust Me on This: Organizational Support for Trust in a World Without Hierarchies" in *The Future of Leadership: Today's Top Leadership Thinkers Speak to Tomorrow's Leaders*, Warren Bennis, Gretchen M. Spreitzer, and Thomas G. Cummings, eds. (San Francisco: Jossey-Bass, 2001), 68.

46. Collins, *Good to Great*, 59.

47. Ibid.

CHAPTER 12

1. A. B. Bruce, *The Training of the Twelve* (London: A. C. Armstrong and Son, 1871; reprint ed., Grand Rapids: Kregel, 1988), 469–70.

2. Collins, *How the Mighty Fall: And Why Some Companies Never Give In.* Collins presents a five stage model: (1) hubris born of success; (2) undisciplined pursuit of more; (3) denial of risk and peril; (4) grasping for salvation; (5) capitulation to irrelevance or death.

3. Kouzes and Posner, *Encouraging the Heart*, 13.

4. McCullough, *Truman*, 564.

5. Ibid., 755.

6. Irwin, *Derailed*.

7. Ibid., 92.

8. H. W. Brands, *TR: The Last Romantic* (New York: Basic Books, 1997), 146.

9. Pollock, *Moody*, 163.

10. De Pree, *Leadership Jazz*, 48.

11. Dotlich and Cairo, *Unnatural Leadership*, 71.

12. Deborah Rhode, "Where Is the Leadership in Moral Leadership?" in *Moral Leadership: The Theory and Practice of Power, Judgment, and Policy*, Deborah Rhode, ed. (San Francisco: Jossey-Bass, 2006), 24–25.

13. Meier, *Caesar*, 312.

14. Graham, *Just As I Am*, 148–51.

15. Reeves, *President Nixon*, 13.

16. Iacocca, *Iacocca: An Autobiography*, 146.

17. Ibid., 285.

18. Jim Bakker, *I Was Wrong* (Nashville: Thomas Nelson, 1996).

19. Watts, *The People's Tycoon*, 269.

20. Kotter, *Leading Change*, 181.

21. De Pree, *Leadership Jazz*, 84.

22. Jinkins and Jinkins, *The Character of Leadership*, 165.

23. Pollock, *Moody*, 169.

24. Ibid., 187.

25. Graham, *Just As I Am*, 852.

26. Chernow, *Titan*, 181–82.

27. Ian H. Murray, *Jonathan Edwards: A New Biography* (Edinburgh: Banner of Truth Trust, 1987; reprint ed., 1992), 313–70.

28. George M. Marsden, *Jonathan Edwards: A Life* (New Haven: Yale University Press, 2003), 368–69.

29. Sanders, *Spiritual Leadership*, 180.

30. Henry Blackaby and Richard Blackaby, *Experiencing God Day-by-Day* (Nashville: B&H Publishing Group, 1997); *Discovering God's Daily Agenda* (Nashville: Thomas Nelson, 2007).

31. Brands, *TR: The Last Romantic*, 521.

32. Graham, *Just As I Am*, 183.

33. Ibid., 852.

34. McCullough, *John Adams*, 555.

35. Chernow, *Titan*, 607.

36. Schroeder, *The Snowball*, 439, 483.

37. Edward J. Renehan, *Commodore: The Life of Cornelius Vanderbilt* (New York: Basic Books, 2007), 301–16.

38. Remini, *The Life of Andrew Jackson*, 359.

39. David Cannadine, *Mellon: An American Life* (New York: Random House, 2006; Vintage Books ed., 2008), 241.

40. Bossidy and Charan, *Execution*, 19.

41. Ibid., 22.

42. Ibid.

43. Ibid., 67.

44. For a good presentation on encouraging vigorous debate on leadership teams, see Lencioni, *Death by Meeting*.

45. Collins, *Good to Great*, 41–45.

46. Gardner, *Leading Minds*, 262.

47. Ibid., 289.

48. Sanders, *Spiritual Leadership*, 232.

49. Ambrose, *Eisenhower*, 394.

50. Ellis, *Founding Brothers*, 130.

51. Ambrose, *Eisenhower*, 246.

52. Henry Blackaby and Richard Blackaby, *God in the Marketplace: 45 Questions Fortune 500 CEOs Ask about Faith, Life, and Business* (Nashville: B&H Publishing Group, 2008).

CHAPTER 13

1. Bruce, *The Training of the Twelve*, 188.

2. Manchester, *Winston Spencer Churchill: The Last Lion, Visions of Glory 1874–1932*, 177.

3. Ibid., 228.

4. Pollock, *Moody*, 271.

5. Ibid., 272.

6. Robin Seager, *Tiberius*, 2nd ed. (London: Eyre Metheun Ltd., 1972; 2nd ed., Oxford: Blackwell Publishing, 2005), 115.

7. Ibid., 207.

8. Ambrose, *Eisenhower*, 12.

9. Ibid., 315.

10. Pollock, *Moody*, 238.

11. W. R. Moody, *The Life of Dwight L. Moody* (London: Morgan and Scott, n.d).

12. Schroeder, *The Snowball*, 761.

13. Kouzes and Posner, *A Leader's Legacy*, 55.

14. Ibid., 58, 60.

15. Kouzes and Posner, *Encouraging the Heart*, 84.

16. Kouzes and Posner, *A Leader's Legacy*, 10.

17. Reeves, *President Nixon*, 385.

18. For a discussion of how Paul chose to always work with others, see Henry Blackaby and Thomas Blackaby, *Anointed to Be God's Servants: Lessons from the Life of Paul and His Companions* (Nashville: Thomas Nelson, 2005).

19. Pollock, *Moody*, 248.

20. Cannadine, *Mellon*, 562.

21. Peter Krass, *Carnegie* (Hoboken, NJ: John Wiley and Sons, 2002), 243.

22. Chernow, *Titan*, 511.

23. His poems, "Pussy-Willows," "The Call," and "An Echo of the First Christmas" were published in *From Overseas: An Anthology of Contemporary Dominions and United States Poetry* (London: Fowler Wright, 1927).

24. Everitt, *Augustus*, xxxvii.

25. Manchester, *Winston Spencer Churchill: The Last Lion, Visions of Glory 1874–1932*, 44.

26. McCullough, *John Adams*, 110.

27. Metaxas, *Amazing Grace*, xv.

28. Markham, *Napoleon*, 137.

29. Pollock, *Moody*, 118.

30. Quoted in Gardner, *Leading Minds*, 280.

31. Greenleaf, *Servant Leadership*, 21.

32. Kouzes and Posner, *Credibility*, 261.

33. Margaret Thatcher, *Margaret Thatcher: The Downing Street Years* (New York: HarperCollins, 1993), 860.

34. Reagan, *Ronald Reagan: An American Life*, 722.

35. Chernow, *Titan*, 554.

36. Chernow, *The House of Morgan*, 374, 385.

FINAL THOUGHTS

1. Meier, *Caesar*, 141.

2. Black, *Franklin Delano Roosevelt*, 402.

3. Goodwin, *Team of Rivals*, 87.

Bibliography

Ambrose, Stephen. *Eisenhower: Soldier and President*. New York: Simon and Schuster, 1990; Touchstone ed., 1991.

Baker, Jean H. *James Buchanan* in The American Presidents. New York: Time Book, 2004.

Bakker, Jim. *I Was Wrong*. Nashville: Thomas Nelson, 1996.

Barbero, Alexander. *Charlemagne: Father of a Continent*. Trans. by Allan Cameron. Berkeley: University of California Press, 2004.

Barna, George. *Leaders on Leadership*. Ventura, CA: Regal Books, 1997.

———. *Today's Pastors*. Ventura, CA: Regal Books, 1983.

———. *Turning Vision into Action*. Ventura, CA: Venture Books, 1996.

Beckett, John. *Loving Monday: Succeeding in Business without Selling Your Soul*. Downers Grove: InterVarsity, 1998.

Bennis, Warren. *On Becoming a Leader*. Reading, MA: Addison-Wesley, 1989.

———. *Why Leaders Can't Lead*. San Francisco: Jossey-Bass, 1989.

Bennis, Warren, and Burt Nanus. *Leaders: Strategies for Taking Charge*. New York: HarperCollins, 1997.

Bernstein, R. B. *Thomas Jefferson*. New York: Oxford University Press, 2003.

Black, Conrad. *Franklin Delano Roosevelt: Champion of Freedom*. New York: Public Affairs, 2003.

Blackaby, Henry, and Richard Blackaby. *Called to Be God's Friend: How God Shapes Those He Loves*. Nashville: Thomas Nelson, 1999.

Blackaby, Henry, and Richard Blackaby. *Called to Be God's Leader: Lessons from the Life of Joshua*. Nashville: Thomas Nelson, 2004.

Blackaby, Henry, and Richard Blackaby. *Discovering God's Daily Agenda*. Nashville: Thomas Nelson, 2007.

Blackaby, Henry, and Richard Blackaby. *Experiencing God Day-by-Day*. Nashville: Broadman and Holman, 1997.

Blackaby, Henry, Richard Blackaby, and Claude V. King. *Experiencing God: Knowing and Doing the Will of God*. Nashville: Lifeway Press, 2007.

Blackaby, Henry, Richard Blackaby, and Claude V. King. *Fresh Encounter: God's Pattern for Spiritual Awakening*. Nashville: B&H Publishing Group, 2009.

Blackaby, Henry, and Richard Blackaby. *God in the Marketplace: 45 Questions Fortune 500 CEOs Ask about Faith, Life, and Business*. Nashville: B&H Publishing Group, 2008.

Blackaby, Henry, and Richard Blackaby. *Hearing God's Voice*. Nashville: B&H Publishing Group, 2002.

Blackaby, Henry, and Thomas Blackaby. *Anointed to Be God's Servants: Lessons from the Life of Paul and His Companions*. Nashville: Thomas Nelson, 2005.

Blackaby, Richard. *Unlimiting God: Increasing Your Capacity to Experience the Divine*. Colorado Springs: Multnomah Publishers, 2008.

Blackaby, Henry, and Richard Blackaby. *When God Speaks: How to Recognize God's Voice and Respond in Obedience*. Nashville: LifeWay Press, 1995.

Blanchard, Ken, and Phil Hodges. *Lead like Jesus: Lessons from the Greatest Leadership Role Model of All Time*. Nashville: Thomas Nelson, 2005.

Bliss, William G. *Leadership Lessons from the Book: Applying Biblical Lessons for Today's Leader*. Anderson, SC: NIN Publishing, 2009.

Bossidy, Larry, and Ram Charan. *Execution: The Discipline of Getting Things Done.* New York: Crown Business, 2002.

Brands, H. W. *TR: The Last Romantic.* New York: Basic Books, 1997.

———. *Woodrow Wilson* in The American Presidents. Arthur M. Schlesinger ed. New York: Times Books, 2003.

Bruce, A. B. *The Training of the Twelve.* London: A. C. Armstrong and Son, 1871; reprint ed. Grand Rapids: Kregel Publications, 1988.

Buckingham, Marcus, and Curt Coffman. *First, Break All the Rules: What the World's Greatest Managers Do Differently.* New York: Simon & Schuster, 1999.

Buckingham, Marcus, and Donald O. Clifton. *Now Discover Your Strengths.* New York: The Free Press, 2001.

Burns, James MacGregor. *Leadership.* New York: Harper Torchbooks, 1978.

Byrne, John. *Chainsaw: The Notorious Career of Al Dunlop in the Era of Profit-at-Any Price.* New York: HarperCollins, 1999.

Cannadine, David. *Mellon: An American Life.* New York: Random House, 2006; Vintage Books ed., 2008.

Canton, James. *The Extreme Future: The Top Trends That Will Reshape the World for the Next 5, 10, and 20 Years.* New York: Dutton Publishing, 2006.

Carlyle, Thomas. *On Heroes, Hero-Worship and the Heroic in History.* London: Collins' Clear-Type Press, 1842.

Champy, James. *Reengineering Management: The Mandate for New Leadership.* New York: HarperBusiness, 1995.

Chang, Jung, and Jon Halliday. *Mao: The Unknown Story.* New York: Alfred A. Knopf, 2005.

Chernow, Ron. *The House of Morgan.* New York: Grove Press, 1990.

———. *Titan: The Life of John D. Rockefeller.* New York: Vintage Books, 1998; 2nd edition 2004.

Churchill, Winston S. *My Early Life.* Glasgow: Fontana Books, 1930; reprint ed., 1963.

————. *Marlborough: His Life and Times, Book One*. London: George G. Harrap, 1933, Chicago: University of Chicago Press, 2002.

————. *Marlborough: His Life and Times, Book Two*. London: George G. Harrap, 1936. Chicago: University of Chicago Press, 2002.

Clinton, Robert. *The Making of a Leader*. Colorado Springs: NavPress, 1988.

Collins, Jim. *Good to Great: Why Some Companies Make the Leap . . . and Others Don't*. New York: HarperCollins, 2001.

————. *How the Mighty Fall: And Why Some Companies Never Give In*. New York: HarperCollins, 2009.

Collins, James C., and Jerry I. Porras. *Built to Last: Successful Habits of Visionary Companies*. New York: HarperCollins, 1994; paperback ed., 1997.

Cottrell, Leonard. *Hannibal: Enemy of Rome*. London: Evans Brothers, 1960; Da Capo Press ed., 1992.

Cray, Ed. *General of the Army: George C. Marshall, Soldier and Statesman*. New York: Cooper Square Press, 1990; reprint ed., 2000.

Crocker, H. W. *Robert E. Lee on Leadership: Executive Lessons in Character, Courage, and Vision*. Rocklin, CA: Forum Publishing, 1999.

D'Antonio, Michael. *Hershey: Milton S. Hershey's Extraordinary Life of Wealth, Empire, and Utopian Dreams*. New York: Simon and Schuster, 2006; paperback ed., 2007.

Davies, Malcom R. "Unlocking the Value of Exceptional Personalities" in *The Perils of Accentuating the Positive*. Robert B. Kaiser, ed. Tulsa: Hogan Press, 2009.

Dean, John W. *Warren G. Harding* in The American Presidents. Arthur M. Schlesinger, ed. New York: Time Books, 2004.

Denning, Stephen. *The Secret Language of Leadership: How Leaders Inspire Action through Narrative*. San Francisco: John Wiley and Sons, 2007.

De Pree, Max. *Leadership Is an Art*. New York: Dell Publishing, 1989.

————. *Leadership Jazz*. New York: Dell Publishing, 1992.

————. *Leading without Power: Finding Hope in Serving Community*. San Francisco: Jossey-Bass, 1997.

Dotlich, David L., and Peter C. Cairo. *Unnatural Leadership: Going against Intuition and Experience to Develop Ten New Leadership Instincts.* San Francisco: Jossey-Bass, 2002.

Drucker, Peter. *The Effective Executive.* New York: HarperBusiness, 1996.

Drucker, Peter F. Foreword to *The Leader of the Future.* Francis Hasselbein, Marshall Goldsmith, and Richard Beckhard, eds. San Francisco: Jossey-Bass, 1996.

Duewel, Wesley L. *Ablaze for God.* Grand Rapids: Francis Asbury, 1989.

Edman, V. Raymond. *They Found the Secret.* Grand Rapids: Zondervan, 1960; reprint ed., 1984.

Ellis, Joseph J. *Founding Brothers: The Revolutionary Generation.* New York: Random House, 2000; Vintage Books ed., 2002.

Everitt, Anthony. *Augustus: The Life of Rome's First Emperor.* New York: Random House, 2006.

Farwell, Byron. *Stonewall: A Biography of General Thomas J. Jackson.* New York: W. W. Norton, 1992; Norton ed., 1993.

Finney, Charles G. *The Autobiography of Charles Finney,* ed. Helen Wessel. Minneapolis: Bethany House, 1977.

Fraser, Antonia. *Cromwell.* New York: Grove Press, 1973.

Freeman, Douglas Southall. *Lee.* New York: Charles Scribner's Sons, 1934; Touchstone ed., 1997.

Friedman, Thomas L. *The World Is Flat: A Brief History of the Twenty-first Century.* New York: Farrar, Straus, and Giroux, 2005; rev. ed., 2006.

Gabler, Neal. *Walt Disney: The Triumph of the American Imagination.* New York: Alfred A. Knopf, 2006.

Gardner, Howard. *Five Minds for the Future.* Boston: Harvard Business School Press, 2007.

———. *Leading Minds: An Anatomy of Leadership.* New York: Basic Books, 1995.

Gardner, John. *On Leadership.* New York: The Free Press, 1990.

Gentry, William A., and Craig T. Chappelow. "Managerial Derailment: Weakness that Can Be Fixed" in *The Perils of Accentuating the Positive*. Robert B. Kaiser ed. Tulsa: Hogan Press, 2009.

Gerber, Michael E. *The E Myth Revisited: Why Most Small Businesses Don't Work and What to Do About It*, 3rd ed. New York: HarperCollins, 1995.

Gladwell, Malcolm. *Outliers: The Story of Success*. New York: Brown, Little and Company, 2008.

————. *The Tipping Point: How Little Things Can Make a Big Difference*. London: Little, Brown, 2000; Abacus ed., 2006.

Godin, Seth. *Tribes: We Need You to Lead Us*. New York: Portfolio, 2008.

Goleman, Daniel. *Primal Leadership: Realizing the Power of Emotional Intelligence*. Boston: Harvard Business School Press, 2002.

————. *Working with Emotional Intelligence*. New York: Bantam Books, 1998.

Goodwin, Doris Kearns. *Team of Rivals: The Political Genius of Abraham Lincoln*. New York: Simon and Schuster, 2005.

Graham, Billy. *Just As I Am*. New York: HarperCollins, 1997; Harper Paperbacks ed., 1998.

Greenleaf, Robert K. *Servant Leadership*. New York: Paulist Press, 1977.

Hamilton, J. R. *Alexander the Great*. Pittsburgh: University of Pittsburgh Press, 1973.

Handy, Charles. *The Age of Paradox*. Boston: Harvard Business School Press, 1995.

Hasselbein, Francis, Marshall Goldsmith, and Richard Beckhard, eds. *The Leader of the Future*. San Francisco: Jossey-Bass, 1996.

Hayward, Steven F. *Churchill on Leadership: Executive Success in the Face of Adversity*. Rocklin, CA: Forum, 1997.

Heifetz, Ronald A. *Leadership without Easy Answers*. Cambridge, MA: Belknap Press, 1994.

Hershey, Paul. *The Situational Leader*. Escondido, CA: Center for Leadership Studies, 1984; reprint ed., 1992.

Hibbert, Christopher. *Disraeli: A Personal History*. New York: HarperCollins, 2004.

Huckabee, Mike. *Character Is the Issue*. Nashville: Broadman & Holman, 1997.

Huntford, Roland. *Shackleton*. New York: Carroll and Graf Publishers, 1985; reprint ed., 2000.

Iacocca, Lee. *Iacocca: An Autobiography*. Toronto: Bantam Books, 1984.

Irwin, Tim. *Derailed: Five Lessons Learned from Catastrophic Failures of Leadership*. Nashville: Thomas Nelson, 2009.

Isaacson, Walter. *Einstein: His Life and Universe*. New York: Simon and Schuster, 2007.

Jinkins, Michael, and Deborah Bradshaw Jinkins. *The Character of Leadership: Political Realism and Public Virtue in Nonprofit Organizations*. San Francisco: Jossey-Bass, 1998.

Johnson, Craig E. *Meeting the Ethical Challenges of Leadership: Casting Light or Shadow*, 3rd ed. Los Angeles: Sage Publications, 2009.

Kaiser, Robert B. "The Rest of What You Need to Know about Strengths-Based Development" in *The Perils of Accentuating the Positive*. Robert B. Kaiser, ed. Tulsa: Hogan Press, 2009.

Kaiser, Robert B., and Robert E. Kaplan. "When Strengths Run Amok." *The Perils of Accentuating the Positive*. Robert Kaiser, ed. Tulsa: Hogan Press, 2009.

Kavaler, Lucy. *The Astors: A Family Chronicle of Pomp and Power*. New York: Dodd, Mead and Company, 1966; reprint ed., Lincoln, NE: iUniverse. com, 2000.

Kelly, Geffrey B., and F. Burton Nelson. *The Cost of Moral Leadership: The Spirituality of Dietrich Bonhoeffer*. Grand Rapids: William B. Eerdmans, 2003.

Kennett, Lee. *Sherman: A Soldier's Life*. New York: HarperCollins, 2001; Perennial ed., 2002.

Kim, W. Chan, and Renee Mauborgne. *Blue Ocean Strategy: How to Create Uncontested Market Space and Make the Competition Irrelevant*. Boston: Harvard Business School Press, 2005.

Koestenbaum, Peter. *Leadership: The Inner Side of Greatness*. San Francisco: Jossey-Bass, 2002.

Kotter, John P. *A Sense of Urgency*. Boston: Harvard Business Press, 2008.

———. *Leading Change*. Boston: Harvard Business School, 1996.

———. *What Leaders Really Do*. Boston: Harvard Business Review, 1999.

Kouzes, James M., and Barry Z. Posner. *A Leader's Legacy*. San Francisco: Jossey-Bass, 2006.

———. *Credibility: How Leaders Gain and Lose It, Why People Demand It*. San Francisco: Jossey-Bass, 1993.

———. *Encouraging the Heart: A Leader's Guide to Rewarding and Recognizing Others*. San Francisco: Jossey-Bass, 1999.

———. *The Leadership Challenge*. San Francisco: Jossey-Bass, 1995.

Krass, Peter. *Carnegie*. Hoboken, NJ: John Wiley and Sons, 2002.

Kurtzman, Joel. *Common Purpose: How Great Leaders Get Organizations to Achieve the Extraordinary*. San Francisco: Jossey-Bass, 2010.

Kytle, Calvin. *Ghandi: Soldier of Nonviolence*. Washington, DC: Seven Locks Press, 1969.

Lande, D. A. *I Was with Patton: First Person Accounts of WW II in George S. Patton's Command*. St. Paul, MN: MBI Publishing Company, 2002.

Lawler III, Edward E. "The Era of Human Capital Has Finally Arrived." *The Future of Leadership*. Warren Bennis, Gretchen M. Spreitzer, and Thomas G. Cummings, eds. San Francisco: Jossey-Bass, 2001.

Leighton, Allan. *On Leadership: Practical Wisdom from the People Who Know*. London: Random House Business Books, 2007.

Leman, Kevin, and William Pentak. *The Way of the Shepherd: 7 Ancient Secrets to Managing Productive People*. Grand Rapids: Zondervan, 2004.

Lencioni, Patrick. *Death by Meeting*. San Francisco: Jossey-Bass, 2004.

———. *The Five Dysfunctions of a Team*. San Francisco: Jossey-Bass, 2002.

Longford, Elizabeth. *Victoria*. London: Wiedenfeld and Nicolson, 1964; Abacus ed., 2000.

Machiavelli Niccolo. *The Prince*. New York: Penguin Books, 1961; reprint ed., 1999.

MacMillan, Pat. *The Performance Factor: Unlocking the Secrets of Teamwork*. Nashville: Broadman and Holman, 2001.

Man, John. *Genghis Khan: Life, Death, and Resurrection*. New York: Thomas Dunne Books, 2004.

Manchester, William. *Winston Spencer Churchill: The Last Lion, Visions of Glory 1874–1932*. New York: Dell Publishing, 1983.

———. *Winston Spencer Churchill: The Last Lion, Alone 1932–1940*. New York: Dell Publishing, 1988.

Markham, Felix. *Napoleon*. New York: New American Library, 1963.

Marsden, George M. *Jonathan Edwards: A Life*. New Haven: Yale University Press, 2003.

Maxwell, John. *Developing the Leader within You*. Nashville: Thomas Nelson, 1993.

McCullough, David. *1776*. New York: Simon and Schuster, 2005.

———. *John Adams*. New York: Simon and Schuster, 2001; Touchstone ed., 2002.

———. *Truman*. New York: Simon and Schuster, 1992; Touchstone ed., 1993.

McFarland, Keith R. *The Breakthrough Company: How Everyday Companies Become Extraordinary Performers*. New York: Crown Publishing, 2008.

McInnis, Edgar. *Canada: A Political and Social History*, 3rd edition. Toronto: Holt, Rinehart and Winston of Canada, 1969.

McIntosh, Gary L., and Samuel D. Rima. *Overcoming the Dark Side of Leadership*. Grand Rapids: Baker Books, 1997.

Meier, Christian. *Caesar*. Berlin: Severin and Siedler, 1982; English ed., London: Fontana Press, 1996.

Metaxas, Eric. *Amazing Grace: William Wilberforce and the Heroic Campaign to End Slavery*. San Francisco: HarperCollins, 2007.

Miller, Basil. *George Muller: The Man of Faith*, 3rd ed. Grand Rapids: Zondervan, 1941.

Monti, James. *The King's Good Servant but God's First: The Life and Writings of St. Thomas More*. San Francisco: Ignatius Press, 1997.

Moody, W. R. *The Life of Dwight L. Moody*. London: Morgan and Scott, n.d.

Murray, Andrew. *Absolute Surrender*. Chicago: Moody, n.d.

Murray, Ian H. *Jonathan Edwards: A New Biography*. Edinburgh: Banner of Truth Trust, 1987; reprint ed., 1992.

Nadel, Laurie. *The Great Streams of History: A Biography of Richard M. Nixon*. New York: Macmillan, 1991.

Nanus, Burt. *Visionary Leadership*. San Francisco: Jossey-Bass, 1992.

Nasaw, David. *The Chief: The Life of William Randolph Hearst*. Boston: Houghton Mifflin, 2000; Mariner Book, ed., 2001.

Nee, Watchman. *Spiritual Authority*. New York: Christian Fellowship Publishers, 1972.

Newman, Peter C. *Renegade in Power: The Diefenbaker Years*. Toronto: McClelland and Stewart, 1963; Power Reporting ed., 1989.

Orr, J. Edwin. *The Event of the Century: The 1857–1858 Awakening*. Wheaton, IL: International Awakening Press, 1989.

Paine, Thomas. *Common Sense, Rights of Man, and Other Essential Writings of Thomas Paine*. New York: Signet Classics, 2003.

Pearce, Terry. *Leading Out Loud: Inspiring Change through Authentic Communication*. San Francisco: Jossey-Bass, 2003.

Peters, Marie. *The Elder Pitt*. London: Longman, 1998.

Peters, Thomas J. and Robert H. Waterman Jr. *In Search of Excellence: Lessons from America's Best Run Companies*. New York: HarperCollins, 1982; HarperBusiness ed., 2004.

Phillips, Donald T. *Lincoln on Leadership: Executive Strategies for Tough Times*. New York: Warner Books, 1992.

———. *Martin Luther King Jr. on Leadership: Inspiration and Wisdom for Challenging Times*. New York: Warner Books, 1999.

Pocock, Tom. *Horatio Nelson*. London: Brockhampton Press, 1987.

Pollock, John. *Moody*. Grand Rapids: Baker Books, 1963.

Quinn, Robert. *Deep Change: Discovering the Leader Within*. San Francisco: Jossey-Bass, 1996.

Rainer, Thom S., and Jess W. *The Millennials: Connecting to America's Largest Generation*. Nashville: B&H Publishing Group, 2011.

Randall, Willard Sterne. *George Washington: A Life*. New York: Henry Holt, 1997.

Reagan, Ronald. *Ronald Reagan: An American Life*. New York: Pocket Books, 1990.

Reeves, Richard. *President Kennedy: Profile of Power*. New York: Simon and Schuster, 1993; Touchstone ed., 1994.

———. *President Nixon: Alone in the White House*. New York: Simon and Schuster, 2001; Touchstone ed., 2002.

Remini, Robert V. *John Quincy Adams* in The American Presidents. Arthur M. Schlesinger, ed. New York: Time Books, 2002.

———. *The Life of Andrew Jackson*. New York: Harper and Row, 1988; Perennial Classics ed., 2001.

Renehan, Edward J. *Commodore: The Life of Cornelius Vanderbilt*. New York: Basic Books, 2007.

Rhode, Deborah. "Where Is the Leadership in Moral Leadership?" *Moral Leadership: The Theory and Practice of Power, Judgment, and Policy*. Deborah Rhode, ed. San Francisco: Jossey-Bass, 2006.

Ritchie, Homer G. *The Life and Legend of J. Frank Norris: The Fighting Parson*. Fort Worth: Homer G. Ritchie, 1991.

Rosenzweig, Phil. *The Halo Effect . . . and the Eight Other Business Delusions That Deceive Managers*. New York: Simon and Schuster, 2007; Free Press ed., 2009.

Rost, Joseph C. *Leadership for the Twenty-First Century*. Westport, CT: Praeger Publishers, 1991; Paperback ed., 1993.

Sample, Stephen B. *The Contrarian's Guide to Leadership*. San Francisco: Jossey-Bass, 2002.

Sanders, Oswald, *Spiritual Leadership*. Chicago: Moody Press, 1967; reprint ed., 1994.

Scarborough, L. R. *With Christ after the Lost*. Nashville: Broadman, 1952.

Schroeder, Alice. *The Snowball: Warren Buffet and the Business of Life*. New York: Bantam Books, 2008.

Schwarzkopf, Norman H., and Petre, Peter. *It Doesn't Take a Hero*. New York: Bantam Books, 1992.

Seager, Robin. *Tiberius*. London: Eyre Metheun Ltd., 1972; 2nd ed., Oxford: Blackwell Publishing, 2005.

Senge, Peter. *The Fifth Discipline: The Art and Practice of the Learning Organization*. New York: Currency Doubleday, 1994.

Shaw, George Bernard. *Man and Superman*. Baltimore: Penguin Books, 1903.

Shirky, Clay. *Cognitive Surplus: Creativity and Generosity in a Connected Age*. New York: Penquin Press, 2010.

Smith, Jean Edward. *Grant*. New York: Simon and Schuster, 2001; Touchstone ed., 2002.

Spreitzer, Gretchen M., and Robert E. Quinn. *A Company of Leaders: Five Disciplines for Unleashing the Power in Your Workforce*. San Francisco: Jossey-Bass, 2001.

Stewart, Thomas A. "Trust Me on This: Organizational Support for Trust in a World without Hierarchies." *The Future of Leadership: Today's Top Leadership Thinkers Speak to Tomorrow's Leaders*. Warren Bennis, Gretchen M. Spreitzer, and Thomas G. Cummings, eds. San Francisco: Jossey-Bass, 2001.

Sullivan, Gordon R., and Michael V. Harper. *Hope Is Not a Method: What Business Leaders Can Learn from America's Army*. New York: Broadway Books, 1997.

Swenson, Richard A. *Margin: Restoring Emotional, Physical, Financial, and Time Reserves to Overloaded Lives*. Colorado Springs: NavPress, 1992.

Szollose, Brad. Liquid *Leadership: From Woodstock to Wikipedia— Multigenerational Management Ideas that Are Changing to Way We Run Things*. Austin, TX: Greenleaf Book Group Press, 2011.

Thatcher, Margaret. *Margaret Thatcher: The Downing Street Years*. New York: HarperCollins, 1993.

Wallace, James, and Jim Erikson. *Hard Drive: Bill Gates and the Making of the Microsoft Empire.* New York: HarperCollins, 1992; HarperBusiness ed., 1993.

Walton, Sam. *Sam Walton: Made in America.* New York: Doubleday, 1992; Bantam Books ed., 1993.

Warren, Rick. *The Purpose Driven Church.* Grand Rapids: Zondervan, 1995.

Watts, Steven. *The People's Tycoon: Henry Ford and the American Century.* New York: Random House, 2005; Vintage Books ed., 2006.

Weir, Alison. *Elizabeth the Queen.* London: Jonathan Cape Ltd., 1998; Pimlico ed., 1999.

———. *Henry VIII: King and Court.* London: Jonathan Cape, 2001; Pimlico ed., 2002.

Wells, Stuart. *Choosing the Future: The Power of Strategic Thinking.* Woburn, MA: Butterworth-Heinemann, 1998.

Widmer, Ted. *Martin Van Buren* in The American Presidents, Arthur Schlesinger, ed. New York: Time Books, 2005.

Wilkes, C. Gene. *Jesus on Leadership: Discovering the Secrets of Servant Leadership.* Wheaton, IL: Tyndale House Publishers, 1998.

Will, Garry. *James Madison* in The American Presidents. Arthur Schlesinger, ed. New York: Times Books, 2002.

Wiseman, Liz. *Multipliers: How the Best Leaders Make Everyone Smarter.* New York: HarperBusiness, 2010.

Subject/Name Index

About the Authors

HENRY T. BLACKABY is a best-selling author and well-known international speaker. He is founder of Blackaby Ministries International, www.blackaby. org.

Henry is a graduate of the University of British Columbia, Vancouver, Canada, and Golden Gate Baptist Theological Seminary in Mill Valley, California. He has four honorary doctor's degrees. He was the pastor of churches in San Francisco and Los Angeles as well as Faith Baptist Church in Saskatoon, Saskatchewan, Canada. Henry served as a director of missions in Vancouver, British Columbia, and ministered for a number of years as a national leader for prayer and spiritual awakening. He has spoken in 114 countries and counsels Christian CEOs of Fortune 500 companies. He has spoken in the White House, the Pentagon, and the United Nations.

Henry has written numerous books including: *Experiencing God: Knowing and Doing the Will of God, What the Spirit is Saying to the Churches, Fresh Encounter: God's Pattern for Spiritual Awakening, The Power of the Call, Called to Be God's Friend: How God Shapes Those He Loves, Anointed to be God's Servants, Chosen to be God's Prophet, Prepared to be God's Vessel, Experiencing God as Couples, A God-Centered Church, Called and Accountable, Holiness, The Man God Uses, Experiencing Prayer with Jesus, Experiencing the Cross, The Ways of God, Worship: Believers Experiencing God, Experiencing The*

Resurrection, Experiencing Pentecost, and *God in the Marketplace: 45 Questions Fortune 500 CEOs Ask about Faith, Life and Business.*

He is married to Marilynn. They have five children: Richard, Thomas, Melvin, Norman, and Carrie and fourteen grandchildren.

RICHARD BLACKABY is Henry's oldest son. He holds a B.A. from the University of Saskatchewan, an M.Div. and a Ph.D. in history from Southwestern Baptist Theological Seminary, and an honorary doctorate from Dallas Baptist University. He has served as a senior pastor and a seminary president. He is currently the president of Blackaby Ministries International (www.blackaby.org). He travels internationally speaking on the Christian life and spiritual leadership. He disciples CEOs of major companies. He is married to Lisa. They have three children: Mike, Daniel, and Carrie. Richard has coauthored numerous books with his father including: *When God Speaks, Experiencing God: Day by Day, The Experience, God's Invitation, Hearing God's Voice, Called to Be God's Leader: Lessons from the Life of Joshua, Reality: 7 Truths from Experiencing God, Blackaby Study Bible; Discovering God's Daily Agenda, Experiencing God, Fresh Encounter: God's Pattern for Spiritual Awakening,* and *God in the Marketplace: 45 Questions Fortune 500 Executives Ask About Faith, Life and Business.* He has also written *CrossSeekers, Putting a Face on Grace: Living a Life Worth Passing On,* and *Unlimiting God: Increasing Your Capacity to Experience the Divine.*

Henry and Richard mentor and teach leaders on their Spiritual Leadership Network. Those interested can contact www.blackaby.org or SLN@blackaby.org.